DEVELOPMENT OF RELIGION AND THOUGHT IN ANCIENT EGYPT

LECTURES DELIVERED ON THE MORSE FOUNDATION
AT UNION THEOLOGICAL SEMINARY

BY

JAMES HENRY BREASTED, Ph.D.

PROFESSOR OF EGYPTOLOGY AND ORIENTAL HISTORY IN THE UNIVERSITY OF CHICAGO—CORRESPONDING MEMBER OF THE ROYAL ACADEMY OF SCIENCES OF BERLIN

ISBN: 978-1-63923-713-5

All Rights reserved. No part of this book maybe reproduced without written permission from the publishers, except by a reviewer who may quote brief passages in a review to be printed in a newspaper or magazine.

Printed: February 2023

Published and Distributed By:
Lushena Books
607 Country Club Drive, Unit E
Bensenville, IL 60106
www.lushenabks.com

ISBN: 978-1-63923-713-5

DEVELOPMENT OF
RELIGION AND THOUGHT IN
ANCIENT EGYPT

TO
ADOLF ERMAN
IN GRATITUDE AND AFFECTION

PREFACE

CONTRARY to the popular and current impression, the most important body of sacred literature in Egypt is not the Book of the Dead, but a much older literature which we now call the "Pyramid Texts." These texts, preserved in the Fifth and Sixth Dynasty Pyramids at Sakkara, form the oldest body of literature surviving from the ancient world and disclose to us the earliest chapter in the intellectual history of man as preserved to modern times. They are to the study of Egyptian language and civilization what the Vedas have been in the study of early East Indian and Aryan culture. Discovered in 1880-81, they were published by Maspero in a pioneer edition which will always remain a great achievement and a landmark in the history of Egyptology. The fact that progress has been made in the publication of such epigraphic work is no reflection upon the devoted labors of the distinguished first editor of the Pyramid Texts. The appearance last year of the exhaustive standard edition of the hieroglyphic text at the hands of Sethe after years of study and arrangement marks a new epoch in the study of earliest Egyptian life and religion. How comparatively inaccessible the Pyramid Texts have been until the appearance of Sethe's edition is best illustrated by the fact that no complete analysis or full account of the Pyramid Texts as a whole has ever appeared in English, much less an English version of them. The great and complicated fabric of life which they reflect to us, the religious and intellectual forces which have left their traces in them, the intrusion of the Osiris faith and the Osirian editing by the hand of the earliest redactor in literary history—all these and many other fundamental disclosures of this earliest body of literature have hitherto been inaccessible to the English reader, and as far as they are new, also to all.

It was therefore with peculiar pleasure that just after the appearance of Sethe's edition of the Pyramid Texts I received President Francis Brown's very cordial invitation to deliver the Morse Lectures at Union Theological Seminary on some subject in Egyptian life and civilization. While it was obviously desirable at this juncture to choose a subject which would involve some account of the Pyramid Texts, it was equally desirable to assign them their proper place in the development of Egyptian civilization. This latter desideratum led to a rather more ambitious subject than the time available before the delivery of the lectures would permit to treat exhaustively, viz., to trace the development of Egyptian religion in its relation to life and thought, as, for example, it has been done for the Hebrews by modern critical and historical study. In the study of Egyptian religion hitherto the effort has perhaps necessarily been to produce a kind of historical encyclopædia of the subject. Owing to their vast extent, the mere bulk of the materials available, this method of study and presentation has resulted in a very complicated and detailed picture in which the great drift of the development as the successive forces of civilization dominated has not been discernible. There has heretofore been little attempt to correlate with religion the other great categories of life and civilization which shaped it. I do not mean that these relationships have not been noticed in certain epochs, especially where they have been so obvious as hardly to be overlooked, but no systematic effort has yet been made to trace from beginning to end the leading categories of life, thought, and civilization as they successively made their mark on religion, or to follow religion from age to age, disclosing especially how it was shaped by these influences, and how it in its turn reacted on society.

I should have been very glad if this initial effort at such a reconstruction might have attempted a more detailed analysis of the basic documents upon which it rests, and if in several places it might have been broadened and extended to include more categories. That surprising group of pamphleteers who made the earliest crusade for social justice and brought about the earliest social regeneration four thousand years ago (Lecture VII) should be further studied in detail in their bearing on the mental and religious attitude of the remarkable age to which they belonged. I am well aware also of the importance and desirability of a full treatment of cult and ritual in such a reconstruction as that here attempted, but I have been obliged to limit the discussion of this subject chiefly to mortuary ritual and observances, trusting that I have not overlooked facts of importance for our purpose discernible in the temple cult. In the space and time at my disposal for this course of lectures it has not been possible to adduce all the material which I had, nor to follow down each attractive vista which frequently opened so temptingly. I have not undertaken the problem of origins in many directions, like that of sacred animals so prominent in Egypt. Indeed Re and Osiris are so largely anthropomorphic that, in dealing as I have chiefly with the Solar and Osirian faiths, it was not necessary. In the age discussed these two highest gods were altogether human and highly spiritualized, though the thought of Re displays occasional relapses, as it were, in the current allusions to the falcon, with which he was so early associated. Another subject passed by is the concept of sacrifice, which I have not discussed at all. There is likewise no systematic discussion of the idea of a god's power, though the material for such a discussion will be found here. I would have been glad to devote a lecture to this subject, especially in its relation to magic as a vague and colossal inexorability to which when invoked even the highest god must bow. Only Amenhotep IV (Ikhnaton) seems to have outgrown it, because Oriental magic is so largely demoniac and Amenhotep IV as a monotheist banished the demons and the host of gods.

It will be seen, then, that no rigid outline of categories has been set up. I have taken those aspects of Egyptian religion and thought in which the development and expansion could be most clearly traced, the endeavor being especially to determine the order and succession of those influences which determine the course and character of religious development. It is of course evident that no such influence works at any time to the exclusion of all the others, but there are epochs when, for example, the influence of the state on religion and religious thought first becomes noticeable and a determining force. The same thing is true of the social forces as distinguished from those of the state organization. This is not an endeavor, then, to trace each category from beginning to end, but to establish the order in which the different influences which created Egyptian religion successively became the determining forces. Beginning shortly after 3000 B. C. the surviving documents are, I think, sufficient to disclose these influences in chronological order as they will be found in the "Epitome of the Development" which follows this preface. Under these circumstances little effort to correlate the phenomena adduced with those of other religions has been made. May I remind the reader of technical attainments also, that the lectures were designed for a popular audience and were written accordingly?

Although we are still in the beginning of the study of Egyptian religion, and although I would gladly have carried these researches much further, I believe that the reconstruction here presented will in the main stand, and that the inevitable alterations and differences of opinion resulting from the constant progress in such a field of research will concern chiefly the details. That the general drift of the religious development in Egypt is analogous to that of the Hebrews is a fact of confirmative value not without interest to students of Comparative Religion and of the Old Testament.

I have been careful to make due acknowledgment in the foot-notes of my indebtedness to the labors of other scholars. The obligation of all scholars in this field to the researches of Erman and Maspero is proverbial, and, as we have said, in his new edition of the Pyramid Texts Sethe has raised a notable monument to his exhaustive knowledge of this subject to which every student of civilization is indebted. May I venture to express the hope that this exposition of religion in the making, during a period of three thousand years, may serve not only as a general survey of the development in the higher life of a great people beginning in the earliest age of man which we can discern at the present day, but also to emphasize the truth that the process of religion-making has never ceased and that the same forces which shaped religion in ancient Egypt are still operative in our own midst and continue to mould our own religion to-day?

The reader should note that half brackets indicate some uncertainty in the rendering of all words so enclosed; brackets enclose words wholly restored, and where the half brackets are combined with the brackets the restoration is uncertain. Parentheses enclose explanatory words not in the original, and dots indicate intentional omission in the translation of an original. Quotations from modern authors are so rare in the volume, and so evident when made, that the reader may regard practically all passages in quotation marks as renderings from an original document. All abbreviations will be intelligible except BAR, which designates the author's *Ancient Records of Egypt* (five volumes, Chicago, 1905–07), the Roman indicating the volume, and the Arabic the paragraph.

In conclusion, it is a pleasant duty to express my indebtedness to my friend and one-time pupil, Dr. Caroline Ransom, of the Metropolitan Museum, for her kindness in reading the entire page-proof, while for a similar service, as well as the irksome task of preparing the index, I am under great obligation to the goodness of Dr. Charles R. Gillett, of Union Theological Seminary.

JAMES HENRY BREASTED.

The University of Chicago,
 April, 1912.

EPITOME OF THE DEVELOPMENT

NATURE furnishes the earliest gods—The *national* state makes early impression on religion—Its forms pass over into the world of the gods—Their origin and function in nature retire into the background—The gods become active in the sphere of human affairs—They are intellectualized and spiritualized till the human arena becomes their domain—The gods are correlated into a general system—In the conception of death and the hereafter we find a glorious celestial realm reserved exclusively for kings and possibly nobles—Herein, too, we discern the emergence of the moral sense and the inner life in their influence on religion—Recognition of futility of material agencies in the hereafter and resulting scepticism—Appearance of the capacity to contemplate society—Recognition of the moral unworthiness of society and resulting scepticism—The cry for social justice—The social forces make their impression on religion—Resulting democratization of the formerly royal hereafter—Magic invades the realm of morals—The Empire (the *international* state) and political universalism so impress religion that the "world-idea" emerges and monotheism results—Earliest manifestation of personal piety growing out of paternal monotheism and the older social justice—The individual in religion—The age of the psalmist and the sage—Sacerdotalism triumphs, resulting in intellectual stagnation, the inertia of thoughtless acceptance, and the development ceases in scribal conservation of the old teachings—The retrospective age—A religious development of three thousand years analogous in the main points to that of the Hebrews.

CONTENTS

LECTURE I

NATURE AND THE STATE MAKE THEIR IMPRESSION
   ON RELIGION—EARLIEST SYSTEMS   3

Natural sources of the content of Egyptian religion chiefly two: the sun and the Nile or vegetation—The Sun-myth and the Solar theology—The *national* state makes its impression on religion—Re the Sun-god becomes the state god of Egypt—Osiris and his nature: he was Nile or the soil and the vegetation fructified by it—The Osiris-myth—Its early rise in the Delta and migration to Upper Egypt—Correlation of Solar and Osirian myths—Early appropriation of the Set-Horus feud by the Osirian myth—Solar group of nine divinities (Ennead) headed by the Sun-god early devised by the priests of Heliopolis—Early intimations of pantheism in Memphite theology—The first pilhosophico-religious system—Its world limited to Egypt.

LECTURE II

LIFE AFTER DEATH—THE SOJOURN IN THE TOMB—
   DEATH MAKES ITS IMPRESSION ON RELIGION   48
(Period: earliest times to 25th century B. C.)

Earliest Egyptian thought revealed in mortuary practices—The conception of a person: *ka* (or protecting genius), *body* and *soul*—Reconstitution of personality after death—Maintenance of the dead in the tomb—Tomb-building—Earliest royal tombs—Tombs of the nobles—Earliest embalmment and burial—Royal aid in mortuary equipment—Tomb endowment—Origin of the pyramid, greatest symbol of the Sun-god—The pyramid and its buildings—Its dedication and protection—Its endowment, ritual, and maintenance—Inevitable decay of the pyramid—Survival of death a matter of material equipment.

LECTURE III

REALMS OF THE DEAD—THE PYRAMID TEXTS—THE
   ASCENT TO THE SKY 70
(Period: 30th to 25th century B. C.)

The Pyramid Texts—The oldest chapter in the intellectual history of man—Earliest fragments before 3400 B. C.—Pyramid Texts represent a period of a thousand years ending in 25th century B. C.—Their purpose to ensure the king felicity hereafter—Their reflection of the life of the age—Their dominant note protest against death—Content sixfold: (1) Funerary and mortuary ritual; (2) Magical charms; (3) Ancient ritual of worship; (4) Ancient religious hymns; (5) Fragments of old myths; (6) Prayers on behalf of the king—Haphazard arrangement—Literary form: parallelism of members—Occasional display of real literary quality—Method of employment—The sojourn of the dead in a distant place—The prominence of the east of the sky—The Stellar and Solar hereafter—The ascent to the sky.

LECTURE IV

Realms of the Dead—The Earliest Celestial Hereafter 118

(Period: 30th to 25th century B. C.)

Reception of the Pharaoh by the Sun-god—Association with the Sun-god—Identification with the Sun-god—The Pharaoh a cosmic figure superior to the Sun-god—Fellowship with the gods—Pharaoh devours the gods—The Pharaoh's food—The Island of the Tree of Life—The Pharaoh's protection against his enemies—Celestial felicity of the Pharaoh—Solar contrasted with Osirian hereafter—Earliest struggle of a state theology and a popular faith.

LECTURE V

The Osirianization of the Hereafter . . . 142

(Period: 30th to 25th century B. C.)

Osirian myth foreign to the celestial hereafter—Osiris not at first friendly to the dead—Osirian kingdom not celestial but subterranean—Filial piety of Horus and the Osirian hereafter—Identity of the dead Pharaoh and Osiris—Osiris gains a celestial hereafter—Osirianization of the Pyramid Texts—Conflict between state and popular religion—Traces of the process in the Pyramid Texts—Fusion of Solar and Osirian hereafter.

LECTURE VI

Emergence of the Moral Sense—Moral Worthiness and the Hereafter—Scepticism and the Problem of Suffering . . . 165

(29th century to 18th century B. C.)

Religion first dealing with the material world—Emergence of the moral sense—Justice—Filial piety—Moral worthiness and the hereafter in tomb inscriptions—Earliest judgment of the dead—Moral justification in the Pyramid Texts—The Pharaoh not exempt from moral requirements in the hereafter—Moral justification not of Osirian but of Solar origin—The limitations of the earliest moral sense—The triumph of character over material agencies of immortality—The realm of the gods begins to become one of moral values—Ruined pyramids and futility of such means—Resulting scepticism and rise of subjective contemplation—Song of the harper—The problem of suffering and the unjustly afflicted—The "Misanthrope," the earliest Job.

LECTURE VII

THE SOCIAL FORCES MAKE THEIR IMPRESSION ON RELIGION—THE EARLIEST SOCIAL REGENERATION 199

(Period: 22d to 18th century B. C.)

Appearance of the capacity to contemplate society—Discernment of the moral unworthiness of society—Scepticism—A royal sceptic—Earliest social prophets and their tractates—Ipuwer and his arraignment—The dream of the ideal ruler—Messianism—The Tale of the Eloquent Peasant and propaganda for social justice—Maxims of Ptahhotep—Righteousness and official optimism—Social justice becomes the official doctrine of the state—The "Installation of the Vizier"—Dialogue form of social and moral discussion and its origin in Egypt—Evidences of the social regeneration of the Feudal Age—Its origin in the Solar faith—Deepening sense of moral responsibility in the hereafter both Solar and Osirian.

LECTURE VIII

POPULARIZATION OF THE OLD ROYAL HEREAFTER—TRIUMPH OF OSIRIS—CONSCIENCE AND THE BOOK OF THE DEAD—MAGIC AND MORALS . 257

(Period: 22d century to 1350 B. C.)

Material equipment for the hereafter not abandoned—Maintenance of the dead—The cemetery festivities of the people illustrated at Siut—Ephemeral character of the tomb and its maintenance evident as before—Value of the uttered word in the hereafter—The "Coffin Texts," the forerunners of the Book of the Dead—Predominance of the Solar and celestial hereafter —Intrusion of Osirian views—Resulting Solar-Osirian hereafter—Democratization of the hereafter—Its innumerable dangers—Consequent growth in the use of magic—Popular triumph of Osiris—His "Holy Sepulchre" at Abydos—The Osirian drama or "Passion Play"—Magic and increased recognition of its usefulness in the hereafter—The Book of the Dead— Largely made up of magical charms—Similar books—The judgment in the Book of the Dead—Conscience in graphic symbols—Sin not confessed as later—Magic enters world of morals and conscience—Resulting degeneration.

LECTURE IX

THE IMPERIAL AGE—THE WORLD-STATE MAKES ITS IMPRESSION ON RELIGION—EARLIEST MONOTHEISM—IKHNATON 312

(Period: 1580 to 1350 B. C.)

Nationalism in religion and thought—It yields to universalism after establishment of Egyptian Empire—Earliest evidences—Solar universalism under Amenhotep III—Opposition of Amon—Earliest national priesthood under High Priest of Amon—Amenhotep IV—His championship of Sun-god as "Aton"—His struggle with Amonite papacy—He annihilates Amon and the gods—He becomes "Ikhnaton"—Monotheism, Aton sole god of the Empire—A return to nature—Ethical content of Aton faith—The intellectual revolution—A world-religion premature—Ikhnaton the earliest "individual."

LECTURE X

THE AGE OF PERSONAL PIETY—SACERDOTALISM AND FINAL DECADENCE 344

(Period: 1350 B. C. on.)

Fall of Ikhnaton—Suppression of the Aton faith—Restoration of Amon—Influences of Aton faith survive—Their appearance in folk-religion of 13th and 12th centuries B. C.—Fatherly care and solicitude of God (as old as Feudal Age), together with elements of Aton faith, appear in a manifestation of personal piety among the common people—New spiritual relation with God, involving humility, confession of sin, and silent meditation—Morals of the sages and moral progress—Resignation to one's lot—Folk theology—Pantheism in a folk-tale—In Theology—Universal spread of mortuary practices—Increasing power of religious institutions—A state within the state—Sacerdotalism triumphs—Religion degenerates into usages, observances, and scribal conservation of the old writings—The retrospective age—Final decadence into the Osirianism of the Roman Empire.

INDEX 371

CHRONOLOGY

BEGINNING OF THE DYNASTIES WITH MENES, ABOUT 3400 B. C.

EARLY DYNASTIES, I AND II, ABOUT 3400 TO 2980 B. C.

OLD KINGDOM OR PYRAMID AGE, DYNASTIES III TO VI, 2980 TO 2475 B.C., ROUGHLY THE FIRST FIVE HUNDRED YEARS OF THE THIRD MILLENNIUM B. C.

MIDDLE KINGDOM OR FEUDAL AGE, DYNASTIES XI AND XII, 2160 TO 1788 B. C.

THE EMPIRE, DYNASTIES XVIII TO XX (FIRST HALF ONLY), ABOUT 1580 TO 1150 B. C.

DECADENCE, DYNASTIES XX (SECOND HALF) TO XXV, ABOUT 1150 TO 660 B. C.

RESTORATION, DYNASTY XXVI, 663 TO 525 B. C.

PERSIAN CONQUEST, 525 B. C.

GREEK CONQUEST, 332 B. C.

ROMAN CONQUEST, 30 B. C.

CORRIGENDA

Page 345, footnote, last line, "Ikhnaton," should read "Tutenkhamon."
Page 363, line 21, "twenty-fifth century," should read "twenty-eighth century."
Page 366, line 8, "which now received its last redaction," should read "still undergoing further redaction."

DEVELOPMENT OF RELIGION AND THOUGHT IN ANCIENT EGYPT

LECTURE I

THE ORIGINS: NATURE AND THE STATE IN THEIR IMPRESSION ON RELIGION—EARLIEST SYSTEMS

THE recovery of the history of the nearer Orient in the decipherment of Egyptian hieroglyphic and Babylonian cuneiform brought with it many unexpected revelations, but none more impressive than the length of the development disclosed. In Babylonia, however, the constant influx of foreign population resulted in frequent and violent interruption of the development of civilization. In Egypt, on the other hand, the isolation of the lower Nile valley permitted a development never seriously arrested by permanent immigrations for over three thousand years. We find here an opportunity like that which the zoologist is constantly seeking in what he calls "unbroken series," such as that of the horse developing in several millions of years from a creature little larger than a rabbit to our modern domestic horse. In all the categories of human life: language, arts, government, society, thought, religion—what you please—we may trace a development in Egypt essentially undisturbed by outside forces, for a period far surpassing in length any such development elsewhere preserved to us; and it is a matter of not a little interest to observe what humankind becomes in the course of five thousand years in such an Island of the Blest as Egypt; to follow him from the flint knife and stone hammer in less than two thousand years to the copper chisel and the amazing extent and accuracy of the Great Pyramid masonry; from the wattle-hut to the sumptuous palace, gorgeous with glazed tile, rich tapestries, and incrusted with gold; to follow all the golden threads of his many-sided life, as it was interwoven at last into a rich and noble fabric of civilization. In these lectures we are to follow but one of these many threads, as its complicated involutions wind hither and thither throughout the whole fabric.

There is no force in the life of ancient man the influence of which so pervades all his activities as does that of the religious faculty. It is at first but an endeavor in vague and childish fancies to explain and to control the world about him; its fears become his hourly master, its hopes are his constant mentor, its feasts are his calendar, and its outward usages are to a large extent the education and the motive toward the evolution of art, literature, and science. Life not only touches religion at every point, but life, thought, and religion are inextricably interfused in an intricate complex of impressions from without and forces from within. How the world about him and the world within him successively wrought and fashioned the religion of the Egyptian for three thousand years is the theme of these studies.

As among all other early peoples, it was in his natural surroundings that the Egyptian first saw his gods. The trees and springs, the stones and hill-tops, the birds and beasts, were creatures like himself, or possessed of strange and uncanny powers of which he was not master. Nature thus makes the earliest impression upon the religious faculty, the visible world is first explained in terms of religious forces, and the earliest gods are the controlling forces of the material world. A social or political realm, or a domain of the spirit where the gods shall be supreme, is not yet perceived. Such divinities as these were local, each known only to the dwellers in a given locality.[1]

As the prehistoric principalities, after many centuries of internal conflict, coalesced to form a united state, the first great national organization of men in history (about 3400 B. C.), this imposing fabric of the state made a profound impression upon religion, and the forms of the state began to pass over into the world of the gods.

At the same time the voices within made themselves heard, and moral values were discerned for the first time. Man's organized power without and the power of the moral imperative within were thus both early forces in shaping Egyptian religion. The moral mandate, indeed, was felt earlier in Egypt than anywhere else. With the development of provincial society in the Feudal Age there ensued a ferment of social forces, and the demand for social justice early found expression in the conception of a gracious and paternal kingship, maintaining high ideals of social equity. The world of the gods, continuing in sensitive touch with the political conditions of the nation, at once felt this influence, and through the idealized kingship social justice passed over into the character of the state god, enriching the ethical qualities which in some degree had for probably a thousand years been imputed to him.

Thus far all was national. As the arena of thought and action widened from national limits to a world of imperial scope, when the Egyptian state expanded to embrace contiguous Asia and Africa, the forces of imperial power consistently reacted upon the thought and religion

---

[1] These remarks are in part drawn from the writer's *History of Egypt*, p. 53.

of the empire. The national religion was forcibly supplanted by a non-national, universal faith, and for the first time in history monotheism dawned. Unlike the social developments of the Feudal Age, this movement was exclusively political, artificial, and imposed upon the people by official pressure from above. The monotheistic movement also failed for lack of nationalism. The Mediterranean world was not yet ripe for a world-religion. In the reversion to the old national gods, much of the humane content of the monotheistic teaching survived, and may be recognized in ideas which gained wide currency among the people. In this process of popularization, the last great development in Egyptian religion took place (1300–1100 B. C.), a development toward deep personal confidence in the goodness and paternal solicitude of God, resulting in a relation of spiritual communion with him. This earliest known age of personal piety in a deep spiritual sense degenerated under the influence of sacerdotalism into the exaggerated religiosity of Græco-Roman days in Egypt.

Such is the imposing vista of development in the religion and thought of Egypt, down which we may look, surveying as we do a period of three thousand years or more. To sum up: what we shall endeavor to do is to trace the progress of the Egyptian as both the world about him and the world within him made their impression upon his thought and his religion, disclosing to us, one after another, nature, the *national* state, the inner life with its growing sense of moral obligation, the social forces, the *world* state, the personal conviction of the presence and goodness of God, triumphant sacerdotalism, scribal literalism, and resulting decay—in short, all these in succession as felt by the Egyptian with profound effect upon his religion and his thought for three thousand years will constitute the survey presented in these lectures.

The fact that a survey of exactly this character has not been undertaken before should lend some interest to the task. The fact that objective study of the great categories mentioned has ranged them chronologically in their effect upon thought and religion in the order above outlined, disclosing a religious development in the main points analogous with that of the Hebrews, though with differences that might have been expected, should also enhance the interest and importance of such a reconstruction. Indeed one of the noticeable facts regarding the religious and intellectual development of the Hebrews has been that the Oriental world in which they moved has heretofore furnished us with no wholly analogous process among kindred peoples.

It will be seen that such a study as we contemplate involves keeping in the main channel and following the broad current, the general drift. It will be impossible, not to say quite undesirable, to undertake an account of all the Egyptian gods, or to study the material appurtenances and outward usages of religion, like the ceremonies and equipment of the cult, which were so elaborately developed in Egypt. Nor shall we follow thought in all its relations to the various incipient sciences, but only those main developments involved in the intimate interrelation between thought and religion.

One characteristic of Egyptian thinking should be borne in mind from the outset: it was always in graphic form. The Egyptian did not possess the terminology for the expression of a system of abstract thought; neither did he develop the capacity to create the necessary terminology as did the Greek. He thought in concrete pict ures, he moved along tangible material channels, and the material world about him furnished nearly all of the terms which he used. While this is probably ultimately true of all terms in any early language, such terms for the most part remained concrete for the Egyptian. We shall discern the emergence of the earliest abstract term known in the history of thought as moral ideas appear among the men of the Pyramid Age in the first half of the third millennium B. C. Let us not, therefore, expect an equipment of precise abstract terms, which we shall find as lacking as the systems which might require them. We are indeed to watch processes by which a nation like the Greeks might have developed such terms, but as we contemplate the earliest developments in human thinking still traceable in contemporary documents, we must expect the vagueness, the crudities, and the limitations inevitable at so early a stage of human development. As the earliest chapter in the intellectual history of man, its introductory phases are, nevertheless, of more importance than their intrinsic value as thought would otherwise possess, while the climax of the development is vital with human interest and human appeal.

As we examine Egyptian religion in its earliest surviving documents, it is evident that two great phenomena of nature had made the most profound impression upon the Nile-dwellers and that the gods discerned in these two phenomena dominated religious and intellectual development from the earliest times. These are the sun and the Nile. In the Sun-god, Re, Atum, Horus, Khepri, and in the Nile, Osiris, we find the great gods of Egyptian life and thought, who almost from the beginning entered upon a rivalry for the highest place in the religion of Egypt— a rivalry which ceased only with the annihilation of Egyptian religion at the close of the fifth century of the Christian era. He who knows the essentials of the story of this long rivalry, will know the main course of the history of Egyptian religion, not to say one of the most important chapters in the history of the early East.

The all-enveloping glory and power of the Egyptian sun is the most insistent fact in the Nile valley, even at the present day as the modern tourist views him for the first time. The Egyptian saw him in different, doubtless originally local forms. At Edfu he appeared as a falcon, for the lofty flight of this bird, which seemed a very comrade of the sun, had led the early fancy of the Nile peasant to believe that the sun must be such a falcon, taking his daily flight across the heavens, and the sun-disk with the outspread wings of the falcon became the commonest symbol of Egyptian religion. As falcon he bore the name Hor (Horus or Horos), or Harakhte, which means "Horus of the horizon." The latter with three other Horuses formed the four Horuses of the eastern sky, originally, doubtless, four different local Horuses.[1] We find them

---

[1] These four Horuses are: (1) "Harakhte," (2) "Horus of the Gods," (3) "Horus of the East," and (4) "Horus-shesemti." On their relation to Osiris, see *infra*, p. 156. Three important Utterances of the Pyramid Texts are built up on them: Ut. 325, 563, and 479. They are also inserted into Ut. 504 (§§ 1085-6). See also § 1105 and § 1206. They probably occur again as curly haired youths in charge of the ferry-boat to the eastern sky in Ut. 520, but in Ut. 522 the four in charge of the ferry-boat are the four genii, the sons of the Osirian Horus, and confusion must be guarded against. On this point see *infra*, p. 157. In Pyr. § 1258 the four Horuses appear with variant names and are perhaps identified with the dead; they are prevented from decaying by Isis and Nephthys. In Pyr. § 1478 also the four Horuses are identified with the dead, who is the son of Re, in a resurrection. Compare also the four children of the Earth-god Geb (Pyr. §§ 1510-11), and especially the four children of Atum who decay not (Pyr. §§ 2057-8), as in Pyr. § 1258.

in the Pyramid Texts as "these four youths who sit on the east side of the sky, these four youths with curly hair who sit in the shade of the tower of Kati."[1]

At Heliopolis the Sun-god appeared as an aged man tottering down the west, while elsewhere they saw in him a winged beetle rising in the east as Khepri. Less picturesque fancy discerned the material sun as Re, that is the "sun." While these were early correlated they at first remained distinct gods for the separate localities where they were worshipped. Survivals of the distinction between the archaic local Sun-gods are still to be found in the Pyramid Texts. Horus early became the son of Re, but in the Pyramid Texts we may find the dead Pharaoh mounting "upon his empty throne between the two great gods" (Re and Horus).[2] They ultimately coalesced, and their identity is quite evident also in the same Pyramid Texts, where we find the compound "Re-Atum" to indicate the identity.[3] The favorite picture of him discloses him sailing across the celestial ocean in the sun-barque, of which there were two, one for the morning and the other for the evening. There were several ancient folk-tales of how he reached the sky when he was still on earth. They prayed that the deceased Pharaoh might reach the sky in the same way: "Give thou to this king Pepi (the Pharaoh) thy two fingers which thou gavest to the maiden, the daughter of the Great God (Re), when the sky was separated from the earth, and the gods ascended to the sky, while thou wast a soul appearing in the bow of thy ship of seven hundred and seventy cubits (length), which the gods of Buto built for thee, which the eastern gods shaped for thee."[4] This separation of

[1] Pyr. Texts, § 1105.
[2] Pyr. § 1125.
[3] Pyr. §§ 1694-5.
[4] Pyr. §§ 1208-9.

earth and sky had been accomplished by Shu the god of
the atmosphere, who afterward continued to support the
sky as he stood with his feet on earth. There, like Atlas
shouldering the earth, he was fed by provisions of the
Sun-god brought by a falcon.[1]

Long before all this, however, there had existed in the
beginning only primeval chaos, an ocean in which the
Sun-god as Atum had appeared. At one temple they said
Ptah had shaped an egg out of which the Sun-god had
issued; at another it was affirmed that a lotus flower had
grown out of the water and in it the youthful Sun-god
was concealed; at Heliopolis it was believed that the Sun-
god had appeared upon the ancient pyramidal "Ben-stone
in the Phœnix-hall in Heliopolis" as a Phœnix.[2] Every
sanctuary sought to gain honor by associating in some
way with its own early history the appearance of the Sun-
god. Either by his own masculine power self-developed,[3]
or by a consort who appeared to him, the Sun-god now
begat Shu the Air-god, and Tefnut his wife. Of these
two were born Geb the Earth-god, and Nut the goddess
of the sky, whose children were the two brothers Osiris
and Set, and the sisters Isis and Nephthys.

In the remotest past it was with material functions that
the Sun-god had to do. In the earliest Sun-temples at
Abusir, he appears as the source of life and increase.
Men said of him: "Thou hast driven away the storm,
and hast expelled the rain, and hast broken up the
clouds."[4] These were his enemies, and of course they
were likewise personified in the folk-myth, appearing in
a tale in which the Sun-god loses his eye at the hands of

[1] Pyr. § 1778.   [2] Pyr. § 1652.
[3] Pyr. § 1818 and § 1248, where the act is described in detail.
[4] Pyr. § 500.

his enemy. Similarly the waxing and waning of the moon, who was also an eye of the Sun-god, gave rise to another version of the lost eye, which in this case was brought back and restored to the Sun-god by his friend Thoth the Moon-god.[1] This "eye," termed the "Horus-eye," became one of the holiest symbols of Egyptian religion, and was finally transferred to the Osirian faith, where it played a prominent part.[2]

As the Egyptian state developed and a uniformly organized nation under a single king embraced and included all the once petty and local principalities, the Sun-god became an ancient king who, like a Pharaoh, had once ruled Egypt. Many folk-myths telling of his earthly rule arose, but of these only fragments have survived, like that which narrates the ingratitude of his human subjects, whom he was obliged to punish and almost exterminate before he retired to the sky.[3]

While the Egyptian still referred with pleasure to the incidents which made up these primitive tales, and his religious literature to the end was filled with allusions to these myths, nevertheless at the beginning of the Pyramid Age he was already discerning the Sun-god in the exercise of functions which lifted him far above such childish fancies and made him the great arbiter and ruler of the Egyptian nation. While he was supreme among the gods, and men said of him, "Thou passest the night in the evening-barque, thou wakest in the morning-barque;

---

[1] Pyr. § 2213 d.
[2] On the two eyes of the Sun-god, see ERMAN's full statement, *Hymnen an das Diadem der Pharaonen*, in *Abhandl. der Kgl. Preuss. Akad.*, 1911, pp. 11-14.
[3] On the sun-myths see ERMAN, *Aegyptische Religion*, pp. 33-38. An insurrection suppressed by the Sun-god is referred to in the Pyramid Texts, Ut. 229 and § 311.

for thou art he who overlooks the gods; there is no god who overlooks thee";[1] he was likewise at the same time supreme over the destinies of men.

This fundamental transition, the earliest known, transferred the activities of the Sun-god from the realm of exclusively *material* forces to the domain of human affairs. Already in the Pyramid Age his supremacy in the affairs of Egypt was celebrated in the earliest Sun-hymn which we possess. It sets forth the god's beneficent maintenance and control of the land of Egypt, which is called the "Horus-eye," that is the Sun-god's eye. The hymn is as follows:

"Hail to thee, Atum!
Hail to thee, Kheprer!
Who himself became (or 'self-generator').
Thou art high in this thy name of 'Height,'
Thou becomest (ḫpr) in this thy name of 'Beetle' (ḫprr).
Hail to thee, Horus-eye (Egypt),
Which he adorned with both his arms.

"He permits thee (Egypt) not to hearken to the westerners,
He permits thee not to hearken to the easterners,
He permits thee not to hearken to the southerners,
He permits thee not to hearken to the northerners,
He permits thee not to hearken to the dwellers in the midst of the earth,
But thou hearkenest unto Horus.

"It is he who has adorned thee,
It is he who has built thee,
It is he who has founded thee.
Thou doest for him everything that he says to thee
In every place where he goes.

[1] Pyr. § 1479.

"Thou carriest to him the fowl-bearing waters that are in thee;
Thou carriest to him the fowl-bearing waters that shall be in thee.
Thou carriest to him every tree that is in thee,
Thou carriest to him every tree that shall be in thee.
Thou carriest to him all food that is in thee,
Thou carriest to him all food that shall be in thee.
Thou carriest to him the gifts that are in thee,
Thou carriest to him the gifts that shall be in thee.
Thou carriest to him everything that is in thee,
Thou carriest to him everything that shall be in thee.
Thou bringest them to him,
To every place where his heart desires to be.

"The doors that are on thee stand fast like Inmutef,[1]
They open not to the westerners,
They open not to the easterners,
They open not to the northerners,
They open not to the southerners,
They open not to the dwellers in the midst of the earth,
They open to Horus.
It was he who made them,
It was he who set them up,
It was he who saved them from every ill which Set did to them.
It was he who settled (grg) thee,
In this thy name of 'Settlements' (grg-wt).
It was he who went doing obeisance (nyny) after thee,
In this thy name of 'City' (nwt)
It was he who saved thee from every ill
Which Set did unto thee."[2]

Similarly the Sun-god is the ally and protector of the king: "He settles for him Upper Egypt, he settles for him Lower Egypt; he hacks up for him the strongholds of Asia, he quells for him all the people,[3] who were fashioned

[1] A priestly title meaning "Pillar of his mother" and containing some mythological allusion.
[2] Pyr. §§ 1587–95.
[3] The word used applies only to the people of Egypt.

under his fingers." [1] Such was his prestige that by the twenty-ninth century his name appeared in the names of the Gizeh kings, the builders of the second and third pyramids there, Khafre and Menkure, and according to a folk-tale circulating a thousand years later, Khufu the builder of the Great Pyramid of Gizeh, and the predecessor of the two kings just named, was warned by a wise man that his line should be superseded by three sons of the Sun-god yet to be born. As a matter of fact, in the middle of the next century, that is about 2750 B. C., the line of Khufu, the Fourth Dynasty, was indeed supplanted by a family of kings, who began to assume the title "Son of Re," though the title was probably not unknown even earlier. This Fifth Dynasty was devoted to the service of the Sun-god, and each king built a vast sanctuary for his worship in connection with the royal residence, on the margin of the western desert. Such a sanctuary possessed no adytum, or holy-of-holies, but in its place there rose a massive masonry obelisk towering to the sky. Like all obelisks, it was surmounted by a pyramid, which formed the apex. The pyramid was, as we shall see, the chief symbol of the Sun-god, and in his sanctuary at Heliopolis there was a pyramidal stone in the holy place, of which that surmounting the obelisk in the Fifth Dynasty sun-temples was perhaps a reproduction. It is evident that the priests of Heliopolis had become so powerful that they had succeeded in seating this Solar line of kings upon the throne of the Pharaohs. From now on the state fiction was maintained that the Pharaoh was the physical son of the Sun-god by an earthly mother, and in later days we find the successive incidents of the Sun-god's terrestrial amour sculptured

[1] Pyr. § 1837.

on the walls of the temples. It has been preserved in two buildings of the Eighteenth Dynasty, the temple of Luxor and that of Der el-Bahri.[1]

The legend was so persistent that even Alexander the Great deferred to the tradition, and made the long journey to the Oasis of Amon in the western desert, that he might be recognized as the bodily son of the Egyptian Sun-god;[2] and the folk-tale preserved in Pseudo-Callisthenes gave the legend currency as a popular romance, which survived until a few centuries ago in Europe. It still remains to be determined what influence the Solar Pharaoh may have had upon the Solar apotheosis of the Cæsars, five hundred years later.

From the foundation of the Fifth Dynasty, in the twenty-eighth century B. C., the position of the Sun-god then, as the father of the Pharaoh and the great patron divinity of the state, was one of unrivalled splendor and power. He was the great god of king and court. When King Neferirkere is deeply afflicted at the sudden death of his grand vizier, who was stricken down with disease at the king's side, the Pharaoh prays to Re;[3] and the court-physician, when he has received a gift from the king for his tomb, tells of it in his tomb inscriptions with the words: "If ye love Re, ye shall praise every god for Sahure's sake who did this for me."[4]

The conception of the Sun-god as a former king of Egypt, as the father of the reigning Pharaoh, and as the protector and leader of the nation, still a kind of ideal king, resulted in the most important consequences for

[1] BAR, II, 187-212.
[2] The material will be found in MASPERO's useful essay, *Comment Alexandre devint dieu en Égypte, École des Hautes Études, annuaire*, 1897.
[3] BAR, I, 247.
[4] BAR, I, 247.

religion. The qualities of the earthly kingship of the Pharaoh were easily transferred to Re. We can observe this even in externals. There was a palace song with which the court was wont to waken the sovereign five thousand years ago, or which was addressed to him in the morning as he came forth from his chamber. It began:

> "Thou wakest in peace,
> The king awakes in peace,
> Thy wakening is in peace."[1]

This song was early addressed to the Sun-god,[2] and similarly the hymns to the royal diadem as a divinity were addressed to other gods.[3] The whole earthly conception and environment of the Egyptian Pharaoh were soon, as it were, the "stage properties" with which Re was "made up" before the eyes of the Nile-dweller. When later on, therefore, the conception of the human kingship was developed and enriched under the transforming social forces of the Feudal Age, these vital changes were soon reflected from the character of the Pharaoh to that of the Sun-god. It was a fact of the greatest value to religion, then, that the Sun-god became a kind of celestial reflection of the earthly sovereign. This phenomenon is, of course, merely a highly specialized example of the universal process by which man has pictured to himself his god with the pigments of his earthly experience. We shall later see how this process is closely analogous to the developing idea of the Messianic king in Hebrew thought.

---

[1] The character and origin, and the later use of this song as a part of temple ritual and worship, were first noticed by ERMAN, *Hymnen an das Diadem der Pharaonen, Abhandl. der Kgl. Preuss. Akad.*, Berlin, 1911, pp. 15 *ff*.

[2] Pyr. §§ 1478, 1518.   [3] See ERMAN, *ibid*.

18 RELIGION AND THOUGHT IN ANCIENT EGYPT

While there is no question whatever regarding the natural phenomenon of which Re, Atum, Horus, and the rest were personifications, there has been much uncertainty and discussion of the same question in connection with Osiris.[1]

The oldest source, the Pyramid Texts, in combination with a few later references, settles the question beyond any doubt. The clearest statement of the nature of Osiris is that contained in the incident of the finding of the dead god by his son Horus, as narrated in the Pyramid Texts: "Horus comes, he recognizes his father in thee, youthful in thy name of 'Fresh Water.'"[2] Equally unequivocal are the words of King Ramses IV, who says to the god: "Thou art indeed the Nile, great on the fields at the beginning of the seasons; gods and men live by the moisture that is in thee."[3]

Similarly in the Pyramid Texts, Osiris is elsewhere addressed: "Ho, Osiris, the inundation comes, the overflow moves, Geb (the earth-god) groans: 'I have sought thee in the field, I have smitten him who did aught against thee ... that thou mightest live and lift thyself up.'"[4] Again when the dead king Unis is identified with Osiris, it is said of him: "Unis comes hither up-stream when the flood inundates.... Unis comes to his pools that are in the region of the flood at the great inundation, to the

---

[1] The material known before the discovery of the Pyramid Texts was put together by LEFEBURE, *Le mythe osirien*, Paris, 1874; review by MASPERO, *Revue critique*, 1875, t. II, pp. 209–210. Without the Pyramid Texts, the oldest source, it is hardly possible to settle the question. The complete material from this source has not hitherto been brought to bear on the question, not even in the latest work on the subject, FRAZER's admirable book, *Adonis Attis Osiris*, London, 1907.

[2] Pyr. § 589.   [3] MARIETTE, *Abydos*, II, 54, l. 7.
[4] Pyr. § 2111.

place of peace, with green fields, that is in the horizon. Unis makes the verdure to flourish in the two regions of the horizon";[1] or "it is Unis who inundates the land."[2]

Likewise the deceased king Pepi I is addressed as Osiris thus: "This thy cavern,[3] is the broad hall of Osiris, O King Pepi, which brings the wind and ⌈guides⌉ the north-wind. It raises thee as Osiris, O King Pepi. The winepress god comes to thee bearing wine-juice. . . . Those who behold the Nile tossing in waves tremble. The marshes laugh, the shores are overflowed, the divine offerings descend, men give praise and the heart of the gods rejoices."[4] A priestly explanation in the Pyramid Texts represents the inundation as of ceremonial origin, Osiris as before being its source: "The lakes fill, the canals are inundated, by the purification that came forth from Osiris";[5] or "Ho this Osiris, king Mernere! Thy water, thy libation is the great inundation that came forth from thee" (as Osiris).[6]

In a short hymn addressed to the departed king, Pepi II, as Osiris, we should discern Osiris either in the life-giving waters or the soil of Egypt which is laved by them. The birth of the god is thus described: "The waters of life that are in the sky come; the waters of life that are in the earth come. The sky burns for thee, the earth trembles for thee, before the divine birth. The two mountains divide, the god becomes, the god takes possession of his body. Behold this king Pepi, his feet are kissed by the pure waters which arose through Atum, which the phallus of Shu makes and the vulva of Tefnut causes to be.

---

[1] Pyr. §§ 507-8. [2] Pyr. § 388.
[3] The word used is tpḥt, the term constantly employed in later religious texts for the cavern from which the Nile had its source.
[4] Pyr. §§ 1551-4. [5] Pyr. § 848. [6] Pyr. § 868.

They come to thee, they bring to thee the pure waters from their father. They purify thee, they cleanse thee, O Pepi. . . . The libation is poured out at the gate of this king Pepi, the face of every god is washed. Thou washest thy arms, O Osiris."[1] As Osiris was identified with the waters of earth and sky, he may even become the sea and the ocean itself. We find him addressed thus: "Thou art great, thou art green, in thy name of Great Green (Sea); lo, thou art round as the Great Circle (Okeanos); lo, thou art turned about, thou art round as the circle that encircles the Haunebu (Ægeans)."[2] "Thou includest all things in thy embrace, in thy name of 'Encircler of the Haunebu' (Ægeans)."[3] Or again: "Thou hast encircled every god in thy embrace, their lands and all their possessions. O Osiris . . . thou art great, thou curvest about as the curve which encircles the Haunebu."[4] Hence it is that Osiris is depicted on the sarcophagus of Seti I, engulfed in waters and lying as it were coiled, with head and heels meeting around a vacancy containing the inscription: "It is Osiris, encircling the Nether-World."[5] We may therefore understand another passage of the Pyramid Texts, which says to Osiris: "Thou ferriest over the lake to thy house the Great Green (sea)."[6]

While the great fountains of water are thus identified with Osiris, it is evidently a particular function of the waters with which he was associated. It was water as a source of fertility, water as a life-giving agency with which

[1] Pyr. §§ 2063–8.
[2] Pyr. §§ 628–9. Osiris is made ruler of the Haunebu also in the Stela No. 20, Bibl. Nat. Cat. Ledrain, pl. xxvi, ll. 19–20.
[3] Pyr. § 1631.   [4] Pyr. § 847.
[5] BONOMI and SHARPE, *Alabaster Sarcophagus of Oimenephah I*, London, 1864, pl. 15.
[6] Pyr. § 1752.

Osiris was identified. It is water which brings life to the soil, and when the inundation comes the Earth-god Geb says to Osiris: "The divine fluid that is in thee cries out, thy heart lives, thy divine limbs move, thy joints are loosed," in which we discern the water bringing life and causing the resurrection of Osiris, the soil. In the same way in a folk-tale thirteen or fourteen hundred years later than the Pyramid Texts, the heart of a dead hero, who is really Osiris, is placed in water, and when he has drunk the water containing his heart, he revives and comes to life.[1]

As we have seen in the last passage from the Pyramid Texts, Osiris is closely associated with the soil likewise. This view of Osiris is carried so far in a hymn of the twelfth century B. C. as to identify Osiris, not only with the soil but even with the earth itself. The beginning is lost, but we perceive that the dead Osiris is addressed as one "with outspread arms, sleeping upon his side upon the sand, lord of the soil, mummy with long phallus. . . . Re-Khepri shines on thy body, when thou liest as Sokar, and he drives away the darkness which is upon thee, that he may bring light to thy eyes. For a time he shines upon thy body mourning for thee. . . . The soil is on thy arm, its corners are upon thee as far as the four pillars of the sky. When thou movest, the earth trembles. . . . As for thee, the Nile comes forth from the sweat of thy hands. Thou spewest out the wind that is in thy throat into the nostrils of men, and that whereon men live is divine. It is ⌜alike in⌝ thy nostrils, the tree and its verdure, reeds—plants, barley, wheat, and the tree of life. When canals are dug, . . . houses and temples are built, when monuments are transported and fields are cultivated, when

[1] The Tale of the Two Brothers; see *infra*, pp. 357–360.

tomb-chapels and tombs are excavated, they rest on thee, it is thou who makest them. They are on thy back, although they are more than can be put into writing. [Thy] back hath not an empty place, for they all lie on thy back; but [thou sayest] not, 'I am weighed down.' Thou art the father and mother of men, they live on thy breath, they eat of the flesh of thy body. The 'Primæval' is thy name."[1]

The earlier views of the Pyramid Texts represent him as intimately associated with vegetable life. We find him addressed thus: "O thou whose ab-tree is green, which (or who) is upon his field; O thou opener of the ukhikh-flower that (or who) is on his sycomore; O thou brightener of regions who is on his palm; O thou lord of green fields."[2] Again it is said to him: "Thou art flooded with the verdure with which the children of Geb (the Earth-god) were flooded.... The am-tree serves thee, the nebes-tree bows its head to thee."[3] In addition to his connection with the wine-press god above, he is called "Lord of overflowing wine."[4] Furthermore, as the inundation began at the rising of Sothis, the star of Isis, sister of Osiris, they said to him: "The beloved daughter, Sothis, makes thy fruits (rnpwt) in this her name of 'Year' (rnpt)."[5] These are the fruits on which Egypt lives; when therefore the dead king is identified with Osiris, his birth is called "his unblemished birth, whereby the Two Lands (Egypt) live," and thereupon he comes as the messenger of Osiris announcing the prosperous yield of the year.[6] In the earliest versions of the Book of the Dead likewise, the deceased says of himself: "I am

---

[1] ERMAN, Zeitschr. für aegypt. Sprache, 38, pp. 30–33.
[2] Pyr. § 699.   [3] Pyr. § 1019.   [4] Pyr. § 1524.
[5] Pyr. § 1065.   [6] Pyr. §§ 1194–5.

Osiris, I have come forth as thou (that is "being thou"), I have entered as thou . . . the gods live as I, I live as the gods, I live as 'Grain,'[1] I grow as 'Grain.' . . . I am barley." With these early statements we should compare the frequent representations showing grain sprouting from the prostrate body of Osiris, or a tree growing out of his tomb or his coffin, or the effigies of the god as a mummy moulded of bruised corn and earth and buried with the dead, or in the grain-field to insure a plentiful crop.

It is evident from these earliest sources that Osiris was identified with the *waters*, especially the inundation, with the *soil*, and with *vegetation*. This is a result of the Egyptian tendency always to think in graphic and concrete forms. The god was doubtless in Egyptian thought the imperishable principle of life wherever found, and this conception not infrequently appears in representations of him, showing him even in death as still possessed of generative power. The ever-waning and reviving life of the earth, sometimes associated with the life-giving waters, sometimes with the fertile soil, or again discerned in vegetation itself—that was Osiris. The fact that the Nile, like the vegetation which its rising waters nourished and supported, waxed and waned every year, made it more easy to see him in the Nile, the most important feature of the Egyptian's landscape, than in any other form.[2] As a matter of fact the Nile was but the source

---

[1] Here personified as god of Grain (Npr). The passage is from the Middle Kingdom Coffin Texts, published by LACAU, *Recueil de trav.* See also "Chapter of Becoming the Nile" (XIX) and *cf.* XLIV.

[2] The later classical evidence from Greek and Roman authors is in general corroborative of the above conclusions. It is of only secondary importance as compared with the early sources employed above. The most important passages will be found in FRAZER's *Adonis Attis Osiris*, London, 1907, pp. 330–345.

and visible symbol of that fertility of which Osiris was the personification.

This ever-dying, ever-reviving god, who seemed to be subjected to human destiny and human mortality, was inevitably the inexhaustible theme of legend and saga. Like the Sun-god, after kings appeared in the land, Osiris soon became an ancient king, who had been given the inheritance of his father Geb, the Earth-god. He was commonly called "the heir of Geb," who "assigned to him the leadership of the lands for the good of affairs. He put this land in his hand, its water, its air, its verdure, all its herds, all things that fly, all things that flutter, its reptiles, its game of the desert, legally conveyed to the son of Nut (Osiris)."[1]

Thus Osiris began his beneficent rule, and "Egypt was content therewith, as he dawned upon the throne of his father, like Re when he rises in the horizon, when he sends forth light for him that is in darkness. He shed forth light by his radiance, and he flooded the Two Lands like the sun at early morning, while his diadem pierced the sky and mingled with the stars—he, leader of every god, excellent in command, favorite of the Great Ennead, beloved of the Little Ennead."[2] In power and splendor and benevolence he ruled a happy people. He "established justice in Egypt, putting the son in the seat of the father." "He overthrew his enemies, and with a mighty arm he slew his foes, setting the fear of him among his adversaries, and extending his boundaries."[3]

His sister Isis, who was at the same time his wife, stood

---

[1] Hymn to Osiris in the Bibliothèque Nationale, Stela No. 20, published by LEDRAIN, *Les monuments égyptiens de la Bibliothèque Nationale*, Paris, 1879, pls. xxi–xxviii, ll. 10–11. Hereafter cited as Bib. Nat. No. 20. It dates from the Eighteenth Dynasty.

[2] Bib. Nat. No. 20, ll. 12–13.   [3] *Ibid.*, 20, ll. 9–10.

loyally at his side; she "protected him, driving away enemies, warding off ⌈danger,⌉ taking the foe by the excellence of her speech—she, the skilful-tongued, whose word failed not, excellent in command, Isis, effective in protecting her brother."[1] The arch enemy of the good Osiris was his brother Set, who, however, feared the good king.[2] The Sun-god warned him and his followers: "Have ye done aught against him and said that he should die? He shall not die but he shall live forever."[3]

Nevertheless his assailants at last prevailed against him, if not openly then by stratagem, as narrated by Plutarch, although there is no trace in the Egyptian sources of Plutarch's story of the chest into which the doomed Osiris was lured by the conspirators and then shut in to die.[4]

The oldest source, the Pyramid Texts, indicates assassination: "his brother Set felled him to the earth in Nedyt";[5] or "his brother Set overthrew him upon his side, on the further side of the land of Gehesti";[6] but another document of the Pyramid Age, and possibly quite as old as the passages quoted from the Pyramid Texts, says: "Osiris was drowned in his new water (the inundation)."[7]

When the news reached the unhappy Isis, she wandered in great affliction seeking the body of her lord, "seeking

[1] Bib. Nat. No. 20, ll. 13–14.
[2] Pyr. § 589. The same intimations are discernible throughout this Utterance (357).
[3] Pyr. § 1471. The Pharaoh's name has been inserted in place of the last pronoun. In the variants of this text (§ 481 and § 944) the enemy is in the singular.
[4] See SCHAEFER, *Zeitschrift für aegypt. Sprache*, 41, 81 ff.
[5] Pyr. § 1256.   [6] Pyr. § 972.
[7] British Museum, Stela 797, ll. 19 and 62. On this monument see *infra*, pp. 41–47.

him unweariedly, sadly going through this land, nor stopping until she found him."[1] The oldest literature is full of references to the faithful wife unceasingly seeking her murdered husband: "Thou didst come seeking thy brother Osiris, when his brother Set had overthrown him."[2] The Plutarch narrative even carries her across the Mediterranean to Byblos, where the body of Osiris had drifted in the waters. The Pyramid Texts refer to the fact that she at last found him "upon the shore of Nedyt,"[3] where we recall he was slain by Set, and it may be indeed that Nedyt is an ancient name for the region of Byblos, although it was later localized at Abydos, and one act of the Osirian passion play was presented at the shore of Nedyt, near Abydos.[4] The introduction of Byblos is at least as old as the thirteenth century B. C., when the Tale of the Two Brothers in an Osirian incident pictures the Osirian hero as slain in the Valley of the Cedar, which can have been nowhere but the Syrian coast where the cedar flourished. Indeed in the Pyramid Texts, Horus is at one point represented as crossing the sea.[5] All this is doubtless closely connected with the identification of Osiris with the waters, or even with the sea, and harmonizes easily with the other version of his death, which represents him as drowning. In that version "Isis and Nephthys saw him. . . . Horus commanded Isis and Nephthys in Busiris, that they seize upon Osiris, and that they prevent him from drowning. They turned around the head (of Osiris) . . . and they

---

[1] Bib. Nat. No. 20, ll. 14–15.
[2] Pyr. § 972.   [3] Pyr. § 1008.
[4] See *infra*, p. 289. Nedyt was conceived as near Abydos even in the Pyramid Texts, see § 754, where Nedyt occurs in parallelism with Thinis the nome of Abydos.
[5] Pyr. §§ 1505, 1508.

brought him to the land."¹ Nephthys frequently accompanies her sister in the long search, both of them being in the form of birds. "Isis comes, Nephthys comes, one of them on the right, one of them on the left, one of them as a het-bird, one of them as a falcon. They have found Osiris, as his brother Set felled him to the earth in Nedyt."²
"'I have found (him),' said Nephthys, when they saw Osiris (lying) on his side on the shore. . . . 'O my brother, I have sought thee; raise thee up, O spirit.'"³ "The het-bird comes, the falcon comes; they are Isis and Nephthys, they come embracing their brother, Osiris. . . . Weep for thy brother, Isis! Weep for thy brother, Nephthys! Weep for thy brother. Isis sits, her arms upon her head; Nephthys has seized the tips of her breasts (in mourning) because of her brother."⁴ The lamentations of Isis and Nephthys became the most sacred expression of sorrow known to the heart of the Egyptian, and many were the varied forms which they took until they emerged in the Osirian mysteries of Europe, three thousand years later.

Then the two sisters embalm the body of their brother to prevent its perishing,⁵ or the Sun-god is moved with pity and despatches the ancient mortuary god "Anubis . . . lord of the Nether World, to whom the westerners (the dead) give praise . . . him who was in the middle of the mid-heaven, fourth of the sons of Re, who was made to descend from the sky to embalm Osiris, because he was so very worthy in the heart of Re."⁶ Then when they have laid him in his tomb a sycomore grows up and

---
¹ Brit. Museum, 797, ll. 62–63.   ² Pyr. §§ 1255–6.
³ Pyr. §§ 2144–5.   ⁴ Pyr. §§ 1280–2.   ⁵ Pyr. § 1257.
⁶ Coffin of Henui, STEINDORFF, *Grabfunde des Mittleren Reichs*, II, 17.

envelops the body of the dead god, like the *erica* in the story of Plutarch. This sacred tree is the visible symbol of the imperishable life of Osiris, which in the earliest references was already divine and might be addressed as a god. Already in the Pyramid Age men sang to it: "Hail to thee, Sycomore, which encloses the god, under which the gods of the Nether Sky stand, whose tips are scorched, whose middle is burned, who art just in ¹suffering¹. . . . Thy forehead is upon thy arm (in mourning) for Osiris. . . . Thy station, O Osiris; thy shade over thee, O Osiris, which repels thy defiance, O Set; the gracious damsel (meaning the tree) which was made for this soul of Gehesti; thy shade, O Osiris." [1]

Such was the life and death of Osiris. His career, as picturing the cycle of nature, could not of course end here. It is continued in his resurrection, and likewise in a later addition drawn from the Solar theology, the story of his son Horus and the Solar feud of Horus and Set, which was not originally Osirian. Even in death the life-giving power of Osiris did not cease. The faithful Isis drew near her dead lord, "making a shadow with her pinions and causing a wind with her wings . . . raising the weary limbs of the silent-hearted (dead), receiving his seed, bringing forth an heir, nursing the child in solitude, whose place is not known, introducing him when his arm grew strong in the Great Hall" (at Heliopolis?).[2]

---

[1] Pyr. §§ 1285–7. Gehesti is the name of the land where Osiris was slain. The reference to the scorching and burning of the tree is doubtless the earliest native mention of the ceremony of enclosing an image of Osiris in a tree and burning it, as narrated by FIRMICUS MATERNUS, *De errore profanarum religionum*, 27; FRAZER, *Adonis Attis Osiris*, pp. 339–340.

[2] Bib. Nat. No. 20, ll. 15–16. The story is told with coarse frankness also in the Pyramid Texts: "Thy sister Isis comes to thee, rejoicing for love of thee. Ponis eam ad phallum tuum, semen tuum

The imagination of the common people loved to dwell upon this picture of the mother concealed in the marshes of the Delta, as they fancied, by the city of Khemmis, and there bringing up the youthful Horus, that "when his arm grew strong" he might avenge the murder of his father. All this time Set was, of course, not idle, and many were the adventures and escapes which befell the child at the hands of Set. These are too fragmentarily preserved to be reconstructed clearly, but even after the youth has grown up and attained a stature of eight cubits (nearly fourteen feet), he is obliged to have a tiny chapel of half a cubit long made, in which he conceals himself from Set.[1] Grown to manhood, however, the youthful god emerges at last from his hiding-place in the Delta. In the oldest fragments we hear of "Isis the great, who fastened on the girdle in Khemmis, when she brought her ⌜censer⌝ and burned incense before her son Horus, the young child, when he was going through the land on his white sandals, that he might see his father Osiris."[2] Again: "Horus comes forth from Khemmis, and (the city of) Buto arises for Horus, and he purifies himself there. Horus comes purified that he may avenge his father."[3]

The filial piety of Horus was also a theme which the imagination of the people loved to contemplate, as he went forth to overthrow his father's enemies and take vengeance upon Set. They sang to Osiris: "Horus hath

emergit in eam." Pyr. § 632, and again less clearly in Pyr. § 1636. At Abydos and Philæ the incident is graphically depicted on the wall in relief.

[1] See SCHAEFER, Zeitschr. f. aegypt. Sprache, 41, 81.
[2] Pyr. § 1214.
[3] Pyr. § 2190. There was also a story of how he left Buto, to which there is a reference in Pyr. § 1373 – § 1089.

come that he might embrace thee. He hath caused Thoth to turn back the followers of Set before thee. He hath brought them to thee all together. He hath turned back the heart of Set before thee, for thou art greater than he. Thou hast gone forth before him, thy character is before him. Geb hath seen thy character, he hath put thee in thy place. Geb hath brought to thee thy two sisters to thy side: it is Isis and Nephthys. Horus hath caused the gods to unite with thee and fraternize with thee. . . . He hath caused that the gods avenge thee. Geb hath placed his foot on the head of thy enemy, who hath retreated before thee. Thy son Horus hath smitten him. He hath taken away his eye from him; he hath given it to thee, that thou mightest become a soul thereby and be mighty thereby before the spirits. Horus hath caused that thou seize thy enemies and that there should be none escaping among them before thee. . . . Horus hath seized Set, he hath laid him for thee under thee, that he (Set) may lift thee up and tremble under thee as the earth trembles. . . . Horus hath caused that thou shouldest recognize him in his inner heart, without his escaping from thee. O Osiris, . . . Horus hath avenged thee."[1] "Horus hath come that he may recognize thee. He hath smitten Set for thee, bound. Thou art his (Set's) ka. Horus hath driven him back for thee; thou art greater than he. He swims bearing thee; he carries in thee one greater than he. His followers behold thee that thy strength is greater than he, and they do not attack thee. Horus comes, he recognizes his father in thee, youthful (rnp) in thy name of 'Fresh Water' (mw-rnpw)."[2] "Loose thou Horus from his bonds, that he may punish the followers of Set. Seize

[1] Pyr. §§ 575–582.   [2] Pyr. §§ 587–9.

them, remove their heads, wade thou in their blood. Count their hearts in this thy name of 'Anubis counter of hearts.'"[1]

The battle of Horus with Set, which as we shall see was a Solar incident, waged so fiercely that the young god lost his eye at the hands of his father's enemy. When Set was overthrown, and it was finally recovered by Thoth, this wise god spat upon the wound and healed it. This method of healing the eye, which is, of course, folk-medicine reflected in the myth, evidently gained wide popularity, passed into Asia, and seems to reappear in the New Testament narrative, in the incident which depicts Jesus doubtless deferring to recognized folk-custom in employing the same means to heal a blind man. Horus now seeks his father, even crossing the sea in his quest,[2] that he may raise his father from the dead and offer to him the eye which he has sacrificed in his father's behalf. This act of filial devotion, preserved to us in the Pyramid Texts (see above, p. 12), made the already sacred Horus-eye doubly revered in the tradition and feeling of the Egyptians. It became the symbol of all sacrifice; every gift or offering might be called a "Horus-eye," especially if offered to the dead. Excepting the sacred beetle, or scarab, it became the commonest and the most revered symbol known to Egyptian religion, and the myriads of eyes, wrought in blue or green glaze, or even cut from costly stone, which fill our museum collections, and are brought home by thousands by the modern tourist, are survivals of this ancient story of Horus and his devotion to his father.

A chapter of the Pyramid Texts tells the whole story of the resurrection. "The gods dwelling in Buto ⌈approach⌉,

[1] Pyr. §§ 1285–7.   [2] Pyr. §§ 1505, 1508.

they come to Osiris¹ at the sound of the mourning of Isis, at the cry of Nephthys, at the wailing of these two horizon-gods over this Great One who came forth from the Nether World. The souls of Buto wave their arms to thee, they strike their flesh for thee, they throw their arms for thee, they beat on their temples for thee. They say of thee, O Osiris:

"'Though thou departest, thou comest (again); though thou sleepest, thou wakest (again); though thou diest, thou livest (again).'

"'Stand up, that thou mayest see what thy son has done for thee. Awake, that thou mayest hear what Horus has done for thee.'

"'He has smitten (ḥy) for thee the one that smote thee, as an ox (yḥ); he has slain (sm') for thee the one that slew thee, as a wild bull (sm'). He has bound for thee the one that bound thee.'

"'He has put himself under thy daughter, the Great One (fem.) dwelling in the East, that there may be no mourning in the palace of the gods.'

"Osiris speaks to Horus when he has removed the evil that was in Osiris on his fourth day, and had forgotten what was done to him on his eighth day. Thou hast come forth from the lake of life, purified in the celestial lake, becoming Upwawet. Thy son Horus leads thee when he has given to thee the gods who were against thee, and Thoth has brought them to thee. How beautiful are they who saw, how satisfied are they who beheld, who saw Horus when he gave life to his father, when he offered satisfaction to Osiris before the western gods."

"Thy libation is poured by Isis, Nephthys has purified

¹ The name of the king for whom the chapter was employed has been inserted here.

THE ORIGINS 33

thee, thy two great and mighty sisters, who have put together thy flesh, who have fastened together thy limbs, who have made thy two eyes to shine (again) in thy head."[1]

Sometimes it is Horus who puts together the limbs of the dead god,[2] or again he finds his father as embalmed by his mother and Anubis: "Horus comes to thee, he separates thy bandages, he throws off thy bonds;"[3] "arise, give thou thy hand to Horus, that he may raise thee up." Over and over again the rising of Osiris is reiterated, as the human protest against death found insistent expression in the invincible fact that he rose. We see the tomb opened for him: "The brick are drawn for thee out of the great tomb,"[4] and then "Osiris awakes, the weary god wakens, the god stands up, he gains control of his body."[5] "Stand up! Thou shalt not end, thou shalt not perish."[6]

The malice of Set was not spent, however, even after his defeat by Horus and the resurrection of Osiris. He entered the tribunal of the gods at Heliopolis and lodged with them charges against Osiris. We have no clear account of this litigation, nor of the nature of the charges, except that Set was using them to gain the throne of Egypt. There must have been a version in which the subject of the trial was Set's crime in slaying Osiris. In dramatic

[1] Pyr. Ut. 670, §§ 1976–82, as restored from Ut. 482 (a shorter redaction), and the tomb of Harhotep and the tomb of Psamtik. (See SETHE, Pyr., vol. II, pp. iii–iv, Nos. 6, 10, 11).
[2] Pyr. §§ 617, 634.   [3] Pyr. §§ 2201–2.
[4] Pyr. § 572.   [5] Pyr. § 2092.
[6] Pyr. § 1299. Commonly so in the Pyramid Texts. It became a frequent means of introducing the formulas of the ritual of mortuary offerings, in order that the dead might be roused to partake of the food offered; see Pyr. § 654 and § 735, or Ut. 413 and 437 entire. The resurrection of Osiris by Re was doubtless a theological device for correlating the Solar and Osirian doctrines (Pyr. § 721).

setting the Pyramid Texts depict the scene. "The sky is troubled, earth trembles, Horus comes, Thoth appears. They lift Osiris from his side; they make him stand up before the two Divine Enneads. 'Remember O Set, and put it in thy heart, this word which Geb spoke, and this manifestation which the gods made against you in the hall of the prince in Heliopolis, because thou didst fell Osiris to the earth. When thou didst say, O Set, "I have not done this to him," that thou mightest prevail thereby, being saved that thou mightest prevail against Horus. When thou didst say, O Set, "It was he who bowed me down" . . . When thou didst say, O Set, "It was he who attacked me" . . . Lift thee up, O Osiris! Set has lifted himself. He has heard the threat of the gods who spoke of the Divine Father. Isis has thy arm, Osiris; Nephthys has thy hand and thou goest between them.'"[1]

But Osiris is triumphantly vindicated, and the throne is restored to him against the claims of Set. "He is justified through that which he has done. . . . The Two Truths[2] have held the legal hearing. Shu was witness. The Two Truths commanded that the thrones of Geb should revert to him, that he should raise himself to that which he desired, that his limbs which were in concealment should be gathered together (again); that he should join those who dwell in Nun (the primeval ocean); and that he should terminate the words in Heliopolis."[3]

---

[1] Pyr. §§ 956-960.
[2] On the Two Truths see the same phrase in the Book of the Dead, *infra*, p. 299 and notes 2 and 3.
[3] Pyr. §§ 316-318. Compare also, "'Set is guilty, Osiris is righteous,' (words) from the mouth of the gods on that good day of going forth upon the mountain" (for the interment of Osiris) (Pyr. §1556), from which it would appear that there was a verdict before the resurrection of Osiris.

The verdict rendered in favor of Orisis, which we translate "justified," really means "true, right, just, or righteous of voice." It must have been a legal term already in use when this episode in the myth took form. It is later used in frequent parallelism with "victorious" or "victory," and possessed the essential meaning of "triumphant" or "triumph," both in a moral as well as a purely material and physical sense. The later development of the Osirian litigation shows that it gained a moral sense in this connection, if it did not possess it in the beginning. We shall yet have occasion to observe the course of the moral development involved in the wide popularity of this incident in the Osiris myth.

The gods rejoice in the triumph of Osiris.

> "All gods dwelling in the sky are satisfied;
> All gods dwelling in the earth are satisfied;
> All gods southern and northern are satisfied;
> All gods western and eastern are satisfied;
> All gods of the nomes are satisfied;
> All gods of the cities are satisfied;

with this great and mighty word that came out of the mouth of Thoth in favor of Osiris, treasurer of life, seal-bearer of the gods."[1]

The penalty laid upon Set was variously narrated in the different versions of the myth. The Pyramid Texts several times refer to the fact that Set was obliged to take Osiris on his back and carry him. "Ho! Osiris! Rouse thee! Horus causes that Thoth bring to thee thy enemy. He places thee upon his back. Make thy seat upon him. Ascend and sit down upon him; let him not escape thee";[2] or again, "The great Ennead avenges thee; they put for

[1] Pyr. §§ 1522-3.   [2] Pyr. §§ 651-2; see also §§ 642, 649.

thee thy enemy under thee. 'Carry one who is greater than thou,' say they of him. . . . 'Lift up one greater than thou,' say they."[1] "'He to whom evil was done by his brother Set comes to us,' say the Two Divine Enneads, 'but we shall not permit that Set be free from bearing thee forever, O king Osiris,' say the Two Divine Enneads concerning thee, O king Osiris."[2] If Osiris is here the earth as commonly, it may be that we have in this episode the earliest trace of the Atlas myth. Another version, however, discloses Set, bound hand and foot "and laid upon his side in the Land of Ru,"[3] or slaughtered and cut up as an ox and distributed as food to the gods;[4] or he is delivered to Osiris "cut into three pieces."[5]

The risen and victorious Osiris receives the kingdom. "The sky is given to thee, the earth is given to thee, the fields of Rushes are given to thee, the Horite regions, the Setite regions, the cities are given to thee. The nomes are united for thee by Atum. It is Geb (the Earth-god) who speaks concerning it."[6] Indeed Geb, the Earth-god and father of Osiris, "assigned the countries to the embrace of Osiris, when he found him lying upon his side in Gehesti."[7] Nevertheless Osiris does not really belong to the kingdom of the living. His dominion is the gloomy Nether World beneath the earth, to which he at once descends. After his death, one of the oldest sources says of him: "He entered the secret gates in the ⸢splendid⸣ precincts of the lords of eternity, at the goings of him who rises in the horizon, upon the ways of Re in the Great Seat."[8] There he is proclaimed king. Horus "proclaimed the royal decree in the

---

[1] Pyr. §§ 626-7, var. § 1628. See also § 1632.
[2] Pyr. § 1699.   [3] Pyr. § 1035.   [4] Pyr. Ut. 580.
[5] Pyr. Ut. 543; see also 1339.   [6] Pyr. § 961.
[7] Pyr. § 1033.   [8] Brit. Mus. Stela 797, l. 63.

places of Anubis.[1] Every one hearing it, he shall not live."[2] It was a subterranean kingdom of the dead over which Osiris reigned, and it was as champion and friend of the dead that he gained his great position in Egyptian religion.

But it will be discerned at once that the Osiris myth expressed those hopes and aspirations and ideals which were closest to the life and the affections of this great people. Isis was the noblest embodiment of wifely fidelity and maternal solicitude, while the highest ideals of filial devotion found expression in the story of Horus. About this group of father, mother, and son the affectionate fancy of the common folk wove a fair fabric of family ideals which rise high above such conceptions elsewhere. In the Osiris myth the institution of the family found its earliest and most exalted expression in religion, a glorified reflection of earthly ties among the gods. The catastrophe and the ultimate triumph of the righteous cause introduced here in a nature-myth are an impressive revelation of the profoundly moral consciousness with which the Egyptian at a remote age contemplated the world. When we consider, furthermore, that Osiris was the kindly dispenser of plenty, from whose prodigal hand king and peasant alike received their daily bounty, that he was waiting over yonder behind the shadow of death to waken all who have fallen asleep to a blessed hereafter with him, and that in every family group the same affections and emotions which had found expression in the beautiful myth were daily and hourly experiences, we shall understand something of the reason for the universal devotion which was ultimately paid the dead god.

The conquest of Egypt by the Osiris faith was, however,

---
[1] An old god of the hereafter.   [2] Pyr. § 1335.

a gradual process. He had once in prehistoric times been a dangerous god, and the tradition of his unfavorable character survived in vague reminiscences long centuries after he had gained wide popularity.[1] At that time the dark and forbidding realm which he ruled had been feared and dreaded.[2] In the beginning, too, he had been local to the Delta, where he had his home in the city of Dedu, later called Busiris by the Greeks. His transformation into a friend of man and kindly ruler of the dead took place here in prehistoric ages, and at an enormously remote date, before the two kingdoms of Upper and Lower Egypt were united under one king (3400 B. C.), the belief in him spread into the southern Kingdom.[3] He apparently first found a home in the south at Siut, and in the Pyramid Texts we read, "Isis and Nephthys salute thee in Siut, (even) their lord in thee, in thy name of 'Lord of Siut.'"[4] But the Osirian faith was early localized at Abydos, whither an archaic mortuary god, known as Khenti-Amentiu, "First of the Westerners," had already preceded Osiris.[5] There he became the "Dweller in Nedyt,"[6] and even in the Pyramid Texts he is identified with the "First of the Westerners."

[1] Pyr. §§ 1266-7.
[2] Pyr. §§ 251, 350; see also *infra*, pp. 142-3.
[3] This is shown in the Pyramid Texts, where the sycomore of Osiris is thus addressed: "Thou hast hurled thy terror into the heart of the kings of Lower Egypt dwelling in Buto" (Pyr. § 1488). Osiris must therefore have reached Upper Egypt, and have become domiciled there at a time when the kings of the North were still hostile.
[4] Pyr. § 630. There is not space here to correlate this fact with MEYER'S results regarding the wolf and jackal gods at Abydos and Siut.
[5] See MASPERO, *Études de mythologie et d'archéologie égyptiennes*, II, pp. 10, 359, etc., and EDUARD MEYER, *Zeitschr. für aegypt. Sprache*, 41, pp. 97 ff.
[6] Pyr. § 754.

"Thou art on the throne of Osiris,
As representative of the First of the Westerners." [1]

As "Lord of Abydos," Osiris continued his triumphant career, and ultimately was better known under this title than by his old association with Busiris (Dedu). All this, however, belongs to the historical development which we are to follow.

In spite of its popular origin we shall see that the Osirian faith, like that of the Sun-god, entered into the most intimate relations with the kingship. In probably the oldest religious feast of which any trace has been preserved in Egypt, known as the "Heb-Sed" or "Sed-Feast," the king assumed the costume and insignia of Osiris, and undoubtedly impersonated him. The significance of this feast is, however, entirely obscure as yet. The most surprising misunderstandings have gained currency concerning it, and the use of it for far-reaching conclusions before the surviving materials have all been put together is premature.

One of the ceremonies of this feast symbolized the resurrection of Osiris, and it was possibly to associate the Pharaoh with this auspicious event that he assumed the rôle of Osiris. In the end the deceased Pharoah became Osiris and enjoyed the same resuscitation by Horus and Isis, all the divine privileges, and the same felicity in the hereafter which had been accorded the dead god.

Some attempt to correlate the two leading gods of Egypt,

[1] Pyr. § 2021; see also § 1996. EDUARD MEYER (*ibid.*, p. 100) states that Osiris is never identified with Khenti-Amentiu in the Pyramid Texts, and it is true that the two names are not placed side by side as proper name and accompanying epithet in the Pyramid Texts, as they are so commonly later, but such a parallel as that above seems to me to indicate essential identity.

the Sun-god and Osiris, was finally inevitable. The harmonization was accomplished by the Solar theologians at Heliopolis, though not without inextricable confusion, as the two faiths, which had already interfused among the people, were now wrought together into a theological system. It is quite evident from the Pyramid Texts that the feud between Horus and Set was originally a Solar incident, and quite independent of the Osiris myth. We find that in the mortuary ceremonies, Set's spittle is used to purify the dead in the same words as that of Horus;[1] and that Set may perform the same friendly offices for the dead as those of Horus.[2] Indeed we find him fraternizing with the dead, precisely as Horus does.[3] We find them without distinction, one on either side of the dead, holding his arms and aiding him as he ascends to the Sun-god.[4] Set was king of the South on equal terms with Horus as king of the North;[5] over and over again in the Pyramid Texts they appear side by side, though implacable enemies, without the least suggestion that Set is a foul and detested divinity.[6] There are even traces of a similar ancient correlation of Osiris himself with Set![7] Set appears too without any unfavorable reflection upon him in connection with the Sun-god and his group,[8] and in harmony with this an old doctrine represents Set as in charge of the ladder by which the dead may ascend to the Sun-god—the ladder up which he himself once climbed.[9] Set was doubtless some natural phenomenon like the others of the group to which he belongs, and it is most probable that he was the darkness. He and Horus divided Egypt between them, Set being most

[1] Pyr. § 850.   [2] Pyr. §§ 1492-3.   [3] Pyr. § 1016-§ 801.
[4] Pyr. § 390.   [5] Pyr. §§ 204-6.
[6] See Pyr. §§ 418, 473, 487, 535, 594, 601, 683, 798, 823, 946, 971, 1148.
[7] Pyr. §§ 832, 865.   [8] Pyr. § 370.   [9] Pyr. §§ 478, 1148, 1253.

commonly represented as taking the South and Horus the North. The oldest royal monuments of Egypt represent the falcon of Horus and the strange animal (probably the *okapi*) of Set, side by side, as the symbol of the kingship of the two kingdoms now ruled by one Pharaoh. It is not our purpose, nor have we the space here, to study the question of Set, further than to demonstrate that he belonged to the Solar group, on full equality with Horus.

By what process Set became the enemy of Osiris we do not know. The sources do not disclose it. When this had once happened, however, it would be but natural that the old rival of Set, the Solar Horus, should be drawn into the Osirian situation, and that his hostility toward Set should involve his championship of the cause of Osiris. An old Memphite document of the Pyramid Age unmistakably discloses the absorption of the Set-Horus feud by the Osirian theology. In dramatic dialogue we discern Geb assigning their respective kingdoms to Horus and Set, a purely Solar episode, while at the same time Geb involves in this partition the incidents of the Osirian story.

"Geb says to Set: 'Go to the place where thou wast born.'"

"Geb says to Horus: 'Go to the place where thy father was drowned.'"

"Geb says to Horus and Set: 'I have separated you.'"

"Set: Upper Egypt."

"Horus: Lower Egypt."

"[Horus and Set]: Upper and Lower Egypt."

"Geb says to the Divine Ennead: 'I have conveyed my heritage to this my heir, the son of my first-born son. He is my son, my child.'"

The equality of Horus and Set, as in the old Solar

theology, is quite evident, but Horus is here made the son of Osiris. An ancient commentator on this passage has appended the following explanation of Geb's proceeding in assigning the kingdoms.

"He gathered together the Divine Ennead and he separated Horus and Set. He prevented their conflict and he installed Set as king of Upper Egypt in Upper Egypt, in the place where he was born in Sesesu. Then Geb installed Horus as king of Lower Egypt, in Lower Egypt in the place where his father was drowned, at (the time of) the dividing of the Two Lands."

"Then Horus stood in (one) district, when they satisfied the Two Lands in Ayan—that is the boundary of the Two Lands."

"Then Set stood in the (other) district, when they satisfied the Two Lands in Ayan—that is the boundary of the Two Lands.

"It was evil to the heart of Geb, that the portion of Horus was (only) equal to the portion of Set. Then Geb gave his heritage to Horus, this son of his first-born son, and Horus stood in the land and united this land." [1]

Here the Osirian point of view no longer permits Set and Horus to rule in equality side by side, but Set is dispossessed, and Horus receives all Egypt. The Solar theologians of Heliopolis certainly did not take this position in the beginning. They built up a group, which we have already noted, of nine gods (commonly called an *ennead*), headed by the ancient Atum, and among this group of nine divinities appears Osiris, who had no real

---

[1] British Museum, Stela No. 797, as reconstructed by ERMAN, *Ein Denkmal memphitischer Theologie* (*Sitzungsber. der Kgl. Preuss. Akad.*, 1911, XLIII), pp. 925–932. On this remarkable monument see also below, pp. 43–47.

original connection with the Solar myth. As Horus had no place in the original ennead, it was the more easy to appropriate him for the Osirian theology. As the process of correlation went on, it is evident also that, like Osiris, the local gods of all the temples were more and more drawn into the Solar theology. The old local Sun-gods had merged, and we find five Solar divinities in a single list in the Pyramid Texts, all addressed as Re.[1] A distinct tendency toward Solar henotheism, or even pantheism, is now discernible. Each of the leading temples and priesthoods endeavored to establish the local god as the focus of this centralizing process. The political prestige of the Sun-god, however, made the issue quite certain. It happens, however, that the system of a less important temple than that of Heliopolis is the one which has survived to us. A mutilated stela in the British Museum, on which the priestly scribes of the eighth century B. C. have copied and rescued a worm-eaten papyrus which was falling to pieces in their day, has preserved for two thousand seven hundred years more, and thus brought down to our time, the only fragment of the consciously constructive thought of the time, as the priests endeavored to harmonize into one system the vast complex of interfused local beliefs which made up the religion of Egypt.

It was the priests of Ptah, the master craftsman of the gods, whose temple was at Memphis, who are at this juncture our guides in tracing the current of religious thought in this remote age. This earliest system, as they wrought it out, of course made Ptah of Memphis the great and central figure. He too had his Memphite ennead made up of a primeval Ptah and eight emanations or manifestations of himself. In the employment of an ennead

[1] Pyr. §§ 1444-9.

to begin with, the theologians of Memphis were betraying the influence of Heliopolis, where the first ennead had its origin. The supremacy of the Solar theology, even in this Memphite system, is further discernible in the inevitable admission of the fact that Atum the Sun-god was the actual immediate creator of the world. But this they explained in this way. One of the members of the Memphite ennead bears the name "Ptah the Great," and to this name is appended the remarkable explanation, "he is the heart and tongue of the ennead," meaning of course the *Memphite* ennead. This enigmatic "heart and tongue" are then identified with Atum, who, perhaps operating through other intermediate gods, accomplishes all things through the "heart and tongue." When we recall that the Egyptian constantly used "heart" as the seat of the mind, we are suddenly aware also that he possessed no word for mind. A study of the document demonstrates that the ancient thinker is using "heart" as his only means of expressing the idea of "mind," as he vaguely conceived it. From Ptah then proceeded "the power of mind and tongue" which is the controlling power in "all gods, all men, all animals, and all reptiles, which live, thinking and commanding that which he wills."[1]

After further demonstrating that the members of Atum, especially his mouth which spake words of power, were made up of the ennead of Ptah, and thus of Ptah himself, our thinker passes on to explain his conception of the function of "heart (mind) and tongue." "When the eyes see, the ears hear, and the nose breathes, they transmit to the

---

[1] The verbal form of "thinking" is questionable, but no other interpretation seems possible. Whether "he" in "he wills" refers to Ptah directly or to the "power of mind and tongue" is not essential, as the latter proceeds from Ptah.

heart. It is he (the heart) who brings forth every issue, and it is the tongue which repeats the thought of the heart. He[1] fashioned all gods, even Atum and his ennead. Every divine word came into existence by the thought of the heart and the commandment of the tongue. It was he who made the kas and ⌈created⌉ the qualities;[2] who made all food, all offerings, by this word; who made that which is loved and that which is hated. It was he who gave life to the peaceful and death to the guilty."

After this enumeration of things chiefly supermaterial, of which the mind and the tongue were the creator, our Memphite theologian passes to the world of material things.

"It was he who made every work, every handicraft, which the hands make, the going of the feet, the movement of every limb, according to his command, through the thought of the heart that came forth from the tongue."

"There came the saying that Atum, who created the gods, stated concerning Ptah-Tatenen: 'He is the fashioner of the gods, he, from whom all things went forth, even offerings, and food and divine offerings and every good thing! And Thoth perceived that his strength was greater than all gods. Then Ptah was satisfied, after he had made all things and every divine word."

---

[1] Heart and tongue have the same gender in Egyptian and the pronoun may equally well refer to either. I use "he" for heart and "it" for tongue, but, I repeat, the distinction is not certain here.

[2] Ḥmswt, which, as BRUGSCH has shown (*Woerterbuch Suppl.*, pp. 996 ff.), indicates the qualities of the Sun-god, here attributed, in origin, to Ptah. These are: "Might, radiance, prosperity, victory, wealth, plenty, augustness, readiness or equipment, making, intelligence, adornment, stability, obedience, nourishment (or taste)." They appear with the kas at royal births, wearing on their heads shields with crossed arrows. So at Der el-Bahri.

"He fashioned the gods, he made the cities, he settled the nomes. He installed the gods in their holy places, he made their offerings to flourish, he equipped their holy places. He made likenesses of their bodies to the satisfaction of their hearts. Then the gods entered into their bodies of every wood and every stone and every metal. Everything grew upon its trees whence they came forth. Then he assembled all the gods and their kas (saying to them): 'Come ye and take possession of "Neb-towe," the divine store-house of Ptah-Tatenen, the great seat, which delights the heart of the gods dwelling in the House of Ptah, the mistress of life . . . whence is furnished the "Life of the Two Lands."'"[1]

In this document we are far indeed from the simple folk-tales of the origin of the world, which make up the mythology of Egypt. Assuming the existence of Ptah in the beginning, the Memphite theologian sees all things as first existing in the thought of the god. This world first

[1] British Museum, Stela No. 797, formerly No. 135, ll. 48–61. This remarkable document long rested in obscurity after its acquirement by the British Museum in 1805. The stone had been used as a nether millstone, almost abrading the inscription and rendering it so illegible that the process of copying was excessively difficult. It was early published by SHARPE (*Inscriptions*, I, 36–38), but the knowledge of the language current in his day made a usable copy impossible. As the signs face the end instead of the beginning as usual, SHARPE numbered the vertical lines backward, making the last line first. Mr. BRYANT and Mr. READ then published a much better copy in the *Proceedings of the Society of Biblical Archæology*, March, 1901, pp. 160 ff. They still numbered the lines backward, however, and so translated the document. In working through the inscriptions of the British Museum for the Berlin Egyptian Dictionary it had soon become evident to me that the lines of this inscription were to be numbered in the other direction. I then published a fac-simile copy of the stone in the *Zeitschrift für aegypt. Sprache*, 39, pp. 39 ff. I stated at the time: "The signs are very faint, and in badly worn places reading is excessively difficult. . . . I have no doubt that

conceived in his "heart," then assumed objective reality by the utterance of his "tongue." The utterance of the thought in the form of a divine fiat brought forth the world. We are reminded of the words in Genesis, as the Creator spoke, "And God said." Is there not here the primeval germ of the later Alexandrian doctrine of the "Logos"?

We should not fail to understand in this earliest philosophico-religious system, that the world which Ptah brought forth was merely the Egyptian Nile valley. As we shall discover in our further progress, the world-idea was not yet born. This Memphite Ptah was far from being a world-god. The world, in so far as it was possible for the men of the ancient Orient to know it, was still undiscovered by the Memphite theologians or any other thinkers of that distant age, and the impression which the world-idea was to make on religion was still over a thousand years in the future when this venerable papyrus of

with a better light than it is possible to get in the museum gallery, more could in places be gotten out." At the same time I ventured to publish a preliminary "rapid sketch" of the content which was undoubtedly premature and which dated the early Egpytian original papyrus of which our stone is a copy at least as early as the Eighteenth Dynasty, adding that "some points in orthography would indicate a much earlier date." Professor ERMAN has now published a penetrating critical analysis of the document (*Ein Denkmal memphitischer Theologie, Sitzungsber. der Kgl. Preuss. Akad.*, 1911, XLIII, pp. 916–950) which places it on the basis of orthography in the Pyramid Age, to which I had not the courage to assign it on the same evidence. With a better knowledge of the Pyramid Texts and Old Kingdom orthography than I had twelve years ago, I wholly agree with ERMAN's date for the document, surprising as it is to find such a treatise in the Pyramid Age. From LEPSIUS's squeeze of the stone, ERMAN has also secured a number of valuable new readings, while the summary of the document given above is largely indebted to his analysis. The discussion in my *History of Egypt*, pp. 356–8, as far as it employs this document, should be eliminated from the Empire.

the Pyramid Age was written. The forces of life which were first to react upon religion were those which spent themselves within the narrow borders of Egypt, and especially those of moral admonition which dominate the inner world and which had already led the men of this distant age to discern for the first time in human history that God "gave life to the peaceful and death to the guilty."

LECTURE II

LIFE AFTER DEATH—THE SOJOURN IN THE TOMB—
DEATH MAKES ITS IMPRESSION ON RELIGION

AMONG no people ancient or modern has the idea of a life beyond the grave held so prominent a place as among the ancient Egyptians. This insistent belief in a hereafter may perhaps have been, and experience in the land of Egypt has led me to believe it was, greatly favored and influenced by the fact that the conditions of soil and climate resulted in such a remarkable preservation of the human body as may be found under natural conditions nowhere else in the world. In going up to the daily task on some neighboring temple in Nubia, I was not infrequently obliged to pass through the corner of a cemetery, where the feet of a dead man, buried in a shallow grave, were now uncovered and extended directly across my path. They were precisely like the rough and calloused feet of the workmen in our excavations. How old the grave was I do not know, but any one familiar with the cemeteries of Egypt, ancient and modern, has found numerous bodies or portions of bodies indefinitely old which seemed about as well preserved as those of the living. This must have been a frequent experience of the ancient Egyptian,[1] and like Hamlet with the skull of Yorick in his hands, he must often have pondered deeply as he contemplated these silent witnesses. The surprisingly perfect state of preservation in which he found his ancestors whenever the digging of a new grave disclosed them, must have greatly stimulated

[1] See also PROF. G. ELLIOT SMITH, *The History of Mummification in Egypt*, Proceedings of the Royal Philosophical Society of Glasgow, 1910.

his belief in their continued existence, and often aroused his imagination to more detailed pictures of the realm and the life of the mysterious departed. The earliest and simplest of these beliefs began at an age so remote that they have left no trace in surviving remains. The cemeteries of the prehistoric communities along the Nile, discovered and excavated since 1894, disclose a belief in the future life which was already in an advanced stage. Thousands of graves, the oldest of which cannot be dated much later than the fifth millennium B. C., were dug by these primitive people in the desert gravels along the margin of the alluvium. In the bottom of the pit, which is but a few feet in depth, lies the body with the feet drawn up toward the chin and surrounded by a meagre equipment of pottery, flint implements, stone weapons, and utensils, and rude personal ornaments, all of which were of course intended to furnish the departed for his future life.

From the archaic beliefs represented in such burials as these it is a matter of fifteen hundred years to the appearance of the earliest written documents surviving to us—documents from which we may draw fuller knowledge of the more developed faith of a people rapidly rising toward a high material civilization and a unified governmental organization, the first great state of antiquity. Much took place in the thought of this remote people during that millennium and a half, but for another half millennium after the beginning of written documents we are still unable to discern the drift of the development. For two thousand years, therefore, after the stage of belief represented by the earliest burials just mentioned, that development went on, though it is now a lost chapter in human thought which we shall never recover.

When we take up the course of the development about

3000 B. C., we have before us the complicated results of a commingling of originally distinct beliefs which have long since interpenetrated each other and have for many centuries circulated thus a tangled mass of threads which it is now very difficult or impossible to disentangle.

✱Certain fundamental distinctions can be made, however. The early belief that the dead lived in or at the tomb, which must therefore be equipped to furnish his necessities in the hereafter, was one from which the Egyptian has never escaped entirely, not even at the present day. As hostile creatures infesting the cemeteries, the dead were dreaded, and protection from their malice was necessary. Even the pyramid must be protected from the malignant dead prowling about the necropolis, and in later times a man might be afflicted even in his house by a deceased member of his family wandering in from the cemetery. His mortuary practices therefore constantly gave expression to his involuntary conviction that the departed continued to inhabit the tomb long after the appearance of highly developed views regarding a blessed hereafter elsewhere in some distant region. We who continue to place flowers on the graves of our dead, though we may at the same time cherish beliefs in some remote paradise of the departed, should certainly find nothing to wonder at in the conflicting beliefs and practices of the ancient Nile-dweller five thousand years ago. ✱Side by side the two beliefs subsisted, that the dead continued to dwell in or near the tomb, and at the same time that he departed elsewhere to a distant and blessed realm.✱

✱In taking up the first of these two beliefs, the sojourn in the tomb, it will be necessary to understand the Egyptian notion of a person, and of those elements of the human personality which might survive death. These views are of course not the studied product of a highly trained and long-developed self-consciousness. On the contrary, we have in them the involuntary and unconscious impressions of an early people, in the study of which it is apparent that we are confronted by the earliest chapter in folk-psychology which has anywhere descended to us from the past.

On the walls of the temple of Luxor, where the birth of Amenhotep III was depicted in sculptured scenes late in the fifteenth century before Christ, we find the little prince brought in on the arm of the Nile-god, accompanied apparently by another child. This second figure, identical in external appearance with that of the prince, is a being called by the Egyptians the "ka"; it was born with the prince, being communicated to him by the god.[1] This curious comrade of an individual was corporeal[2] and the fortunes of the two were ever afterward closely associated; but the ka was not an element of the personality, as is so often stated. It seems to me indeed from a study of the Pyramid Texts, that the nature of the ka has been fundamentally misunderstood. He was a kind of superior genius intended to guide the fortunes of the individual *in the hereafter*, or it was in the world of the hereafter that he chiefly if not exclusively had his abode, and there he awaited the coming of his earthly companion. In the oldest inscriptions the death of a man may be stated by saying that "he goes to his ka";[3] when Osiris dies he "goes to his ka."[4] Hence the dead are referred to as those 'who have gone to their kas.'[5] Moreover, the ka was really

[1] On the creation of the kas in the beginning by the god see Brit. Mus. 797, *infra*, p. 45.
[2] Pyr. § 372.   [3] BAR, I, 187, 253.
[4] Pyr. §§ 826, 832, 836; *cf.* also "he goes *with* his ka," Pyr. § 17.
[5] PETRIE, *Deshasheh*, 7; LEPSIUS, *Denkmaeler*, Text I, 19; Pyr. § 829.

separated from its *protégé* by more than the mere distance to the cemetery, for in one passage the deceased "goes to his ka, to the sky."[1] Similarly the sojourn in the hereafter is described as an association with the ka,[2] and one of the powers of the blessed dead was to have dominion over the other kas there.[3] (In their relations with each other the ka was distinctly superior to his mundane companion.) In the oldest texts the sign for the ka, the uplifted arms, are frequently borne upon the standard which bears the signs for the gods. "Call upon thy ka, like Osiris, that he may protect thee from all anger of the dead,"[4] says one to the deceased; and to be the ka of a person is to have entire control over him. Thus in addressing Osiris it is said of Set, "He (Horus) has smitten Set for thee, bound; thou art his (Set's) ka."[5] In the hereafter, at least, a person is under the dominion of his own ka. The ka assists the deceased by speaking to the great god on his behalf, and after this intercession, by introducing the dead man to the god (Re).[6] He forages for the deceased and brings him food that they both may eat together,[7] and like two guests they sit together at the same table.[8] (But the ka is ever the protecting genius. / The dead king Pepi "lives with his ka; he (the ka) expels the evil that is before Pepi, he removes the evil that is behind Pepi, like the boomerangs of the lord of Letopolis, which remove the evil that is before him and expel the evil that is behind him."[9] Notwithstanding their intimate association, there was danger that the ka might fail

---

[1] Pyr. § 1431.
[2] "How beautiful it is with thy ka (that is, in the company of thy ka = in the hereafter) forever," Pyr. § 2028.
[3] Pyr. § 267 and § 311.
[4] Pyr. § 63.
[5] Pyr. § 587. See also § 1609 and § 1623.
[6] Pyr. Ut. 440.
[7] Pyr. § 564.
[8] Pyr. § 1357.
[9] Pyr. § 908.

to recognize his *protégé*, and the departed therefore received a garment peculiar to him, by means of which the ka may not mistake him for an enemy whom he might slay.[1] So strong was the ka, and so close was his union with his *protégé*, that to have control over a god or a man it was necessary to gain the power over his ka also,[2] and complete justification of the deceased was only certain when his ka also was justified.[3] Thus united, the deceased and his protecting genius lived a common life in the hereafter, and they said to the dead: "How beautiful it is in the company of thy ka!"[4] The mortuary priest whose duty it was to supply the needs of the deceased in the hereafter was for this reason called "servant of the ka," and whatever he furnished the ka was shared by him with his *protégé*, as we have seen him foraging for his charge, and securing for him provisions which they ate together. Eventually, that is after a long development, we find the tombs of about 2000 B. C. regularly containing prayers for material blessings in the hereafter ending with the words: "for the ka of X" (the name of the deceased).

While the relation of the ka to the dead is thus fairly clear, it is not so evident in the case of the living. (His protecting power evidently had begun at the birth of the individual, though he was most useful to his *protégé* after earthly life was over.) We find the ka as the protecting genius of a mortuary temple dwelling on earth, but it is certainly significant that it is a mortuary building which he protects. Moreover the earliest example of such a *local* genius is Osiris, a mortuary god, who is said to become the ka of a pyramid and its temple, that they may enjoy

[1] Pyr. Ut. 591.
[3] Pyr. § 929.
[2] Pyr. § 776.
[4] Pyr. § 2028.

his protection.¹ As we stated above, however, the ka was not an element of the personality, and we are not called upon to explain him physically or psychologically as such. He is roughly parallel with the later notion of the guardian angel as found among other peoples, and he is of course far the earliest known example of such a being. It is of importance to note that in all probability the ka was originally the exclusive possession of kings, each of whom thus lived under the protection of his individual guardian genius, and that by a process of slow development the privilege of possessing a ka became universal among all the people.²

The actual personality of the individual in life consisted, according to the Egyptian notion, in the visible body, and the invisible intelligence, the seat of the last being considered the "heart" or the "belly," ³ which indeed furnished the chief designations for the intelligence. Then the vital principle which, as so frequently among other peoples, was identified with the breath which animated the body, was not clearly distinguished from the intelligence. The two together were pictured in one symbol, a

¹ Pyr. Texts. A later example is found in the temple of Seti I, latter half of the fourteenth century B. C., in a relief where the ka is depicted as a woman, with the ka sign of uplifted arms on her head, embracing the name of Seti's Gurna temple. CHAMPOLLION, *Monuments*, pl. 151, Nos. 2 and 3.

² I owe this last remark to STEINDORFF, who has recently published a reconsideration of the ka (*Zeitschrift für aegypt. Sprache*, 48,151 *ff.*), disproving the old notion that the mortuary statues in the tombs, especially of the Old Kingdom, are statues of the ka. He is undoubtedly right. After the collection of the above data it was gratifying to receive the essay of STEINDORFF and to find that he had arrived at similar conclusions regarding the nature and function of the ka, though in making the ka so largely mortuary in function I differ with him.

³ See above, pp. 44-45; and my essay, *Zeitsch. für aegypt. Sprache*, 39, pp. 39 *ff*.

human-headed bird with human arms, which we find in the tomb and coffin scenes depicted hovering over the mummy and extending to its nostrils in one hand the figure of a swelling sail, the hieroglyph for wind or breath, and in the other the so-called *crux ansata*, or symbol of life. This curious little bird-man was called by the Egyptians the "ba." The fact has been strangely overlooked that originally the ba came into existence really for the first time at the death of the individual. All sorts of devices and ceremonies were resorted to that the deceased might at death become a ba, or as the Pyramid Texts, addressing the dead king, say, "that thou mayest become a ba among the gods, thou living as (or 'in') thy ba."[1] There was a denominative verb "ba," meaning "to become a ba." Ba has commonly been translated as "soul," and the translation does indeed roughly correspond to the Egyptian idea. It is necessary to remember, however, in dealing with such terms as these among so early a people, that they had no clearly defined notion of the exact nature of such an element of personality. It is evident that the Egyptian never wholly dissociated a person from the body as an instrument or vehicle of sensation, and they resorted to elaborate devices to restore to the body its various channels of sensibility, after the ba, which comprehended these very things, had detached itself from the body. He thought of his departed friend as existing in the body, or at least as being in outward appearance still possessed of a body, as we do, if we attempt to picture our departed friend at all. Hence, when depicted in mortuary paintings, the departed of course appears as he did in life.[2]

[1] Pyr. § 1943 b.
[2] There were other *designations* of the dead, but there were not additional elements of his personality besides the *ba* and the *body*, as we find it so commonly stated in the current discussions of this subject. Thus the dead were thought of as "glorious" (y'ḫw),

'In harmony with these conceptions was the desire of the surviving relatives to insure physical restoration to the dead. Gathered with the relatives and friends of the deceased, on the flat roof of the massive masonry tomb, the mortuary priest stood over the silent body and addressed the departed: "Thy bones perish not, thy flesh sickens not, thy members are not distant from thee."[1] Or he turns to the flesh of the dead itself and says: "O flesh of this king Teti, decay not, perish not; let not thy odor be evil."[2] He utters a whole series of strophes, each concluding with the refrain: "King Pepi decays not, he rots not, he is not bewitched by your wrath, ye gods."[3]

However effective these injunctions may have been, they were not considered sufficient. The motionless body must be resuscitated and restored to the use of its members and senses. This resurrection might be the act of a favoring god or goddess, as when accomplished by Isis or Horus, or the priest addresses the dead and assures him that the Sky-

---

and in the Pyramid Texts are frequently spoken of as the "glorious" just as we say the "blessed." The fact that they later spoke of "his y'ḫw," that is "his glorious one," does not mean that the y'ḫw was another element in the personality. This is shown in the reference to Osiris when he died, as "going to his y'ḫw" (Pyr. § 472), which is clearly a substitution of y'ḫw for ka, in the common phrase for dying, namely, "going to his ka." The use of y'ḫw with the pronoun, namely, "his y'ḫw," is rare in the Pyramid Texts, but came into more common use in the Middle Kingdom, as in the Misanthrope, who addresses his soul as his y'ḫw. Similarly the "shadow" is only another symbol, but not another element of the personality. There is no ground for the complicated conception of a person in ancient Egypt as consisting, besides the body of a ka, a ba (soul), a y'ḫw (spirit), a shadow, etc. Besides the body and the ba (soul), there was only the ka, the protecting genius, which was not an element of the personality as we have said.

[1] Pyr. § 725.   [2] Pyr. § 722.
[3] Pyr. Ut. 576; see also preservation from decay by Isis and Nephthys, Pyr. § 1255.

goddess will raise him up: "She sets on again for thee thy head, she gathers for thee thy bones, she unites for thee thy members, she brings for thee thy heart into thy body."[1] Sometimes the priest assumes that the dead does not even enter the earth at interment and assures the mourning relatives: "His abomination is the earth, king Unis enters not Geb (the Earth-god). When he perishes, sleeping in his house on earth, his bones are restored, his injuries are removed."[2] But if the inexorable fact be accepted that the body now lies in the tomb, the priest undauntedly calls upon the dead: "Arise, dwellers in your tombs. Loose your ⸢bandages,⸣ throw off the sand from thy (*sic!*) face. Lift thee up from upon thy left side, support thyself on thy right side. Raise thy face that thou mayest look at this which I have done for thee. I am thy son, I am thy heir."[3] He assures the dead: "Thy bones are gathered together for thee, thy members are prepared for thee, thy ⸢impurities⸣ are thrown off for thee, thy bandages are loosed for thee. The tomb is opened for thee, the coffin is broken open for thee."[4] And yet the insistent fact of death so inexorably proclaimed by the unopened tomb led the priest to call upon the dead to waken and arise before each ceremony which he performed. As he brings food and drink we find him calling: "Raise thee up, king Pepi, receive to thee thy water. Gather to thee thy bones, stand thou up upon thy two feet, being a glorious one before the glorious. Raise thee up for this thy bread which cannot dry up, and thy beer which cannot become stale."[5]

But even when so raised the dead was not in possession

[1] Pyr. § 835. [2] Pyr. § 308.
[3] Pyr. §§ 1878–9. [4] Pyr. § 2008–9.
[5] Pyr. §§ 858–9; see also the resuscitation before purification, Pyr. §§ 837, 841, and not uncommonly.

of his senses and faculties, nor the power to control and use his body and limbs. His mourning friends could not abandon him to the uncertain future without aiding him to recover all his powers. "King Teti's mouth is opened for him, king Teti's nose is opened for him, king Teti's ears are opened for him,"[1] says the priest, and elaborate ceremonies were performed to accomplish this restoration of the senses and the faculty of speech.[2]

All this was of no avail, however, unless the unconscious body received again the seat of consciousness and feeling, which in this restoration of the mental powers was regularly the heart. "The heart of king Teti is not taken away,"[3] says the ritual; or if it has gone the Sky-goddess "brings for thee thy heart into thy body (again)."[4]

Several devices were necessary to make of this unresponsive mummy a living person, capable of carrying on the life hereafter. He has not become a ba, or a soul merely by dying, as we stated in referring to the nature of the ba. It was necessary to aid him to become a soul. Osiris when lying dead had become a soul by receiving from his son Horus the latter's eye, wrenched from the socket in his conflict with Set. Horus, recovering his eye, gave it to his father, and on receiving it Osiris at once became a soul. From that time any offering to the dead might be, and commonly was, called the "eye of Horus," and might thus produce the same effect as on Osiris.

---

[1] Pyr. § 712.
[2] See also Pyr. §§ 9, 10, and for the opening of the mouth, especially Ut. 20, 21, 22, 34, 38; for the opening of the eyes, Ut. 638, 639; for the opening of eyes, ears, nose, and mouth, see Pyr. § 1673.
[3] Pyr. § 748.
[4] Pyr. § 828 = § 835; the heart may also be restored to the body by Horus, Pyr. Ut. 595, or by Nephthys, Ut. 628.

"Raise thee up," says the priest, "for this thy bread, which cannot dry up, and thy beer which cannot become stale, *by which thou shalt become a soul.*"[1] The food which the priest offered possessed the mysterious power of effecting the transformation of the dead man into a soul as the "eye of Horus" had once transformed Osiris. And it did more than this, for the priest adds, "by which thou shalt become one prepared."[2] To be "one prepared" or, as the variants have it, "one equipped," is explained in the tombs of the Old Kingdom, where we find the owner boasting, "I am an excellent, equipped spirit, I know every secret charm of the court."[3] This man, a provincial noble, is proud of the fact that he was granted the great boon of acquaintance with the magical mortuary equipment used for the king at the court, an equipment intended to render the dead invulnerable and irresistible in the hereafter. We are able then to understand another noble of the same period when he says: "I am an excellent equipped spirit (literally, 'glorious one') whose mouth knows,"[4] meaning his mouth is familiar with the mortuary magical equipment, which he is able to repeat whenever needed. Similarly one of the designations of the departed in the Pyramid Texts is "the glorious by reason of their equipped mouths."[5] Finally this strangely potent bread and beer which the priest offers the dead, not only makes him a "soul" and makes him "prepared," but it also gives him "power" or makes him a "mighty one."[6] The "power" conferred was in the first place intended to control the body of the dead and guide its actions, and without this power intended for this specific purpose it is evident the Egyptian believed the dead to be helpless.[7] This "power" was also

[1] Pyr. § 859. [2] *Ibid.* [3] BAR, I, 378. [4] BAR, I, 329.
[5] Pyr. Ut. 473. [6] Pyr. § 859. [7] Pyr. § 2096.

intended to give the dead ability to confront successfully the uncanny adversaries who awaited him in the beyond. It was so characteristic of the dead, that they might be spoken of as the "mighty" as we say the "blessed," and it was so tangible a part of the equipment of the departed that it underwent purification together with him.[1] This "power" finally gave the deceased also "power" over all other powers within him, and the priest says to him, "Thou hast power over the powers that are in thee."[2]

From these facts it is evident that the Egyptians had developed a rude psychology of the dead, in accordance with which they endeavored to reconstitute the individual by processes *external to him*, under the control of the survivors, especially the mortuary priest who possessed the indispensable ceremonies for accomplishing this end. We may summarize it all in the statement that after the resuscitation of the body, there was a mental restoration or a reconstitution of the faculties one by one, attained especially by the process of making the deceased a "soul" (ba), in which capacity he again existed as a *person*, possessing all the powers that would enable him to subsist and survive in the life hereafter. It is therefore not correct to attribute to the Egyptians a belief in the *immortality* of the soul strictly interpreted as imperishability or to speak of his "ideas of immortality."[3]

[1] Pyr. § 837.   [2] Pyr. § 2011.
[3] The above does not exhaust the catalogue of qualities which were thought valuable to the dead and were communicated to him in the Pyramid Texts. Thus they say of the deceased: "His *fearfulness* (b'w) is on his head, his *terror* is at his side, his *magical charms* are before him" (Pyr. § 477). For "fearfulness" a variant text has "lion's-head" (Pyr. § 940), which was a mask placed over the head of the deceased. With this should be compared the equipment of the deceased with a jackal's face, not infrequently occurring (e. g., Pyr. § 2098), which of course is a survival of the influence of the ancient mortuary

That life now involved an elaborate material equipment, a monumental tomb with its mortuary furniture. The massive masonry tomb, like a truncated pyramid with very steep sides, was but the rectangular descendant of the prehistoric tumulus, with a retaining wall around it, once of rough stones, now of carefully laid hewn stone masonry, which has taken on some of the incline of its ancient ancestor, the sand heap, or tumulus, still within it. In the east side of the superstructure, which was often of imposing size, was a rectangular room, perhaps best called a chapel, where the offerings for the dead might be presented and these ceremonies on his behalf might be performed. For, notwithstanding the elaborate reconstitution of the dead as a person, he was not unquestionably able to maintain himself in the hereafter without assistance from his surviving relatives. All such mortuary arrangements were chiefly Osirian, for in the Solar faith the Sun-god did not die among men, nor did he leave a family to mourn for him and maintain mortuary ceremonies on his behalf. To be sure, the oldest notion of the relation

god, of the jackal head, Anubis. Two other variant passages (§ 992 and § 1472) have "ba" (soul) instead of "fearfulness" above. This threefold equipment was that of Osiris. It is found several times, e. g., in § 1559, where the text states: "His *power* is within him, his *soul* (ba) is behind him, his *preparation* (or equipment) is upon him, which Horus gave to Osiris." Again it is fourfold, as in Pyr. § 1730, where the appropriate recitation is enjoined

"that he may be a *glorious one* thereby,
that he may be a *soul* thereby,
that he may be an *honored one* thereby,
that he may be a *powerful* (or mighty) one thereby"
(Pyr. § 1730).

Similarly the ceremony of offering ointment to the dead is performed, and as a result the priest says, "Thou art a soul thereby, thou art a mighty one thereby, thou art an honored one thereby" (Pyr. § 2075), omitting the "equipment" or "preparation." It is also omitted in Pyr. § 2096 and § 2098.

of Osiris to the dead, which is discernible in the Pyramid Texts, represents him as hostile to them, but this is an archaic survival of which only a trace remains.[1] As a son of Geb the Earth-god, it was altogether natural to confide the dead to his charge.[2]

It was the duty of every son to arrange the material equipment of his father for the life beyond—a duty so naturally and universally felt that it involuntarily passed from the life of the people into the Osiris myth as the duty of Horus toward his father Osiris. It was an obligation which was sometimes met with faithfulness in the face of difficulty and great danger, as when Sebni of Elephantine received news of the death of his father, Mekhu, in the Sudan, and at once set out with a military escort to penetrate the country of the dangerous southern tribes and to rescue the body of his father. The motive for such self-sacrifice was of course the desire to recover his father's body that it might be embalmed and preserved, in order that the old man might not lose all prospect of life beyond. Hence it was that when the son neared the frontier on his return, he sent messengers to the court with news of what had happened, so that as he re-entered Upper Egypt he was met by a company from the court, made up of the embalmers, mortuary priests, and mourners, bearing fragrant oil, aromatic gums, and fine linen, that all the ceremonies of embalmment, interment, and complete equipment for the hereafter might be completed at once, before the body should further perish.[3]

The erection of the tomb was an equally obvious duty incumbent upon sons and relatives, unless indeed that father was so attached to his own departed father that he desired to rest in his father's tomb, as one noble of the

[1] Ut. 534. [2] Ut. 592. [3] BAR, I, 362-374.

twenty-sixth century B. C. informs us was his wish. He says: "Now I caused that I should be buried in the same tomb with this Zau (his father's name) in order that I might be with him in the same place; not, however, because I was not in a position to make a second tomb; but I did this in order that I might see this Zau every day, in order that I might be with him in the same place."[1] This pious son says further: "I buried my father, the count Zau, surpassing the splendor, surpassing the goodliness of any ⌈equal⌉ of his who was in this South" (meaning Upper Egypt).[2]

From the thirty-fourth century on, as the tombs of the First Dynasty at Abydos show, it had become customary for favorite officials and partisans of the Pharaoh to be buried in the royal cemetery, forming a kind of mortuary court around the monarch whom they had served in life. Gradually the king became more and more involved in obligations to assist his nobles in the erection of their tombs and to contribute from the royal treasury to the splendor and completeness of their funerals. The favorite physician of the king receives a requisition on the treasury and the royal quarries for the labor and the transportation necessary to procure him a great and sumptuous false door of massive limestone for his tomb, and he tells us the fact with great satisfaction and much circumstance in his tomb inscriptions.[3] We see the Pharaoh in the royal palanquin on the road which mounts from the valley to the desert plateau, whither he has ascended to inspect his pyramid, now slowly rising on the margin of the desert overlooking the valley. Here he discovers the unfinished

---

[1] BAR, I, 383; other examples of filial piety in the same respect, BAR, I, 181-7, 248, 274
[2] BAR, I, 382.   [3] BAR, I, 237-240.

tomb of Debhen, one of his favorites, who may have presumed upon a moment of royal complaisance to call attention to its unfinished condition. The king at once details fifty men to work upon the tomb of his *protégé*, and afterward orders the royal engineers and quarrymen who are at work upon a temple in the vicinity to bring for the fortunate Debhen two false doors of stone, the blocks for the façade of the tomb, and likewise a portrait statue of Debhen to be erected therein.[1] One of the leading nobles who was flourishing at the close of the twenty-seventh century B. C. tells us in his autobiography how he was similarly favored: "Then I besought . . . the majesty of the king that there be brought for me a limestone sarcophagus from Troja (royal quarries near Cairo, from which much stone for the pyramids of Gizeh was taken). The king had the treasurer of the god (= Pharaoh's treasurer) ferry over, together with a troop of sailors under his hand, in order to bring for me this sarcophagus from Troja; and he arrived with it in a large ship belonging to the court (that is, one of the royal galleys), together with its lid, the false door . . . (several other blocks the words for which are not quite certain in meaning), and one offering-tablet."[2]

In such cases as these, and indeed quite frequently, the king was expected to contribute to the embalmment and burial of a favorite noble. We have already seen how the Pharaoh sent out his body of mortuary officials, priests, and embalmers to meet Sebni, returning from the Sudan with his father's body.[3] Similarly he despatched one of his commanders to rescue the body of an unfortunate noble who with his entire military escort had been massacred by the Bedwin on the shores of the Red Sea, while building

[1] BAR, I, 210-212. [2] BAR, I, 308. [3] See above, p. 61.

a ship for the voyage to Punt, the Somali coast, in all likelihood the land of Ophir of the Old Testament. Although the rescuer does not say so in his brief inscription, it is evident that the Pharaoh desired to secure the body of this noble also in order to prepare it properly for the hereafter.[1] Such solicitude can only have been due to the sovereign's personal attachment to a favorite official. This is quite evident in the case of Weshptah, one of the viziers of the Fifth Dynasty about 2700 B. C. The king, his family, and the court were one day inspecting a new building in course of construction under Weshptah's superintendence, for, besides being grand vizier, he was also chief architect. All admire the work and the king turns to praise his faithful minister when he notices that Weshptah does not hear the words of royal favor. The king's exclamation alarms the courtiers, the stricken minister is quickly carried to the court, and the priests and chief physicians are hurriedly summoned. The king has a case of medical rolls brought in, but all is in vain. The physicians declare his case hopeless. The king is smitten with sorrow and retires to his chamber, where he prays to Re. He then makes all arrangements for Weshptah's burial, ordering an ebony coffin made and having the body anointed in his own presence. The dead noble's eldest son was then empowered to build the tomb, which the king furnished and endowed.[2] The noble whose pious son wished to rest in the same tomb with him (p. 64) enjoyed similar favor at the king's hands. His son says: "I requested as an honor from the majesty of my lord, the king of Egypt, Pepi II, who lives forever, that there be levied a coffin, clothing, and festival perfume for this Zau (his dead father). His majesty caused that the custodian

[1] BAR, I, 360.   [2] BAR, I, 242-9.

of the royal domain should bring a coffin of wood, festival perfume, oil, clothing, two hundred pieces of first-grade linen and of fine southern linen . . . taken from the White House (the royal treasury) of the court for this Zau."[1]

Interred thus in royal splendor and equipped with sumptuous furniture, the maintenance of the departed, in theory at least, *through all time* was a responsibility which he dared not intrust exclusively to his surviving family or eventually to a posterity whose solicitude on his behalf must continue to wane and finally disappear altogether. The noble therefore executed carefully drawn wills and testamentary endowments, the income from which was to be devoted exclusively to the maintenance of his tomb and the presentation of oblations of incense, ointment, food, drink, and clothing in liberal quantities and at frequent intervals. The source of this income might be the revenues from the noble's own lands or from his offices and the perquisites belonging to his rank, from all of which a portion might be permanently diverted for the support of his tomb and its ritual.[2]

In a number of cases the legal instrument establishing these foundations has been engraved as a measure of safety on the wall inside the tomb-chapel itself and has thus been preserved to us. At Siut Hepzefi the count and baron of the province has left us ten elaborate contracts on the inner wall of his tomb-chapel, intended to perpetuate the service which he desired to have regularly celebrated at his tomb or on his behalf.[3]

The amount of the endowment was sometimes surpris-

[1] BAR, I, 382.
[2] BAR, I, 200-9, 213-222, 226-230, 231, 349, 378, 535-593.
[3] BAR, I, 535-593. They will be found in substance *infra*, pp. 259-269.

ingly large. In the twenty-ninth century B. C., the tomb of prince Nekure, son of king Khafre of the Fourth Dynasty, was endowed from the prince's private fortune with no less than twelve towns, the income of which went exclusively to the support of his tomb. A palace steward in Userkaf's time, in the middle of the twenty-eighth century B. C., appointed eight mortuary priests for the service of his tomb, and a baron of Upper Egypt two centuries and a half later endowed his tomb with the revenues from eleven villages and settlements. The income of a mortuary priest in such a tomb was, in one instance, sufficient to enable him to endow the tomb of his daughter in the same way. In addition to such private resources, the death of a noble not infrequently resulted in further generosity on the part of the king, who might either increase the endowment which the noble had already made during his life, or even furnish it entirely from the royal revenues.[1]

The privileges aeeruing to the dead from these endowments, while they were intended to secure him against all apprehension of hunger, thirst, or cold in the future life, seem to have consisted chiefly in enabling him to share in the most important feasts and celebrations of the year. Like all Orientals the Egyptian took great delight in religious celebrations, and the good cheer which abounded on such occasions he was quite unwilling to relinquish when he departed this world. The calendar of feasts, therefore, was a matter of the greatest importance to him, and he was willing to divert plentiful revenues to enable him to celebrate all its important days in the hereafter as he had once so bountifully done among his friends on earth. He really expected, moreover, to celebrate these

[1] So with the vizier, Weahptah, above, p. 66; see also BAR, I, 378, 241, 213–230.

joyous occasions among his friends in the temple just as he once had been wont to do, and to accomplish this he had a statue of himself erected in the temple court. Sometimes the king, as a particular distinction granted to a powerful courtier, commissioned the royal sculptors to make such a statue and station it inside the temple door. In his tomb likewise the grandee of the Pyramid Age set up a sumptuous stone portrait statue of himself, concealed in a secret chamber hidden in the mass of the masonry. Such statues, too, the king not infrequently furnished to the leading nobles of his government and court. It was evidently supposed that this portrait statue, the earliest of which we know anything in art, might serve as a body for the disembodied dead, who might thus return to enjoy a semblance at least of bodily presence in the temple, or again in the same way return to the tomb-chapel, where he might find other representations of his body in the secret chamber close by the chapel.[1]

We discern in such usages the emergence of a more highly developed and more desirable hereafter, which has gradually supplanted the older and simpler views. The common people doubtless still thought of their dead either as dwelling in the tomb, or at best as inhabiting the gloomy realm of the west, the subterranean kingdom ruled by the old mortuary gods eventually led by Osiris. But for the great of the earth, the king and his nobles at least, a happier destiny had now dawned. They might dwell at will with the Sun-god in his glorious celestial kingdom. In the royal tomb we can henceforth discern the emergence of this Solar hereafter (*cf.* pp. 140–1).

[1] The supposition that these statues were intended to be those of the ka in particular is without foundation. Ka statues are nowhere mentioned in the Pyramid Texts, nor does the inscription regularly placed on such a statue ever refer to it as a statue of the ka. Later see also STEINDORFF, *Zeitschr. für aegypt. Sprache*, 48, 152–9.

LECTURE III

THE REALMS OF THE DEAD—THE PYRAMID TEXTS—THE ASCENT TO THE SKY

THE Pharaoh himself might reasonably expect that his imposing tomb would long survive the destruction of the less enduring structures in which his nobles were laid, and that his endowments, too, might be made to outlast those of his less powerful contemporaries. The pyramid as a stable form in architecture has impressed itself upon all time. Beneath this vast mountain of stone, as a result of its mere mass and indestructibility alone, the Pharaoh looked forward to the permanent survival of his body, and of the personality with which it was so indissolubly involved. Moreover, the origin of the monument, hitherto overlooked, made it a symbol of the highest sacredness, rising above the mortal remains of the king, to greet the Sun, whose offspring the Pharaoh was.

The pyramid form may be explained by an examination of the familiar obelisk form. The obelisk, as is commonly known, is a symbol sacred to the Sun-god. So far as I am aware, however, little significance has heretofore been attached to the fact that the especially sacred portion of the obelisk is the pyramidal apex with which it is surmounted. An obelisk is simply a pyramid upon a lofty base which has indeed become the shaft. In the Old Kingdom Sun-temples at Abusir, this is quite clear, the diameter of the shaft being at the bottom quite one-third of its height. Thus the shaft appears as a high base, upon which the surmounting pyramid is supported. This pyramidal top is the essential part of the monument and the significant symbol which it bore. The Egyptians called it a *benben* (or *benbenet*), which we translate "pyramidion," and the shaft or high base would be without significance without it. Thus, when Sesostris I proclaims to posterity the survival of his name in his Heliopolis monuments, he says:

> "My beauty shall be remembered in his house,
> My name is the pyramidion and my name is the lake."[1]

His meaning is that his name shall survive on his great obelisks, and in the sacred lake which he excavated. The king significantly designates the obelisk, however, by the name of its pyramidal summit. Now the long recognized fact that the obelisk is sacred to the sun, carries with it the demonstration that it is the *pyramid* surmounting the obelisk which is sacred to the Sun-god. Furthermore, the sanctuary at Heliopolis was early designated the "Benben-house," that is the "pyramidion-house."[2] The symbol, then, by which the sanctuary of the Sun-temple at Heliopolis was designated was a pyramid. Moreover, there was in this same Sun-temple a pyramidal object called a "ben," presumably of stone standing in the "Phœnix-house"; and upon this pyramidal object the Sun-god in the form of a Phœnix had in the beginning first appeared. This object was already sacred as far back as the middle of the third millennium B. C.,[3] and will doubtless have

[1] BAR, I, 503.
[2] BAR, III, 16, l. 5; Cairo Hymn to Amon, V, ll. 1–2, VIII, ll. 3–4; Piankhi Stela, l. 105 = BAR, IV, 871.
[3] Pyr. § 1652.

been vastly older. We may conjecture that it was one of those sacred stones, which gained their sanctity in times far back of all recollection or tradition, like the *Ka'aba* at Mecca. In hieroglyphic the Phœnix is represented as sitting upon this object, the form of which was a universally sacred symbol of the Sun-god. Hence it is that in the Pyramid Texts the king's pyramid tomb is placed under the protection of the *Sun-god* in two very clear chapters,[1] the second of which opens with a reference to the fact that the Sun-god when he created the other gods was sitting aloft on the *ben* as a Phœnix, and hence it is that the king's pyramid is placed under his protection. (See pp. 76–77.)

The pyramidal form of the king's tomb therefore was of the most sacred significance. The king was buried under the very symbol of the Sun-god which stood in the holy of holies in the Sun-temple at Heliopolis, a symbol upon which, from the day when he created the gods, he was accustomed to manifest himself in the form of the Phœnix; and when in mountainous proportions the pyramid rose above the king's sepulchre, dominating the royal city below and the valley beyond for many miles, it was the loftiest object which greeted the Sun-god in all the land, and his morning rays glittered on its shining summit long before he scattered the shadows in the dwellings of humbler mortals below. We might expect to find some hint of all this on the pyramids themselves, and in this expectation we are not disappointed, in spite of the fact that hitherto no exterior inscription has ever been found actually in position in the masonry of a pyramid, so sadly have they suffered at the hands of time and vandals. A magnificent

[1] Ut. 599 and 600. Their content with quotations is given below, pp. 76–77.

pyramidal block of polished granite, found lying at the base of Amenemhet III's pyramid at Dahshur, is, however, unquestionably the ancient apex of that monument, from which it has fallen down as a result of the quarrying by modern natives.[1]

On the side which undoubtedly faced the east appears a winged sun-disk, surmounting a pair of eyes, beneath which are the words "beauty of the sun," the eyes of course indicating the idea of beholding, which is to be understood with the words "beauty of the sun." Below is an inscription[2] of two lines beginning: "The face of king Amenemhet III is opened, that he may behold the Lord of the Horizon when he sails across the sky." [3]

Entirely in harmony with this interpretation of the significance of the pyramid form is its subsequent mortuary use. A large number of small stone pyramids, each cut from a single block, has been found in the cemeteries of later times. On opposite sides of such a pyramid is a niche in which the deceased appears kneeling with upraised hands, while the accompanying inscriptions represent him as singing a hymn to the Sun-god, on one side to the rising and on the other to the setting sun. The larger museums of Europe possess numbers of these small monuments.

---

[1] It was published, without indication of its original position, by MASPERO, *Annales du Service des antiquités*, III, pp. 206 ff. and plate; see SCHAEFER, *Zeitschrift für aegypt. Sprache*, 41, 84, who demonstrates its original position. This had also been noted in the author's *History of Egypt*, Fig. 94.

[2] The same inscription is found accompanying the eyes on the outside of the Middle Kingdom coffin of Sebek-o at Berlin. (See STEINDORFF, *Grabfunde des Mittleren Reichs*, II, 5, 1.)

[3] It is evident that the identification of Osiris with the pyramid and temple in Pyr. §§ 1657-8 is secondary and another evidence of his intrusion in the Solar faith of which the Pyr. Texts furnish so many examples.

74   RELIGION AND THOUGHT IN ANCIENT EGYPT

In the selection of the pyramid, the greatest of the Solar symbols, as the form of the king's tomb, we must therefore recognize another evidence of the supremacy of the Solar faith at the court of the Pharaohs.[1] It is notable in this connection that it was chiefly against Osiris and the divinities of his cycle that protection was sought at the dedication of a royal pyramid tomb.[2]

The imposing complex of which the pyramid was the chief member has only been understood in recent years as a result of the excavations of the Deutsche Orient-Gesellschaft at Abusir. The pyramid occupied a prominent position on the margin of the desert plateau overlooking the Nile valley. On its east side, properly called the front of the monument, and abutting on the masonry of the pyramid, rose an extensive temple, with a beautiful colonnaded court in front, storage chambers on either side, and in the rear a holy place. The back wall of this "holy of holies" was the east face of the pyramid itself, in which was a false door. Through this the dead king might step forth to receive and enjoy the offerings presented to him here. A covered causeway of massive masonry led up from the valley below to the level of the plateau where pyramid and temple stood, and extended to the very door

---

[1] There is possibly another connection in which the pyramid form may be discerned as belonging to the Sun-god. The triangle of zodiacal light which some have claimed to be able to discover in the east at sunrise at certain times, and the writing of the Solar god, Soped's name with a triangle or pyramid after it, may have some connection with the use of the pyramid as a Solar symbol. The architectural evolution of the form through the compound mastaba, the terraced structure, like the so-called "terraced pyramid" of Sakkara, has long been understood.

[2] Pyr. Ut. 534, all of which is a long prayer intended to prevent the appropriation of pyramid, temple, and their possessions by Osiris or the gods of his cycle. This important Utterance is taken up again in connection with the dedication of the pyramid, pp. 75-76.

in the front of the temple, with whose masonry it engaged. The lower end of the causeway was adorned with a sumptuous colonnaded entrance, a monumental portal, which served as a town or residence temple of the pyramid and was probably within the walls of the royal residence city below. These temples were of course the home of the mortuary ritual maintained on behalf of the king, and were analogous in origin to the chapel of the noble's tomb already discussed (p. 62). The whole group or complex, consisting of pyramid, temple, causeway, and town temple below, forms the most imposing architectural conception of this early age and its surviving remains have contributed in the last few years an entirely new chapter in the history of architecture. They mark the culmination of the development of the material equipment of the dead.

Each Pharaoh of the Third and Fourth Dynasties spent a large share of his available resources in erecting this vast tomb, which was to receive his body and insure its preservation after death. It became the chief object of the state and its organization thus to insure the king's survival in the hereafter. More than once the king failed to complete the enormous complex before death, and was thus thrown upon the piety of his successors, who had all they could do to complete their own tombs. When completed the temple and the pyramid were dedicated by the royal priests with elaborate formulæ for their protection. The building was addressed and adjured not to admit Osiris or the divinities of his cycle, when they came, "with an evil coming," that is of course with evil designs upon the building. On the other hand, the building was charged to receive hospitably the dead king at his coming. The priest addressing the building said: "When this king

Pepi, together with his ka, comes, open thou thy arms to him." At the same time Horus is supposed to say: "Offer this pyramid and this temple to king Pepi and to his ka. That which this pyramid and this temple contain belongs to king Pepi and to his ka."[1] Besides this the buildings were protected by doors with boukrania upon or over them, and "sealed with two evil eyes," and the great hall being "purer than the sky," the place was thus inviolable[2] even by the mortuary patron god Osiris if he should come with malicious intent.

Similarly the pyramid and temple were protected from decay for all time. When the dead king appears in the hereafter he is at once hailed with greetings by Atum, the ancient Sun-god; Atum then summons the gods: "Ho, all ye gods, come, gather together; come, unite as ye gathered together and united for Atum in Heliopolis, that he might hail you. Come ye, do ye everything which is good for king Pepi II for ever and ever." Atum then promises generous offerings "for all gods who shall cause every good thing to be king Pepi II's; who shall cause to endure this pyramid and this building like that where king Pepi II loved to be for ever and ever. All gods who shall cause to be good and enduring this pyramid and this building of king Pepi II they shall be equipped (or prepared), they shall be honored, they shall become souls, they shall become mighty; to them shall be given royal mortuary offerings, they shall receive divine offerings; to them shall joints be presented, to them shall oblations be made."[3]

Again the priest addresses the Sun-god under his earliest name, Atum, and recalls the time when the god sat high on the sacred *ben*, the pyramidal symbol at Heliopolis,

[1] Pyr. §§ 1276–7.   [2] Pyr. § 1266.   [3] Pyr. Ut. 599.

and created the other gods. This then is a special reason why he should preserve the pyramid of the king forever. "Thou wast lofty," says the priest, "on the height; thou didst shine as Phœnix of the *ben* in the Phœnix-hall in Heliopolis. That which thou didst spew out was Shu; that which thou didst spit out was Tefnut (his first two children). Thou didst put thy arms behind them as a ka-arm, that thy ka might be in them. O Atum, put thou thy arms behind king Mernere, behind this building, and behind this pyramid, as a ka-arm, that the ka of king Mernere may be in it enduring for ever and ever. Ho, Atum! Protect thou this king Mernere, this his pyramid and this building of king Mernere."[1] The priest then commends the pyramid to the whole Ennead, and finally proceeds to another long Utterance, which takes up the names of all the gods of the Ennead one after the other, affirming that, "as the name of the god so-and-so is firm, so is firm the name of king Mernere; so are firm this his pyramid and this his building likewise for ever and ever."[2]

Resting beneath the pyramid, the king's wants were elaborately met by a sumptuous and magnificent ritual performed on his behalf in the temple before his tomb. Of this ritual we know nothing except such portions of it as have been preserved in the Pyramid Texts. These show that the usual calendar of feasts of the living was celebrated for the king,[3] though naturally on a more splendid scale. Evidently the observances consisted chiefly in the presentation of plentiful food, clothing, and the like. One hundred and seventy-eight formulæ or utterances, forming about one-twentieth of the bulk of the Pyramid Texts,[4] contain the words spoken by the royal mortuary

[1] Pyr. Ut. 600.
[2] Pyr. Ut. 601.
[3] Pyr. § 2117.
[4] Ut. 26–203.

priests in offering food, drink, clothing, ointment, perfume, and incense, revealing the endless variety and splendid luxury of the king's table, toilet, and wardrobe in the hereafter. The magnificent vases discovered by Borchardt at Abusir in the pyramid-temple of Neferirkere (twenty-eighth century B. C.) are a further hint of the royal splendor with which this ritual of offerings was maintained, while the beauty and grandeur of the pyramid-temples themselves furnished an incomparable setting within which all this mortuary magnificence was maintained.

All this system of mortuary maintenance early came under the complete domination of the Osirian faith, though the very tomb at which it was enacted was a symbol of the Sun-god. Osiris had died not in the distant sky like Re, but on earth as men die. The human aspects of his life and death led to the early adoption of the incidents in his story as those which took place in the life and death of every one. Horus had offered to his father the eye which Set had wrenched out, and this evidence of the son's self-sacrifice for the father's sake had made Osiris a "soul," and proven of incalculable blessing. The "Horus-eye" became the primal type of all offerings, especially those offered to the dead, Osiris having been dead when he received the eye. Thus every offering presented to the king in the ritual of the pyramids was called the "Horus-eye," no matter what the character of the offering might be. In presenting linen garments the priest addressed the dead king thus: "Ho! This king Pepi! Arise thou, put on thee the Horus-eye, receive it upon thee, lay it to thy flesh; that thou mayest go forth in it, and the gods may see thee clothed in it. . . . The Horus-eye is brought to thee, it removes not from thee for ever and ever."[1] Again in offering ointment the priest assuming the office of Horus says: "Horus comes filled with ointment. He has embraced his father Osiris. He found him (lying) upon his side in Gehesti. Osiris filled himself with the eye of him whom he begat. Ho! This king Pepi II! I come to thee steadfast, that I may fill thee with the ointment that came forth from the Horus-eye. Fill thyself therewith. It will join thy bones, it will unite thy members, it will join to thee thy flesh, it will dissolve thy evil sweat to the earth. Take its odor upon thee that thy odor may be sweet like (that of) Re, when he rises in the horizon, and the horizon-gods delight in him. Ho! This king Pepi II! The odor of the Horus-eye is on thee; the gods who follow Osiris delight in thee."[2]

The individual formulæ in the long offering-ritual are very brief. The prevailing form of offering is simply: "O king X! Handed to thee is the Horus-eye which was wrested from Set, rescued for thee, that thy mouth might be filled with it. Wine, a white jar."[3] The last words prescribe the offering which the formula accompanies. Similarly the method of offering or the accompanying acts may be appended to the actual words employed by the priest. Thus through the lengthy ritual of six or eight score such utterances, besides some others scattered through the Pyramid Texts, the priest lays before the dead king those creature comforts which he had enjoyed in the flesh.[4] In doing so he entered the mysterious

---

[1] Pyr. Ut. 453. [2] Pyr. Ut. 637. [3] Pyr. Ut. 54.
[4] The ritual of offerings, properly so called, in the Pyramid Texts, begins at Ut. 26 and continues to Ut. 203. This ritual as a whole has received an Osirian editing and only Ut. 44 and 50 are clearly Solar. Each *Spruch*, or Utterance, contains the words to be used by the priest, with some designation of the offering, sometimes no more than the words "Horus-eye." Not infrequently directions as to the place

80 RELIGION AND THOUGHT IN ANCIENT EGYPT

chamber behind the temple court, where he stepped into the presence of the pyramid itself, beneath which the king lay. Before the priest rose the great false door through which the spirit of the king might re-enter the temple from his sepulchre far beneath the mountain of masonry now towering above it. Standing before the false door the priest addressed the king as if present and presented a vast array of the richest gifts, accompanying each with the precribed formula of presentation which we have already discussed. But the insistent fact of death cannot be ignored even in these utterances which exist solely because the dead is believed to live and feels the needs of the living. In the silent chamber the priest feels the unresponsiveness of the royal dead yonder far beneath the mountainous pyramid, and hence from time to time calls upon him to rise from his sleep and behold the food and the gifts spread out for him. In order that none of these may be omitted, the priest summarizes them all in the promise to the king: "Given to thee are all offerings, all oblations, (even) thy desire, and that by which it is well for thee with the god forever."[1] Added to all this elaborate ritual of gifts there were also charms potent to banish hunger from the vitals of the king, and these, too, the priest from time to time recited for the Pharaoh's benefit.[2]

The kings of the early Pyramid Age in the thirtieth cen-

where the offering is to be put accompany the formula, with memoranda also of the quantity and the like. A little group of prayers and charms (Ut. 204–212) follows the offering-ritual. This group also concerns offerings, but it is all Solar except the first and last utterance. The other texts concerning material needs scattered through the Pyramid Texts, conceive the king as dwelling no longer in the tomb in most cases (e. g., Ut. 413). There is a group of twelve Utterances on food (Ut. 338–349), and a larger group concerned chiefly with the physical necessities (Ut. 401–426).

[1] Pyr. §§ 101 c, d.   [2] Pyr. § 204.

tury B. C. evidently looked confidently forward to indefinite life hereafter maintained in this way. In a lament for the departed Pharaoh, which the priest as Horus recited, Horus says: "Ho! king Pepi! I have wept for thee! I have mourned for thee. I forget thee not, my heart is not weary to give to thee mortuary offerings every day, at the (feast of the) month, at the (feast of the) half-month, at the (feast of) 'Putting-down-the-Lamp,' at the (feast of) Thoth, at the (feast of) Wag, at the period of thy years and thy months which thou livest as a god."[1] But would the posterity of an Oriental sovereign never weary in giving him mortuary offerings every day? We shall see.

Such maintenance required a considerable body of priests in constant service at the pyramid-temple, though no list of a royal pyramid priesthood has survived to us. They were supported by liberal endowments, for which the power of the royal house might secure respect for a long time. The priesthood and the endowment of the pyramid of Snefru at Dahshur (thirtieth century B. C.) were respected and declared exempt from all state dues and levies by a royal decree issued by Pepi II of the Sixth Dynasty, three hundred years after Snefru's death. Moreover, there had been three changes of dynasty since the decease of Snefru. But such endowments, accumulating as they did from generation to generation, must inevitably break down at last. In the thirtieth century B. C., Snefru himself had given to one of his nobles "one hundred loaves every day from the mortuary temple of the mother of the king's children, Nemaathap."[2] This queen had died at the close of the Second Dynasty, some

[1] Pyr. §§ 2117–18, restored from Pap. Schmitt.
[2] BAR, I, 173.

two generations earlier. Snefru, while he may not have violated her mortuary income, at least disposed of it after it had served its purpose at her tomb, in rewarding his partisans. In the same way Sahure, desiring to reward Persen, one of his favorite nobles, finds no other resources available and diverts to Persen's tomb an income of loaves and oil formerly paid to the queen Neferhotepes every day.[1] There is in these acts of Snefru and Sahure a hint of one possible means of meeting the dilemma as the number of tomb endowments increased, viz., by supplying one tomb with food-offerings which had already served in another. Even so the increasing number of royal tombs made it more and more difficult as a mere matter of management and administration to maintain them. Hence even the priests of Sahure's pyramid in the middle of the twenty-eighth century B. C., unable properly to protect the king's pyramid-temple, found it much cheaper and more convenient to wall up all the side entrances and leave only the causeway as the entrance to the temple. They seem to have regarded this as a pious work, for they left the name of the particular phyle of priests who did it, on the masonry of the doorways which they thus closed up.[2] After this the accidentally acquired sanctity of a figure of the goddess Sekhmet in the temple, a figure which enjoyed the local reverence and worship of the surrounding villages, and continued in their favor for centuries, resulted in the preservation of a large portion of the temple which otherwise would long before have fallen into ruin. Sahure's successor, Neferirkere, fared much worse. A few years after his death a successor of the same dynasty (Nuserre) broke away the causeway leading up to the

[1] BAR, I, 241.
[2] BORCHARDT, *Das Grabdenkmal des Koenigs Sahure*, pp. 94 *ff*.

pyramid-temple that he might divert it to his own temple near by. The result was that the mortuary priests of Neferirkere, unable longer to live in the valley below, moved up to the plateau, where they grouped their sundried brick dwellings around and against the façade of the temple where they ministered. As their income dwindled these dwellings became more and more like hovels, they finally invaded the temple court and chambers, and the priests, by this time in a state of want, fairly took possession of the temple as a priestly quarter. Left at last without support, their own tumble-down hovels were forsaken and the ruins mingled with those of the temple itself. When the Middle Kingdom opened, six hundred years after Neferirkere's death, the temple was several metres deep under the accumulation of rubbish, and the mounds over it were used as a burial ground, where the excavations disclosed burials a metre or two above the pavement of the temple. The great Fourth Dynasty cemetery at Gizeh experienced the same fate. The mortuary priests whose ancestors had once administered the sumptuous endowments of the greatest of all pyramids, pushed their intrusive burials into the streets and areas between the old royal tombs of the extinct line, where they too ceased about 2500 B. C., four hundred years after Khufu laid out the Gizeh cemetery. Not long after 2500 B. C., indeed the whole sixty-mile line of Old Kingdom pyramids from Medûm on the south to Gizeh on the north had become a desert solitude.[1] This melancholy condition is discernible also in the reflections of the thoughtful in the Feudal Age five hundred years later as they contemplated the wreck of these massive tombs. (See pp. 181–4.)

What was so obvious centuries after the great Pharaohs

[1] Confer REISNER, *Boston Mus. of Fine Arts Bulletin*, IX, 16.

of the Pyramid Age had passed away was already discernible long before the Old Kingdom fell. The pyramids represent the culmination of the belief in *material equipment* as completely efficacious in securing felicity for the dead. The great pyramids of Gizeh represent the effort of titanic energies absorbing all the resources of a great state as they converged upon one supreme endeavor to sheath eternally the body of a single man, the head of the state, in a husk of masonry so colossal that by these purely material means the royal body might defy all time and by sheer force of mechanical supremacy make conquest of immortality. The decline of such vast pyramids as those of the Fourth Dynasty at Gizeh, and the final insertion of the Pyramid Texts in the pyramids beginning with the last king of the Fifth Dynasty about 2625 B. C., puts the emphasis on well-being elsewhere, a belief in felicity in some distant place not so entirely dependent upon material means, and recognizes in some degree the fact that piles of masonry cannot confer that immortality which a man must win in his own soul.

The Pyramid Texts as a whole furnish us the oldest chapter in human thinking preserved to us, the remotest reach in the intellectual history of man which we are now able to discern. It had always been supposed that the pyramids were all without inscription, until the native workmen employed by Mariette at Sakkara in 1880, the year before his death, penetrated the pyramid of Pepi I, and later that of Mernere. For the first edition of the Pyramid Texts we are indebted to Maspero, who displayed great penetration in discerning the general character of these texts, which he published during the next ten years. Nevertheless, it has been only since the appearance of Sethe's great edition in 1910 that it has been possible to undertake the systematic study of these remarkable documents.[1]

Written in hieroglyphic they occupy the walls of the passages, galleries, and chambers in five of the pyramids of Sakkara: the earliest, that of Unis, belonging at the end of the Fifth Dynasty in the latter half of the twenty-seventh century B. C., and the remaining four, those of the leading kings of the Sixth Dynasty, Teti, Pepi I, Mernere, and Pepi II, the last of whom died early in the twenty-fifth century B. C. They thus represent a period of about one hundred and fifty years from the vicinity of 2625 to possibly 2475 B. C., that is the whole of the twenty-sixth century and possibly a quarter of a century before and after it.

It is evident, however, that they contain material much older than this, the age of the copies which have come down to us. The five copies themselves refer to material then in existence which has not survived. We read in them of "the Chapter of Those Who Ascend," and the "Chapter of Those Who Raise Themselves Up," which purport to have been used on the occasion of various incidents in the myths.[2] They were thus regarded as older than our Pyramid Texts. Such older material, therefore, existed, whether we possess any of it or not. We find conditions of civilization also in the Pyramid Texts which were far older than the Fifth and Sixth Dynasties. In

---

[1] MASPERO's edition appeared in his journal, the *Recueil*, in volumes 3, 4, 5, 7, 8, 9, 10, 11, 12, and 14; it later appeared in a single volume. SETHE's edition of the hieroglyphic text in two volumes (*Die Altaegyptischen Pyramidentexte von Kurt Sethe*, Leipzig, 1908–10) will be accompanied by further volumes containing translation and discussion of the texts, and with palæographic material by H. SCHAEFER.

[2] Pyr. § 1245; see also § 1251.

summoning the dead to rise he is bidden: "Throw off the sand from thy face,"¹ or "Remove thy earth."² Such passages as these must have arisen in a time when the king was buried in a primitive grave scooped out of the desert sand. Similarly when the king's tomb is opened for him that he may rise he is assured: "The brick are drawn for thee out of the great tomb,"³ a passage which must have come into use when the kings used brick tombs like those at Abydos in the First and Second Dynasties. Like the sand grave or the brick tomb, is the common representation of the king crossing the celestial waters on the two reed floats, used by the peasants of Nubia to this day.

Parallel with these hints in the conditions of civilization are others referring to the political conditions, which plainly place some of the Pyramid Texts in the days before the rise of the dynasties, in the age when South and North were warring together for supremacy, that is before 3400 B. C. We find a sycomore-goddess addressed thus: "Thou hast placed the terror of thee in the heart of the kings of Lower Egypt, dwelling in Buto" (the capital of the prehistoric Delta kingdom),⁴ a passage evidently written from the point of view of the South in hostility toward the North. We read of Horus "who smote the Red Crowns";⁵ again "the White (southern) Crown comes forth, it has devoured the Great (northern) Crown;"⁶ or "the horizon burns incense to Horus of Nekhen (capital of the South), . . . the flood of its flame is against you, ye wearers of the Great (northern) Crown."⁷ It is said of the king that

---

¹ Pyr. § 1878 b. ² Pyr. § 747, same in § 1732. ³ Pyr. § 572.
⁴ Pyr. § 1488; this passage was first remarked by SETHE as showing the early date of the document, *Zeitschr. für aegypt. Sprache*, 38, 64.
⁵ Pyr. § 2037. ⁶ Pyr. § 239. ⁷ Pyr. § 295.

"he has eaten the Red (crown), he has swallowed the Green" (Buto goddess of the North);[1] and in the hereafter he is crowned with the White (southern) Crown.[2] There too he receives the southern (Upper Egyptian) district of the blessed Field of Rushes,[3] and he descends to the southern district of the Field of Offerings.[4] As priest of Re in the hereafter the king has a libation jar "which purifies the Southland."[5] Finally, "it is king Unis who binds with lilies the papyrus (the two flowers of North and South); it is king Unis who reconciles the Two Lands; it is king Unis who unites the Two Lands."[6] It is evident therefore that the Pyramid Texts contain passages which date from before the union of the Two Lands, that is before the thirty-fourth century B. C.; and also others which belong to the early days of the union when the hostilities had not yet ceased, but the kings of the South were nevertheless maintaining control of the North and preserving the united kingdom. All these are written from the southern point of view. It should not be forgotten also that some of them were composed as late as the Old Kingdom itself, like the formulæ intended to protect the pyramid,[7] which of course are not earlier than the rise of the pyramid-form in the thirtieth century B. C. Within the period of a century and a half covered by our five copies also, differences are noticeable. Evidences of editing in the later copies, which, however, are not found in the earlier copies, are clearly discernible. The processes of thought and the development of custom and belief which brought them forth were going on until the last copy was produced in the early twenty-fifth century B. C. They therefore represent a period of at least a

---

[1] Pyr. § 410. [2] Pyr. Ut. 524. [3] Pyr. § 1084.
[4] Pyr. § 1087. [5] Pyr. § 1179. [6] Pyr. § 388.
[7] Pyr. Ut. 599–600; see *infra*, pp. 75–76.

thousand years, and a thousand years, it should not be forgotten, which was ended some four thousand five hundred years ago. Such a great mass of documents as this from the early world exists nowhere else and forms a storehouse of experience from the life of ancient man which largely remains to be explored.

While their especial function may be broadly stated to be *to insure the king felicity in the hereafter*, they constantly reflect, as all literature does, the ebb and flow of the life around them, and they speak in terms of the experience of the men who produced them, terms current in the daily life of palace, street, and bazaar, or again terms which were born in the sacred solitude of the inner temple. To one of quick imagination they abound in pictures from that long-vanished world of which they are the reflection. While they are concerned chiefly with the fortunes of the king, these do not shut out the world around. Of the happiness of the king beyond the grave it is said: "This that thou hast heard in the houses and learned in the streets on this day when king Pepi was summoned to life."[1] Of this life in the houses and on the streets of five thousand years ago we catch fleeting glimpses: the swallows twittering on the wall,[2] the herdman wading the canal immersed to his middle and bearing across the helpless young of his flock,[3] the crooning of the mother to her nursing child at twilight,[4] "the hawk seen in the evening traversing the sky,"[5] the wild goose withdrawing her foot and escaping the hand of the baffled fowler in the marsh,[6] the passenger at the ferry with nothing to offer the boatmen for a seat in the crowded ferry-boat, but who is allowed to embark and work his passage wearily bailing the leaky craft;[7]

[1] Pyr. § 1189. [2] Pyr. § 1216. [3] Pyr. § 1348. [4] Pyr. § 912.
[5] Pyr. § 1048.   [6] Pyr. § 1484.   [7] Pyr. § 335.

the noble sitting by the pool in his garden beneath the shade of the reed booth;[1] these pictures and many others are alive with the life of the Nile-dweller's world. The life of the palace is more fully and picturesquely reflected than that of the world outside and around it. We see the king in hours heavy with cares of state, his secretary at his side with writing kit and two pens, one for black and the other for the red of the rubrics;[2] again we discern him in moments of relaxation leaning familiarly on the shoulder of a trusted friend and counsellor,[3] or the two bathe together in the palace pool and royal chamberlains approach and dry their limbs.[4] Often we meet him heading a brilliant pageant as he passes through the streets of the residence with outrunners and heralds and messengers clearing the way before him;[5] when he ferries over to the other shore and steps out of the glittering royal barge, we see the populace throwing off their sandals, and then even their garments, as they dance in transports of joy at his coming;[6] again we find him surrounded by the pomp and splendor of his court at the palace gate, or seated on his gorgeous throne, adorned with lions' heads and bulls' feet.[7] In the palace-hall "he sits upon his marvellous throne, his marvellous sceptre in his hand; he lifts his hand toward the children of their father and they rise before this king Pepi; he drops his hand toward them and they sit down (again)."[8] To be sure these are depicted as incidents of the life beyond the grave, but the subject-matter and the colors with which it is portrayed are drawn from the life here and the experience here. It is the gods who cast off their sandals and their raiment to dance for joy at the arrival of the king, as he crosses the heavenly

[1] Pyr. § 130. [2] Pyr. § 954. [3] Pyr. § 730. [4] Pyr. Ut. 323.
[5] Pyr., passim. [6] Pyr. § 1197. [7] Pyr. § 1123. [8] Pyr. § 1563.

Nile; but they of course are depicted as doing that which the Pharaoh's subjects were accustomed to do along the earthly Nile. It is the gods who dry the Pharaoh's limbs as he bathes with the Sun-god in the "lake of rushes," but here too the gods do for the Pharaoh what his earthly chamberlains had been wont to do for him.

But notwithstanding the fact that these archaic texts are saturated with the life out of which they have come, they form together almost a *terra incognita*. As one endeavors to penetrate it, his feeling is like that of entering a vast primeval forest, a twilight jungle filled with strange forms and elusive shadows peopling a wilderness through which there is no path. | An archaic orthography veils and obscures words with which the reader may be quite familiar in their later and habitual garb. They serve too in situations and with meanings as strange to the reader as their spelling. Besides these disguised friends, there is a host of utter strangers, a great company of archaic words which have lived a long and active life in a world now completely lost and forgotten. Hoary with age they totter into sight for a brief period, barely surviving in these ancient texts, then to disappear forever, and hence are never met with again. They vaguely disclose to us a vanished world of thought and speech, the last of the unnumbered æons through which prehistoric man has passed till he finally comes within hailing distance of us as he enters the historic age. But these hoary strangers, survivors of a forgotten age, still serving on for a generation or two in the Pyramid Texts, often remain strangers until they disappear; we have no means of making their acquaintance or forcing them to reveal to us their names or the message which they bear, and no art of lexicography can force them all to yield up their secrets. Combined with these

REALMS OF THE DEAD—PYRAMID TEXTS 91

words, too, there is a deal of difficult construction, much enhanced by the obscure, dark, and elusive nature of the content of these archaic documents; abounding in allusions to incidents in lost myths, to customs and usages long since ended, they are built up out of a fabric of life, thought, and experience largely unfamiliar or entirely unknown to us.

We have said that their function is essentially to insure the king's felicity in the hereafter. The chief and dominant note throughout is insistent, even passionate, protest against death. They may be said to be the record of humanity's earliest supreme revolt against the great darkness and silence from which none returns. The word death never occurs in the Pyramid Texts except in the negative or applied to a foe. Over and over again we hear the indomitable assurance that the dead lives. "King Teti has not died the death, he has become a glorious one in the horizon";[1] "Ho! King Unis! Thou didst not depart dead, thou didst depart living";[2] "Thou hast departed that thou mightest live, thou hast not departed that thou mightest die";[3] "Thou diest not";[4] "This king Pepi dies not";[5] "King Pepi dies not by reason of any king . . . (nor) by reason of any dead";[6] "Have ye said that he would die? He dies not; this king Pepi lives forever";[7] "Live! Thou shalt not die";[8] "If thou landest (euphemism for "diest"), thou livest (again)";[9] "This king Pepi has escaped his day of death";[10]—such is the constant refrain of these texts. Not infrequently the utterance concludes with the assurance: "Thou livest, thou livest, raise thee up";[11] or "Thou diest not, stand up,

---

[1] Pyr. § 350. [2] Pyr. § 134. [3] Pyr. § 833. [4] Pyr. § 775.
[5] Pyr. § 1464 c. [6] Pyr. § 1468 c–d. [7] Pyr. § 1477 b. [8] Pyr. § 2201 c.
[9] Pyr. § 1975 b. [10] Pyr. § 1453 a–h. [11] Pyr. § 1262.

raise thee up"; [1] or "Raise thee up, O this king Pepi, thou diest not"; [2] or an appendix is added as a new utterance by itself: "O lofty one among the Imperishable Stars, thou perishest not eternally." [3] When the inexorable fact must be referred to, death is called the "landing" or the "mooring" as we have seen it above, [4] or its opposite is preferred, and it is better to mention "not living" than to utter the fatal word; [5] or with wistful reminiscence of lost felicity once enjoyed by men, these ancient texts recall the blessed age "before death came forth." [6]

While the supreme subject of the Pyramid Texts is life, eternal life for the king, they are a compilation from the most varied sources. Every possible agency and influence was brought to bear to attain the end in view, and all classes of ancient lore deemed efficacious or found available for this purpose were employed by the priests who put together this earliest surviving body of literature. Speaking chronologically, there are strata here representing the different centuries for a thousand years or more as we have seen; but speaking in terms of subject-matter, we must change the figure and regard the Pyramid Texts as a fabric into which the most varied strands have been woven. Whether we make a vertical or a horizontal section, whether we cut across the fabric transversely or longitudinally these varied elements are exposed and contrasted. Cutting transversely we discover the varied constituents side by side, the strands of the warp running in most cases from end to end of the fabric; whereas when we cut longitudinally we disclose the changes due to time as the woof is wrought into the fabric. We shall make the transverse cut first and ascertain the character of the

[1] Pyr. § 867. [2] Pyr. § 875. [3] Pyr. Ut. 464.
[4] See also Pyr. § 1090. [5] Pyr. § 1335. [6] Pyr. § 1466 d.

constituent strands, without reference to the time element. Our question is, what is the content of the Pyramid Texts?

It may be said to be in the main sixfold:

1. A funerary ritual and a ritual of mortuary offerings at the tomb.
2. Magical charms.
3. Very ancient ritual of worship.
4. Ancient religious hymns.
5. Fragments of old myths.
6. Prayers and petitions on behalf of the dead king.

There is of course some miscellaneous matter and some which falls under several of the above classes at once. Taking up these six classes we find that the priestly editors have arranged their materials in sections often of some length, each section headed by the words: "Utter (or Recite) the words." Each such section has been called by Sethe in his edition a "Spruch," and we call them "Utterances." Of these the first of the five pyramids, that of Unis, contains two hundred and twenty-eight, while the others contain enough additional "Utterances" to make up a total of seven hundred and fourteen. In their modern published form, including the variants, they fill two quarto volumes containing together over a thousand pages of text.[1]

With the exception of the funerary and offering ritual, which is at the head of the collection, and with which we have already dealt in the preceding lectures, the material was arranged by the successive editors almost at haphazard. If such an editor had the materials before him in groups he made no effort to put together groups of like content, but he copied as he happened to come upon his

[1] Exactly 1051.

sources. He must have had before him a series of ancient books, each containing a number of groups of Utterances falling into all six of the above classes, but he copied each book from beginning to end before he took up the next one. Thus it is that we find groups of charms, or prayers, or hymns devoted to the same subject embedded in various places widely separated, or distributed throughout the entire collection, without any attempt to bring them together.

※There can be no doubt that a considerable portion of the Pyramid Texts were intended to be employed as charms. Some of these were used by the mortuary priest at the interment; others were wielded by the deceased himself in self-defence. "King Pepi is a magician, King Pepi is one who is possessed of magic,"[1] say the texts. The dead are called "the glorious by reason of (or 'by means of') their equipped mouths,"[2] meaning that their mouths are equipped with the charms, prayers, and ritual of the Pyramid Texts. It is evident that the dead king was supposed to employ magic power, and the agency of this power was the Pyramid Texts themselves. They are sometimes unequivocally called magical charms. "This charm that is in the belly of king Pepi is on him when he ascends and lifts himself to the sky" affirms one passage,[3] and the Utterance referred to is an accompanying list of the limbs of the king, which are thus protected. Again in a remarkable passage the ancient text insists: "It is not this king Pepi who says this against you, ye gods; it is the charm which says this against you, ye gods,"[4] and "this" is the text of the accompanying Utterance. The possession of such charms was vitally important, so that a special charm was included to prevent the departed

[1] Pyr. § 924 b.   [2] Pyr. § 930 a.   [3] Pyr. § 1318 c.   [4] Pyr. § 1324.

Pharaoh from being deprived of his charm or his magical power.[1]

The distinction between a charm and a prayer in these texts is difficult for the reason that a text of a character originally in no way connected or identified with magical formulæ may be employed as such. We find a Sun-hymn[2] called a "charm" in the Pyramid Texts. Again the archaic hymn to Nut,[3] a fragment of ancient ritual, is later employed as a household charm.[4] The question is not infrequently one of function rather than one of content. The serpent-charms are distinguishable as such in the Pyramid Texts at the first glance in most cases; but the question whether a hymn or a prayer may not be designed to serve as a charm is sometimes not easily decided. The question is an important one, because some have averred that the whole body of Pyramid Texts is simply a collection of magical charms, and that therefore the repetition of any Utterance was supposed to exert magical power. Such a sweeping statement cannot be demonstrated. An ancient hymn supposed to be repeated by the dead king, when it is accompanied by no express statement that it is a charm, may have served the same function with regard to the god to whom it is addressed, which it served in the ancient ritual from which it was taken; and because some such hymns have been inserted in charms is no sufficient reason for concluding that all such hymns in the Pyramid Texts are necessarily charms. The Pyramid Texts themselves are one of the most important documents in which we may observe the gradual invasion of mortuary religious beliefs by the power of magic, but when the last of the Pyramid Texts was edited

[1] Pyr. Ut. 678. [2] Pyr. Ut. 456. [3] Pyr. Ut. 429-435.
[4] ERMAN, Zauberspr. für Mutter und Kind, 5, 8-6, 8.

in the twenty-fifth century B. C. the triumph of magic in the realm of such beliefs was still a thousand years away.

Besides the funerary and offering ritual employed at the tomb, and besides the charms unquestionably present, there is then a large residuum of ancient religious literature, consisting of ritual of worship, religious hymns, fragments of old myths, and finally prayers on behalf of the dead (Nos 3, 4, 5, and 6, above). An Osirian Utterance in the Pyramid Texts[1] occurs over a thousand years later as part of the ritual at Abydos on the wall of the Atum chapel in the Seti temple of Osiris. There can be little doubt that it was temple ritual also in the Pyramid Age. It is not unlikely that the religious hymns embedded in this compilation, like the impressive Sun-hymn in Utterance 456,[2] or the archaic hymn to the Sky-goddess,[3] or the hymn to Osiris as Nile,[4] also belonged to temple rituals. In this case they fall in the same class with temple ritual and should not be made a class by themselves. In so far as the fragments of the old myths fall into poetic form they too are not distinguishable from the religious hymns. These fragments in most cases recite current incidents in which some god enjoys some benefit or passes through some desirable experience or attains some triumph, and the same good fortune is now desired for the deceased king. Many of them, as we have already seen, relate to matters which unhappily are unintelligible without a full knowledge of the myth from which they are drawn.

While the *content* of the Pyramid Texts may be thus indicated in a general way, a precise and full analysis is a far more difficult matter. The *form* of the literature contained

---

[1] Pyr. Ut. 637.
[2] See above, pp. 13–14.
[3] Pyr. Ut. 427–435.
[4] Pyr. Ut. 581.

is happily more easily disposed of. Among the oldest literary fragments in the collection are the religious hymns, and these exhibit an early poetic form, that of couplets displaying parallelism in arrangement of words and thought—the form which is familiar to all in the Hebrew psalms as "parallelism of members." It is carried back by its employment in the Pyramid Texts into the fourth millennium B. C., by far earlier than its appearance anywhere else. It is indeed the oldest of all literary forms known to us. Its use is not confined to the hymns mentioned, but appears also in other portions of the Pyramid Texts, where it is, however, not usually so highly developed.

Besides this form, which strengthens the claim of these fragments to be regarded as literature in our sense of the term, there is here and there, though not frequently, some display of literary quality in thought and language. There is, for example, a fine touch of imagination in one of the many descriptions of the resurrection of Osiris: "Loose thy bandages! They are not bandages, they are the locks of Nephthys,"[1] the weeping goddess hanging over the body of her dead brother. The ancient priest who wrote the line sees in the bandages that swathe the silent form the heavy locks of the goddess which fall and mingle with them. There is an elemental power too in the daring imagination which discerns the sympathetic emotion of the whole universe as the dread catastrophe of the king's death and the uncanny power of his coming among the gods of the sky are realized by the elements. "The sky weeps for thee, the earth trembles for thee" say the ancient mourners for the king,[2] or when they see him in imagination ascending the vault of the sky they say:

[1] Pyr. § 1363. [2] Pyr. § 1365.

"Clouds darken the sky,
The stars rain down,
The Bows (a constellation) stagger,
The bones of the hell-hounds tremble,
The ⌈porters⌉ are silent,
When they see king Unis,
Dawning as a soul."[1]

A fundamental question which arises as one endeavors to interpret these ancient documents is that of the method of employment. How were they used? In all likelihood the entire collection was recited by the mortuary priests on the day of burial. The entire offering ritual (including in the different pyramids one hundred and seventy-eight "Utterances") was furthermore recited on all feast days, and probably also on all other days. The fact that each "Utterance" is headed by the words "recite the words" also indicates this manner of employing them. A large proportion are personal equipment of the dead king to be recited by him as occasion demanded. This is shown by the curious fact that a number of long sections were in the first person originally, and were so engraved on the pyramid walls; but these passages were afterward altered to the third person, usually by the insertion of the king's name over the old personal pronoun. It is evident that many of the charms were designed for use by the dead, as when a Sun-hymn is accompanied by directions stating that the king is to employ it as a charm, which, if he knows it, will secure him the friendship of the Sun-god.[2] When the whole collection was recited by the priest he of course personified the king, in all passages where the king speaks in the first person, just as he personified so many of the gods who are depicted speaking and acting in these texts; but the fact that a large body

[1] Pyr. § 393.   [2] Pyr. Ut. 456.

of texts address the dead king in the second person clearly shows that they were uttered by the priest or some one on the king's behalf. In one case the speaker is the living and still reigning king who offers eye-paint to his departed royal ancestor.[1]

On one other question in this connection there can be no doubt. These mortuary texts were all intended for the king's exclusive use, and as a whole contain beliefs which apply only to the king.[2] This is not to say, however, that some archaic texts in use among the people have not here and there crept into the collection. To these may possibly belong the addresses to the dead as if buried in the desert sand, or a few others like simple serpent charms, or passages according the king hereafter a destiny not strictly peculiar to him and one which ordinary mortals already believed attainable by them. It is a significant fact that the nobles of the age made practically no use of the Pyramid Texts in their own tombs.

While the Pyramid Texts have not been able to shake off the old view of the sojourn at the tomb, they give it little thought, and deal almost entirely with a blessed life in a distant realm. Let it be stated clearly at the outset that this distant realm is the sky, and that the Pyramid Texts know practically nothing of the hereafter in the Nether World. Echoes of other archaic notions of the place of the dead have been preserved here and there.

---

[1] Pyr. Ut. 605.
[2] The presence of the word "mn"="so and so" instead of the king's name (Pyr. § 147) does not necessarily indicate the use of the passage by *any* one, but simply shows that the priestly copyist, when first recording this text in his manuscript, did not know for what king it was to be employed. Then in copying it on the wall the draughtsman by oversight transferred the "so and so" from his manuscript to the wall, instead of changing it to the king's name.

The oldest doubtless is contained in that designation of the dead which claims ignorance as to their whereabouts, and calls them "those whose places are hidden."[1] Another ancient belief conceives the dead as somewhere in the distant "west," but this belief plays practically no part in the Pyramid Texts, and is discernible there only in an archaic title of the mortuary Anubis of Siut, who occasionally has appended to his name the words "First or Lord of the Westerners,"[2] a designation which served as the name of an old mortuary god at Abydos, who was later identified with Osiris, and his name appropriated by him also occurs a number of times in the Pyramid Texts.[3] But the "west" hardly attains even a subordinate rôle in the beliefs which dominate the Pyramid Texts. We hear of it once as a means of gaining access to the Sun-god: "These thy four ways which are before the tomb of Horus, wherein one goes to the (Sun-) god, as soon as the sun goes down. He (the Sun-god) grasps thy arm. . . ."[4] In one passage, too, the dead is adjured to go to the "west" in preference to the east, in order to join the Sun-god, but in this very passage he appears as one whose function was in the east.[5] An analogous passage affirms: "King Unis rests from life (dies) in the west, . . . King Unis dawns anew in the east."[6] The west is mentioned casually, also along with the other celestial regions where the Sun-god in his course finds the translated Pharaoh.[7] It is the *east* which with constant reiteration is affirmed to be the most sacred of all regions, and that to which the dead king

---

[1] Pyr. § 873 et al.   [2] Pyr. §§ 745 a, 1833, 2198 b.
[3] E. g., §§ 650, 759. See *infra*, p. 38.   [4] Pyr. § 1355.
[5] Pyr. §§ 1531-2; see also § 1703, where, by total inversion of the myth, the king is born in the west. Similarly in § 470 it is the western horn of the sky-bull that is removed for the passage of the dead.
[6] Pyr. § 306.   [7] Pyr. § 919.

should fare. Indeed he is explicitly cautioned against the west: "Go not on those currents of the west; those who go thither, they return not (again)."[1] In the Pyramid Texts it may be fairly said that the old doctrine of the "west" as the permanent realm of the dead, a doctrine which is later so prominent, has been quite submerged by the pre-eminence of the east.

This "east," therefore, is the east of the sky, and the realm of the dead is a celestial one, using the term with none of its frequent theological significance in English. Two ancient doctrines of this celestial hereafter have been commingled in the Pyramid Texts: one represents the dead as a star, and the other depicts him as associated with the Sun-god, or even becoming the Sun-god himself. It is evident that these two beliefs, which we may call the stellar and the Solar hereafter, were once in a measure independent, and that both have then entered into the form of the celestial hereafter which is found in the Pyramid Texts. In the cloudless sky of Egypt it was a not unnatural fancy which led the ancient Nile-dweller to see in the splendor of the nightly heavens the host of those who had preceded him; thither they had flown as birds, rising above all foes of the air,[2] and there they now swept across the sky as eternal stars.[3] It is especially those stars which are called "the Imperishable Ones" in which the Egyptian saw the host of the dead. These are said to be in the north of the sky,[4] and the suggestion that the circumpolar stars, which never set or disappear, are the ones which are meant is a very probable one.[5] While there are Utterances in the Pyramid Texts which define

[1] Pyr. § 2175.
[2] Pyr. § 1216.
[3] See the author's *History of Egypt*, p. 64.
[4] Pyr. § 1080.
[5] BORCHARDT, in ERMAN, *Handbuch der aegypt. Rel.*, p. 107.

the stellar notion of the hereafter without any reference to the Solar faith,[1] and which have doubtless descended from a more ancient day when the stellar belief was independent of the Solar, it is evident that the stellar notion has been absorbed in the Solar. There is a trace of the process in the endeavor to reconcile the northern station of the "Imperishables" with the "east" as the place of the dead in the Solar faith. We find provision made that the deceased king "may ferry over to Re, to the horizon . . . to his station on the east side of the sky, in its northern region among the Imperishable (Stars)."[2] Thus the stellar and the Solar elements were combined, though the Solar beliefs predominate so strongly that the Pyramid Texts as a whole and in the form in which they have reached us may be said to be of Solar origin.

The Solar destiny was perhaps suggested by the daily disappearance and reappearance of the sun. We find the texts assuring us, "This king Pepi lives as lives he (=the Sun-god) who has entered the west of the sky, when he rises in the east of the sky."[3] It should be noted that the place of living again is, however, the east, and it is not only the east, but explicitly the east of the *sky*. Death was on earth; life was to be had only in the sky.

>"Men fall,
>   Their name is not.
>   Seize thou king Teti by his arm,
>   Take thou king Teti to the sky,
>   That he die not on earth,
>   Among men."[4]

This idea that life was in the sky is the dominant notion, far older than the Osirian faith in the Pyramid Texts.

[1] Pyr. Ut. 328, 329, 503.
[2] Pyr. § 1000.
[3] Pyr. § 1469.
[4] Pyr. § 604.

So powerful was it that Osiris himself is necessarily accorded a celestial and a Solar hereafter in the secondary stage, in which his myth has entered the Pyramid Texts.

The prospect of a glorious hereafter in the splendor of the Sun-god's presence is the great theme of the Pyramid Texts. Even the royal tomb, as we have seen, assumed the form of the Sun-god's most sacred symbol. The state theology, which saw in the king the bodily son and the earthly representative of Re, very naturally conceived him as journeying at death to sojourn forever with his father, or even to supplant his father, and be his successor in the sky as he had been on earth. The Solar hereafter is properly a royal destiny, possible solely to a Pharaoh; it is only later that ordinary mortals gradually assume the right to share it, though, as we shall see, this could be done only by assuming also the royal character of every such aspirant.

Passing as the king did to a new kingdom in the sky, even though the various notions of his status there were not consistent, he was called upon to undergo a purification, which is prescribed and affirmed in the texts with wearisome reiteration. It may take place after the king's arrival in the sky, but more often it follows directly upon his resuscitation from the sleep of death. It may be accomplished by libations or by bathing in the sacred lake in the blessed fields, with the gods even officiating at the royal bath with towels and raiment, or by the fumes of incense which penetrate the limbs of the royal dead.[1] Sometimes it is the water of the traditional Nile sources at Elephantine which, as especially sacred and pure, should be employed,[2] or the dead king appears there and the goddess of the cataract, Satis, performs the ceremonies

---

[1] Pyr. §§ 27-29, 275, 920-1; Ut. 323.   [2] Pyr. § 864.

of purification.[1] That this purification might have moral aspects we shall later (p. 171) see. But it was chiefly intended to produce ceremonial cleanness, and when this was attained the king was prepared to undertake the journey to the sky.

We have already had occasion to remark that the region toward which he fared was the east of the sky, which in the Pyramid Texts is far more sacred than the west (pp. 100–102). Not only was the Sun-god born there every day as we have seen, but also the other gods. Over there was "this field, where the gods were begotten, over which the gods rejoice on these their New Year's Days,"[2] and there likewise they were born.[3] Similarly according to one view, not infrequently occurring, the deceased king is born there.[4] It was there too that the eye of Horus fell when it was wrenched out by Set.[5] In this sacred place are the doors of the sky,[6] before which stands "that tall sycomore east of the sky whereon the gods sit."[7] Again we hear of "the two sycomores which are on yonder side of the sky," which the king seizes when "they ferry him over and set him on the east side of the sky."[8] Here in this sacred place too the dead king finds the Sun-god, or is found by him,[9] here he ascends to the sky,[10] and here the ferry lands which has brought him over.[11]

[1] Pyr. § 1116.   [2] Pyr. § 1187.   [3] Pyr. § 928.   [4] Pyr. § 607.
[5] Pyr. §§ 594–6, 947.   [6] Pyr. §§ 1343, 1440.   [7] Pyr. § 916.
[8] Pyr. § 1433.   [9] Pyr. § 919.   [10] Pyr. §§ 326, 883, 1530.

[11] Pyr. § 1541. The supremacy of the east is such that even the Osirian Isis and Nephthys appear as "the great and mighty pair, who are in the east of the sky" (Pyr. § 2200). In spite of the fact that Osiris is "First of the Westerners" he goes to the east in the Pyramid Texts, and the pair, Isis and Nephthys, carry the dead into the east (Pyr. Ut. 702). In Pyr. §§ 1496–8 the east combines with the south and "the middle of the sky" as places where the ascent to the sky may be made.

When the deceased Pharaoh turned his face eastward toward this sacred region he was confronted by a lake lying along the east which it was necessary for him to cross in order to reach the realm of the Sun-god. It was on the further, that is eastern, shore of this lake that the eye of Horus had fallen in his combat with Set.[1] It was called the "Lily-lake," and it was long enough to possess "windings," [2] and must have stretched far to the north and south along the eastern horizon.[3] Beyond it lay a strange wonder-land, alive with uncanny forces on every hand. *All* was alive, whether it was the seat into which the king dropped, or the steering-oar to which he reached out his hand,[4] or the barque into which he stepped,[5] or the gates through which he passed. To all these, or to anything which he found, he might speak; and these uncanny things might speak to him, like the swan-boat of Lohengrin. Indeed it was a wonder-world like that in the swan-stories or the Nibelungen tales of the Germanic traditions, a world like that of the Morte d'Arthur, where prodigies meet the wayfarer at every turn.

To the dweller along the Nile the most obvious way to cross the Lily-lake is to embark in a ferry-boat. We find it among the rushes of the lake-shore with the ferryman standing in the stern poling it rapidly along. To do so he faces backward, and is therefore called "Face-behind," or "Look-behind." [6] He rarely speaks, but stands in silence awaiting his passenger. Numerous are the pleas and the specious petitions by which the waiting Pharaoh

---
[1] Pyr. § 595 b.   [2] Pyr. § 2061 c.
[3] Pyr. §§ 802, 1376–7. On the eastern position of this lake see also Pyr. Ut. 359. The chief references on the subject are Pyr. §§ 469 a, 543 b, 802 a, 1102 d, 1138 d, 1162 d, 1228 d, 1376 c, 1345 c, 1441 a, 1084 b; Ut. 359.
[4] Pyr. § 6021.   [5] Pyr. § 926.   [6] Pyr. §§ 1201, 1227.

seeks to cajole this mysterious boatman with averted face.
We hear him assured that "this king Pepi is the herdman
of thy cattle who is over thy breeding-place,"[1] and who
must therefore be ferried over at once in the ferryman's
own interests. Or the king brings with him a magic jar
the power of which the boatman cannot resist,[2] or the ferryman is assured that the Pharaoh is "righteous in the sight
of the sky and of the earth" and of the isle to which they
go.[3] Again the king is the dwarf or pygmy of the royal
dances "who gladdens the (king's) heart before the great
throne,"[4] and he must therefore be hastened across to the
court of Re to gladden the Sun-god. Indeed this is matter
of common knowledge, as the ferryman is now told:
"This is what thou hast heard in the houses and learned in
the streets on this day when this king Pepi was summoned
to life. . . . Lo, the two who are on the throne of the
Great God (Re), they summon this king Pepi to life and
satisfaction forever: they are Prosperity and Health.
(Therefore) ferry over this king Pepi to the field of the
good seat of the Great God."[5] We hear the boatman's
challenge of the new-comer: "Whence hast thou come?"
and the dead king must prove his royal lineage.[6] Or appeal may be made directly to Re: "O Re! Commend
king Teti to 'Look-behind' ferryman of the Lily-lake, that
he may bring that ferry-boat of the Lily-lake, for king
Teti, in which he ferries the gods to yonder side of the
Lily-lake, that he may ferry king Teti to yonder side of
the Lily-lake, to the east side of the sky."[7] If in spite of
all the king's efforts the shadowy boatman proves ob-
durate and refuses to bring his boat to the shore, then the
king addresses the oar in the ferryman's hand: "Ho!

[1] Pyr. § 1183.   [2] Pyr. § 1185.   [3] Pyr. § 1188.   [4] Pyr. § 1189.
[5] Pyr. §§ 1189-91.   [6] Pyr. § 1091.   [7] Pyr. §§ 599-600.

Thou who art in the fist of the ferryman,"[1] and if his words are powerful enough, the oar brings in the boat for the king. Sometimes it is on the opposite shore in charge of four curly haired guardians. These four are peremptorily summoned to bring it over to the king: "If ye delay to ferry over the ferry-boat to this king Pepi, this king Pepi will tell this your name to the people, which he knows;[2] . . . king Pepi will pluck out these locks that are in the middle of your heads like lotus flowers in the garden."[3]

Again, as so frequently in these texts, an unknown speaker in the king's behalf stands forth and threatens the boatman: "If thou dost not ferry over king Unis, then he will place himself upon the wing of Thoth. He, (even) he will ferry over king Unis to yonder side of the horizon."[4] There is also another ferryman of a boat bearing the remarkable name of "Eye of Khnum,"[5] who may be called upon in emergency; and should all other means fail the sceptres of the Imperishable Stars may serve as ferryman[6] or the two sycomores in the east may be prevailed upon to perform the same office for the king.[7] Even Re himself is not unwilling to appear and ferry the dead king across.[8] In any case the dead cannot be left without a ship, for he possesses the cunning charm which brings them all together: "The knots are tied, the ferryboats are brought together for the son of Atum. The

---

[1] Pyr. Ut. 616.
[2] To know the name of a god is to be able to control him.
[3] Pyr. § 1223. See also: Pyr. §§ 597, 599, 697, 925, 946, 999, 1091, 1441, 1769, 1429, and Ut. 310, 516–522, 616.
[4] Pyr. § 387; see also §§ 595–7, 1489, 1175.
[5] This is of course parallel with the designation, "Eye of Horus," which may also be applied to the boat. See Pyr. §§ 946, 445, 1769.
[6] Pyr. § 1432. [7] Pyr. § 1433. [8] Pyr. § 363.

son of Atum is not without a boat; king Mernere is with the son of Atum; the son of Atum is not without a boat."[1]

From the earliest days the prehistoric peasant might cross the Nile on two reed floats bound firmly together side by side like two huge cigars.[2] One of the earliest folk-tales of the Sun-god's voyage depicted him as crossing the celestial waters on such a pair of floats, and however primitive they might be, their use by the Sun-god had become common and involuntary belief. It required but the proper "sympathetic" transference of their use by Re to the dead Pharaoh, to insure him certain passage like that of the Sun-god. Horus (who, we recall, is but another form of the Sun-god) ferries over to the east of the sky on the two floats and he commends the dead king to "these four youths who sit on the east side of the sky, these four youths who sit in the shade of the tower of Kati,"[3] "these four youths who stand on the east side of the sky . . . (and) who bind together the two floats for Re, . . ." will also "bind together the two floats for this king Pepi."[4] Thus just as "the two floats of the sky are placed for Re that he may ferry over therewith to the horizon," so "the two floats of the sky are placed for

---

[1] Pyr. § 1472.
[2] The writer was once, like the Pharaoh, without a boat in Nubia, and a native from a neighboring village at once hurried away and returned with a pair of such floats made of dried reeds from the Nile shores. On this somewhat precarious craft he ferried the writer over a wide channel to an island in the river. It was the first time that the author had ever seen this contrivance, and it was not a little interesting to find a craft which he knew only in the Pyramid Texts of 5000 years ago still surviving and in daily use on the ancient river in far-off Nubia. There can be no doubt that this is the craft so often called the "two shnwy" (dual) in the Pyr. Texts.
[3] Pyr. § 1105.
[4] Pyr. § 1026.

king Unis that he may ferry over therewith to the horizon to Re."¹

But even these many devices for crossing the eastern sea might fail and then the king must commit himself to the air and make the ascent to the sky. "Thy two wings are spread out like a falcon with thick plumage, like the hawk seen in the evening traversing the sky," says the mysterious speaker to the king.² "He flies who flies; this king Pepi flies away from you, ye mortals. He is not of the earth, he is of the sky. . . . This king Pepi flies as a cloud to the sky, like a masthead bird; this king Pepi kisses the sky like a falcon, this king Pepi reaches the sky like the Horizon-god (Harakhte)."³ The variant text has like a grasshopper, and in accordance with this we find that the dead king was born with the back of a grasshopper.⁴ As the Egyptian grasshopper flies like a bird to vast heights, the back of a grasshopper was undoubtedly an appropriate adjunct to the royal anatomy. But it was the falcon, the sacred bird of the Sun-god, whose lofty flight was especially desired for the king. He is "the great falcon upon the battlements of the house of him of the hidden name."⁵ "Thy bones are falconesses, goddesses dwelling in the sky," say they to the king;⁶ or again, "Thou ascendest to the sky as a falcon, thy feathers are (those of) geese."⁷ The speaker also sees him escaping from the hands of men as the wild goose escapes the hand of the fowler clutching his feet and flies away to the sky;⁸ "the tips of his wings are those of the

¹ Pyr. § 337. The floats were a favorite means of crossing; they are found frequently in the Pyramid Texts. See besides the above passages also §§ 342, 351, 358, 464, 926–7, 932–5, 999–1000, 1085–6, 1103, 1705.
² Pyr. § 1048.   ³ Pyr. §§ 890–1.   ⁴ Pyr. § 1772.
⁵ Pyr. § 1778.   ⁶ Pyr. § 137.   ⁷ Pyr. § 913.   ⁸ Pyr. § 1484.

great goose."¹ Thus he "flies as a goose and flutters as a beetle."² "His face is (that of) falcons and his wings are (those of) geese";³ "king Unis flaps his wings like a zeret-bird,"⁴ and the wind bears him on high. "King Unis goes to the sky, king Unis goes to the sky! On the wind! On the wind!"⁵ "The clouds of the sky have taken him away, they exalt king Unis to Re."⁶ He "has ascended upon the rain-cloud."⁷ Or the priest sees strange forms in the cloud of incense that soars above him and he cries: "He ascends upon the smoke of the great incense-burning."⁸

In the oblique rays of the sun also, shooting earthward through some opening in the clouds, they beheld a radiant stairway let down from the sky that the king might ascend. "King Pepi has put down this radiance as a stairway under his feet, whereon king Pepi ascended to this his mother, the living Uræus that is on the head of Re."⁹ "Thou climbest, thou mountest the radiance," says the speaker¹⁰ as he beholds the king grasping the Solar rays.¹¹ Thus "stairs to the sky are laid for him that he may ascend thereon to the sky."¹² It is of course with the city of the sun that this stairway is associated: "The spirits of Heliopolis, they set up for him a stairway in order to reach the top."¹³ Sometimes the Solar splendor seems stretched out to him like vast arms, and the king "is a flame (moving) before the wind to the ends of the sky, to the ends of the earth when the arm of the sunbeams is lifted with king Unis."¹⁴ Lest any portion of the king's body should fail to rise with him, all of his members, or at least the more impor-

---

¹ Pyr. § 1122. ² Pyr. § 366. ³ Pyr. § 461. ⁴ Pyr. § 463.
⁵ Pyr. § 309. ⁶ Pyr. § 336. ⁷ Pyr. § 1774. ⁸ Pyr. § 365.
⁹ Pyr. § 1108. ¹⁰ Pyr. § 751. ¹¹ Pyr. § 547.
¹² Pyr. § 365. ¹³ Pyr. § 1090. ¹⁴ Pyr. § 324.

tant ones, twenty-six in number, are enumerated by name, beginning with the crown of his head and descending through face, eyes, nose, mouth, etc., to his toes, each member being identified with a different god, "when he ascends and lifts himself to the sky." This canny device is of irresistible magical potency, so that "every god who shall not lay steps for this king Pepi when he ascends" shall suffer loss of all his offerings. Moreover, the gods are bidden to remember that "It is not this king Pepi who says this against you, it is the charm which says this against you, ye gods." On the other hand, "every god who shall lay steps for king Pepi when he ascends" is promised all offerings, and if he extends a helping hand to the king as he climbs up, this god's "ka shall be justified by Geb."[1]

Again the broad sunbeams slanting earthward seem like a ladder to the imagination of this remote people and they say, "King Unis ascends upon the ladder which his father Re (the Sun-god) made for him."[2] Indeed we find the Sun-god making the ladder: "Atum has done that which he said he would do for this king Pepi II, binding for him the rope-ladder, joining together the (wooden) ladder for this king Pepi II; (thus) this king is far from the abomination of men."[3] Again it is the four sons of

---

[1] All the preceding from Pyr. Ut. 539. It seems impossible to separate these primitive means of reaching the sky from the similar or identical means employed in later astral theology in the Mediterranean. They have survived in the grotesque tale of the ascent of Alexander in the late western (Latin) version of Pseudo-Callisthenes, from which they passed even into art. See *Burlington Magazine*, vol. VI, pp. 395 *ff*. The ladder of the next paragraph was a common device in astral mortuary theology. (See CUMONT, *Astrology and Religion*, p. 184.)

[2] Pyr. § 390; similarly the ladder is associated with Heliopolis in Pyr. § 978. [3] Pyr. § 2083.

Horus who "bind a rope-ladder for this king Pepi II; they join together a (wooden) ladder for king Pepi II. They send up king Pepi II to Khepri (the Sun-god) that he may arrive on the east side of the sky. Its timbers are hewn by Shesa, the ropes that are in it are joined together with cords of Gasuti, the Bull of the Sky (Saturn); the uprights at its sides are fastened with leather of ⌜—⌝, born of the Heset-cow; a great support is placed under it by 'Him-who-Binds-the-Great-One.' Lift ye up the ka of this king Pepi II; lead ye him to the two lions; make him ascend to Atum."[1] An old Solar legend places the ladder in charge of Set, or at least associates it closely with him. We find it called the "ladder which carried the Ombite (Set)";[2] but it also appears occasionally under the guardianship of Kebehet, daughter of Anubis.[3] Sometimes the Sun-god summons all his divine subjects to assist in making the ladder. "It is done for this king Pepi by Atum as it was done for himself (Atum). He brings to this Pepi the gods belonging to the sky, he brings to him the gods belonging to the earth. They place their

✓ [1] Pyr. §§ 2078–81. The exhortation at the end is addressed to the four sons of Horus of Letopolis, Imset, Hapi, Dewamutef, and Kebehsenuf, who made the ladders. Some of the names and epithets are obscure; the two lions are Shu and Tefnut, see § 696 c and parallels. The Solar character of the ladder is evident in this passage also, which is one of the indications that the four sons of Horus are of Solar origin. Even in Osirianized passages the Solar origin of the ladder is unequivocal. See especially Pyr. § 472; also § 971 and infra, p. 153.
[2] Pyr. § 1253. In § 971 it is called "ladder of Set," though as a pendant to this it is also called "ladder of Horus." Throughout this Utterance (478), however, it is afterward called the "ladder of Set," and it is evidently regarded as his, even though Osiris climbs it. Is this another form of the tradition that Set was forced to carry Osiris?
[3] Pyr. § 468; besides the preceding references see also Pyr. § 1431, where the ladder is called "Ascender to the sky."

arms under him. They make a ladder for king Pepi that he may ascend upon it to the sky."¹ The spectacle of the ascending king calls forth the admiration of the gods: "'How beautiful to see, how satisfying to behold,' say the gods, 'when this god (meaning the king) ascends to the sky. His fearfulness is on his head, his terror is at his side, his magical charms are before him.'² Geb has done for him as was done for himself (Geb). The gods and souls of Buto, the gods and souls of Hierakonpolis, the gods in the sky and the gods on earth come to him. They make supports for king Unis on their arm(s). Thou ascendest, O king Unis, to the sky. Ascend upon it in this its name 'Ladder.'"³

Men and gods together are called upon in mighty charms to lift the king. "O men and gods! Your arms under king Pepi! Raise ye him, lift ye him to the sky, as the arms of Shu are under the sky and he raises it. To the sky! To the sky! To the great seat among the gods!"⁴ Or the daughter of the ancient mortuary Anubis offers him her shoulder: "Kebehet places him on her shoulder, she puts him down among the gardens (like) the herdmen of the calves,"⁵ a picture which we often see in the mastaba reliefs, as the cowherd wades cautiously across the canal, immersed to the waist, with a calf borne tenderly upon his shoulders, while the solicitous mother beast follows anxiously behind licking the flanks of the calf. Should all other means fail, Isis and Nephthys will offer their hips upon which the king mounts, while his father Atum reaches down and seizes the arm of the Pharaoh;⁶ or the earth itself may rise under the feet of the

---

¹ Pyr. §§ 1473–4.
² For the interpretation of this equipment, see p. 61, note 3.
³ Pyr. §§ 476–9.   ⁴ Pyr. § 1101.   ⁵ Pyr. § 1348.   ⁶ Pyr. §§ 379–380.

waiting king and lift him to the sky, where Tefnut grasps his arm[1] and leads him into the celestial fields.

But the possibility remained that the gates of the celestial country might not be opened to the new-comer. Over and over again we find the assurance that the double doors of the sky are opened before the Pharaoh: "Opened are the double doors of the horizon; unlocked are its bolts"[2] is a constant refrain in the Pyramid Texts. That art which opened the door for Ali Baba and the Forty Thieves had opened many a gate in the ancient East, thousands of years before the Arabian Nights made it familiar to us of the western world. The king faces the gates with these words: "O lofty one, (Gate) whom no one names! Gate of Nut! King Teti is Shu who came forth from Atum. O Nun! (the primeval waters) cause that this (gate) be opened for king Teti."[3] "He causes that those double doors of the sky be opened for king Teti (by the following charm):

"'Men fall,
Their name is not.
Seize thou king Teti by his arm;
Take thou king Teti to the sky,
That he die not on earth,
Among men.'"[4]

A similar method appealed to the fact that the sky-gates had once opened to each of the four eastern Horuses, and by sympathetic analogy they must now inevitably do the same for the king. "The double doors of the sky are opened, the double doors of the firmament are thrown open to Horus of the gods. . . . The double doors of the sky are opened to this king Pepi, the double doors of the

[1] Pyr. § 990. [2] Pyr. § 194. [3] Pyr. § 603. [4] Pyr. § 604.

firmament are thrown open to this king Pepi."[1] In the same way the approaching king is identified with the four eastern Horuses one after the other, after which Re may be appealed to as his father: "O father of king Pepi, O Re! Take thou this king Pepi with thee for life to thy mother Nut, who opens the double doors of the sky to this king Pepi, who throws open the double doors of the firmament to this king Pepi."[2]

The difficulty of the gates and the ascension might, however, be met by an appeal of men directly to the Sun-god: "'Ho Re,' say men, when they stand beside this king Pepi on earth while thou appearest in the east of the sky, 'give thy arm to king Pepi; take thou him with thee to the east side of the sky.'"[3]

It will be seen that in spite of the conviction of life, abounding life, with which the Pyramid Texts are filled, they likewise reveal the atmosphere of apprehension which enveloped these men of the early world as they contemplated the unknown and untried dangers of the shadow world. Whichever way the royal pilgrim faced as he looked out across the eastern sea he was beset with apprehensions of the possible hostility of the gods, and there crowded in upon him a thousand fancies of danger and opposition which clouded the fair picture of blessedness beyond. There is an epic touch in the dauntless courage, with which the solitary king, raising himself like some elemental colossus, and claiming sway over the gods themselves, confronts the celestial realm and addresses the

[1] Pyr. § 1408.
[2] Pyr. §§ 1479–80. There are four Utterances which are built up on the four Horuses: 325, 563, and 479, which are of the same general structure; and 573 of different structure, in which the identification of the king with the four Horuses perhaps takes place. On the latter see also *infra*, pp. 154–6.   [3] Pyr. § 1496.

Sun-god: "I know thy name. I am not ignorant of thy name.¹ 'Limitless' is thy name. The name of thy father is 'Possessor-of-Greatness.' Thy mother is 'Satisfaction,' who bears thee every morning. The birth of 'Limitless' in the horizon shall be prevented, if thou preventest this king Pepi from coming to the place where thou art." ² The king wielding his magical power thus makes himself sovereign of the universe and will stop the very rising ("birth") of the sun if he is halted at the gate of the Sun-god's realm. Far less impressive is the king's threat directed against the gods who oppose him as he mounts the ladder. "Every spirit and every god who shall oppose his arm to this king Pepi, when he ascends to the sky on the ladder of the god, the earth shall not be hoed for him, an offering shall not be brought for him, he shall not ferry over to the evening meal in Heliopolis, he shall not ferry over to the morning meal in Heliopolis." ³ Likewise Kebehet, the daughter of Anubis, perched on the two uprights of the ladder, is adjured to "open the way of king Unis, that king Unis may pass by," and in the same words the "Ostrich on the shore of the Lily-lake" and the "Bull of Re, having four horns," one toward each of the cardinal points, are warned to make way for him.⁴

And so at last the departed king draws near the eastern shore of the Lily-lake,⁵ and "this king Pepi finds the glorious by reason of their equipped mouths,⁶ sitting on

¹ To know the name of a god was to hold sway over him.
² Pyr. §§ 1434-5. Compare similar threatening of the Sun-god, *infra*, p. 308.
³ Pyr. § 978.
⁴ Pyr. §§ 468-471; see also §§ 504, 1432, and 914.
⁵ This was the case whether he ferried over by boat or employed the ladder; for the latter was set up in the east, and the ascent was made there; *e. g.*, Pyr. § 928.
⁶ For the explanation of this term see p. 94.

the two shores of the lake, ... the drinking-place of every glorious one by reason of his equipped mouth." Then they challenge the new arrival and the king replies: "I am a glorious one by reason of his equipped mouth." "'How has this happened to thee,' say they to king Pepi, ... 'that thou hast come to this place more august than any place?' 'Pepi has come to this place more august than any place, because the two floats of the sky were placed,' says the morning-barque, 'for Re'";[1] and at the story of his successful crossing as Re had crossed, the celestials break out into jubilee.[2] Thereupon the Pharaoh lands, takes up their manner of life, and sits before the palace ruling them.[3] Again we hear a solitary voice issuing from the world of the dead and challenging the king as he ascends and passes through the gates of the sky, led by Geb: "Ho! Whence comest thou, son of my father?" And another voice answers: "He has come from the Divine Ennead that is in the sky, that he may satisfy them with their bread." Again comes the challenge: "Ho! Whence comest thou, son of my father?" and we hear the reply: "He has come from the Divine Ennead that is on earth, that he may satisfy them with their bread." The questioner is still unsatisfied: "Ho! Whence comest thou, son of my father?" "He has come from the Zenedzender-barque." And then we hear the question for the last time: "Ho! Whence comest thou, son of my father?" "He has come from these his two mothers, the two vultures with long hair and hanging breasts, who are on the mountain of Sehseh. They draw their breasts over the mouth of king Pepi, but they do not wean him forever." Thereafter the challenging voice is silent[4] and the Pharaoh enters the kingdom of the sky.

[1] Pyr. §§ 930-2. [2] Pyr. § 935. [3] Pyr. §§ 936-8. [4] Pyr. §§ 1116-19.

LECTURE IV

REALMS OF THE DEAD—THE EARLIEST CELESTIAL HEREAFTER

WE have followed the royal pilgrim as he passed through the celestial gates, where he awaited announcement of his arrival to the Sun-god, in whose realm he must now abide. We behold his heralds hastening to announce his advent. "Thy messengers go, thy swift messengers run, thy heralds make haste. They announce to Re that thou hast come, (even) this king Pepi."[1] We hear their message as they shout, "'Behold, he comes! Behold, he comes!' says Sehpu. 'Behold the son of Re comes, the beloved of Re comes,' says Sehpu, 'who was made to come by Horus.'"[2] The gods crowd down to the shore. "This king Pepi found the gods standing, wrapped in their garments, their white sandals on their feet. They cast off their white sandals to the earth, they throw off their garments. 'Our heart was not glad until thy coming,' say they."[3] Again they are overcome with awe as they hear the proclamation of the heralds and behold the king approaching. Re stands before the gates of the horizon leaning upon his sceptre, while the gods are grouped about him. "The

---

[1] Pyr. §§ 1539-40; this passage has been Osirianized, but it will be found in its original form in §§ 1991-2.

[2] Pyr. § 1492; the same formula is repeated with the names of Set, Geb, the souls of Heliopolis and the souls of Buto in the place of the name of Horus.

[3] Pyr. § 1197.

gods are silent before thee, the Nine Gods have laid their hands upon their mouths," says the herald voice.[1]

It may be, however, that the king finds himself without any messenger to despatch to Re, and in this case the ferryman may be induced to announce his coming.[2] Otherwise, as he approaches the gate the gate-keeper is called upon to perform this office. "Ho, Methen! Keeper of the great gate! Announce this king Pepi to these two great gods" (Re and Horus).[3] He may even be obliged to intrust his case to the good offices of Re's body servant, affording an interesting side-light on the possible methods of gaining the royal ear in this distant age. "O ye who are over the offering and the libation! Commit king Unis to Fetekta, the servant of Re, that he may commit him to Re himself."[4] More often the gods themselves, who have greeted him with acclamation, or have stood in awed silence at his coming, proclaim it far and near, after they have announced him to Re: "O Re-Atum! This king Unis comes to thee, an imperishable glorious-one, lord of the affairs of the place of the four pillars (the sky). Thy son comes to thee. This king Unis comes to thee." Then Set and Nephthys hasten to the south, where they proclaim his coming "to the gods of the south and their spirits": "This king Unis comes indeed, an imperishable glorious-one. When he desires that ye die, ye die; when he desires that ye live, ye live." To the north Osiris and Isis say: "This king Unis comes indeed, an imperishable glorious-one, like the morning star over the Nile. The spirits dwelling in the water praise him. When he desires that he live, he lives; when he desires that he die, he dies." Thoth hastens to the west with the words: "This king

[1] Pyr. §§ 253–5.
[2] Pyr. § 597.
[3] Pyr. § 952.
[4] Pyr. § 120.

Unis comes indeed, an imperishable spirit, adorned with the jackal on the sceptre before the western height.[1] He numbers the hearts, he takes possession of the hearts. When he desires that he live, he lives; when he desires that he die, he dies." Finally Horus, speeding to the east, proclaims: "This king Unis comes indeed, an imperishable spirit. When he desires that he live, he lives; when he desires that he die, he dies." In conclusion of this fourfold announcement at the cardinal points, the voice again cries to Re, "O Re-Atum! Thy son comes to thee, Unis comes to thee. Lift him up to thee, enfold thou him in thy embrace. He is thy bodily son forever."[2]

Thus received by his father, the question of the status of the royal pilgrim at once arises. His ambitions sometimes seem lowly enough, and he is even amusingly unceremonious in carrying them out. Yonder sits Re at his "divan" with his secretary at his side, the scribe having his two pens thrust behind his ears, while a large roll of papyrus is spread across his knees. As the king approaches a voice is heard: "O scribe, scribe! Break thy writing kit, smash thy two pens, destroy thy papyrus rolls. O Re! Expel him from his post and put king Pepi in his place."[3] Thus ensconced in a snug post as secretary of the ruler of the celestial realm, "King Unis sits before him (Re), king Unis opens his chests (of papers), king Unis breaks open his edicts, king Unis seals his decrees, king Unis despatches his messengers who weary not, king Unis does what he (Re) says to king Unis."[4] Thus the king becomes the counsellor of the Sun-god, "the wise one bearing the divine book on the right of

---

[1] The jackal is an old god of the west, and the reference is to a jackal's head, which commonly appears on the head of a sceptre.
[2] Pyr. Ut. 217.   [3] Pyr. § 954.   [4] Pyr. §§ 490–1.

Re."[1] Again we find the dead Pharaoh serving as a priest "before Re, bearing this jar, which purifies the Southland before Re, when he comes forth from his horizon."[2] He may even appear as Uneg, the son and body-servant of Re,[3] and we behold him as "a star . . . long of stride, bringing the provisions of the (daily) journey to Re every day."[4]

More often the greatest intimacy and familiarity now develop between the Sun-god and the newly arrived king; "every beautiful place where Re goes, he finds this king Pepi there."[5] Should there be any difficulties in the way, the dead king recites a magical hymn[6] in praise of the Sun-god, which smoothes the way to perfect fellowship with Re. The priestly editor has added the assurance: "Now he who knows this chapter of Re, and he doeth them, (even) these charms of Harakhte (the Horizon-god), he shall be the familiar of Re, he shall be the friend of Harakhte. King Pepi knows it, this chapter of Re; king Pepi doeth them, these charms of Harakhte. King Pepi is the familiar of Re, king Pepi is the companion of Harakhte."[7] Thus the departed Pharaoh may "sit at his (Re's) shoulder, and Re does not permit him to throw himself upon the earth (in obeisance), knowing that he (the king) is greater than he (Re)."[8] In the quaint imagination of the priestly editor, the king may even become the lotus flower, which the god holds to his nose.[9]

But that association with Re in which the Egyptian took the greatest delight was the voyage with him across the sky in his daily journey to the west. As the cool Nile breezes and the picturesque life of the refreshing river

[1] Pyr. § 267.
[2] Pyr. § 1179.
[3] Pyr. § 952.
[4] Pyr. § 263.
[5] Pyr. § 918.
[6] See above, pp. 13–14.
[7] Pyr. §§ 855–6.
[8] Pyr. § 813.
[9] Pyr. § 266.

were the central picture in his earthly life, so he looked forward to finding the celestial Nile the source of the same joy in the life hereafter. "Thou embarkest in this barque of Re, to which the gods love to ascend, in which they love to embark, in which Re is rowed to the horizon."[1] The simplest form of this belief places the dead king among the crew of the Solar barque. "King Pepi receives to himself his oar, he takes his seat, he seats himself in the bow of the ship, . . . he rows Re to the west."[2] If there is no other way to secure passage in the beautiful "sunbeam-barque,"[3] the once splendid Pharaoh is permitted to come along as little better than a stowaway and to bail out the craft.[4]

The theological theory of the state in the Pyramid Age, as we have seen, represents the Pharaoh as the son of the Sun-god. The Pyramid Texts of course take full advantage of this circumstance, and often call upon Re to recognize and protect his son. The dead Pharaoh boldly approaches the Sun-god with the words: "I, O Re, am this one of whom thou didst say, . . . 'My son!' My father art thou, O Re. . . . Behold king Pepi, O Re. This king Pepi is thy son. . . . This king Pepi shines in the east like Re, he goes in the west like Kheprer. This king Pepi lives on that whereon Horus (son of Re) lord of the sky lives, by command of Horus lord of the sky."[5] As Re, however, was his own son, begotten every day and born every morning, the sonship of the Pharaoh ultimately leads to his identity with Re, and the priestly elaborators of the Pyramid Texts had no hesitation in reaching this result. This was the more easy in that they had made the king divine by subtle ceremonies, especially the burning

---

[1] Pyr. § 1687.   [2] Pyr. § 906 = §§ 1573–4. See also § 889.
[3] Pyr. § 1346.   [4] Pyr. § 335 = § 950.   [5] Pyr. §§ 886–8.

of incense, at his interment.¹ Even without encroaching upon the position of Re the dead Pharaoh is pictured as divine, and his divinity is proclaimed to the denizens of the other world. "Lift up your faces, gods dwelling in Dewat.² King Unis has come that ye may see him become a great god. . . . Protect yourselves all of you. King Unis commands men; king Unis judges the living in the court of the region of Re. King Unis speaks to this pure region which he has visited, that he may dwell therein with the judge of the two gods. King Unis is mighty beside him (Re). King Unis bears the sceptre; it purifies king Unis. King Unis sits with them that row Re; king Unis commands good that he may do it. King Unis is a great god."³

This divinity is unmistakably defined more than once. "King Teti is this eye of Re, that passes the night, is conceived and born every day."⁴ "His mother the sky bears him living every day like Re. He dawns with him in the east, he sets with him in the west, his mother Nut (the sky) is not void of him any day. He equips king Pepi II with life, he causes his heart joy, he causes his heart pleasure."⁵ "Thou camest forth as king Pepi, king Pepi came forth as thou."⁶ The dead king does not merely receive the office and station of Re, he actually becomes Re. "Thy body is in king Pepi, O Re; preserve alive thy body in king Pepi, O Re."⁷ "King Teti is thou (Re), thou art king Teti; thou shinest in king Teti, king Teti shines in thee."⁸ He is even identified with Atum limb by limb,⁹ or with Atum and the Solar gods, who are themselves identified with Atum.¹⁰ Thus he becomes king

---

¹ Pyr. § 25.
² See p. 144, n. 2.
³ Pyr. Ut. 252.
⁴ Pyr. § 698; also § 704.
⁵ Pyr. §§ 1835–6.
⁶ Pyr. § 1875.
⁷ Pyr. § 1461 b.
⁸ Pyr. § 703–4.
⁹ Pyr. § 135.
¹⁰ Pyr. §§ 147–9.

of the sky in Re's place. "Thou embarkest therein (in the Sun-barque) like Re; thou sittest down on this throne of Re, that thou mayest command the gods; for thou art Re, who came forth from Nut, who begets Re every day."[1] There are indeed hints that the Pharaoh takes forcible possession of the Sun-god's throne,[2] and their identity does not exclude the idea of his being dispossessed, or even of his continued benefits to the Pharaoh, though these are sometimes mutual. The voice says to Re: "Make king Teti sound, and Teti will make thee sound; make king Teti green (fresh, youthful), and Teti will make thee green," and thus a mystical relationship with Hathor, the eye of Re, is established, "which turns back the years from king Teti" and they pass over him without increasing his age.[3]

Perhaps the finest fragment of literature preserved in the Pyramid Texts is a Sun-hymn[4] in which the king is identified with the Sun-god. The hymn addresses Egypt in a long and imposing enumeration of the benefits which she enjoys under the protection and sovereignty of the Sun-god. Hence Egypt offers him her wealth and produce. Now in view of the fact that the Pharaoh is identified with the Sun-god, the Pharaoh, therefore, confers the same benefits on Egypt, and must therefore receive the same gifts from Egypt. The entire hymn is therefore repeated with the insertion of the Pharaoh's name wherever that of Re or Horus occurs in the original hymn,[5] and

---

[1] Pyr. § 1688.   [2] Pyr. § 306
[3] Pyr. §§ 704–5. Compare also Utterance 573, in which the king is probably identified with the four Horuses, that Re may protect and preserve him alive.
[4] Pyr. Ut. 587; see *infra*, pp. 13–14.
[5] This entire Utterance, 587, is really but a longer example of the sympathetic operation of the god's activities, of which we have innumerable examples throughout the Pyramid Texts. The god

thus the king appropriates to himself all the homage and offerings received by the Sun-god from Egypt.

But the imagination of the priests does not stop here. Equality or identity with Re is not enough, and we behold the translated Pharaoh a cosmic figure of elemental vastness, even superior to the Sun-god in the primeval darkness. The mysterious voice cries: "Father of king Teti! Father of king Teti in darkness! Father of king Teti, Atum in darkness! Bring thou king Teti to thy side that he may kindle for thee the light; that he may protect thee, as Nun (the primeval ocean) protected these four goddesses on the day when they protected the throne, (even) Isis, Nephthys, Neit, and Serket."[1] The dead king sweeps the sky as a devouring fire as soon as "the arm of the sunbeams is lifted with king Unis."[2] Again we see him towering between earth and sky: "This his right arm, it carries the sky in satisfaction; this his left arm, it supports the earth in joy."[3] The imagination runs riot in figures of cosmic power, and the king becomes "the outflow of the rain, he came forth at the origin of water";[4] or he gains the secret and the power of all things as "the scribe of the god's-book, which says what is and causes to be what is not."[5] He came forth before the world or death existed. "The mother of king Pepi became pregnant with him, O Dweller in the ⌜nether sky⌝; this king Pepi was born by his father Atum before the sky came forth, before the earth came forth, before men came forth, before gods were born, before death came forth. This king Pepi escapes the day of death as Set

crosses the Lily-lake, the king crosses; the god is purified, the king is purified; the god sails the sky, the king sails the sky, etc., etc.
[1] Pyr. Ut. 362.   [2] Pyr. § 324.
[3] Pyr. § 1156.   [4] Pyr. § 1146.   [5] Pyr. § 1146.

escaped the day of death. This king Pepi belongs to your ⸢company⸣, ye gods of the ⸢nether sky⸣, who cannot perish by their enemies; this king Pepi perishes not by his enemies. (Ye) who die not by a king, this king Pepi dies not by a king; (ye) who die not by any dead, king Pepi dies not by any dead."[1] When in process of time the gods were born, the king was present at their birth.

The mergence of the king into the very body and being of Re is analogous to his assimilation by the gods as a group. One of the most remarkable passages in the Pyramid Texts employs the ceremony and the suggestiveness of incense-burning as a sympathetic agency by which, as the odorous vapor arises from earth to the gods, it bears aloft the fragrance of the king to mingle with that of the gods, and thus to draw them together in fellowship and association. The passage is of importance as a very early priestly interpretation of the significance of incense as fellowship with the gods. The passage reads:

> "The fire is laid, the fire shines;
> The incense is laid on the fire, the incense shines.
> Thy fragrance comes to king Unis, O Incense;
> The fragrance of king Unis comes to thee, O Incense.
> Your fragrance comes to king Unis, O ye gods;
> The fragrance of king Unis comes to you, O ye gods.
> King Unis is with you, ye gods;
> Ye are with king Unis, ye gods.
> King Unis lives with you, ye gods;
> Ye live with king Unis, ye gods.
> King Unis loves you, ye gods;
> Love ye him, ye gods."[2]

[1] Pyr. §§ 1466-8.
[2] Pyr. §§ 376-8. The variant in the last line has: "Ye love this Pepi, ye gods." The poem was of course accompanied by the burning of incense; also by an offering of bread which immediately followed. A formula of the ascension, as frequently with the burning of incense, then follows.

This fellowship thus mystically symbolized is in sharp contrast with a dark and forbidding picture, surviving from vastly remote prehistoric days, in which we see the savage Pharaoh ferociously preying upon the gods like a blood-thirsty hunter in the jungle. The passage begins with the terrifying advent of the Pharaoh in the sky:

> "Clouds darken the sky,
> The stars rain down,
> The Bows (a constellation) stagger,
> The bones of the hell-hounds tremble,
> The ⌜porters⌝ are silent,
> When they see king Unis dawning as a soul,
> As a god living on his fathers,
> Feeding on his mothers.
> King Unis is lord of wisdom,
> Whose mother knows not his name.
> The honor of king Unis is in the sky,
> His might is in the horizon,
> Like Atum his father who begat him.
> When he begat him, he was stronger than he.
> . . . .[1]
> King Unis is one who eats men and lives on gods,
> Lord of messengers, who ⌜despatches⌝ his messages;
> It is 'Grasper-of-Forelocks' living in Kehew
> Who binds them for king Unis.
> It is the serpent 'Splendid-Head'
> Who watches them for him and repels them for him.
> It is 'He-who-is-upon-the-Willows'
> Who lassoes them for him.
> It is 'Punisher-of-all-Evil-doers'
> Who stabs them for king Unis.
> He takes out for him their entrails,
> He is a messenger whom he (king Unis) sends to ⌜punish⌝.

[1] The passage omitted is an obscure description of the equipment of the dead king, which, however, contains an important statement that the king "lives on the being of every god, eating their organs who come with their belly filled with charms."

Shesmu cuts them up for king Unis
And cooks for him a portion of them
In his evening kettles (or 'as his evening kettles = meal').
King Unis is he who eats their charms,
And devours their glorious ones (souls).
Their great ones are for his morning portion,
Their middle(-sized) ones are for his evening portion,
Their little ones are for his night portion.
Their old men and their old women are for his incense-burning.
It is the 'Great-Ones-North-of-the-Sky'
Who set for him the fire to the kettles containing them,
With the legs of their oldest ones (as fuel).
The 'Dwellers-in-the-Sky' revolve for king Unis (in his service).
⌜The kettles are replenished⌝ for him with the legs of their women.
He has encircled all the Two Skies (corresponding to the Two Lands),
He has revolved about the two regions.
King Unis is the 'Great Mighty-One'
Who overpowers the 'Mighty Ones'
. . . .
Whom he finds in his way, him he devours. . . .[1]
The protection of king Unis is before all the noble (dead)
Who dwell in the horizon.
King Unis is a god, older than the eldest.
Thousands revert to him,
Hundreds are offered to him.
Appointment as 'Great One' is given to him
By Orion, father of gods.
King Unis has dawned again in the sky,
⌜Shining⌝ as lord of the horizon.
. . . .
He has taken the hearts of the gods;
He has eaten the Red,
He has swallowed the Green.
King Unis is nourished on satisfied organs,
He is satisfied, living on their hearts and their charms.
. . . .
Their charms are in his belly.
The dignities of king Unis are not taken away from him;

---

[1] This line is found three times: §§ 278 a, 407, 444 e.

THE EARLIEST CELESTIAL HEREAFTER 129

> He hath swallowed the knowledge of every god.
> The lifetime of king Unis is eternity,
> His limit is everlastingness in this his dignity of:
> 'If-he-wishes-he-does,
> If-he-wishes-not-he-does-not,'[1]
> Who dwells in the limits of the horizon for ever and ever.
> Lo, their (the gods') soul is in the belly of king Unis,
> Their Glorious Ones are with king Unis.
> The plenty of his portion is more than (that of) the gods.
> . . . .
> Lo, their soul is with king Unis."[2]

In this remarkable picture the motive of the grotesque cannibalism is perfectly clear. The gods are hunted down, lassoed, bound, and slaughtered like wild cattle, that the king may devour their substance, and especially their internal organs, like the heart where the intelligence had its seat, in the belief that he might thus absorb and appropriate their qualities and powers. When "he has taken the hearts of the gods," "he has swallowed the knowledge of every god," and "their charms are in his belly"; and because the organs of the gods which he has devoured are plentifully satisfied with food, the king cannot hunger, for he has, as it were, eaten complete satiety.

This introduces us to a subject to which the Pyramid Texts devote much space—the question of the food supply in the distant realm of the Sun-god. To explain the apparently aimless presentation of food at the tomb, where, in the Solar belief the dead no longer tarried, it was assumed that the food offered there was transmitted to the dead in various ways. Sometimes it is Thoth who conveys the food from the tomb to the sky and delivers

[1] This is a name or rank expressed in a couplet.
[2] Pyr. Ut. 273.

it to the dead king;[1] again it is the two Solar barques who transport it thither.[2] The "Imperishable Stars" too may convey the food offered on earth to the kas in the sky[3] or the ferryman may be prevailed upon to do so.[4] In any case the chief dread felt by the Egyptian for the hereafter was fear of hunger, and especially the danger that he might be reduced to the detestable extremity of consuming his own uncleanness. "The abomination of king Unis is offal; he rejects urine, he eats it not."[5]

More commonly the celestial region where he tarries furnishes all his necessities. As son of Re, born of the Sky-goddess, he is frequently represented as suckled by one of the Sky-goddesses or some other divinity connected with Re, especially the ancient goddesses of the prehistoric kingdoms of South and North. These appear as "the two vultures with long hair and hanging breasts; . . . they draw their breasts over the mouth of king Pepi, but they do not wean him forever";[6] or we find them as the two crowns of the two kingdoms personified as goddesses: "This king Pepi knows his mother, he forgets not his mother: (even) the White Crown shining and broad that dwells in Nekheb, mistress of the southern palace . . . and the bright Red Crown, mistress of the regions of Buto. O mother of this king Pepi . . . give thy breast to this king Pepi, suckle this king Pepi therewith." To this the goddess responds: "O my son Pepi, my king, my breast is extended to thee, that thou mayest suck it, my king, and live, my king, as long as thou art little."[7] This

---

[1] Pyr. § 58.   [2] Pyr. § 717.   [3] Pyr. § 1220.
[4] Pyr. Ut. 521. Hence it is that even in the sky the deceased Pharaoh is concerned that the food supply of his "altars that are on earth" shall be continued. See Pyr. § 1482.
[5] Pyr. § 718.   [6] Pyr. §§ 1118-19.   [7] Pyr. §§ 910-913.

THE EARLIEST CELESTIAL HEREAFTER 131

incident exhibits more of the naturally and warmly human than anything else in the Solar theology.

Besides this source of nourishment, and the very bodies of the gods themselves,[1] there were also the offerings of all Egypt, as we have seen in the ancient Sun-hymn, where the dead king receives all that is offered by Egypt to Re (pp. 13–14). It is taken for granted that the celestial revenues belong to the king, and that they will meet all his wants. We hear the voice calling for the mortuary revenues in his behalf: "An offering which the king gives! An offering which Anubis gives! Thy thousand of young antelope from the highland, they come to thee with bowed head. An offering which the king gives! An offering which Anubis gives! Thy thousand of bread! Thy thousand of beer! Thy thousand of incense, that came forth from the palace hall! Thy thousand of everything pleasant! Thy thousand of cattle! Thy thousand of everything thou eatest, on which thy desire is set!"[2] The Pyramid Texts delight to picture the plenty which the king is to enjoy. "Plenty has extended her arm toward king Teti. The two arms of king Teti have embraced fisher and fowler, (even) all that the field furnishes to her son, the fisher-fowler."[3] We even see him going about with sack and basket collecting quantities of food,[4] food of the gods which cannot perish, "bread which cannot dry up" and "beer which cannot grow stale."[5] For the voice prays to the Sun-god: "Give thou bread to this king Pepi from this thy eternal bread, thy everlasting beer,"[6] and we read that "this king Pepi receives his

---

[1] As above (pp. 127–9). The phrase "Whom he finds in his way he eats him for himself," referring to divine victims whom he devours as food, is found no less than three times (Pyr. §§ 278 a, 407, 444 e).
[2] Pyr. §§ 806–7.   [3] Pyr. § 555.   [4] Pyr. § 556.
[5] Pyr. § 859.   [6] Pyr. § 1117.

provision from that which is in the granary of the Great God (Re)"[1] and his "bread is the bread of the god which is in the palace hall."[2] There in "the good seat of the Great God, in which he does the things to be done with the revered (dead), he appoints them to food and assigns them to fowling . . .; he appoints king Pepi to food, he assigns king Pepi to fowling."[3] He is surrounded by plenty: "He who is behind him belongs to food, he who is before him belongs to snared fowl,"[4] and thus "that land into which king Unis goes—he thirsts not in it, he hungers not in it forever,"[5] for there "Appetite belongs to the morning meal of the king, Plenty belongs to his evening meal."[6] Again a voice summons him: "Ho, king Pepi! . . . Raise thee up! Arise! Sit down to thy thousand of bread, thy thousand of beer, thy thousand of oxen, thy thousand of geese, thy thousand of everything whereon the god lives."[7] There can be no failure of the source of supply: "a god does not escape from what he has said. (Therefore) he will furnish to thee thy thousand of bread, thy thousand of beer, thy thousand of oxen, thy thousand of geese, thy thousand of everything on which the god lives."[8]

There were, to be sure, certain contingencies to be guarded against, lest some one else should secure the provisions intended for the king. "This king Pepi eats this his sole bread alone; he does not give it to the one behind him;"[9] nor does he permit the fowl of the air to plunder him of his portion.[10] If necessary he may resort to magical means, so cunningly devised that he is enabled to banish hunger and thirst and drive them far away.

[1] Pyr. § 1182. [2] Pyr. § 866.   [3] Pyr. §§ 1191-2.
[4] Pyr. § 1394. [5] Pyr. § 382.   [6] Pyr. § 1876.
[7] Pyr. §§ 2026-7. [8] Pyr. § 2006. [9] Pyr. § 1226. [10] Ibid.

"Hunger! Come not to king Teti. Hasten to Nun (the primeval flood), go to the flood. King Teti is sated; he hungers not by reason of this bread of Horus which he has eaten, which his eldest daughter made for him. He is satisfied therewith, he takes this land therewith. King Teti thirsts not by reason of Shu; he hungers not by reason of Tefnut. Hapi, Dewamutef, Kebehsenuf, and Imset (the four sons of Horus), they expel this hunger which is in the body of king Teti, and this thirst which is in the lips of king Teti." [1]

Finally one of the most, if not the most, important of the numerous sources from which the departed Pharaoh hoped to draw his sustenance in the realm of Re was the tree of life in the mysterious isle in the midst of the Field of Offerings, in search of which he sets out in company with the Morning Star. The Morning Star is a gorgeous green falcon, a Solar divinity, identified with "Horus of Dewat." He has four faces, corresponding to the four Horuses of the East, with whom he is doubtless also identified.[2] We find him standing in the bow of his celestial barque of seven hundred and seventy cubits in length, and there the voice addresses him: "Take thou this king Pepi with thee in the cabin of thy boat. . . . Thou takest this thy favorite harpoon, thy staff which ⌜pierces⌝ the canals, whose points are the rays of the sun, whose barbs are the claws of Mafdet. King Pepi cuts off therewith the heads of the adversaries, dwelling in the Field of Offerings, when he has descended to the sea. Bow thy head, decline thy arms, O Sea! The children of Nut are these

---

[1] Pyr. Ut. 338; see also Ut. 339, 340, 400, 438. The charm quoted above may be Osirian, in view of "the bread of Horus," but the distinction between Osirian and Solar elements is here of slight consequence.   [2] Pyr. § 1207.

(Pepi and the Morning Star) who have descended to thee, wearing their garlands on their heads, wearing their garlands at their throats." Here the homage of the sea is claimed because Pepi and the Morning Star are bent upon a beneficent errand for Isis and Horus.[1] The story then proceeds: "This king Pepi opened his path like the fowlers, he exchanged greetings with the lords of the kas, he went to the great isle in the midst of the Field of Offerings over which the gods make the swallows fly. The swallows are the Imperishable Stars. They give to this king Pepi this tree of life, whereof they live, that ye (Pepi and the Morning Star) may at the same time live thereof."[2]

But the most sinister enemies may contrive to deprive the king of the sustenance which we have seen to be so elaborately provided. They may even lurk in his own body, especially in his nostrils, where they may appropriate the food intended for the king.[3] In this early age, however, enemies and dangers in the hereafter have not been multiplied by the priests as they were later in the Book of the Dead. There are precautions against them, like the dread name received by the king, a name so potent that his enemies all fear it and flee away. "Re calls thee in this thy name of which all the Glorious are afraid. Thy terror is against hearts like the terror of Re when he rises in the horizon."[4] Besides the name the dead king also receives a peculiar costume or a "recognizance," which at once distinguishes and protects him against attack from those who might mistake him for an enemy.[5]

---

[1] This introduction of an Osirian incident here does not alter the clearly Solar character of the story, in which Pepi goes in search of the tree of life with the Morning Star, a Sun-god, carrying a spear of sunbeams. [2] Pyr. §§ 1209-16.
[3] Pyr. § 484.   [4] Pyr. § 2025.   [5] Pyr. §§ 2044, 2004.

Charms, as we have already shown, were among the equipment furnished by the Pyramid Texts, and not a few of these are of a protective character. The enemy against which these are most often directed in the Pyramid Texts is serpents. It was of course natural that the dead, who were buried in the earth, out of which serpents come forth, should be especially exposed to this danger. In the case of the king also, there was another reason. In the myth of Re, he was stung by a serpent and forced to reveal his name to Isis. The departed Pharaoh who is identified with Re must necessarily meet the same danger, and from it he is protected by numerous serpent charms in the Pyramid Texts. In such charms it is quite in accordance with the Solar tale to find Re invoked to exorcise the dangerous reptile. "O serpent, turn back, for Re sees thee" were words which came very naturally to the lips of the Egyptian of this age.[1] While all the great goddesses of Egypt are said to extend their protection over the king, it is especially the Sky-goddess Nut who shields him from all harm.[2]

The men in whose hands the Pyramid Texts grew up took the greatest delight in elaborating and reiterating in ever new and different pictures the blessedness enjoyed by the king, thus protected, maintained, and honored in the Sun-god's realm. Their imagination flits from figure to figure, and picture to picture, and allowed to run like some wild tropical plant without control or guidance, weaves a complex fabric of a thousand hues which refuse

[1] Pyr. § 226; see also § 231 and other serpent charms in Ut. 226–237, 240, 242 et al.
[2] Pyr. Ut. 443–7, 450–2, 484, 589, 681, and § 2107. Many of these are strongly colored by Osirian theology; indeed Ut. 443–7 are largely Osirian, but the original character of Nut's functions in the celestial and Solar theology is clear.

to merge into one harmonious or coherent whole. At one moment the king is enthroned in Oriental splendor as he was on earth, at another he wanders in the Field of Rushes in search of food; here he appears in the bow of the Solar barque, yonder he is one of the Imperishable Stars acting as the servant of Re. There is no endeavor to harmonize these inconsistent representations, although in the mass we gain a broad impression of the eternal felicity of a godlike ruler, "who puts his annals (the record of his deeds) among his people, and his love among the gods."[1] "The king ascends to the sky among the gods dwelling in the sky. He stands on the great ⌈dais⌉, he hears (in judicial session) the (legal) affairs of men. Re finds thee upon the shores of the sky in this lake that is in Nut (the Sky-goddess). 'The arriver comes!' say the gods. He (Re) gives thee his arm on the stairway to the sky. 'He who knows his place comes,' say the gods. O Pure One, assume thy throne in the barque of Re and sail thou the sky. . . . Sail thou with the Imperishable Stars, sail thou with the Unwearied Stars. Receive thou the ⌈tribute⌉ of the Evening Barque, become thou a spirit dwelling in Dewat. Live thou this pleasant life which the lord of the horizon lives."[2] "This king Pepi goes to the Field of Life, the birthplace of Re in the sky. He finds Kebehet approaching him with these her four jars with which she refreshes the heart of the Great God (Re) on the day when he awakes (or 'by day when he awakes'). She refreshes the heart[3] of this king Pepi therewith to life, she purifies him, she cleanses him. He receives his provision from that which is in the granary of the Great God;

[1] Pyr. § 1160. [2] Pyr. §§ 1169–72.
[3] Confer the reanimation of the heart of the dead Bata by the use of a jar of water in the Tale of the Two Brothers, *infra*, p. 359.

he is clothed by the Imperishable Stars."[1] To Re and Thoth (the sun and the moon) the voice cries: "Take ye this king Unis with you that he may eat of that which ye eat, and that he may drink of that which ye drink, that he may live on that whereon ye live, that he may sit in that wherein ye sit, that he may be mighty by that whereby ye are mighty, that he may sail in that wherein ye sail. The booth of king Unis is plaited (erected) in the reeds, the pool of king Unis is in the Field of Offerings. His offering is among you, ye gods. The water of king Unis is wine like (that of) of Re. King Unis circles the Sky like Re, he traverses the sky like Thoth."[2] The voice summons the divine nourishment of the king: "Bring the milk of Isis for king Teti, the flood of Nephthys, the circuit of the lake, the waves of the sea, life, prosperity, health, happiness, bread, beer, clothing, food, that king Teti may live therefrom."[3] "Lo, the two who are on the throne of the Great God (Re), they summon this king Pepi to life and satisfaction forever; they (the two) are Prosperity and Health."[4] Thus "it is better with him to-day than yesterday,"[5] and we hear the voice calling to him: "Ho! King Pepi, pure one! Re finds thee standing with thy mother Nut. She leads thee in the path of the horizon and thou makest thy abiding place there. How beautiful it is together with thy ka for ever and ever."[6]

Over and over again the story of the king's translation to the sky is brought before us with an indomitable conviction and insistence which it must be concluded were thought to make the words of inevitable power and effect. Condensed into a paragraph the whole sweep of the king's

[1] Pyr. §§ 1180–2.   [2] Pyr. §§ 128–130.   [3] Pyr. § 707.
[4] Pyr. § 1190.   [5] Pyr. § 122.   [6] Pyr. § 2028.

celestial career is brought before us in a few swift strokes, each like a ray of sunshine touching for but an instant the prominences of some far landscape across which we look. Long successions of such paragraphs crowd one behind another like the waves of the sea, as if to overwhelm and in their impetuous rush to bear away as on a flood the insistent fact of death and sweep it to utter annihilation. It is difficult to convey to the modern reader the impression made by these thousands of lines as they roll on in victorious disregard of the invincibility of death, especially in those epitomizations of the king's celestial career which are so frequent, the paragraphs here under discussion. In so far as they owe their impressiveness to their mere bulk, built up like a bulwark against death, we can gain the impression only by reading the whole collection through. The general character of such individual epitomizing paragraphs is perhaps suggested by such as the following. The voice addresses the king: "Thy seats among the gods abide; Re leans upon thee with his shoulder. Thy odor is as their odor, thy sweat is as the sweat of the Eighteen Gods. Thou dawnest, O king Teti, in the royal hood; thy hand seizes the sceptre, thy fist grasps the mace. Stand, O king Teti, in front of the two palaces of the South and the North. Judge the gods, (for) thou art of the elders who surround Re, who are before the Morning Star. Thou art born at thy New Moons like the moon. Re leans upon thee in the horizon, O king Teti. The Imperishable Stars follow thee, the companions of Re serve thee, O king Teti. Thou purifiest thyself, thou ascendest to Re; the sky is not empty of thee, O king Teti, forever."[1] "King Teti purifies himself; he receives to himself his pure seat that is in the sky. He

[1] Pyr. §§ 730–3.

abides, the beautiful seats of king Teti abide. He receives to himself his pure seat that is in the barque of Re. The sailors who row Re, they (also) row king Teti. The sailors who carry Re around behind the horizon, they carry (also) king Teti around behind the horizon."[1] "O king Neferkere! the mouth of the earth opens to thee, Geb (the Earth-god) speaks to thee: 'Thou art great like a king, mighty like Re.' Thou purifiest thyself in the Jackal-lake, thou cleansest thyself in the lake of Dewat. 'Welcome to thee,' say the Eighteen Gods. The eastern door of the sky is opened to thee by Yemen-kau; Nut has given to thee her arms, O king Neferkere, she of the long hair and pendent breasts. She guides thee to the sky, she does not put king Neferkere down (again) to the earth. She bears thee, O king Neferkere, like Orion; she makes thy abiding place before the Double Palace (of Upper and Lower Egypt transferred to the sky). King Neferkere descends into the barque like Re, on the shores of the Lily-lake. King Neferkere is rowed by the Unwearied Stars, he commands the Imperishable Stars."[2]

Such in the main outlines were the beliefs held by the Egyptian of the Old Kingdom (2980–2475 B. C.) concerning the Solar hereafter. There can bo no doubt that at some time they were a fairly well-defined group, separable as a group from those of the Osirian faith. To the Osirian faith, moreover, they were opposed, and evidences of their incompatibility, or even hostility, have survived. We find it said of Re that "he has not given him (the king) to Osiris, he (the king) has not died the death; he has become a Glorious One in the horizon";[3] and still more unequivocal is the following: "Re-Atum does not give thee to Osiris. He (Osiris) numbers not thy heart, he

[1] Pyr. Ut. 407.   [2] Pyr. §§ 2169–73.   [3] Pyr. § 350.

gains not power over thy heart. Re-Atum gives thee
not to Horus (son of Osiris). He numbers not thy heart,
he gains not power over thy heart. Osiris! thou hast
not gained power over him, thy son (Horus) has not gained
power over him. Horus! thou hast not gained power
over him, thy father (Osiris) has not gained power over
him."[1] It is evident that to the devotee of the Solar
faith, Osiris once represented the realm and the dominion
of death, to which the follower of Re was not delivered
up. In harmony with this is the apprehension that the
entire Osirian group might enter the pyramid with evil
intent. As a great Solar symbol it was necessary to protect the pyramid from the possible aggressions of Osiris,
the Osirian Horus, and the other divinities of the Osirian
group.[2] At a very early age the beliefs of both the Solar
and the Osirian religion merged as we have seen in the
first lecture. While the nucleus of each group of myths
is fairly distinguishable from the other, the coalescence
of the Solar and Osirian conceptions of the hereafter has
left us a very difficult process of analysis if we undertake
to separate them. There is a certain body of beliefs regarding the hereafter which we may designate as Solar,
and another group which are unquestionably Osirian,
but the two faiths have so interpenetrated each other
that there is much neutral territory which we cannot
assign to either, to the entire exclusion of the other. It
is clear that in the Solar faith we have a state theology,
with all the splendor and the prestige of its royal patrons
behind it; while in that of Osiris we are confronted by a
religion of the people, which made a strong appeal to the
individual believer. It is not impossible that the history
of the early sequence of these beliefs was thus: We

[1] Pyr. §§ 145-6.   [2] See above, p. 75.

should begin with a primitive belief in a subterranean kingdom of the dead which claimed all men. As an exclusive privilege of kings at first, and then of the great and noble, the glorious celestial hereafter which we have been discussing, finally emerged as a Solar kingdom of the dead. When the growing prestige of Osiris had displaced the older mortuary gods (like Anubis) Osiris became the great lord of the Nether World, and Osiris and his realm entered into competition with the Solar and celestial hereafter. In the mergence of these two faiths we discern for the first time in history the age-long struggle between the state form of religion and the popular faith of the masses. It will be the purpose of the next lecture to disengage as far as may be the nucleus of the Osirian teaching of the after life, and to trace the still undetermined course of its struggle with the imposing celestial theology whose doctrine of the royal dead we have been following.

LECTURE V

THE OSIRIANIZATION OF THE HEREAFTER

PROBABLY nothing in the life of the ancient Nile-dwellers commends them more appealingly to our sympathetic consideration than the fact that when the Osirian faith had once developed, it so readily caught the popular imagination as to spread rapidly among all classes. It thus came into active competition with the Solar faith of the court and state priesthoods. This was especially true of its doctrines of the after life, in the progress of which we can discern the gradual Osirianization of Egyptian religion, and especially of the Solar teaching regarding the hereafter.

There is nothing in the Osiris myth, nor in the character or later history of Osiris, to suggest a celestial hereafter. Indeed clear and unequivocal survivals from a period when he was hostile to the celestial and Solar dead are still discoverable in the Pyramid Texts. We recall the exorcisms intended to restrain Osiris and his kin from entering the pyramid, a Solar tomb, with evil intent (p. 75).[1] Again we find the dead king as a star in the sky, thus addressed: "Thou lookest down upon Osiris commanding the Glorious (=the dead). There thou standest, being far from him, (for) thou art not of them (the dead), thou belongest not among them."[2] Likewise it is said of the Sun-god: "He has freed king Teti from Kherti, he has

[1] Pyr. §§ 1266-7.   [2] Pyr. § 251.

not given him to Osiris." [1] It is perhaps due to an effort to overcome this difficulty that Horus, the son of Osiris, is represented as one "who puts not this Pepi over the dead, he puts him among the gods, he being divine." [2] The prehistoric Osiris faith, probably local to the Delta, thus involved a forbidding hereafter which was dreaded and at the same time was opposed to celestial blessedness beyond. To be sure, the Heliopolitan group of gods, the Divine Ennead of that city, makes Osiris a child of Nut, the Sky-goddess. But his father was the Earth-god Geb, a very natural result of the character of Osiris as a Nile-god and a spirit of vegetable life, both of which in Egyptian belief came out of the earth. Moreover, the celestial destiny through Nut the Sky-goddess is not necessarily Osirian. It is found, along with the frequent and non-Osirian or even pre-Osirian co-ordination of Horus and Set, associated in the service of the dead.[3] The appearance of these two together assisting the dead cannot be Osirian.[4] To be protected and assisted by Nut, therefore, does not necessarily imply that she is doing this for the dead king, because he is identified with Osiris, her son. It is thus probable that as a Sky-goddess intimately associated with Re, Nut's functions in the celestial life hereafter were originally Solar and at first not connected with the Osirian faith.

When Osiris migrated up the Nile from the Delta, we recall how he was identified with one of the old mortuary gods of the South, the "First of the Westerners" (Khenti-Amentiu), and his kingdom was conceived as situated in the West, or below the western horizon, where it merged into the Nether World. He became king of a realm of

[1] Pyr. § 350.
[2] Pyr. § 969.
[3] Pyr. Ut. 443.
[4] See *infra*, pp. 152-3.

the dead below the earth, and hence his frequent title, "Lord of Dewat," the "Nether World," which occurs even in the Pyramid Texts.[1] It is as lord of a subterranean kingdom of the dead that Osiris later appears.[2]

[1] Pyr. § 8 d.
[2] The situation of Dewat is a difficult problem. As the Nile flows out of it, according to later texts, especially the Sun-hymns, and the common designation of the universe in the Empire is "sky, earth, and Dewat," it is evident that it was later understood to be the Nether World. Such is the conclusion of SETHE in his still unpublished *Antrittsvorlesung*. See also JÉQUIER, *Le livre de ce qu'il y a dans l'Hades*, Paris, 1894, especially pp. 3–6; also LEFEBURE, in *Sphinx*, vol. I, pp. 27–46. In the Pyramid Texts it is evidently in the sky in a considerable number of passages. It can be understood in no other way in passages where it is parallel with "sky," like the following:

"The sky conceived thee together with Orion;
Dewat bears thee together with Orion."
(Pyr. § 820 = the same in Pyr. § 1527.)

Or again:
"Who voyages the sky with Orion,
Who sails Dewat with Osiris."
(Pyr. § 882.)

Similarly "Dewat seizes thy hand, (leads thee) to the place where Orion (= the sky) (Pyr. § 802); and Orion and Sothis in the "horizon" are encircled by Dewat (Pyr. § 151). Here Dewat is in the horizon, and likewise we find the dead "descends among" the dwellers in Dewat after he has ascended to the sky (Pyr. § 2084 c). It was thus sufficiently accessible from the sky, so that the dead, after he ascended, bathed in the "lake of Dewat" (Pyr. § 1164), and while in the sky he became a "glorious one dwelling in Dewat" (Pyr. § 1172 b). When he has climbed the ladder of Re, Horus and Set take him to Dewat (Pyr. § 390). It is parallel with 'kr, where 'kr is a variant of Geb, the earth (Pyr. § 1014 = § 796), which carries it down to earth again. It might appear here that Dewat was a lower region of the sky, in the vicinity of the horizon, below which it also extended. It is notable that in the Coffin Texts of the Middle Kingdom there appears a "lower Dewat" (LACAU, *Rec.* 27, 218, l. 47). The deceased says: "My place is in the barque of Re in the middle of lower Dewat" (*ibid.*, l. 52). Dewat thus merged into the Nether World, with which it was ultimately identified, or, being originally the Nether World, it had its counterpart in the sky.

As there was nothing then in the myth or the offices of Osiris to carry him to the sky, so the simplest of the Osirian Utterances in the Pyramid Texts do not carry him thither. There are as many varying pictures of the Osirian destiny as in the Solar theology. We find the dead king as a mere messenger of Osiris announcing the prosperous issue and plentiful yield of the year, the harvest year, which is associated with Osiris.[1] That group of incidents in the myth which proves to be especially available in the future career of the dead king is his relations with Horus, the son of Osiris, and the filial piety displayed by the son toward his father. We may find the dead king identified with Horus and marching forth in triumph from Buto, with his mother, Isis, before him and Nephthys behind him, while Upwawet opened the way for them.[2] More often, however, the dead king does all that Osiris did, receiving heart and limbs as did Osiris,[3] or becoming Osiris himself. This was the favorite belief of the Osiris faith. The king became Osiris and rose from the dead as Osiris did.[4] This identity began at birth and is described in the Pyramid Texts with all the wonders and prodigies of a divine birth.

> "The waters of life that are in the sky come;
> The waters of life that are in the earth come.
> The sky burns for thee,
> The earth trembles for thee,
> Before the divine birth.
> The two mountains divide,
> The god becomes,

[1] Pyr. §§ 1195 ff.
[2] Pyr. §§ 1089–90; §§ 1373–5. Both these passages merge into an ascension of Solar character.
[3] Pyr. § 364, followed by celestial ascent and association with Re.
[4] Pyr. Ut. 373.

> The god takes possession of his body.
> The two mountains divide,
> This king Neferkere becomes,
> This king Neferkere takes possession of his body."

Osiris as Nile is thus born between the two mountains of the eastern and western Nile shores, and in the same way, and as the same being, the king is born.[1] Hence we find the king appearing elsewhere as the inundation.[2] It is not the mere assumption of the form of Osiris,[3] but complete identity with him, which is set forth in this doctrine of the Pyramid Texts. "As he (Osiris) lives, this king Unis lives; as he dies not, this king Unis dies not; as he perishes not, this king Unis perishes not." These asseverations are repeated over and over, and addressed to every god in the Ennead, that each may be called upon to witness their truth. Osiris himself under various names is adjured, "Thy body is the body of this king Unis, thy flesh is the flesh of this king Unis, thy bones are the bones of this king Unis."[4] Thus the dead king receives the throne of Osiris, and becomes, like him, king of the dead. "Ho! king Neferkere (Pepi II)! How beautiful is this! How beautiful is this, which thy father Osiris has done for thee! He has given thee his throne, thou rulest those of the hidden places (the dead), thou leadest their august ones, all the glorious ones follow thee."[5]

The supreme boon which this identity of the king with Osiris assured the dead Pharaoh was the good offices of Horus, the personification of filial piety. All the pious

---

[1] Pyr. §§ 2063-5.
[2] Pyr. §§ 507-9.
[3] Pyr. § 1804.
[4] Pyr. Ut. 219.
[5] Pyr. §§ 2022-3. There is little distinction between the passages where the dead king receives the throne of Osiris, because identified with him and others in which he receives it as the heir of Osiris. He may take it even from Horus, heir of Osiris, e. g., Pyr. Ut. 414.

THE OSIRIANIZATION OF THE HEREAFTER   147

attentions which Osiris had once enjoyed at the hands of his son Horus now likewise become the king's portion. The litigation which the myth recounts at Heliopolis is successfully met by the aid of Horus, as well as Thoth, and, like Osiris, the dead king receives the predicate "righteous of voice," or "justified," an epithet which was later construed as meaning "triumphant."[1] Over and over again the resurrection of Osiris by Horus, and the restoration of his body, are likewise affirmed to be the king's privilege. "Horus collects for thee thy limbs that he may put thee together without any lack in thee."[2] Horus then champions his cause, as he had done that of his father, till the dead king gains the supreme place as sovereign of all. "O Osiris king Teti, arise! Horus comes that he may reclaim thee from the gods. Horus loves thee, he has equipped thee with his eye. . . . Horus has opened for thee thy eye that thou mayest see with it. . . . The gods . . . they love thee. Isis and Nephthys have healed thee. Horus is not far from thee; thou art his ka. Thy face is gracious unto him. . . . Thou hast received the word of Horus, thou art satisfied therewith. Hearken unto Horus, he has caused the gods to serve thee. . . . Horus has found thee that there is profit for him in thee. Horus sends up to thee the gods; he has given them to thee that they may illuminate thy face. Horus has placed thee at the head of the gods. He has caused thee to take every crown. . . . Horus has seized for thee the gods. They escape not from thee, from the place where thou hast gone. Horus counts for thee the gods. They retreat not from thee, from the place which thou hast seized. . . . Horus avenged thee; it was not long till he avenged thee. Ho, Osiris king Teti! thou art

[1] Pyr. Ut. 260. See above, p. 35.   [2] Pyr. § 635.

a mighty god, there is no god like thee. Horus has given to thee his children that they might carry thee. He has given to thee all gods that they may serve thee, and thou have power over them."[1] A long series of Utterances in the Pyramid Texts sets forth this championship of the dead king as Osiris by his son Horus.[2] In all this there is little or no trace of the celestial destiny, or any indication of the place where the action occurs. Such incidents and such Utterances are appropriated from the Osirian theology and myth, with little or no change. But the Osirian doctrine of the hereafter, absorbed into these royal mortuary texts by the priesthood of Heliopolis, could not, in spite of its vigorous popularity, resist the prestige of the state (or Solar) theology. Even in the Osirian Utterances on the good offices of Horus just mentioned we twice find the dead king, although he is assumed to be Osiris, thus addressed: "Thou art a Glorious One (Y'ḫwty) in thy name of 'Horizon (Y'ḫt) from which Re comes forth.'"[3] The Osirian hereafter was thus celestialized, as had been the Osirian theology when it was correlated with that of Heliopolis. We find the Sky-goddess Nut extending to the Osirian dead her protection and the privilege of entering her realm. Nut "takes him to the sky, she does not cast him down to the earth."[4] The ancient hymn in praise of the Sky-goddess embedded in the Pyramid Texts[5] has received an introduction, in which the king as Osiris is commended to her protection, and the hymn is broken up by petitions inserted at intervals craving a celestial destiny for the dead king, although this archaic hymn had originally no demonstrable con-

---

[1] Pyr. Ut. 364. See also 1683-6.
[2] Pyr. Ut. 356, 357, 364, 367-372.
[3] Pyr. § 621 = § 636.　　[4] Pyr. § 1345.　　[5] Pyr. Ut. 427-435.

nection with Osiris, and was, as far as any indication it contains is concerned, written before the priestly theology had made Osiris the son of the Sky-goddess.[1] Similarly Anubis, the ancient mortuary god of Siut, "counts Osiris away from the gods belonging to the earth, to the gods dwelling in the sky";[2] and we find in the Pyramid Texts the anomalous ascent of Osiris to the sky: "The sky thunders (lit. speaks), earth trembles, for fear of thee, Osiris, when thou makest ascent. Ho, mother cows yonder! Ho, suckling mothers (cows) yonder! Go ye behind him, weep for him, hail him, acclaim him, when he makes ascent and goes to the sky among his brethren, the gods."[3] His transition to the Solar and celestial destiny is effected in one passage by a piece of purely mortuary theologizing which represents Re as raising Osiris from the dead.[4] Thus is Osiris celestialized until the Pyramid Texts even call him "lord of the sky,"[5] and represent him as ruling there. The departed Pharaoh is ferried over, the doors of the sky are opened for him, he passes all enemies as he goes, and he is announced to Osiris in the sky precisely as in the Solar theology. There he is welcomed by Osiris,[6] and he joins the "Imperishable Stars, the followers of Osiris,"[7] just as in the Solar faith. In the same way he emerges as a god of primeval origin and elemental powers. "Thou bearest the sky in thy hand, thou layest down the earth with thy foot."[8] Celestials and men acclaim the dead, even "thy wind is incense, thy north wind is smoke,"[9] say they.

While the Heliopolitan priests thus solarized and celes-

[1] The protection and assistance of Nut are further elaborated in Ut. 444–7 and 450–2.
[2] Pyr. § 1523.
[3] Pyr. Ut. 337.
[4] Pyr. § 721.
[5] Pyr. §§ 964, 968.
[6] Pyr. § 2000.
[7] Pyr. § 749.
[8] Pyr. § 2067.
[9] Pyr. § 877.

tialized the Osirian mortuary doctrines, although they were essentially terrestrial in origin and character, these Solar theologians were in their turn unable to resist the powerful influence which the popularity of the Osirian faith brought to bear upon them. The Pyramid Texts were eventually Osirianized, and the steady progress of this process, exhibiting the course of the struggle between the Solar faith of the state temples and the popular beliefs of the Osirian religion thus discernible in the Pyramid Texts, is one of the most remarkable survivals from the early world, preserving as it does the earliest example of such a spiritual and intellectual conflict between state and popular religion. The dying Sun and the dying Osiris are here in competition. With the people the human Osiris makes the stronger appeal, and even the wealthy and subsidized priesthoods of the Solar religion could not withstand the power of this appeal. What we have opportunity to observe in the Pyramid Texts is specifically the gradual but irresistible intrusion of Osiris into the Solar doctrines of the hereafter and their resulting Osirianization.

Even on his coffin, preserved in the pyramid sepulchre, the departed king is called "Osiris, lord of Dewat."[1] The Osirian influence is superficially evident in otherwise purely Solar Utterances of the Pyramid Texts where the Osirian editor has inserted the epithet "Osiris" before the king's name, so that we have "Osiris king Unis," or "Osiris king Pepi."[2] This was at first so mechanically done that in the offering ritual it was placed only at the head of each Utterance. In the earliest of our five versions of the Pyramid Texts, that of Unis, we find "Osiris" inserted before the king's name wherever that name stands at the

---

[1] Pyr. § 8 d.   [2] Pyr. Ut. 578 and 579.

head of the Utterance, but not where it is found in the body of the text. Evidently the Osirian editor ran hastily and mechanically through the sections, inserting "Osiris" at the head of each one which began with the king's name, but not taking the trouble to go through each section seeking the king's name and to insert "Osiris" wherever necessary in the body of the text also.¹

In this way the whole Offering Ritual was Osirianized in Unis's pyramid, but the editor ceased this process of mechanical insertion at the end of the ritual. A similar method may be observed where the same Utterance happens to be preserved in two different pyramids, one exhibiting the mechanical insertion of "Osiris" before the king's name, while the other lacks such editing. This is especially significant where the content of the Utterances is purely Solar.²

But the Osirianization of the Pyramid Texts involves more than such mechanical alteration of externals. We find one Utterance³ in its old Solar form, without a single reference to Osiris or to Osirian doctrine, side by side with the same Utterance in expanded form filled with Osirian elements. The traces of the Osirian editor's work are evident throughout, but they are interestingly demonstrable

---

¹ "Osiris Unis" occurs in the body of the Utterance in 18 c (once) and 30 b (once); but the following references will show how regularly it is found at the head of the Utterance and not in the body of the text in the pyramid of Unis. In Ut. 45–49, once each at beginning; in Ut. 72–76 and 78–79, once each at beginning; omitted in Ut. 77, 81, and 93, where Unis's name does not begin the Utterance. In Ut. 84, 85, 87–92, 94, 108–171, and 199 "Osiris-Unis" heads each Utterance. After Ut. 200 "Osiris-Unis" does not occur at all. It is evident that this mechanical method of Osirianization did not extend beyond the Offering Ritual, which also terminates at this place.

² Pyr. Ut. 579 and 673. ³ Pyr. Ut. 571.

in a series of five stanzas each addressed to a different god, whose name begins the stanza. The last stanza of the five begins with *two* gods' names, however, the second being "Sekhem, son of Osiris," although in the apostrophe, which constitutes this fifth stanza, the two gods are addressed by pronouns in the *singular number!* It is evident that, like the other four stanzas, the fifth also began with the name of a single god, but that the Osirian editor has inserted the name of an Osirian god as a second name, forgetting to change the pronouns.[1] The insertion is enhanced in significance by the fact that all five gods in these five stanzas are Solar gods, and the last one, after which the name of Osiris was inserted, is identified with Re.

The process was carried so far that it was sometimes applied to passages totally at variance with the Osirian doctrine. In the old Solar teaching we not infrequently find Horus and Set side by side on an equal basis, and both represented as engaged in some beneficent act for the dead.[2] Now when the dead king is identified with Osiris, by the insertion of the name "Osiris" before that of the king, we are confronted by the extraordinary assumption that Set performs pious mortuary offices for Osiris, although the Osiris myth represents Set as mutilating the body of the dead Osiris and scattering his limbs far and wide. Thus an old purification ceremony in the presence of the gods and nobles of Heliopolis (and hence clearly Solar) represents the dead as cleansed by the spittle of Horus and the spittle of Set. This ceremony

---

[1] Pyr. Ut. 570.
[2] See above, pp. 40 f. The best examples are: Pyr. §§ 204, 206, 370, 390, 418, 473, 487, 594, 535, 601, 683, 798, 801 = §§ 1016, 823, 848–850, 946, 971, 1148.

had, of course, nothing to do with the Osirian ritual, but when the ritual introducing this ceremony was Osirianized, we find "King Osiris, this Pepi" inserted before the formula of purification, thus assuming that Osiris was purified by his arch-enemy, the foul Set![1] Similarly, Set may appear alone in old Solar Utterances on familiar and friendly terms with the dead king, so that the king may be addressed thus: "He calls to thee on the stairway of the sky; thou ascendest to the god; Set fraternizes with thee," even though the king has just been raised as Osiris from the dead![2]

The ladder leading to the sky was originally an element of the Solar faith. That it had nothing to do with Osiris is evident, among other things, from the fact that one version of the ladder episode represents it in charge of Set.[3] The Osirianization of the ladder episode is clearly traceable in four versions of it, which are but variants of the same ancient original.[4] The four represent a period of nearly a century, at least of some eighty-five years. In the oldest form preserved to us, in the pyramid of Unis,[5] dating from the middle of the twenty-seventh century, the Utterance opens with the acclamation of the gods as Unis ascends. "'How beautiful to see, how satisfying to behold,' say the gods, 'when this god ascends to the sky, when Unis ascends to the sky. . . .' The gods in the sky and the gods on earth come to him; they make supports for Unis on their arm. Thou ascendest, O Unis,

---

[1] Pyr. §§ 848–850.   [2] Pyr. § 1016.
[3] Pyr. § 478; compare also "Set lifts him (the dead) up" (Pyr. § 1148). In Pyr. § 1253 we find "ladder which carried the Ombite (Set)."
[4] Pyr. Ut. 306 (Unis, Mernere, Pepi II), 480 (Teti), 572 (Pepi, Mernere), 474 (Pepi).
[5] Pyr. Ut. 306.

to the sky. Ascend upon it in this its name of 'Ladder.' The sky is given to Unis, the earth is given to him by Atum." Such is the essential substance of the Utterance.[1] The ladder here barely emerges and the climber is the Pharaoh himself, though Atum is prominent. A generation later, in the pyramid of Teti the ladder is more developed and the original climber is Atum, the Sun-god; but the Osirian goddesses, Isis and Nephthys, are introduced. Finally, in the pyramid of Pepi I, at least eighty-five years after that of Unis, the opening acclamation of the old gods as they behold the ascent of the Pharaoh is put into the mouths of Isis and Nephthys, and the climber has become Osiris.[2] Thus Osiris has taken possession of the old Solar episode and appropriated the old Solar text. This has taken place in spite of embarrassing complications. In harmony with the common co-ordination of Horus and Set in the service of the dead, an old Solar doctrine represented them as assisting him at the ascent of the ladder which Re and Horus set up. But when the ascending king becomes Osiris, the editor seems quite unconscious of the incongruity, as Set, the mortal enemy and slayer of Osiris, assists him to reach his celestial abode![3]

Nowhere is the intrusion of Osiris in the Pyramid Texts more striking than in the Utterances devoted to the services of the four Eastern Horuses on behalf of the dead. A favorite means of ascension, of opening the sky-gates,

[1] The brief intimation of a mysterious enemy plotting against the life of the king, appended at the end of the Utterance, is perhaps an intrusive Osirian reference; but it does not affect the clearly celestial and Solar character of the Utterance. It is omitted in Ut. 480, but appears more fully developed in the Osirianized Utterances 572 and 474, but in none of the Utterances to which it is appended is the name of Osiris mentioned, while the epithet which is employed, "Ymnw (Hidden one?) of the Wild Bull," is usually Solar.

[2] Pyr. Ut. 474.   [3] Pyr. Ut. 305.

of ferrying over, of purification and the like, was to have all these things first done for each of the four Horuses in succession, and then by sympathetic inevitability also for the dead king. Four considerable Utterances are built up in this way, each containing an account of the things done by each of the four Horuses, and then likewise by the king.[1]

In the oldest form of these Utterances, as found in the pyramid of Teti, the quartette comprise the following:

1. Horus of the Gods.
2. Horus of the Horizon (Harakhte).
3. Horus of the Shesmet.
4. Horus of the East.[2]

The exclusively Solar character of each of these Horuses is evident from the connections in which they appear in the Pyramid Texts, while in the case of two of them (Horus of the Horizon and Horus of the East) the name renders it evident. Indeed, in the Teti pyramid the four appear as heralds announcing the name of Teti to the Sun-god, in a passage which is hostile to Osiris, and affirms that the Sun-god "has not given him (the king)

---

[1] These Utterances are 325, 563, 479, and 573. In Ut. 573 variant forms of their names appear. In 1085–6 the four Horuses appear ferrying over on the two floats of the sky; they are found again in 1105 and in 1206, "these four youths who stand on the east side of the sky" bind the two floats for Re and then for the dead. We should doubtless recognize them also in the four curly haired youths who are in charge of the ferry-boat to the eastern sky in Ut. 520. (But in Ut. 522 the four in charge of the ferry-boat are the four genii, the "sons of Horus," and confusion must be guarded against.) The four Horuses in 1258 (Ut. 532), who are identified with the dead and kept from decay by Isis and Nephthys, are treated above. For the sake of completeness, compare the four children of Geb in Pyr. §§ 1510–11, and especially the four children of Atum who decay not (Pyr. §§ 2057–8), just as in 1258.

[2] Pyr. Ut. 325 and 563.

to Osiris."[1] Two generations after Teti we find the same four Horuses, unaltered,[2] side by side with a further development of the group exhibiting an intruder; it appears thus:

1. Horus of the Gods.
2. Horus of the East.
3. Horus of the Shesmet.
4. Osiris.[3]

Osiris has thus pushed his way into this Solar group to the displacement of the most unequivocally Solar of them all, Horus of the Horizon (Harakhte). The intrusion of Osiris here is the most convincing example of his power, and the most clearly discernible in the whole range of the process which Osirianized the Pyramid Texts. We can now understand why it is that when the dead is identified with the four Horuses, he is preserved from decay by Isis and Nephthys as the four Horuses had been likewise preserved by the same Osirian goddesses. When once the group has been Osirianized it is to be expected that they shall enjoy the good offices of the wife and sister of Osiris.[4] The exclusion of one of the four Horuses, by the intrusion of Osiris, leaving really only three, is doubtless the reason why we find in another Osirianized Utterance that only three of them appear.[5]

As the four Solar Horuses of the East were Osirianized, so in all probability were the four mortuary genii, commonly known as the "four sons of Horus." We find this second four (whom we shall call the four genii to distinguish them from the four Solar Horuses) figuring prominently in the ascension. Indeed they make the ladder, which is a purely celestial and Solar matter, as we have

[1] Pyr. § 348. [2] Pyr. Ut. 563. [3] Pyr. Ut. 479.
[4] Pyr. Ut. 532. [5] Pyr. §§ 1132-8.

THE OSIRIANIZATION OF THE HEREAFTER 157

seen (p. 111), and they make it together with Atum, the primeval Sun-god. Similarly we find them all in a list of Solar gods,[1] and they appear also in charge of the Solar ferry-boat,[2] in which they ferry over the dead.[3] The four Horuses also have much to do with the celestial ferry, and it would appear, though this is merely a conjecture, that the four genii are an artificial creation parallel with the four Horuses, and perhaps their sons.[4] In any case the dead may be identified with one of them as with the four Horuses.[5] The four genii were, however, fully Osirianized, they avenge Osiris and smite Set,[6] and they carry the body of the dead king as Osiris.[7] In the later mortuary ritual of the Osirian faith they played a prominent rôle, and are especially well known as the four genii who had charge of the viscera of the dead, which they protect in the hereafter in the four so-called "Canopic" jars, each one of which is surmounted by the head of one of the four genii. This function in the Osirian faith is foreshadowed in the Pyramid Texts in a passage where we find them expelling hunger and thirst from the belly and lips of the dead.[8]

As the four Horuses and the four genii, who had so much to do with the ascension and the celestial ferry, were Osirianized, so eventually was the ancient Solar ferryman "Face-Behind-Him," who receives the title "Doorkeeper of Osiris" and the Solar ferry becomes the prop-

---

[1] Pyr. §§ 147-9.   [2] Pyr. Ut. 522.   [3] Pyr. § 1092.
[4] I am aware that the four genii are called "the offspring of Horus of Letopolis" (Pyr. § 2078).
[5] Pyr. § 1483.   [6] Pyr. Ut. 541.
[7] Pyr. Ut. 544-6, 645, 648. We find them bringing to the dead his name "Imperishable," at which time they are called the "souls" of Horus (Pyr. § 2102).
[8] Pyr. § 552.

erty of Osiris, to whom the ferryman is adjured to say, "Let this thy (Osiris's) ship be brought for this king Pepi."[1] The two floats of reeds suffered much the same fate. These, as we have seen (p. 108), are clearly Solar when they first appear.[2] Indeed, in the pyramid of Teti they are found in an Utterance[3] explicitly hostile to Osiris, in which it is stated that the Sun-god does not deliver the dead king to Osiris. Nevertheless the reed floats are also completely Osirianized in the Pyramid Texts. We find them laid down for Osiris, by the gods of the cardinal points, in an Utterance purely Osirian in character,[4] and within a century after they appear still purely Solar in the pyramid of Unis, they were employed in that of Pepi I for the crossing of Osiris.[5]

If the ladder, the ferry-boat, and the reed floats, the instrumentalities for reaching the skies, a place with which Osiris had properly nothing to do, were thus early Osirianized, we cannot wonder that the sky itself and its denizens were likewise appropriated by Osiris till the "Imperishable Stars" are called "followers of Osiris." In the same way, when the king is born, like Osiris, as Nile,[6] we may find him transferred to the sky and flooding the heavens as the Nile inundation; he makes all the sky fresh and verdant. "King Unis comes to his pools that are in the region of the flood at the great inundation, to the place of peace with green fields, that is in the horizon. Unis makes the verdure to flourish in the two regions of the horizon."[7] Finally Osiris is not only identified with the dead king, but also even with his temple and pyramid,[8] the great Solar symbol, from which these

[1] Pyr. § 1201.
[2] Pyr. Ut. 263–6.
[3] Pyr. Ut. 264.
[4] Pyr. Ut. 303.
[5] Pyr. § 556.
[6] Pyr. §§ 2063–5.
[7] Pyr. §§ 508–9.
[8] Pyr. §§ 1657–8.

same Pyramid Texts contain formulæ for exorcising Osiris and his kin (see p. 75).[1]

An important link between the celestial and the Osirian doctrine of the hereafter was the fact that the Sun-god died every day in the west. There was at Abydos, as we have already seen (p. 38), an old mortuary god known as "First of the Westerners," who was early absorbed by Osiris, so that "First of the Westerners" became an epithet appended to the name of Osiris. Before this conquest by Osiris took place, however, the "First of the Westerners" as a local god of Abydos had already become involved in the celestial hereafter. An ancient Abydos offering formulary preserved in the Pyramid Texts addresses the dead thus: "The earth is hacked up for thee, the offering is placed before thee. Thou goest upon that way whereon the gods go. Turn thee that thou mayest see this offering which the king has made for thee, which the First of the Westerners has made for thee. Thou goest to those northern gods, the Imperishable Stars."[2] It is evident that the First of the Westerners is closely associated with the celestial hereafter in this passage. Later, when Osiris was identified with the First of the Westerners, the latter's connection with the celestial hereafter will have assisted in celestializing the Osirian mortuary beliefs.

Now, while all this also resulted in Osirianizing the celestial and Solar mortuary teachings, they still remained celestial. When the dead Osiris is taken up by Re,[3] it is evident that Re's position in these composite mortuary doctrines is still the chief one. The fact remains, then, that the *celestial* doctrines of the hereafter dominate the Pyramid Texts throughout, and the later *subterranean*

[1] Pyr. §§ 1266-7. [2] Pyr. Ut. 441. [3] Pyr. § 819.

kingdom of Osiris and Re's voyage through it are still entirely in the background in these royal mortuary teachings. Among the *people* Re is later, as it were, dragged into the Nether World to illumine there the subjects of Osiris in his mortuary kingdom, and this is one of the most convincing evidences of the power of Osiris among the lower classes. In the *royal* and *state temple* theology, Osiris is lifted to the sky, and while he is there Solarized, we have just shown how he also tinctures the Solar teaching of the celestial kingdom of the dead with Osirian doctrines. The result was thus inevitable confusion, as the two faiths interpenetrated.

In both faiths we recall that the king is identified with the god, and hence we find him unhesitatingly called Osiris and Re in the same passage. The following extensive passages well illustrate the often inextricable confusion resulting from the interweaving of these unharmonized elements. The text opens with the resurrection of Osiris at the hands of Horus, but we soon perceive that this incident has been engrafted upon ancient Solar doctrines. "Arise for me, O king. Arise for me, O Osiris king Mernere. I am he, I am thy son, I am Horus. I come to thee, I purify thee, I make thee alive, I gather for thee thy bones. . . . For I am Horus, thy avenger. I have smitten for thee him who smote thee. I have avenged thee, king Osiris Mernere, on him who did thee evil. I have come to thee with a commission of Heru. He has put thee, king Osiris Mernere, upon the throne of Re-Atum, that thou mayest lead the people. Thou embarkest in this barque of Re, to which the gods love to descend, in which they love to embark, in which Re is rowed to the horizon. Thou embarkest therein like Re, thou sittest down on this throne of Re that thou mayest

THE OSIRIANIZATION OF THE HEREAFTER   161

command the gods. For thou art Re who came forth from Nut, who begets Re every day. This Mernere is born every day like Re." Then follows a picture of enthronement and felicity in the realm of Re, in which there is no reference to Osiris. It then proceeds: "They (the 'two great gods who are in charge of the Field of Rushes') recite for thee this chapter which they recited for Re-Atum who shines every day. They put this Mernere upon their thrones before every Divine Ennead, like Re and like his successor. They cause this Mernere to become like Re in this his name of Kheprer (Sun-god). Thou ascendest to them like Re in this his name of Re. Thou wanderest away from them like Re in this his name of Atum.[1] The two Divine Enneads rejoice, O king Osiris Mernere. They say, 'Our brother here comes to us,' say the two Divine Enneads concerning Osiris Mernere, O king Osiris Mernere. 'One of us comes to us,' say the two Divine Enneads concerning thee, O king Osiris Mernere. 'The first-born of his mother!' say the two Divine Enneads concerning thee, O king Osiris Mernere. 'He to whom evil was done by his brother Set comes to us,' say the two Divine Enneads. 'But we shall not permit that Set be delivered from bearing thee forever, O king Osiris Mernere,' say the two Divine Enneads concerning thee, O king Osiris Mernere. Lift thee up, O king Osiris Mernere. Thou livest."[2] It will be noticed that the Osirian passage which follows so abruptly upon the Solar is Osirian in *content*, and its Osirian character does not consist in the simple insertion of the name of Osiris before that of the king.

[1] "Ascendest" and "wanderest" are in Egyptian puns on the names of Re and Atum.
[2] Pyr. Ut. 606.

Perhaps even worse confusion is exhibited by the following Utterance:

"O this Pepi! Thou hast departed. Thou art a Glorious One, thou art mighty as a god, like the successor of Osiris. Thy soul hast thou in the midst of thee. Thy power (or 'control') hast thou behind thee. Thy crown hast thou on thy head. . . . The servants of the god are behind thee, the nobles of the god are before thee."

"They recite: 'The god comes! The god comes! This Pepi comes upon the throne of Osiris. This Glorious One comes, the Dweller in Nedyt, the mighty one, the dweller in Thinis (Osiris).'"

"Isis speaks to thee, Nephthys greets thee. The Glorious come to thee, bowing down; they kiss the earth at thy feet, because the terror of thee, O this Pepi, is in the cities of Seya."

"Thou ascendest to thy mother Nut; she seizes thy arm. She gives to thee the way to the horizon, to the place where Re is. The double doors of the sky are opened for thee, the double doors of Kebehu (the sky) are opened for thee."

"Thou findest Re standing (there); he greets thee. He seizes thy arm, he leads thee into the double palace of the sky. He places thee upon the throne of Osiris."

"Ho, this Pepi! The Horus-eye comes to thee, it addresses thee. Thy soul that is among the gods comes to thee; thy power (or 'control') that is among the Glorious comes to thee. The son has avenged his father, Horus has avenged Osiris. Horus has avenged Pepi on his enemies."

"Thou risest, O this Pepi, avenged, equipped as a god, endued with the form of Osiris, upon the throne of the First of the Westerners. Thou doest what he was ac-

THE OSIRIANIZATION OF THE HEREAFTER 163

customed to do among the Glorious, the Imperishable Stars."

"Thy son stands on thy throne equipped with thy form. He does what thou wast accustomed to do formerly before the living, by command of Re, the great god. He ploughs barley, he ploughs spelt, he presents thee therewith."

"'Ho, this Pepi! All satisfying life is given to thee, eternity is thine,' says Re. Thou speakest thyself; receive to thee the form of the god wherewith thou shalt be great among the gods who are in control of the lake."

"Ho, this Pepi! Thy soul stands among the gods, among the Glorious. The fear of thee is on their hearts."

"Ho, this Pepi! This Pepi stands upon thy throne before the living. The terror of thee is on their hearts."

"Thy name lives upon earth, thy name grows old upon earth. Thou perishest not, thou passest not away for ever and ever."[1]

While there is some effort here to correlate the functions of Re and Osiris, it can hardly be called an attempt at harmonization of conflicting doctrines. This is practically unknown in the Pyramid Texts. Perhaps we may regard it as an explanation of Osiris's presence in the sky when we find a reference to the fact that "he ascended . . . to the sky that he might join the suite of Re."[2] But the fact that both Re and Osiris appear as supreme kings of the hereafter cannot be reconciled, and such mutually irreconcilable beliefs caused the Egyptian no more

[1] Pyr. Ut. 422.
[2] Pyr. § 971 e. The only passage which may fairly be called an effort to harmonize conflicting doctrine is that on p. 102, where the place of the Imperishable Stars in the north is pushed over toward the east to harmonize with the doctrine of the eastern sky as the place of the abode of the celestial dead. Pyr. § 1000.

discomfort than was felt by any early civilization in the maintenance of a group of religious teachings side by side with others involving varying and totally inconsistent suppositions. Even Christianity itself has not escaped this experience.

There is a marked difference between Osiris and Re. Osiris is in function passive. Rarely does he become an active agent on behalf of the dead (as, *e. g.*, in Pyr. Ut. 559). The blessedness of the Osirian destiny consisted largely in the enjoyment of the good offices of Horus, who appears as the son of the dead as soon as the latter is identified with Osiris. On the other hand, Re is a mighty sovereign, often directly interposing in favor of the dead, while it is the services of *others* on behalf of Osiris (not *by* Osiris) which the dead (as Osiris) enjoys. Osiris is a god of the dead; Re, on the other hand, is the great power in the affairs of living men, and there we behold his sovereignty expanding and developing to hold sway in a more exalted realm of moral values—a realm of which we shall gain the earliest glimpses anywhere vouchsafed us as we endeavor to discover more than the merely material agencies, and the material ends, which we have seen dominating the Egyptian conception of the hereafter.

LECTURE VI

THE EMERGENCE OF THE MORAL SENSE—MORAL WORTHINESS AND THE HEREAFTER—SCEPTICISM AND THE PROBLEM OF SUFFERING

NOWHERE in ancient times has the capacity of a race to control the material world been so fully expressed in surviving material remains as in the Nile valley. In the abounding fulness of their energies they built up a fabric of material civilization, the monuments of which it would seem time can never wholly sweep away. But the manifold substance of life, interfused of custom and tradition, of individual traits fashioned among social, economic, and governmental forces, ever developing in the daily operations and functions of life—all that made the stage and the setting amid which necessity for hourly *moral* decisions arises—all that creates the attitude of the individual and impels the inner man as he is called upon to make these decisions—all these constitute an elusive higher atmosphere of the ancient world which tomb masonry and pyramid orientation have not transmitted to us. Save in a few scanty references in the inscriptions of the Pyramid Age, it has vanished forever; for even the inscriptions, as we have seen, are concerned chiefly with the *material* welfare of the departed in the hereafter. What they disclose, however, is of unique interest, preserving as it does the earliest chapter in the moral development of man as known to us, a chapter marking perhaps the most important fundamental step in the evolution of civilization. Moreover, these materials from the Pyramid Age have never been put together, and in gathering them together for these lectures I have been not a little surprised to find them as numerous as they are.

They are, indeed, sufficiently numerous, and so unequivocal as to demonstrate the existence nearly three thousand years before Christ of a keen moral discernment, already so far developed that we must conclude it had begun far back in the fourth millennium B. C. Indeed the Egyptian of the Pyramid Age had already begun to look back upon a time when sin and strife did not exist, to "that first body" of "the company of the just," "born before arose," "strife," "voice," "blasphemy," "conflict," or the frightful mutilations inflicted upon each other by Horus and Set.[1] With this age of innocence, or at least of righteousness and peace, we must associate also the time of which they spoke, "before death came forth."[2] The development of moral discernment had indeed gone so far in the Pyramid Age that the thought of the age was dealing with the origin of good and evil, the source of human traits. We recall that our Memphite philosopher and theologian attributed all these things to the creative word of his god, "which made that which is loved and that which is hated," "which gave life to the peaceful and death to the guilty."[3] Akin to this is the emergence, in this age, of the earliest abstract term discernible in the ancient world, the word for "truth, right, righteousness, justice," all of which are connoted by one word.

Furthermore, in the daily secular life of this remote age, even in administration, moral ideals already had great

[1] Pyr. § 1463.   [2] Pyr. § 1466 d.   [3] See above, p. 45.

influence. In the Feudal Age, a thousand years after the rise of the Old Kingdom, at the installation of the vizier, that official used to be referred to the example of an ancient vizier who had already become proverbial in the Pyramid Age. The cause of his enduring reputation was that he had decided a case, in which his relatives were involved, against his own kin, no matter what the merits of the case might be, lest he should be accused of partial judgment in favor of his own family.[1] A similar example of respect for moral ideals in high places is doubtless to be recognized in the Horus-name of king Userkaf (twenty-eighth century B. C.). He called himself "Doer-of-Righteousness" (or Justice).

Among the people the most common virtue discernible by us is filial piety. Over and over again we find the massive tombs of the Pyramid Age erected by the son for the departed father, as well as a splendid interment arranged by the son.[2] Indeed one of the sons of this age even surpasses the example of all others, for he states in a passage of his tomb inscription: "Now I caused that I should be buried in the same tomb with this Zau (his father), in order that I might be with him in the same place; not, however, because I was not in a position to make a second tomb; but I did this in order that I might see this Zau every day, in order that I might be with him in the same place."[3]

It is especially in the tomb that such claims of moral worthiness are made. This is not an accident; such claims are made in the tomb in this age with the logical purpose of securing in the hereafter any benefits accruing from such virtues. Thus, on the base of a mortuary

---
[1] SETHE, *Untersuchungen*, V, 99.
[2] BAR, I, 382.   [3] BAR, I, 383.

statue set up in a tomb, the deceased represented by the portrait statue says: "I had these statues made by the sculptor and he was satisfied with the pay which I gave him."[1] The man very evidently wished it known that his mortuary equipment was honestly gotten. A nomarch of the twenty-seventh century B. C. left the following record of his upright life: "I gave bread to all the hungry of the Cerastes-Mountain (his domain); I clothed him who was naked therein. I filled its shores with large cattle and its ⌜lowlands⌝ with small cattle. I satisfied the wolves of the mountain and the fowl of the sky with ⌜flesh⌝ of small cattle. . . . I never oppressed one in possession of his property so that he complained of me because of it to the god of my city; (but) I spake and told that which was good. Never was there one fearing because of one stronger than he, so that he complained because of it to the god. . . . I was a benefactor to it (his domain) in the folds of the cattle, in the settlements of the fowlers. . . . I speak no lie, for I was one beloved of his father, praised of his mother, excellent in character to his brother, and amiable to [his sister]."[2]

Over and over these men of four thousand five hundred to five thousand years ago affirm their innocence of evildoing. "Never did I do anything evil toward any person,"[3] says the chief physician of king Sahure in the middle of the twenty-eighth century before Christ, while a priest a little later says essentially the same thing: "Never have I done aught of violence toward any person."[4] A century later a citizen of little or no rank places the following address to the living upon the front

---

[1] Statue in the Leipzig University Collection. STEINDORFF, *Zeitschr. für aegypt. Sprache*, 48, 156.
[2] BAR, I, 281. [3] BAR, I, 240. [4] BAR, I, 252.

of his tomb: "O ye living, who are upon earth, who pass by this tomb . . . let a mortuary offering of that which ye have come forth for me, for I was one beloved of the people. Never was I beaten in the presence of any official since my birth; never did I take the property of any man by violence; I was a doer of that which pleased all men."[1] It is evident from such addresses to the living as this that one motive for these affirmations of estimable character was the hope of maintaining the goodwill of one's surviving neighbors, that they might present mortuary offerings of food and drink at the tomb.

It is equally clear also that such moral worthiness was deemed of value in the sight of the gods and might influence materially the happiness of the dead in the hereafter. An ethical ordeal awaited those who had passed into the shadow world. Both the motives mentioned are found combined in a single address to the living on the front of the tomb of the greatest of early African explorers, Harkhuf of Elephantine, who penetrated the Sudan in the twenty-sixth century B. C. He says: "I was . . . one (beloved) of his father, praised of his mother, whom all his brothers loved. I gave bread to the hungry, clothing to the naked, I ferried him who had no boat. O ye living who are upon earth, [who shall pass by this tomb whether] going down-stream or going up-stream, who shall say, 'A thousand loaves, a thousand jars of beer for the owner of this tomb!' I will intercede for their sakes in the Nether World. I am a worthy and equipped Glorious One, a ritual priest whose mouth knows. As for any man who shall enter into (this) tomb as his mortuary possession, I will seize him like a wild fowl; he shall be judged for it by the Great God. I was one saying good

[1] BAR, I, 279.

things and repeating what was loved. Never did I say aught evil to a powerful one against anybody. I desired that it might be well with me in the Great God's presence. Never did I [judge two brothers] in such a way that a son was deprived of his paternal possession."[1] Here the threat of judgment is not only used to deter the lawless who might take possession of the dead man's tomb, but the thought of that judgment, meaning moral responsibility beyond the grave, is affirmed to have been the motive of the great explorer's exemplary life. That motive is thus carried back to the actual course of his daily, earthly life as when he says: "I desired that it might be well with me in the Great God's presence."[2] Throughout his life, then, he looked forward to standing in that dread presence to answer for the ethical quality of his conduct. As the earliest evidence of moral responsibility beyond the tomb, such utterances in the cemeteries of the Pyramid Age, nearly five thousand years ago, are not a little impressive. In other lands, for over two thousand years after this, good and bad alike were consigned to the same realm of the dead, and no distinction whatever was made between them. It is, as it were, an isolated moral vista down which we look, penetrating the early gloom as a shaft of sunshine penetrates the darkness.

It is of great importance to identify these ideas of a moral searching in the hereafter with one or the other of the two dominant theologies, that is with Re or Osiris. Unfortunately the god whose judgment is feared is not mentioned by name, but an epithet, "Great God," is employed instead. This is expanded in one tomb to "Great

[1] BAR, I, 328-331. The threat will also be found, BAR, I, 253 and 338.
[2] This statement is also found in another Aswan tomb, BAR, I, 357.

God, lord of the sky."[1] It is hardly possible that any other than Re can be meant. To be sure, the celestializing of Osiris has in one or two rare instances brought even him the title "lord of the sky" (see above, p. 149), but the unprejudiced mind on hearing the words "Great God, lord of the sky" would think of no other than Re, to whom it was and had been for centuries incessantly applied; and this conclusion is confirmed by all that we find in the Pyramid Texts, where, as we shall see, Re is over and over again the lord of the judgment. It is he who is meant when Inti of Deshasheh says: "But as for all people who shall do evil to this (tomb), who shall do anything destructive to this (tomb), who shall damage the writing therein, judgment shall be had with them for it by the Great God, the lord of judgment in the place where judgment is had."[2]

We have already followed the elaborate provision for all the contingencies of the hereafter which we find in the Pyramid Texts, and we recall how indispensable was the purification of the dead at some point in his transition from the earthly to the celestial realm. We stated in reference to that purification that its significance was not exhausted in purely physical and ceremonial cleansing. That to some extent it signified moral purification is evident from the fact that when the dead king in one passage is washed by "the Followers of Horus," "they recite the 'Chapter of the Just' on behalf of this king Pepi (whom they are washing); they recite the 'Chapter of Those Who Have Ascended to Life and Satisfaction' on behalf of this king Pepi."[3] The "Followers of Horus" who perform this ceremony are of course Solar, and thus moral purity in the hereafter is associated with the Sun-

[1] BAR, I, 338.   [2] PETRIE, *Deshasheh*, pl. vii.   [3] Pyr. § 921.

god at the very beginning. This connection between the Sun-god and moral requirements is clearly recognized in a number of important passages in the Pyramid Texts. "'Let him come, he is pure,' says the priest of Re concerning king Mernere. The door-keeper of the sky, he announces him (Mernere) to these four gods (the four Horuses) who are over the lake of Keneset. They recite (the chapter), 'How just is king Mernere for his father Geb!'¹ They recite (the chapter), 'How just is king Mernere for his father Re!'"²

The king, then, is not exempt from the requirement which the tombs of his nobles disclose them as so anxious to fulfil, and the god whom he satisfies, as in the case of his subjects, is Re. "There is no evil which king Pepi has done. Weighty is this word in thy sight, O Re."³ In a typical Solar Utterance, an appendix to an untouched Solar Utterance preceding it, we find Re's ferryman thus addressed: "O thou who ferriest over the just who is without a ship, ferryman of the Field of Rushes, king Merire (Pepi) is just before the sky and before the earth. King Pepi is just before that island of the earth to which he has swum and arrived there."⁴ When the righteous king has safely crossed, he furthermore finds a Solar Horus in charge of the celestial doors, who presides in

¹ The Osirian editor of the only other text of this Utterance (510), that of Pepi, has inserted Osiris over Geb here, and then incorrectly added "Pepi," making "Osiris Pepi." The text thus made nonsense, viz., "How just is king Pepi for Osiris Pepi!" The passage incidentally furnishes one of the best examples of Osirian editing. That the text had nothing to do with Osiris in this passage, but concerned solely Geb and Re, is shown by the following context: "His (the king's) boundaries exist not, his landmarks are not found; while Geb, with his arm to the sky and his (other) arm to the earth, announces king Mernere to Re."

' ² Pyr. §§ 1141-2.   ³ Pyr. § 1238.   ⁴ Pyr. § 1188.

what is evidently a building, of uncertain character, to which is appended the phrase "of righteousness."[1] Re has two barques of "Truth" or "Righteousness,"[2] and we remember that the goddess of Truth or Righteousness, a personification of one of the few abstractions existent in this early age, was a daughter of Re.

Similarly, the Morning Star, a Solar deity, takes due note of the moral status of the dead Pharaoh. "Thou (O Morning Star) makest this Pepi to sit down because of his righteousness and to rise up because of his reverence."[3] Sometimes his guiltlessness applies to matters not wholly within the moral realm from our modern point of view. Having become the son of Re, rising and setting like Re, receiving the food of Horus (son of Re), ministering to Re and rowing Re across the sky, it is said of the king: "This Pepi blasphemes not the king, he ⌈defames⌉ not Bastet, he does not make merry in the sanctuary."[4]

The moral worthiness of the deceased must of course, in accordance with the Egyptian's keen legal discernment, be determined in legal form and by legal process. We have seen that the nobles refer to the judgment in their tombs, and it would seem that even the king was subject to such judgment. Indeed not even the gods escaped it; for it is stated that every god who assists the Pharaoh to the sky "shall be justified before Geb."[5] In the same way the punishment of a refractory god is "that he shall not ascend to the house of Horus that is in the sky on that day of the (legal) hearing."[6] In a series of three Solar Utterances concerning the two celestial reed floats,[7]

---

[1] Pyr. § 815.   [2] Pyr. §1785 b.   [3] Pyr. §1219 a.
[4] Pyr. Ut. 467.   Does the blaspheming refer to Re? For Pepi is himself the king!
[5] Pyr. § 1327.   [6] Pyr. § 1027.   [7] Pyr. Ut. 263–5.

the last one concludes with a refrain three times uttered: "This king Pepi is justified, this king Pepi is praised, the ka of this king Pepi is praised." When we note that the second of this coherent series of three Utterances is anti-Osirian, it is evident that the justification occurring in this connection is not Osirian but Solar, like the Utterance in which it is found. This conclusion is confirmed by another Solar Utterance on the two reed floats which affirms: "This Pepi is justified, the ka of this Pepi is justified." [1]

The translated Pharaoh, who is thus declared just, continues to exhibit the same qualities in the exercise of the celestial sovereignty which he receives. "He judges justice before Re on that day of the feast, (called) 'First of the Year.' The sky is in satisfaction, the earth is in joy, having heard that king Neferkere (Pepi II) has placed justice [in the place of injustice]. They are satisfied who sit with king Neferkere in his court of justice with the just utterance which came forth from his mouth." [2] It is significant that the king exercises this just judgment in the presence of Re the Sun-god. Similarly in a Solar Utterance we find it affirmed that "king Unis has set justice therein (in the isle where he is) in the place of injustice." [3]

There can be no doubt that in the Old Kingdom the sovereignty of Re had resulted in attributing to him the moral requirements laid upon the dead in the hereafter, and that in the surviving literature of that age he is chiefly the righteous god rather than Osiris. Righteous-

---

[1] Pyr. § 929 a. [2] Pyr. §§ 1774 a–1776 b.
[3] Pyr. § 265. "Justice" in both these passages may be translated also "truth" or "righteousness." As the correlated opposite means "falsehood," it is perhaps more nearly correct to render "truth" and "falsehood."

ness is a quality which is associated with several gods in the Old Kingdom, but none of the others approaches the prominence of Re in this particular. We find the four genii, the sons of Horus, who, as we have seen, were not improbably Solar in origin, though later Osirianized, called "these four gods who live in righteousness, leaning upon their sceptres, guarding the Southland."[1] These gods are once associated with Letopolis,[2] and it is perhaps a connected fact that officiating before Khenti-yerti of Letopolis we find a god called "Expeller of Deceit," using the word for "deceit" which is correlated with "Truth or Righteousness" in the Pyramid Texts as its opposite.[3] These four sons of Horus are mortuary gods, and one of the old mortuary gods of Memphis, Sokar, possessed a barque which was called the "Barque of Truth (or Righteousness)."[4] To this barque or its presiding divinity the dead king is compared: "The tongue of this king Pepi is (that of) 'The-Righteous-One (a god) -Belonging-to-the-Barque-of-Righteousness.'"[5] The Osirian Horus once receives the epithet "the justified" in the Pyramid Texts;[6] and Osiris likewise is, though very rarely, called "Lord of Truth (or Righteousness)."[7] In connection with the Osirian litigation at Heliopolis three statements regarding the legal triumph of the king are made which, because of the legal character of the victory, may not be exclusively ethical. The passage says of the king: "He is justified through that which he has done."[8] Again, he "comes forth to the truth (or 'righteousness' in the sense of legal victory), that he may take it with him";[9] and finally the king "goes forth on this day that he may

[1] Pyr. § 1483.   [2] Pyr. § 2078.   [3] Pyr. § 2086.
[4] Pyr. § 1429 c.   [5] Pyr. § 1306 c.   [6] Pyr. § 2089 a.
[7] Pyr. § 1520 a.   [8] Pyr. § 316.   [9] Pyr. § 319.

bring the truth with him."¹ The later rapid growth of ethical teaching in the Osiris faith and the assumption of the rôle of judge by Osiris is not yet discernible in the Pyramid Age, and the development which made these elements so prominent in the Middle Kingdom took place in the obscure period after the close of the Pyramid Age. Contrary to the conclusion generally accepted at present, it was the Sun-god, therefore, who was the earliest champion of moral worthiness and the great judge in the hereafter. A thousand years later Osiris, as the victorious litigant at Heliopolis, as the champion of the dead who had legally triumphed over all his enemies, emerged as the great moral judge. In the usurpation of this rôle by Osiris we have another evidence of the irresistible process which Osirianized Egyptian religion. To these later conditions from which modern students have drawn their impressions, the current conclusion regarding the early moral supremacy of Osiris is due. The greater age of the Solar faith in this as in other particulars is, however, perfectly clear.²

These early moral aspirations had their limitations. Let us not forget that we are dealing with an age lying between five thousand and forty-five hundred years ago. The chief conquests of man in this remote age had been gained in a struggle with material forces. In this struggle he had issued a decisive victor, but nevertheless it was

¹ Pyr. § 323.
² In my *History of Egypt* I have accepted the conclusion that the Osirian litigation at Heliopolis is the incident in the career of Osiris which resulted in the introduction of powerful ethical motives into Egyptian religion. A further study of the Pyramid Texts and the collection of all the data they contain on the subject, as presented above, demonstrate in my judgment the incorrectness of this conclusion as well as the early moral superiority of the Solar religion.

amid the tangle of a host of obscuring influences into which we cannot enter here; it was, as it were, through the dust of an engrossing conflict that he had caught but faintly the veiled glory of the moral vision. Let us not imagine, then, that the obligations which this vision imposed were all-embracing or that it could include all that we discern in it. The requirements of the great judge in the hereafter were not incompatible with the grossest sensuality. Not only was sensual pleasure permitted in the hereafter as depicted by the Pyramid Texts, but positive provision was made for supplying it.[1] The king is assured of sensual gratification in the grossest terms, and we hear it said of him that he "is the man who takes women from their husbands whither he wills and when his heart desires."[2]

Nevertheless that was a momentous step which regarded felicity after death as in any measure dependent upon the ethical quality of the dead man's earthly life; and it must have been a deep and abiding moral consciousness which made even the divine Pharaoh, who was above the mandates of earthly government, amenable to the celestial judge and subject to moral requirements. This step could not have been taken at once. It is possible that even in the brief century and a half covered by the Pyramid Texts we may discern some trace of the progress of ethical consciousness as it was involving even the king in its imperious demands. We have already noted above the statement regarding the king, "This king Pepi is justified." Now, it happens that the Utterance in which this statement occurs is found in a variant

[1] In Pyr. § 123 the Pharaoh is supplied with a mistress in the hereafter.
[2] Pyr. § 510.

form in the pyramids of Unis and Teti, two kings earlier than Pepi. Neither of these earlier forms contains this statement of justification, and within a period of sixty to eighty years the editors deemed it wise to insert it.[1]

As we have so often said, it is not easy to read the spiritual and intellectual progress of a race in monuments so largely material as contrasted with literary documents. It is easy to be misled and to misinterpret the meagre indications furnished by purely material monuments. Behind them lies a vast complex of human forces and of human thinking which for the most part eludes us. Nevertheless it is impossible to contemplate the colossal tombs of the Fourth Dynasty, so well known as the Pyramids of Gizeh, and to contrast them with the comparatively diminutive royal tombs which follow in the next two dynasties, without, as we have before hinted, discerning more than exclusively political causes behind this sudden and startling change. The insertion of the Pyramid Texts themselves during the last century and a half of the Pyramid Age is an evident resort to less material forces enlisted on behalf of the departed Pharaoh as he confronted the shadow world. On the other hand, the Great Pyramids of Gizeh represent, as we have said before, the struggle of titanic material forces in the endeavor by purely material means to immortalize the king's physical body, enveloping it in a vast and impenetrable husk of masonry, there to preserve forever all that linked the spirit of the king to material life. The Great Pyramids of Gizeh, while they are to-day the most imposing surviving witnesses to the earliest emergence of organized man and the triumph of concerted effort, are

---

[1] The Utterances are 263 (Unis), 264 (Teti), and 265-6 (Pepi). Unis, the oldest king, died about 2625 B. C., and Pepi I about 2570.

likewise the silent but eloquent expression of a supreme endeavor to achieve immortality by sheer physical force. For merely physical reasons such a colossal struggle with the forces of decay could not go on indefinitely; with these reasons political tendencies too made common cause; but combined with all these we must not fail to see that the mere insertion of the Pyramid Texts in itself in the royal tombs of the last century and a half of the Pyramid Age was an abandonment of the titanic struggle with material forces and an evident resort to less tangible agencies. The recognition of a judgment and the requirement of moral worthiness in the hereafter was a still more momentous step in the same direction. It marked a transition from reliance on agencies external to the personality of the dead to dependence on inner values. Immortality began to make its appeal as a thing achieved in a man's own soul. It was the beginning of a shift of emphasis from objective advantages to subjective qualities. It meant the ultimate extension of the dominion of God beyond the limits of the material world, that he might reign in the invisible kingdom of the heart. It was thus also the first step in the long process by which the individual personality begins to emerge as contrasted with the mass of society, a process which we can discern likewise in the marvellous portrait sculpture of the Pyramid Age. The vision of the possibilities of individual character had dimly dawned upon the minds of these men of the early world; their own moral ideals were passing into the character of their greatest gods, and with this supreme achievement the development of the five hundred years which we call the Pyramid Age had reached its close.

When Egypt emerged from the darkness which followed the Pyramid Age, and after a century and a half of preparatory development reached the culmination of the Feudal Age (Twelfth Dynasty), about 2000 B. C., the men of this classic period looked back upon a struggle of their ancestors with death—a struggle whose visible monuments were distributed along a period of fifteen hundred years. The first five hundred years of this struggle was still represented by the tombs of the first two dynasties in Abydos and vicinity, but it was veiled in mist, and to the men of the Feudal Age its monuments were mingled with the memorials of the gods who once ruled Egypt. Of the thousand years which had elapsed since the Pyramid Age began, the first five hundred was impressively embodied before their eyes in that sixty-mile rampart of pyramids sweeping along the margin of the western desert. There they stretched like a line of silent outposts on the frontiers of death. It was a thousand years since the first of them had been built, and five hundred years had elapsed since the architects had rolled up their papyrus drawings of the latest, and the last group of workmen had gathered up their tools and departed. The priesthoods too, left without support, had, as we have already seen, long forsaken the sumptuous temples and monumental approaches that rose on the valley side. The sixty-mile pyramid cemetery lay in silent desolation, deeply encumbered with sand half hiding the ruins of massive architecture, of fallen architraves and prostrate colonnades, a solitary waste where only the slinking figure of the vanishing jackal suggested the futile protection of the old mortuary gods of the desert. Even at the present day no such imposing spectacle as the pyramid cemeteries of Egypt is to be found anywhere in the ancient world, and we easily recall something of the reverential awe with which they oppressed us when we first looked upon them. Do we ever realize that this impression was felt by their descendants only a few centuries after the builders had passed away? and that they were already ancient to the men of 2000 B. C.? On the minds of the men of the Feudal Age the Pyramid cemetery made a profound impression. If already in the Pyramid Age there had been some relaxation in the conviction that by sheer material force man might make conquest of immortality, the spectacle of these colossal ruins now quickened such doubts into open scepticism, a scepticism which ere long found effective literary expression.

Discernment of moral requirements had involved subjective contemplation. For the first time in history man began to contemplate *himself* as well as his destiny, to "expatiate free o'er all this scene of man." It is a ripe age which in so doing has passed beyond the unquestioning acceptance of traditional beliefs as bequeathed by the fathers. Scepticism means a long experience with inherited beliefs, much rumination on what has heretofore received unthinking acquiescence, a conscious recognition of personal power to believe or disbelieve, and thus a distinct step forward in the development of self-consciousness and personal initiative. It is only a people of ripe civilization who develop scepticism. It is never found under primitive conditions. It was a momentous thousand years of intellectual progress, therefore, of which these sceptics of the Feudal Age represented the culmination. Their mental attitude finds expression in a song of mourning, doubtless often repeated in the cemetery, and as we follow the lines we might conclude that the author had certainly stood on some elevated point over-

182 RELIGION AND THOUGHT IN ANCIENT EGYPT

looking the pyramid cemetery of the Old Kingdom as he wrote them. We possess two fragmentary versions of the song, one on papyrus, the other on the walls of a Theban tomb.[1] But the papyrus version was also copied from a tomb, for the superscription reads: "Song which is in the house (tomb-chapel) of king Intef [2] the justified, which is in front of the singer with the harp." The song reads:

> "How prosperous is this good prince! [3]
> It is a goodly destiny, that the bodies diminish,
> Passing away while others remain,
> Since the time of the ancestors,
> The gods who were aforetime,
> Who rest in their pyramids,
> Nobles and the glorious departed likewise,
> Entombed in their pyramids.
> Those who built their (tomb)-temples,
> Their place is no more.
> Behold what is done therein.
> I have heard the words of Imhotep and Hardedef, [4]

---

[1] They have been edited by W. M. MUELLER in his *Liebespoesie*. The first version is found among the love-songs of Papyrus Harris, 500, in the British Museum, pl. vi, l. 2, to pl. vii, l. 3 (part of a duplicate on a fragment of tomb wall in Leyden). See MUELLER, pls. xii-xv. The other version is in the tomb of Neferhotep, MUELLER, pl. i. For the older publications see MUELLER.

[2] This is one of the Eleventh Dynasty Intefs.

[3] Meaning the dead king in whose tomb the song was written.

[4] Imhotep was grand vizier, chief architect, and famous wise man under king Zoser of the Third Dynasty (thirtieth century B. C.). He was the first great architect in stone-masonry construction, the father of stone architecture. The futility of the massive building methods which he introduced is thus brought out with double effectiveness. He has not escaped the fate of all the rest in the Old Kingdom cemetery. Hardedef was a royal prince, son of Khufu of Gizeh, and hence connected with the greatest pyramid. He lived about a century after Imhotep. Both of them had thus become proverbial wise men a thousand years after they had passed away.

(Words) greatly celebrated as their utterances.
Behold the places thereof;
Their walls are dismantled,
Their places are no more,
As if they had never been.

"None cometh from thence
That he may tell (us) how they fare;
That he may tell (us) of their fortunes,
That he may content our heart,
Until we (too) depart
To the place whither they have gone.

"Encourage thy heart to forget it,
Making it pleasant for thee to follow thy desire,
While thou livest.
Put myrrh upon thy head,
And garments on thee of fine linen,
Imbued with marvellous luxuries,
The genuine things of the gods.

"Increase yet more thy delights,
And let [not] thy heart languish.
Follow thy desire and thy good,
Fashion thine affairs on earth
After the mandates of thine (own) heart.
(Till) that day of lamentation cometh to thee,
When the silent-hearted hears not their lamentation,
Nor he that is in the tomb attends the mourning.

"Celebrate the glad day,
Be not weary therein.
Lo, no man taketh his goods with him.
Yea, none returneth again that is gone thither."

Such were the feelings of some of these men of the Feudal Age as they looked out over the tombs of their ancestors and contemplated the colossal futility of the vast pyramid cemeteries of the Old Kingdom. Even the names of some of the wise men of a thousand years before, whose sayings had become proverbial, and who thus had attained more than a sepulchral immortality in some colossal tomb, arose in the recollection of the singer. It can hardly be a matter of chance that Imhotep, the first of the two whom the singer commemorates, was the earliest architect in stone masonry on a large scale, the father of architecture in stone. As the architect of king Zoser of the thirtieth century B. C., he was the builder of the oldest superstructure of stone masonry still surviving from the ancient world, the so-called "terraced pyramid" of Sakkara. It was a peculiarly effective stroke to revert to the tomb of this first great architect, and to find it in such a state of ruin that the places thereof were "as if they had never been." Indeed, to this day its place is unknown. Hardedef, too, the other wise man whom the poem recalls, was a son of Khufu, and therefore connected with the greatest of the pyramids. The fact, too, that these two ancient sages had survived only in their wise sayings was another illustration of the futility of material agencies as a means of immortality. At the same time the disappearance of such souls as these to a realm where they could no longer be discerned, whence none returned to tell of their fate, strikes the sombrest and most wistful note in all these lines. It is a note of which we seem to hear an echo in the East three thousand years later in the lines of Omar Khayyam:

> "Strange, is it not? that of the myriads who
> Before us passed the door of Darkness through,
> Not one returns to tell us of the Road
> Which to discover we must travel too."[1]

[1] FITZGERALD, *Rubaiyat*, 64.

Here is bared a scepticism which doubts *all* means, material or otherwise, for attaining felicity or even survival beyond the grave. To such doubts there is no answer; there is only a means of sweeping them temporarily aside, a means to be found in sensual gratification which drowns such doubts in forgetfulness. "Eat, drink, and be merry, for to-morrow we die."

The other version of the song, from the tomb of the "divine father (priest) of Amon, Neferhotep," at Thebes, is hardly as effective as the first, and unhappily is very fragmentary. It contains, however, some valuable lines which should not be overlooked.

> "How rests this just prince!
> The goodly destiny befalls,
> The bodies pass away
> Since the time of the god,
> And generations come into their places.
>
> "Re shows himself at early morn,
> Atum goes to rest in Manu.[1]
> Men beget and women conceive,
> Every nostril breathes the air.
> Morning comes, they bear numerously,
> They (the new-born) come to their (appointed) places.
>
> "Celebrate the glad day, O divine father.
> Put the finest spices together at thy nose,
> Garlands of lotus flowers at thy shoulder, at thy neck.
> Thy sister who dwells in thy heart,
> She sits at thy side.
> Put song and music before thee,
> Behind thee all evil things,
> And remember thou (only) joy.

[1] These two lines merely recall the ceaseless rising and setting of the sun. Manu is the mountain of the west.

"Till comes that day of mooring,
At the land that loveth silence,
. . . .
(Where) the heart is quiet
Of the son whom he loves.

"Celebrate the glad day, O Neferhotep, justified, divine father,
Excellent and pure of hands.
I have heard all that befell
Those . . .
Their houses are dismantled,
The place of them is no more,
They are as if they had never been,
Since the time of the god,
Those lords . . .

"[Wilt thou plant for thee pleasant trees] [1]
Upon the shore of thy pool,
That thy soul may sit under them,
That he may drink their water?
Follow thy desire wholly,
. . . .
Give bread to him who hath no field.
So shalt thou gain a good name
For the future forever. [2]

"Thou hast seen [ʳthe tombs of the greatʳ]
[ʳWhere priests offer, wearing skins ofʳ] the panther;
Their libation vessels are on the ground,
And their bread of their food-offerings.

---

[1] As MUELLER has noticed, there was some reference to the well-known mortuary grove in this lacuna; he refers to MASPERO, in *Recueil de travaux*, II, pp. 105–7; ROUGÉ, *Inscr. hierogl.*, CV; *Mém. Miss. franç.*, V, 300, 330. But I cannot agree with MUELLER in making it an injunction to equip the futile tomb with a grove equally futile, and supposing it to be an insertion by a later *orthodox* scribe. This can be avoided by making it a question.

[2] While a tomb and the grove attached to it are fruitless trouble, moral worthiness, kindness to the poor, and the resulting good name shall endure.

Songstresses ⌈weep⌉ . . .
Their mummies are set up before Re,
Their people are in lamentation without (ceasing).

". . . comes in her season;
Fate numbers his days.
Thou hast waked . . .
. . . ."

The song continues with reflections on the vanity of riches, as if in expansion of the single line in the other version referring to the fact that no man may take his goods with him when he departs. Wealth is fruitless, for the same fate has overtaken

"Those who had granaries,
Besides bread for offerings,
And those [who had none] likewise."

Hence the rich man is admonished:

"Remember thou the day
When thou art dragged
To the land of . . .
[Follow thy desire] wholly.
There is none that returns again."[1]

It is evident that the men of this age were reflecting deeply on the human state. The singer of this second version finds no hope in the contemplation of death, but suggests that it is well in any case to leave an enduring good name behind; not because it necessarily insures the good man anything in the world to come, but rather that it may abide in the minds of those who remain behind. Indeed, the obligation to a moral life imposed by the

[1] The upper ends of the remaining six lines are too fragmentary to yield any certain or connected sense.

"Great God" whose judgment is yet to come, as well as the benefits in the world of the dead, resulting from the fulfilment of this obligation, play no part in this sceptic's thought. The gods are largely ignored. The only one mentioned is the Sun-god, who appears even in connection with the mummy, where we should have expected the appearance of Osiris. Self-indulgence and a good name *on earth* hereafter may be said to summarize the teaching of these sceptics, who have cast away the teaching of the fathers.

Nevertheless there were those who rejected even these admonitions as but a superficial solution of the dark problem of life. Suppose that the good name be innocently and unjustly forfeited, and the opportunities for self-indulgence cut off by disease and misfortune. It is exactly this situation which is presented to us in one of the most remarkable documents surviving from this remote age. We may term it "The Dialogue of a Misanthrope with his Own Soul," though no ancient title has survived. The general subject is the despair resulting from the situation mentioned, a despair which turns to death as the only escape. It is perhaps hardly necessary to call attention to the remarkable choice of such a subject in so remote an age, a subject which is essentially a state of mind, the inner experience of an unjust sufferer. It is our earliest Book of Job, written some fifteen hundred years before a similar experience brought forth a similar book among the Hebrews.

The introduction narrating the circumstances which brought about this spiritual convulsion is unhappily lost.[1] The prologue of the book is therefore lacking, but some

---

[1] The document is a papyrus of the Middle Kingdom in Berlin (P. 3024). It was first published by Lepsius over fifty years ago

of the facts which it must have contained, setting forth the reasons for the reflections offered by the book, can be drawn from these reflections themselves. Our unfortunate (we never learn his name) was a man of gentle spirit who nevertheless was overtaken by blighting misfortunes. He fell sick only to be forsaken by his friends, and even by his brothers, who should have cared for him in his illness. No one proved faithful to him, and in the midst of his distress his neighbors robbed him. The good that he had done yesterday was not remembered, and although a wise man, he was repelled when he would have plead his cause. He was unjustly condemned, and his name, which should have been revered, became a stench in the nostrils of men.

At this juncture, when in darkness and despair he determines to take his own life, the document as preserved to us begins. Then, as he stands on the brink of the grave, his soul shrinks back from the darkness in horror and refuses to accompany him. In a long dialogue which now sets in, we discern the unfortunate man discoursing with himself, and conversing with his soul as with another person. The first reason for his soul's unwillingness is apprehension lest there should be no tomb in which to dwell after death. This, at first, seems strange enough in view of the scepticism with which such material preparation for death was viewed by just such men as our unfortunate proved himself to be. We soon discover, however, that this, like another which follows, was but a literary device intended to offer opportunity for ex-

(*Denkmaeler*, VI, Taf., 111–112). Its content is so difficult that it remained unintelligible until republished by ERMAN in 1896, "*Gespraech eines Lebensmueden mit seiner Seele,*" Abhandl. der koenigl. Preuss. Akad., Berlin, 1896. From ERMAN's treatise the above presentation draws substantially.

posing the utter futility of all such preparations. It would seem that the soul itself had before advised death by fire; but that it had then itself shrunk back from this terrible end. As there would be no surviving friend or relative to stand at the bier and carry out the mortuary ceremonies, the misanthrope then proceeded to adjure his own soul to undertake this office. The soul, however, now refuses death in any form and paints the terrors of the tomb. "My soul opened its mouth and answered what I had said: 'If thou rememberest burial it is mourning, it is a bringer of tears, saddening a man; it is taking a man from his house and casting him upon the height (the cemetery plateau). Thou ascendest not up that thou mayest see the sun. Those who build in red granite, who erect the ⌈sepulchre⌉ in the pyramid, those beautiful in this beautiful structure, ⌈who have become like⌉ gods, the offering-tables thereof are as empty as (those of) these weary ones who die on the dike without a survivor, (when as he lies half immersed on the shore) the flood has taken (one) end of him, the heat likewise; those to whom the fish along the shore speak (as they devour the body). Hearken to me—lo, it is good for men to hearken—follow the glad day and forget care.'"[1]

This then is the reply of the soul when the conventional view of death has been held up before it. The misanthrope has affirmed that he is fortunate "who is in his pyramid over whose coffin a survivor has stood," and he has besought his soul to be the one "who shall be my ⌈burier,⌉ who shall make offering, who shall stand at the tomb on the day of burial, that he may ⌈prepare⌉ the bed in the cemetery."[2] But like the harper in the two songs we have read, his soul remembers the dismantled

[1] Misanthrope, ll. 56–68.   [2] *Ibid.*, ll. 52–55.

tombs of the great, whose offering-tables are as empty as those of the wretched serfs dying like flies among the public works, along the vast irrigation dikes, and who lie there exposed to heat and devouring fish as they await burial. There is but one solution: to live on in forgetfulness of sorrow and drown it all in pleasure.

Up to this point the Dialogue, with its philosophy of "Eat, drink, and be merry, for to-morrow we die," has gone no further than the Song of the Harper. It now proceeds to a momentous conclusion, going far beyond that song. It undertakes to demonstrate that life, far from being an opportunity for pleasure and unbridled indulgence, is more intolerable than death. The demonstration is contained in four poems which the unhappy man addresses to his own soul. These constitute the second half of the document,[1] and are fortunately much more intelligible than the first half.[2] The first poem portrays the unjust abhorrence in which our unfortunate's name is held by the world. Each three-line strophe begins with the refrain, "My name is abhorred," and then, to enforce this statement, adduces for comparison some detestible thing from the daily life of the people, especially the notorious stench of fish and fowl so common in the life of the Nile-dweller.

THE UNJUST ABHORRENCE OF HIS NAME

"Lo, my name is abhorred,
  Lo, more than the odor of birds
  On summer days when the sky is hot.

[1] Lines 85–147.
[2] In structure these poems are as follows:
  The first has eight three-line strophes.
  The second has sixteen three-line strophes.
  The third has six three-line strophes.
  The fourth has three three-line strophes.

> "Lo, my name is abhorred,
> Lo, more than a fish-receiver
> On the day of the catch when the sky is hot.
>
> "Lo, my name is abhorred,
> Lo, more than the odor of fowl
> On the willow-hill full of geese.
>
> "Lo, my name is abhorred,
> Lo, more than the odor of fishermen
> By the shores of the marshes when they have fished.
>
> "Lo, my name is abhorred,
> Lo, more than the odor of crocodiles,
> More than sitting under the ⌈bank⌉ full of crocodiles.
>
> "Lo, my name is abhorred,
> Lo, more than a woman,
> Against whom a lie is told her husband."

Two more strophes follow, but they are too obscure to be rendered. They exhibit the same structure, and evidently were similar in content to the others. While this poem is but a reiteration of the fact that the unhappy man's name has become a stench in the nostrils of his fellows, in the second poem he turns from himself to characterize those who are responsible for his misery. He looks out over the society of his time and finds only corruption, dishonesty, injustice, and unfaithfulness even among his own kin. It is a fearful indictment, and as he utters it he asks himself in an ever-recurring refrain which opens each strophe, "To whom do I speak to-day?" His meaning probably is, "What manner of men are those to whom I speak?" and following each repetition of this question is a new condemnation.

THE CORRUPTION OF MEN

"To whom do I speak to-day?
 Brothers are evil,
 Friends of to-day are ⌜not of love⌝.

"To whom do I speak to-day?
 Hearts are thievish,
 Every man seizes his neighbor's goods.

"To whom do I speak to-day?
 The gentle man perishes,
 The bold-faced goes everywhere.

"To whom do I speak to-day?
 He of the peaceful face is wretched,
 The good is disregarded in every place.

"To whom do I speak to-day?
 When a man arouses wrath by his evil conduct,
 He stirs all men to mirth, (although) his iniquity is wicked.

"To whom do I speak to-day?
 Robbery is practised,
 Every man seizes his neighbor's (goods).

"To whom do I speak to-day?
 The pest is faithful,
 (But) the brother who comes with it becomes an enemy.

"To whom do I speak to-day?
 Yesterday is not remembered,
 Nor is . . . in this hour.

"To whom do I speak to-day?
 Brothers are evil,
 . . . .

"To whom do I speak to-day?
 Faces pass away,
 Every man with face lower than (those of) his brothers.

"To whom do I speak to-day?
Hearts are thievish,
The man upon whom one leans has no understanding.

"To whom do I speak to-day?
There are no righteous,
The land is left to those who do iniquity.

"To whom do I speak to-day?
There is dearth of the faithful,
. . . .

"To whom do I speak to-day?
There is none here of contented heart;
Go with him (the apparently contented) and he is not here.

"To whom do I speak to-day?
I am laden with wretchedness,
Without a faithful one.

"To whom do I speak to-day?
Evil smites the land,
It hath no end."

The soul of the sufferer had shrunk back from death, and, like the Song of the Harper, proposed a life of pleasure as a way of escape. Then moved by the terror of death, and the hopelessness of material preparations to meet it, the unhappy man recoiled for a moment and turned to contemplate life. The two poems we have just read depict what he sees as he thus turns. What follows is the logical rebound from any faint hope that life may be possible, to the final conviction that death alone is the release from the misery in which he is involved. This third poem is a brief hymn in praise of death. It is not an exalted contemplation of the advantages of death, such as we find fifteen hundred years later in Plato's story of the death of Socrates; nor is it comparable to the lofty pessimism of the afflicted Job; but as the earliest utterance of the unjustly afflicted, as the first cry of the righteous sufferer echoing to us from the early ages of the world, it is of unique interest and not without its beauty and its wistful pathos. It is remarkable that it contains no thought of God; it deals only with glad release from the intolerable suffering of the past and looks not forward. It is characteristic of the age and the clime to which the poem belongs, that this glad release should appear in the form of concrete pictures drawn from the daily life of the Nile-dweller.

DEATH A GLAD RELEASE

"Death is before me to-day
 [Like] the recovery of a sick man,
 Like going forth into a garden after sickness.

"Death is before me to-day
 Like the odor of myrrh,
 Like sitting under the sail on a windy day.

"Death is before me to-day
 Like the odor of lotus flowers,
 Like sitting on the shore of drunkenness.

"Death is before me to-day
 Like the course of the freshet,
 Like the return of a man from the war-galley to his house.

"Death is before me to-day
 Like the clearing of the sky,
 Like a man ⌜fowling therein toward⌝ that which he knew not.

"Death is before me to-day
 As a man longs to see his house
 When he has spent years in captivity."

In spite of the fact that these pictures are drawn from the life of a distant world, for the most part unfamiliar to us, they do not altogether fail of their effect. Life as a long sickness from which we recover at death as the convalescent enters a beautiful garden; death as the odor of myrrh borne on the fresh Nile wind, while the voyager sits beneath the bellying sail; death as the return of a war-worn wanderer in far waters approaching his home, or the glad restoration of the captive from foreign exile—these are figures of universal appeal in any age or clime.[1]

The forward glance into the ultimate future, which is so noticeably lacking in the preceding song, is the theme of the fourth poem. Each of its three strophes begins with the refrain, "He who is yonder," a common phrase, especially in the plural, "those who are yonder," for "the dead." "He who is yonder" shall himself be a god and "inflict the punishment of wickedness on the doer of it," *not*, as in the life of our misanthrope, on the innocent. "He who is yonder" embarks with the Sun-god in his celestial ship, and shall see that the best of offerings are offered to the temples of the gods, and not (by implication) be spent in corrupt rewards or diverted by thieving officials. "He who is yonder" is a respected sage, not repelled as he appeals to the corrupt officials, but directing to the Sun-god (Re) his appeals for which his daily presence with the god affords him opportunity.

---

[1] Two of the figures are obscure: "the course of the freshet" is perhaps a reference to the dry water-course comparable with life, while its sudden filling by the waters of the freshet is the welcome refreshing corresponding to death. "A man fowling therein toward that which he knew not" may perhaps refer to the approach of the hunter to unfamiliar regions. "Sitting on the shore of drunkenness" is a picture of sensual pleasure in a drinking-booth on the dike or highway, here called "the shore."

Earlier in the struggle with his soul, the sufferer had expressed the conviction that he should be justified hereafter.[1] He now returns to this conviction in this fourth poem, with which the remarkable document closes. It therefore concludes with a solution likewise found among those discerned by Job—an appeal to justification hereafter, although Job does not necessarily make this a reason for seeking death, thus making death the vestibule to the judgment-hall and therefore to be sought as soon as possible.

THE HIGH PRIVILEGES OF THE SOJOURNER YONDER

"He who is yonder
Shall seize (the culprit) as a living god,
Inflicting punishment of wickedness on the doer of it.

"He who is yonder
Shall stand in the celestial barque,
Causing that the choicest of the offerings there be given to the temples.

"He who is yonder
Shall be a wise man who has not been repelled,
Praying to Re when he speaks."

Thus longing for the glad release which death affords and confident of the high privileges he shall enjoy beyond, the soul of the unhappy man at last yields, he enters the shadow and passes on to be with "those who are yonder." In spite of the evident crudity of the composition it is not without some feeling that we watch this unknown go, the earliest human soul, into the inner chambers of which we are permitted a glimpse across a lapse of four thousand years.

[1] Lines 23-27.

It is evident that the men of the Feudal Age took great pleasure in such literary efforts. This particular Berlin papyrus was copied by a book-scribe, whose concluding remark is still legible at the end of the document: "It is finished from beginning to end like that which was found in writing."[1] He copied it therefore from an older original, and doubtless many such copies were to be found on the shelves of the thinking men of the time. The story of the Misanthrope was one which owed its origin to individual experiences through which the men of this time were really passing, and they found profit in perusing it. It is a distinct mark in the long development of self-consciousness, the slow process which culminated in the emergence of the individual as a moral force, an individual appealing to conscience as an ultimate authority at whose mandate he may confront and arraign society. In this document, then, we discern the emergence of a new realm, the realm of social forces; for while it is the tragedy of the individual unjustly afflicted, his very affliction places him in the inexorable grip of social forces, calling for a crusade of social righteousness. The dawn of that social crusade and the regeneration which followed are still to be considered.

[1] Lines 154-5.

LECTURE VII

THE SOCIAL FORCES MAKE THEIR IMPRESSION ON RELIGION —THE RISE OF SOCIAL REFORMERS—THE EARLIEST SOCIAL REGENERATION

THE story of the Misanthrope, although that of an *individual* experience, nevertheless involves contemplation of society to whose failings this individual experience of the writer was largely due. But the subject himself remained the chief or exclusive concern. On the other hand, concern for social misfortune, the ability to contemplate and discern the unworthiness of men, the calamities that befall society, and the chronic misery which afflicts men as a body also appear as the subject of dark and pessimistic reflections in this remarkable age of growing self-consciousness and earliest disillusionment. A priest of Heliopolis, named Khekheperre-sonbu, born under Sesostris II (1906–1887 B. C.), gave expression to his sombre musings on society in a composition which was still circulating some four hundred years later when a scribe of the Eighteenth Dynasty copied it upon a board now preserved in the British Museum.[1] It is of especial interest, as indicating at the outset that such men of the Feudal Age were perfectly conscious that they were thinking upon new lines, and that they had departed far

---

[1] British Museum, 5645. Although long exhibited, its content was first discerned and published by GARDINER, in his *Admonitions of an Egyptian Sage*, as an Appendix, pp. 95–112 and pls. 17–18. The above rendering is chiefly that of GARDINER.

from the wisdom of the fathers. The little tractate reads as follows:

"The collection of words, the gathering of sayings, the pursuit of utterances with searching of heart, made by the priest of Heliopolis, . . . Khekheperre-sonbu, called Onkhu. He says: 'Would that I had unknown utterances, sayings that are unfamiliar, even new speech that has not occurred (before), free from repetitions, not the utterance of what has ⸢long⸣ passed, which the ancestors spake. I squeeze out my breast[1] for what is in it, in dislodging all that I say; for it is but to repeat what has been said when what has (already) been said has been said. There is no ⸢support⸣ for the speech of the ancestors when the descendants find it. . . .'"

"'I have spoken this in accordance with what I have seen, beginning with the first men down to those who shall come after. Would that I might know what others have not known, even what has not been repeated, that I might speak them and that my heart might answer me; that I might make clear to it (my heart) concerning my ill, that I might throw off the burden that is on my back. . . .'"

"'I am meditating on the things that have happened, the events that have occurred in the land. Transformations go on, it is not like last year, one year is more burdensome than the next. . . . Righteousness is cast out, iniquity is in the midst of the council-hall. The plans of the gods are violated, their dispositions are disregarded. The land is in distress, mourning is in every place, towns and districts are in lamentation. All men alike are under wrongs; as for respect, an end is made of it. The lords of quiet are disquieted. A morning comes every day and

[1] Literally "body" or "belly," the seat of mind.

turns back again to what has been (formerly). When I would speak ⌈thereof⌉, my limbs are heavy laden. I am distressed because of my heart, it is suffering to hold my peace concerning it. Another heart would bow down, (but) a brave heart in distress is the companion of its lord. Would that I had a heart able to suffer. Then would I rest in it. I would load it with words of . . . that I might dislodge through it my malady.'"

"He said to his heart: 'Come then, my heart, that I may speak to thee and that thou mayest answer for me my sayings and mayest explain to me that which is in the land. . . . I am meditating on what has happened. Calamities come in to-day, to-morrow ⌈afflictions⌉ are not past. All men are silent concerning it, (although) the whole land is in great disturbance. Nobody is free from evil; all men alike do it. Hearts are sorrowful. He who gives commands is as he to whom commands are given; the heart of both of them is content. Men awake to it in the morning daily, (but) hearts thrust it not away. The fashion of yesterday therein is like to-day and resembles it ⌈because of⌉ many things. . . . There is none so wise that he perceives, and none so angry that he speaks. Men awake in the morning to suffer every day. Long and heavy is my malady. The poor man has no strength to save himself from him that is stronger than he. It is painful to keep silent concerning the things heard, (but) it is suffering to reply to the ignorant man. To criticise an utterance causes enmity, (for) the heart receives not the truth, and the reply to a matter is not endured. All that a man desires is his own utterance. . . .'"

"'I speak to thee, my heart; answer thou me, (for) a heart assailed is not silent. Lo, the affairs of the servant are like (those of) the master. Manifold is the burden upon thee.'"

Here is a man deeply stirred by the corruption of his fellows. He contemplates society as a whole, and while he constantly gives expression to his own misery in view of such a prospect, it is not his own suffering which is the chief burden of his utterance. His concern is for society, shackled by its own inertia, incapable of discerning its own misery, or, if at all conscious of it, without the initiative to undertake its own regeneration. Many of his reflections might find appropriate place in the mouth of a morally sensitive social observer of our own times. It is evident, then, that we have reached an age when for the first time in history men have awakened to a deep sense of the moral unworthiness of society. Nor was this conviction confined to the reflections of an humble Heliopolitan priest. It speaks also in the disillusionment of Amenemhet I, the great founder of the dynasty under which these momentous developments in thought were taking place. He strikes the same sombre note to which, as we have seen, even the harper at their feasts attuned his instrument. This king has left us a brief word of counsel addressed to his son, Sesostris I, who was to succeed him—counsel very evidently uttered after a base attempt upon the old king's life by those whom he trusted.[1]

---

[1] The text is preserved in seven corrupt hieratic manuscripts of the Empire dating from the age near the end of the reign of Ramses II. The latest and best treatment and text are by GRIFFITH (*Zeitschr. für aegyptische Sprache*, 34, 35–49). An excellent translation of the clearer passages by ERMAN in *Aus den Papyrus des koeniglichen Museums zu Berlin*, 44–45. The above version is indebted to both; see BAR, I, 474–483. For the old bibliography see MASPERO, *Dawn of Civilization*, 467, n. 2.

"He saith, while distinguishing righteousness,
For his son . . . .
. . . .
Hearken to that which I say to thee,
That thou mayest be king of the earth,
That thou mayest be ruler of the lands,
That thou mayest increase good.
⌈Harden⌉ thyself against all subordinates.
The people give heed to him who terrorizes them.
Approach them not alone,
Fill not thy heart with a brother,
Know not a friend,
Nor make for thyself intimates,
Wherein there is no end.
When thou sleepest, guard for thyself thine own heart;
For a man has no people
In the day of evil.
I gave to the beggar, I nourished the orphan;
I admitted the insignificant as well as him who was of great account.
(But) he who ate my food made insurrection;
He to whom I gave my hand aroused fear therein."

This is all followed by the story of the attempt on his life, an incident which accounts to some extent for the disillusionment of the embittered old king.

The unrelieved pessimism of the Misanthrope, of our Heliopolitan priest, and of Amenemhet I was not, however, universal. There were men who, while fully recognizing the corruption of society, nevertheless dared dream of better days. Another moral prophet of this great age has put into dramatic setting not only his passionate arraignment of the times, but also constructive admonitions looking toward the regeneration of society and the golden age that might ensue. This, perhaps the most remarkable document of this group of social and moral tractates of the Feudal Age, may be called the Admonitions of Ipuwer.[1] The beginning of the papyrus containing the narrative introduction setting forth the circumstances under which the sage utters his reflections is unfortunately lost. The situation in its chief externals is, however, clear. The wise man Ipuwer, in the presence of the king himself and some others, possibly the assembled court, delivers a long and impassioned arraignment of the times concluding with counsel and admonition. A brief rejoinder by the king follows, and a few words of reply by the sage conclude the pamphlet. Of the long oration by the wise man, constituting the bulk of the document, over two-thirds is occupied by this arraignment; that is, nearly ten out of nearly fourteen pages. This indictment displays no logical arrangement of content, though there has been evident effort to dispose the utterances of the sage in strophic form, each strophe beginning with the same phrase, just as in the poems of the Misanthrope. In the following paragraphs we shall endeavor to summarize by subjects the chief content of the arraignment, with sufficient quotation to indicate the character of the wise man's utterances. The fragmentary condition of the papyrus, and the intense difficulty

[1] So GARDINER. A papyrus in the Leiden Museum, No. 344. It is 378 centimetres long and 18 centimetres high, and contains seventeen pages of writing. Although early published by LEEMANS in his *Aegyptische Monumenten* (pls. cv-cxiii), it is in such a bad state of preservation, and is furthermore so obscure and difficult in language and subject-matter, that it resisted the attempts of scholars to determine its content until 1903, when H. O. LANGE published a sketch of the document, with selected translations, showing it to be a socio-prophetic tractate: *Prophezeiungen eines aegyptischen Weisen*, in *Sitzungsber. der Kgl. Preuss. Akad.*, 1903, 601 ff. In 1909 the papyrus was published *in extenso*, in what will remain the standard edition, by ALAN H. GARDINER (*The Admonitions of an Egyptian Sage*, Leipzig, 1909), with fuller discussion and closer determination of the exact character of the document.

of the language employed make a continuous translation, even with copious commentary, quite out of the question.[1]

With searching vision the sage sweeps his eye over the organized life of the Nile-dwellers and finds all in confusion. Government is practically suspended, "the laws of the judgment-hall are cast forth, men walk upon [them] in the public places, the poor break them open in the midst of the streets. Indeed, the poor man (thus) attains to the power of the Divine Ennead; that (old and respected) procedure of the Houses of the Thirty (Judges) is divulged. Indeed, the great judgment-hall is ⌈thronged⌉, poor men go and come in the Great Houses (law-courts)" (6, 9–12). "Indeed, as for the ⌈splendid⌉ judgment-hall, its writings are carried away; the private office that was is exposed. . . . Indeed, departmental offices are opened, their writings are carried away,[2] (so that) serfs become lords of ⌈serfs⌉. Indeed, officials are slain, their writings are carried away. Woe is me for the misery of this time. Indeed, the scribes of the ⌈produce⌉, their writings are rejected; the grain of Egypt is any comer's" (6, 5–9). "Behold, the district councils of the land are expelled from the land, the . . . are expelled from the royal houses" (7, 9–10).

This disorganization of government is due to a state of violence and warfare within the land. "A man smites his brother of the same mother. What is to be done?"

[1] The above translations are chiefly those of GARDINER, who has been commendably cautious in his renderings. Besides his own thorough work on the document, he has incorporated the proverbially penetrating observations and renderings of SETHE.

[2] This was particularly heinous from the orderly Egyptian's point of view; the withdrawing of writings and records from the public offices for purposes of evidence or consultation was carefully regulated. The regulations governing the vizier's office have survived; see BAR, II, 684.

(5, 10). "Behold a man is slain by the side of his brother, while he (the brother) ⌈forsakes⌉ him to save his own limbs" (9, 3). "A man regards his son as his enemy" (1, 5). "A man goes to plough bearing his shield. . . . Indeed, . . . the archer is ready, the violent is in every place. There is no man of yesterday" (2, 2). "Behold the man (who gains) a noble lady as wife, her father protects him; he who is without [such protection], they slay him" (8, 8–9). "Blood is everywhere; there is no ⌈lack⌉ of death; the swathing (of the dead) speaks, before one comes near it" (2, 6). "Behold a few lawless men are endeavoring to deprive the land of the kingship. Behold men are endeavoring to revolt against the Uræus (the royal serpent) . . . which pacifies the Two Lands" (7, 2–4). "Indeed, Elephantine and ⌈Thinis⌉ are the [⌈domain⌉] of Upper Egypt, (but) civil war pays no revennes" (3, 10–11).

To this condition of disorganization and revolt within are added the terrors of foreign invasion. "Indeed, the desert is in the land; the districts (of Egypt) are devastated; foreign bowmen come to Egypt" (3, 1). "Indeed, the Marshes (of the Delta) throughout are not hidden. Although Lower Egypt is proud of (its) trodden highways, what is to be done? . . . Behold, it is ⌈in the hand⌉ of those who knew it not like those who knew it. Asiatics are skilled in the workmanship of the Marshes" (4, 5–8).

A prey to internal disorder and revolt, helpless before the raids of the Asiatics on the eastern frontiers of the Delta, the property of Egypt is destroyed and the economic processes of the land cease. "Behold, all the craftsmen, they do no work; the enemies of the land impoverish its crafts. [Behold, he who reaped] the har-

SOCIAL FORCES AND RELIGION 207

vest knows naught of it; he who has not ploughed [⌈fills his granaries. When the harvest⌉] occurs, it is not reported. The scribe [⌈idles in his bureau, there is no work for⌉] his hands therein" (9, 6-8). "Indeed, when the Nile overflows, no one ploughs for him (the Nile). Every man says, 'We know not what has happened in the land'" (2, 3). "Behold, cattle are left straying; there is none gathering them together. Every man brings for himself those that are branded with his name" (9, 2-3). As meat thus disappears, men eat "of herbs washed down with water.... Indeed, grain has perished on every side. Men are deprived of clothing, ⌈perfumes⌉, and ointments. All men say, 'There is none.' The storehouse is laid waste; its keeper is stretched on the ground" (6, 1-4). "Civil war pays no taxes. Scanty are ⌈grain⌉, charcoal, ...¹ the labor of the craftsmen.... For what is a treasury without its revenues?" (3, 10-11).

Under such economic conditions at home, foreign commerce decays and disappears. "Men sail not northward to [Byb]los to-day. What shall we do for cedars for our mummies, with the tribute of which priests are buried; and with the oil of which [princes] are embalmed as far as Keftyew.² They return no more. Scanty is gold, ended are the ... of all crafts. ... What a great thing that the natives of the oases (still) come bearing their festal produce!" (3, 6-9).³

Such conditions might be expected, for the public safety of men and merchandise has vanished. "Although the

---
¹ Three sorts of wood follow.
² Vocalize Kaftoyew, Caphtor (as first suggested by SPIEGELBERG), that is Crete.
³ This last remark is of course ironical in reference to the fact that the only traffic with the outside world left to Egypt is the scanty produce of the oases which still filters in.

roads are guarded, men sit in the thickets until the benighted traveller comes, in order to seize his burden. That which is upon him is taken away. He is beaten with blows of a stick and wickedly slain" (5, 11-12). Indeed, the land turns around (the order of things is overturned) as does a potter's wheel. He who was a robber is lord of wealth, [⌈the rich man⌉] is (now) one plundered (2, 8-9). "Indeed, chests of ebony are smashed and luxurious acacia-wood is split into ⌈billets⌉" (3, 4-6). "Indeed, gates, columns, and ⌈walls⌉ are burned up" (2, 10). As in the Song of the Harper and the despair of the Misanthrope, the provisions for the dead are violated and serve no purpose. "Behold, though one be buried as a (royal) falcon on the bier, that which the pyramid concealed (the sepulchre) has become empty" (7, 2). When even the royal tombs are not respected men make but little attempt to build a tomb. "Indeed, many dead are buried in the river; the stream is a tomb and the embalming place has become a stream" (2, 6-7). "Those who were in the embalming place are laid away on the high ground" (instead of in a tomb) (4, 4). "Behold, the owners of tombs are driven out upon the high ground."

Thus, as the figure of the "potter's wheel" suggests, all is overturned. Social conditions have suffered complete upheaval. In the longest series of utterances all similarly constructed, in the document, the sage sets forth the altered conditions of certain individuals and classes of society, each utterance contrasting what was with what now is. "Behold, he who had no yoke of oxen is (now) possesser of a herd; and he who found no plough-oxen for himself is (now) owner of a herd. Behold, he who had no grain is (now) owner of granaries; and he who used to fetch grain for himself, (now) has it issued (from his own granary)" (9, 3-5). "Behold, the owner of wealth (now) passes the night thirsting (instead of banqueting); and he who used to beg for himself his dregs is now owner of ⌜overflowing⌝ bowls. Behold, the owners of robes are (now) in rags; and he who wove not for himself is (now) owner of fine linen" (7, 10-12). Thus the sage goes on with one contrast after another. In such a state as this society is perishing. "Men are few; he who lays away his fellow in the earth is everywhere" (2, 13-14). "There is dearth of women and no conception (of children); Khnum (creator of man) fashions not (men) by reason of the state of the land."

In the general ruin moral decadence is, of course, involved, though it is not emphasized as the cause of the universal misery. "The man of virtues walks in mourning by reason of what has happened in the land" (1, 8); others say, "If I knew where the god is, then would I make offerings to him" (5, 3). "Indeed, [righteousness] is in the land (only) in this its name; what men do, in appealing to it, is iniquity"[1] (5, 3-4). Little wonder that there is universal despair. "Indeed, mirth has perished, it is no longer made; it is sighing that is in the land, mingled with lamentations" (3, 13-14). "Indeed, great and small [say], 'I would that I might die.' Little children say, 'Would there were none to keep me alive'" (4, 2-3). "Indeed, all small cattle, their hearts weep; the cattle sigh by reason of the state of the land" (5, 5). The sage cannot view all this dispassionately; he, too, is

[1] The restoration of "righteousness" is due to SETHE, and in view of its frequent occurrence, as the opposite of the word here used as "inquity" (ysft), from the Pyramid Texts on, the restoration fits the context admirably, but GARDINER states that the traces in the lacuna do not favor the restoration. The original hieratic of the passage is not included in his publication.

deeply affected by the universal calamity and prays for the end of all. "Would that there might be an end of men, that there might be no conception, no birth. If the land would but cease from noise, and strife be no more" (5, 12–6, 1). He even chides himself that he has not endeavored to save the situation before. "Would that I had uttered my voice at that time, that it might save me from the suffering wherein I am" (6, 5). "Woe is me for the misery in this time!" (6, 8).

Such is the dark picture painted by the Egyptian sage. This arraignment, occupying, as we have said, nearly two-thirds of the document as preserved, must be regarded as setting forth the conditions in Egypt at a very definite time. The close relationship in language, thought, and point of view between this tractate of Ipuwer and the other social pamphlets known to belong to the Feudal Age, leave little question as to the date of our document. The unhappy state of Egypt depicted by the sage must have existed in the obscure and little-known period immediately preceding the Feudal Age (Middle Kingdom).

As might be imagined from the intense grief with which Ipuwer views the misery of the time, he is not content to leave his generation in this hopeless state. He now turns to exhortation, urging his countrymen first to destroy the enemies of the king. Five short utterances (10, 6–11) begin with the words: "Destroy the enemies of the august residence" (of the king), although the papyrus is too fragmentary at this point to determine clearly what followed each repetition of the injunction. At least eight similar injunctions follow, each beginning with the word "Remember!" (10, 12–11, 10) and calling upon all men to resume all sacred observances on behalf of the gods. This second group of exhortations is gradually involved in ever-increasing obscurity as the fragmentary condition of the papyrus grows worse. Out of a large lacuna at last [1] there emerges the most important passage in the entire speech of the sage, and one of the most important in the whole range of Egyptian literature.

In this remarkable utterance the sage looks forward to the restoration of the land, doubtless as a natural consequence of the admonitions to reform which he has just laid upon the hearts of his countrymen. He sees the ideal ruler for whose advent he longs. That ideal king once ruled Egypt as the Sun-god, Re, and as the sage recalls that golden age, he contrasts it with the iniquitous reign under which the land now suffers. "He brings cooling to the flame. It is said he is the shepherd [2] of all men. There is no evil in his heart. When his herds are few, he passes the day to gather them together, their hearts being fevered.[3] Would that he had discerned their character in the first generation. Then would he have smitten evil. He would have stretched forth his arm against it. He would have smitten the ⌜seed⌝ thereof and their inheritance. . . . Where is he to-day? Doth he sleep perchance? Behold his might is not seen" (11, 13–12, 6).

While there is no unquestionably predictive element in this passage, it is a picture of the ideal sovereign, the righteous ruler with "no evil in his heart," who goes about like a "shepherd" gathering his reduced and thirsty herds.

---

[1] Latter part of p. 11.
[2] Or "herdman." The Sun-god is called "a valiant herdman who drives his cattle" in a Sun-hymn of the Eighteenth Dynasty (see below, p. 316), and this, it seems to me, makes quite certain GARDINER's conclusion (on other grounds) that this passage is a description of the reign of Re.
[3] This probably means thirsty, perhaps a symbol for afflicted. Compare the hearts of the cattle "weeping" above, p. 209.

Such a righteous reign, like that of David, has been, and may be again. The element of hope, that the advent of the good king is imminent, is unmistakable in the final words: "Where is he to-day? Doth he sleep perchance? Behold his might is not seen." With this last utterance one involuntarily adds, "as yet." The peculiar significance of the picture lies in the fact that, if not the social programme, at least the social ideals, the golden dream of the thinkers of this far-off age, already included the ideal ruler of spotless character and benevolent purposes who would cherish and protect his own and crush the wicked. Whether the coming of this ruler is definitely predicted or not, the vision of his character and his work is here unmistakably lifted up by the ancient sage—lifted up in the presence of the living king and those assembled with him, that they may catch something of its splendor. This is, of course, Messianism nearly fifteen hundred years before its appearance among the Hebrews.[1]

[1] LANGE first called attention to the Messianic character of this passage. His interpretation, however, was that the passage definitely *predicts* the coming of the Messianic king. GARDINER has successfully opposed LANGE's conclusion as far as *prediction* is concerned, and by his full and careful commentary has contributed much to our understanding of the passage. But no student of Hebrew prophecy can follow GARDINER in his next step, viz., that by the elimination of the predictive element we deprive the document of its prophetic character. This is simply to import a modern English meaning of the word prophecy as *prediction* into the interpretation of these ancient documents, particularly Hebrew literature. GARDINER's final conclusion is: "I must once more affirm that there is no certain or even likely trace of prophecies in any part of this book" (*Admonitions*, p. 17). In the same paragraph he states the "specific problem" of the document to be "the conditions of social and political well-being." This is, of course, the leading theme of Hebrew prophecy. On the basis of any sufficient definition of Hebrew prophecy, including the contemplation of social and political evils, and admonitions for their amelioration, the utterances of

In the mind of the sage the awful contrast between the rule of the ideal king and that of the living Pharaoh in whose presence he stands now calls forth the fiercest denunciation of his sovereign. Like Nathan[1] with his biting words, "Thou art the man," he places the responsibility for all that he has so vividly recalled upon the shoulders of the king. "Taste, Knowledge, and Righteousness are with thee," he says, (but) "it is strife which thou puttest in the land, together with the sound of tumult. Lo, one makes attack upon another. Men conform to that which thou hast commanded. If three men go upon a road, they are found to be two, (for) they who are many slay the few. Is there a herdman who loves death, (that is, for his herds)? Wherefore thou com-

---

Ipuwer are prophecy throughout (see *infra*, p. 215). With reference to the "Messianic" passage above, its Messianic character does not in the slightest depend upon its *predictive* character. GARDINER is surely right (against LANGE) in making the long arraignment not prediction, but a description of actually existent conditions. The admonitions which follow, however, definitely look to the future, in which the sage expects the people to carry out his injunctions. The "Messianic" passage follows directly upon these admonitions, and itself is followed by a rebuke to the king merging into a picture which, in GARDINER's words, describes "the joy and prosperity of the land in a happier age" (*ibid.*, p. 87). Indeed in GARDINER's own opinion the "Messianic" passage concludes with a "return to a consideration of the future prospects of Egypt," so that at the end "we touch firm ground in three sentences that clearly refer to the looked-for (but not necessarily prophesied) redeemer: 'Where is he to-day? Doth he sleep perchance? Behold ye, his might is not seen'" (*ibid.*, p. 80). The parenthesis is GARDINER's, and what he means is, of course, that the "redeemer" is looked for, but not necessarily *predicted*. It is solely this entirely insufficient conception of Hebrew prophecy as "prediction" which eventuates in GARDINER's conclusion, "that there is too much uncertainty about the matter for it to be made the basis of any far-reaching conclusions as to the influence of Egyptian upon Hebrew literature" (*ibid.*, p. 15). The "uncer-

[1] The similarity was noticed by GARDINER.

mandest to make answer: 'It is because one man loves, (but) another hates' . . . (Nay, I say) thou hast (so) done as to bring forth these things. Thou hast spoken lies" (12, 12–13, 2). Having thus given the king the lie in response to his supposed reply, the wise man for a moment reverts to description of the desolate condition of society which occupied him in the long arraignment. The progress of his thought, however, is toward the future betterment to which he admonished after the conclusion of the arraignment, and his bitter denunciation of the king; now, therefore, the misery for which he is responsible merges into a final picture of "joy and prosperity" (13, 9–14, 5) in eight strophes, each beginning with a refrain of somewhat uncertain meaning.

The sage has completed his long address, and the king now actually replies, though we are unable to recover it from the broken fragments of the tattered page on which

---

tainty," as GARDINER here specifies it, concerns solely LANGE's interpretation of the "Messianic" passage as predictive; though even, according to GARDINER, the latter part of the "Messianic" passage looks forward to a "redeemer" yet to come. The Messianic vision with the Hebrew prophets was often but a great hope, sometimes rising to conviction that the hope would be realized. It was a vision toward the realization of which they desired to contribute. It was but an early form of social idealism, which evidently began (so far as we know) in Egypt, and emerged in lofty form among the Hebrews also. A unique detachment and capacity to contemplate society, emerging for the first time in history in the Feudal Age in Egypt, produced these social tractates above discussed. If the story of the Two Brothers, after centuries of circulation in Egypt, reached Palestine to find embodiment in the tale of Joseph, it is more than possible that the pamphlets of Ipuwer and the men of his class similarly entered Palestine and suggested to the idealists of Israel the conception of the righteous king and redeemer. I ought, perhaps, to add that in a letter to me GARDINER disclaims regarding prediction as constituting "prophecy," but I have had to deal with his argument as I found it in his admirable volume.

it appears. A brief reply of Ipuwer ensues, beginning, "That which Ipuwer said when he replied to the majesty of the sovereign." It is very obscure, but seems to remind the king ironically that he has but done what the inertia and indifference of a corrupt generation desired, and here, as Gardiner shows, the tractate probably ended.

In recognizing the depths to which a degenerate and corrupt society and government have descended, our sage has much in common with the Misanthrope. The latter, however, found his individual fortunes so fatally involved in the general catastrophe that there was no hope, and he desired death as the only solution. Ipuwer, on the other hand, quite unmistakably looks toward a future redemption of society. The appearance in this remote age of the necessary detachment and the capacity to contemplate society, things before unknown in the thought of man, is a significant phenomenon. Still more significant, however, is this vision of the possible redemption of society, and the agent of that redemption as a righteous king, who is to shield his own and to purge the earth of the wicked. This is but the earliest emergence of a social idealism which among the Hebrews we call "Messianism." Such a conception might go far in the early East. After centuries of circulation in Egypt, the tale picturing the trial of the virtue of a good youth, as we have it in the Story of the Two Brothers, passed over into Palestine, to be incorporated in the mosaic which has descended to us as the story of Joseph. How such materials migrated among the peoples of the eastern Mediterranean has been demonstrated by the recent recovery of the Aramaic original of the Story of Akhikar. Under these circumstances it is more than possible that the imagination of the literary prophets of the Hebrews was first touched by some knowledge of the Egyptian vision of the ideal age and the ideal king set forth in such a tractate as that of Ipuwer, and wandering into Palestine, as did the Tale of the Two Brothers.

We see, then, that not all of the social thinkers at the court of the Pharaoh in the Feudal Age shared the unqualified pessimism which we had thus far found in their earlier teachings; nor, on the other hand, did they follow exclusively the fair but elusive vision of this Messianic dreamer. Not an ideal king only, but a body of just officials should usher in the era of social justice in the thought of some. The men of this school as they scanned life, held wholesome and practical principles of right living applicable to the daily situation of the average member of the official class. These views have found expression in at least two tractates which have descended to us: *The Eloquent Peasant* and the *Wisdom of Ptahhotep*. The first, whose author, as so commonly in this impersonal age, we do not know, is in the form of a picturesque Oriental tale, conceived solely to furnish a dramatic setting for a series of disquisitions on the proper character and spirit of the just official, and the resulting social and administrative justice toward the poor. It is not a little interesting to discern this ancient thinker of four thousand years ago wrestling with a difficulty which has since then continued to be one of the most refractory problems of all administrators in the East, a problem which has not been wholly solved even under the skilled and experienced administration of England in Egypt at the present day.

The tale of the Eloquent Peasant is as follows.[1] A

[1] The tale of the Eloquent Peasant is preserved in six papyri, three of which are now in the Berlin Museum (P. 10499, P. 3023, P. 3025); one in the British Museum (Papyrus Butler 527, Brit. Mus., No.

peasant of the Fayum region in the Natron district, living in a village called the Salt-Field, loads a small train of donkeys with the produce of his village and goes down to Heracleopolis, near the mouth of the Fayum, to trade for grain. On the way thither he is obliged to pass the establishment of one Thutenakht, a subordinate official among the people of Rensi,[1] who was grand steward of the Pharaoh himself, Heracleopolis being the royal residence at the time in which the action is placed (Ninth or Tenth Dynasty). Now, when Thutenakht sees the donkeys of the peasant approaching, he at once devises a plan for seizing them. Sending a servant hastily to the house, he secures thence some pieces of linen, which he spreads out in the highway so as to fill it entirely from the edge of the grain-field on the upper side to the water of the canal on the lower. The unsuspecting peasant approaches, as the tale, with a discernible touch of the writer's indignation, states, "on the way belonging to every one," which Thutenakht has thus blocked. Fearing the water below, the peasant turns upward to skirt the edge of the grain-

---

10274, *recto*, containing only forty lines); and two in the Amherst collection (consisting of fragments belonging to Berlin, P. 3023 and P. 3025). The Berlin papyri, P. 3023 and P. 3025, were published by LEPSIUS, *Denkmaeler*, VI, 108–110. A final standard publication, including all three of the Berlin papyri, was issued by the Berlin Museum in 1908 (*Die Klagen des Bauern*, bearbeitet von F. VOGELSANG und ALAN H. GARDINER, Leipzig, 1908). It contains a careful translation. See also GARDINER, *Eine neue Handschrift des Sinuhegedichtes* (*Sitzungsber. der Kgl. Preuss. Akad.*, 1907, p. 142), on the discovery of Berlin P. 10499. Papyrus Butler was published by GRIFFITH in *Proceedings of the Soc. of Bibl. Arch.*, XIV, 1892, pp. 451 ff. The Amherst fragments were published by NEWBERRY in *The Amherst Papyri*, London, 1899.

[1] This name was formerly read "Meruitensi." The proper reading, "Rensi," was established by SETHE, *Zeitschr. für aegypt. Sprache*, 49, 95 ff.

field. As the donkeys pass, one of them nips a mouthful of the tempting grain, at once affording the wily Thutenakht the opportunity he desired. The peasant pathetically maintains the attitude and the speech of deprecatory but not servile courtesy, until with loud complaint Thutenakht seizes the asses. Thereupon the peasant repeats his former courteous remonstrance, but adds a bold protest. "My way is right. One side is blocked. I bring my ass along the edge thereof, and thou seizest him because he has plucked a mouthful of the grain. Now, I know the lord of this domain. It belongs to the grand steward, Meru's son, Rensi. Now, it is he who drives off every robber in this whole land. Shall I then be robbed in his domain!" Infuriated by the peasant's boldness, Thutenakht seizes a branch of green tamarisk, mercilessly beats his victim, and, in spite of the peasant's cries and protests, drives off the asses to his own quarters. After four days of fruitless pleading for the return of the asses, the unhappy peasant, all the time knowing that his family at home is on the verge of starvation, determines to apply to the grand steward himself, on whose domain the outrage occurred. He is the more encouraged in so doing by the proverbial reputation for justice which the grand steward enjoys. As the peasant approaches the city, he fortunately meets the grand steward issuing from the shore-gate of his estate and going down to embark in his state barge on the canal. By the most ceremonious politeness and complete command of the current diplomacy of address, the peasant gains the ear of the great man for a moment as he passes, so that he sends a body-servant to hear the peasant's story. When the servant has returned and communicated Thutenakht's theft to Rensi, the grand steward lays the affair before his suite of officials.

Their reply is the author's skilfully created occasion for bringing before the reader, without comment, the current and conventional treatment of such complaints of the poor in official circles. The colleagues of the grand steward at once range themselves on the side of their subordinate, the thievish Thutenakht. They reply to Rensi, with much indifference, that the case is probably one of a peasant who has been paying his dues to the wrong superior officer, and that Thutenakht has merely seized dues which rightfully belonged to him. They ask with indignation, "Shall Thutenakht be punished for a little natron and a little salt? (Or at most) let it be commanded him to replace it and he will replace it." It is characteristic of their class that they quite ignore the asses, the loss of which means starvation to the peasant and his family.

Meantime the peasant stands by and hears his fatal loss thus slurred over and ignored by those in authority. The grand steward meanwhile stands musing in silence. It is a tableau which epitomizes ages of social history in the East: on the one hand, the brilliant group of the great man's sleek and subservient suite, the universal type of the official class; and, on the other, the friendless and forlorn figure of the despoiled peasant, the pathetic personification of the cry for social justice. This scene is one of the earliest examples of that Oriental skill in setting forth abstract principles in concrete situations, so wonderfully illustrated later in the parables of Jesus. Seeing that the grand steward makes no reply, the peasant makes another effort to save his family and himself from the starvation which threatens them all. He steps forward and with amazing eloquence addresses the great man in whose hands his case now rests, promising him a fair voyage as he embarks on the canal and voicing the fame of the grand steward's benevolence on which he had reckoned. "For thou art the father of the orphan, the husband of the widow, the brother of the forsaken, the kilt of the motherless. Let me put thy name in this land above every good law, O leader free from avarice, great man free from littleness, who destroys falsehood and brings about truth. Respond to the cry which my mouth utters, when I speak, hear thou. Do justice, thou who art praised, whom the praised praise. Relieve my misery. Behold me, I am heavy laden; prove me, lo I am in sorrow."[1]

The grand steward is so pleased with the peasant's extraordinary readiness in speech, that he leaves him without giving any decision in his case, and proceeds at once to the court, where he says to the king: "My lord, I have found one of these peasants who is verily beautiful of speech." The king, greatly pleased, charges the grand steward to lead the peasant on without giving him a decision, in order that he may deliver himself of further addresses. The king likewise commands that what the peasant says shall be carefully written down, and that meantime he shall be supplied with food and maintenance and that a servant be sent to his village to see that his family suffers no want in the interval. As a result of these arrangements, the peasant makes no less than eight successive appeals to Rensi.

These addresses to the grand steward at first reflect the grievous disappointment of the peasant in view of the great man's reputation for unswerving justice. He therefore begins his second address with reproaches, which

[1] In the older Berlin papyrus the conclusion reads: "Count me (or 'prove me'), lo, I am few."

Rensi interrupts with threats. The peasant, like Ipuwer in his arraignment of the king, is undaunted and continues his reproof. The third speech reverts to praises like those of his first appeal to Rensi. "O grand steward, my lord! Thou art Re, lord of the sky together with thy court. All the affairs of men (are thine). Thou art like the flood (inundation), thou art the Nile that makes green the fields and furnishes the waste lands. Ward off the robber, protect the wretched, become not a torrent against him who pleads. Take heed, (for) eternity draws near. Prefer acting as it is (proverbially) said, 'It is the breath of the nostrils to do justice' (or 'right, righteousness, truth'). Execute punishment on him to whom punishment is due, and none shall be like thy correctness. Do the balances err? Does the scale-beam swerve to one side? . . . Speak not falsehood, (for) thou art great (and therefore responsible). Be not light, (for) thou art weighty. Speak not falsehood, for thou art the balances. Swerve not, for thou art a correct sum. Lo, thou art at one with the balances. If they tip (falsely) thou tippest (falsely). . . . Thy tongue is the index (of the balances), thy heart is the weight, thy two lips are the beam thereof" (ll. 140–167).

These comparisons of the grand steward's character and functions with the balances appear repeatedly in the speeches of the peasant.[1] Their lesson is evident. The norm of just procedure is in the hands of the ruling class. If they fail, where else shall it be found? It is expected that they shall weigh right and wrong and reach a just decision with the infallibility of accurate balances. They form a symbol which became widely current in Egyptian

[1] It is a comparison which the great nobles of the Feudal Age were fond of using on their tomb stelæ; *e. g.*, BAR, I, 745, 531.

life, till the scales appear as the graphic means of depicting the judgment of each soul in the hereafter. Indeed in the hands of blind Justice they have survived even into our own day. But this symbol had its origin among these social thinkers of the Feudal Age in Egypt four thousand years ago. It should be noticed, too, that the peasant reminds the grand steward of his own appearance before the judgment of the impartial balances. "Take heed," says he, "(for) eternity draws near." This is one of few appeals against injustice to the future responsibility of the oppressor. It is found once more also in this document, in the second speech of the peasant.[1]

The threats of the peasant now prove too keen for the grand steward as he stands before the palace, and he despatches two servants to flog the unhappy man. Nevertheless he awaits Rensi's coming, as he issues from the state temple of the residence, to address him in a fourth speech, and proceeds then in a fifth to even sharper denunciation. "Thou art appointed," he says, "to hear causes, to judge two litigants, to ward off the robber. But thou makest common cause with the thief. Men love thee, although thou art a transgressor. Thou art set for a dam for the afflicted, to save him from drowning."[2]

Still there is no response from Rensi, and the peasant begins a sixth address with renewed appeal to the great man's sense of justice and his reputation for benevolence. "O grand steward, my lord! ⌈Destroy⌉ falsehood, bring about justice. Bring about every good thing, destroy [every evil] thing; like the coming of satiety, that it may end hunger; (or) clothing, that it may end nakedness; like the peaceful sky after the violent tempest, that it may

[1] Berlin, P. 3023, l. 95.   [2] Ibid., ll. 234-8.

warm those who suffer cold; like fire that cooks what is raw; like water that quenches thirst." [1]

As Rensi remains unresponsive to this appeal, the wretched peasant is again goaded to denunciation. "Thou art instructed, thou art educated, thou art taught, but not for robbery. Thou art accustomed to do like all men and thy kin are (likewise) ensnared. (Thou) the rectitude of all men, art the (chief) transgressor of the whole land. The gardener of evil, waters his domain with iniquity that his domain may bring forth falsehood, in order to flood the estate with wickedness." [2] Even such denunciation seems now to leave the grand steward entirely indifferent and the peasant approaches for his seventh speech. He begins with the usual florid encomium in which the grand steward is the "rudder of the whole land according to whose command the land sails," [3] but turns soon to his own miserable condition. "My body is full, and my heart is burdened," he complains; "there is a break in the dam and the waters thereof rush out. (Thus) my mouth is opened to speak." Then as the indifference of this man of just and benevolent reputation continues, the unhappy peasant's provocation is such that the silence of the grand steward appears as something which would have aroused the speech of the most stupid and faltering of pleaders. "There is none silent whom thou wouldst not have roused to speech. There is none sleeping whom thou wouldst not have wakened. There is none unskilled whom thou wouldst not have made efficient. There is no closed mouth which thou wouldst not have opened. There is none ignorant

[1] *Ibid.*, ll. 240–8.
[2] *Ibid.*, ll. 260–5 = Berlin, P. 3025, ll. 14–20.
[3] *Ibid.*, ll. 267–8.

whom thou wouldst not have made wise. There is none foolish whom thou wouldst not have taught."[1] Unable to restrain the tide of his indignation, therefore, the peasant goes on to his eighth speech and continued denunciation. "Thy heart is avaricious; it becomes thee not. Thou robbest; it profiteth thee not. . . . The officials who were installed to ward off iniquity are a refuge for the unbridled, (even) the officials who were installed to ward off falsehood."[2] The appeal to justice, however, is not abandoned, and the peasant returns to it in the most remarkable utterances in this remarkable tractate. "Do justice for the sake of the lord of justice . . . thou (who art) Pen and Roll and Writing Palette, (even) Thoth[3] who art far from doing evil. . . . For justice (or 'righteousness, right, truth') is for eternity. It descends with him that doeth it into the grave, when he is placed in the coffin and laid in the earth. His name is not effaced on earth; he is remembered because of good. Such is the exact summation of the divine word." Upon these impressive words follows naturally the question whether, in spite of this, injustice is still possible; and so the peasant asks: "Do the balances indeed swerve? Do the scales indeed incline to one side?" Or is it merely that no decision at all has been reached to right the shameful wrong which he has suffered? And yet the just magistrate who might have righted it has been present from the beginning. "Thou hast not been sick, thou hast not fled, thou hast not ⌈hidden thyself⌉! (But) thou hast not given me requital for this good word which came out of

[1] *Ibid.*, ll. 285-8. The negative has been omitted by the scribe in the second half (the relative clause) of each one of these sentences. This is doubtless due to the customary confusion in many languages in sentences where two negatives occur.

[2] *Ibid.*, ll. 292-8. [3] God of writing and legal procedure.

the mouth of Re himself: 'Speak the truth, do the truth.[1] For it is great, it is mighty, it is enduring. The reward thereof shall find thee, and it shall follow (thee) unto blessedness hereafter.'"[2]

No response from Rensi follows these noble words. The peasant lifts up his voice again in a final despairing plea, his ninth address. He reminds the grand steward of the dangers of consorting with deceit; he who does so "shall have no children and no heirs on earth. As for him who sails with it (deceit), he shall not reach the land, and his vessel shall not moor at her haven. . . . There is no yesterday for the indifferent. There is no friend for him who is deaf to justice. There is no glad day for the avaricious. . . . Lo, I make my plea to thee, but thou hearest it not. I will go and make my plea because of thee to Anubis." In view of the fact that Anubis is a god of the dead, the peasant doubtless means that he goes to take his own life. The grand steward sends his servants to bring him back as he departs, and some unintelligible words pass between them. Meantime, Rensi "had committed to a roll every petition (of the peasant) unto [this] day." It is supposably a copy of this roll which has descended to us; but, unfortunately, the conclusion has been torn off. We can only discern that the roll prepared by Rensi's secretaries is taken by him to the king, who found "it more pleasant to (his) heart than anything in this whole land."[3] The king commands

[1] In such an utterance as this it is important to remember that "truth" is always the same word which the Egyptian employs for "right, righteousness, justice," according to the connection in which it is used. In such an injunction as this we cannot distinguish any particular one of these concepts to the exclusion of the rest.

[2] *Ibid.*, ll. 307-322. The word rendered "blessedness hereafter" means "reverence," the state of the revered dead.

[3] The same words are used regarding the vizier's wisdom in Pap. Prisse (2, 6-7). See below, p. 228.

the grand steward to decide the peasant's case, the attendants bring in the census-rolls, which determine where he officially belongs, his exact legal and social status, the number of people in his household, and the amount of his property. Less than a dozen broken words follow, from which it is probable that Thutenakht was punished, and that the possessions of that greedy and plundering official were bestowed upon the peasant.

The high ideal of justice to the poor and oppressed set forth in this tale is but a breath of that wholesome moral atmosphere which pervades the social thinking of the official class. It is remarkable, indeed, to find these aristocrats of the Pharaoh's court four thousand years ago sufficiently concerned for the welfare of the lower classes to have given themselves the trouble to issue what are very evidently propaganda for a régime of justice and kindness toward the poor. They were pamphleteers in a crusade for social justice. They have made this particular pamphlet, too, very pleasant reading for the patrician class to whom it was directed. In spite of the constant obscurity of the language, the florid style, and the bold and extreme figures of speech, it enjoyed a place as literature of a high order in its day. It is evidently in the approved style of its age, and the pungent humor which here and there reaches the surface could but enhance the literary reputation of the tractate in the estimation of the humor-loving Egyptians. But it was literature with a moral purpose.

It is probable that the Wisdom of Ptahhotep,[1] the other

---

[1] The Wisdom of Ptahhotep is preserved in five manuscripts: (1) the Papyrus Prisse in the Bibliothèque Nationale, Paris, Nos. 183–194; (2) the three papyri in the British Museum, Nos. 10371, 10435, and 10509; a wooden writing-tablet, or board, in the Cairo Museum, known as the Tablette Carnarvon, No. 41790. The Papyrus Prisse was published by the owner, E. PRISSE D'AVENNES (*Fac-similé d'un*

social tractate of the official class, did not enjoy the same popularity. It is not so clearly cast in the form of a tale, though it does not lack dramatic setting. Like the Eloquent Peasant, the action is placed under an earlier king. Indeed, the most important manuscript of Ptahhotep purports to contain also the wisdom of a still earlier sage who lived a thousand years before the Feudal Age. The composition attributed to the earlier wise man preceded that of Ptahhotep in the roll and probably formed its beginning and first half. All but a few passages at the end have been torn off, but its conclusion is instructive as furnishing part of the historical setting of earlier days in which this school of sages were wont to place their teachings. Following the last fourteen lines of his instruction, all that is preserved, we find the conclusion of the unknown sage's life:

"The vizier (for such he purports to have been) caused his children to be summoned, after he had discerned the

papyrus égyptien, Paris, 1847). It was republished, together with all the other manuscripts (except B. M., 10509), by G. JÉQUIER (*Le Papyrus Prisse, et ses variantes*, Paris, 1911). The Carnarvon tablet was published in transcription, with discussion of its relation to the Papyrus Prisse by MASPERO, in *Recueil de travaux*, XXXI, 146–153, and afterward by the EARL OF CARNARVON in his beautiful volume, *Five Years' Excavations at Thebes*, Oxford Univ. Press, 1912 (discussed by GRIFFITH, pp. 36–37, and reproduced pl. xxvii). The five columns contained in Brit. Mus. Pap., No. 10509, were published by BUDGE, *Fac-similes of Egyptian Hieratic Papyri in the British Museum*, London, 1910, pls. xxxiv–xxxviii, pp. xvii–xxi. This reached me too late to be employed above. Like the other Wisdom literature, or semi-philosophical tractates discussed above, Papyrus Prisse is excessively difficult. The old translations, as their divergences from each other show, are too conjectural to be used with safety. An exhaustive study on the basis of modern grammatical knowledge would undoubtedly render much of it intelligible, although a large proportion of it is too obscure and too corrupt in text ever to be translated with certainty.

fashion of men and their character ⌜came to him⌝.¹ ...
He said to them: 'As for everything that is in writing in
this roll, hear it as I say it ⌜as an added obligation⌝.' They
threw themselves upon their bellies, they read it according to that which was in writing. It was pleasanter to
their hearts than anything that is in this whole land.²
Then they rose up and they sat down accordingly. Then
the majesty of the king of Upper and Lower Egypt Huni
died, and the majesty of the king of Upper and Lower
Egypt Snefru was established as excellent king in this
whole land. Then Kegemne was appointed to be governor of the (residence) city and vizier. It (the book)
is ended."³ Presumably, the career of the nameless old
vizier and sage of the Third Dynasty, into whose mouth
the wisdom of the Twelfth Dynasty was put, ended with
the life of his king and the advent of a new vizier.⁴ It
is evident that social ethics as taught by the sages of the
Twelfth Dynasty (Feudal Age) was also commonly attributed by them to the viziers of the Pyramid Age, for
we shall find that this was the case also with the Wisdom
of Ptahhotep, which was the next roll taken up by the
copyist as he resumed this pen, leaving an interval to
mark the end of the old book which he had just finished.

The Wisdom of Ptahhotep begins: "The instruction
of the governor of the city and vizier, Ptahhotep, under
the majesty of the king of Upper and Lower Egypt,
Isesi, who lives for ever and ever. The governor of the
city and vizier Ptahhotep says, 'O king, my lord, infirmity comes on, old age advances, the limbs weaken,

[1] On the rendering, see GARDINER, *Admonitions*, p. 107, n. 1.
[2] The same statement is made regarding the roll containing the speeches of the Eloquent Peasant. See above, p. 225.
[3] Papyrus Prisse, pp. 1 and 2.
[4] This vizier, Kegemne, was also a famous wise man.

⌜feebleness⌝ is renewed, strength perishes because of the languor of the heart (understanding). The mouth is silent and speaks not; the eyes wax small, the ears are dulled. The languid heart sleeps every day. The heart forgets, it remembers not yesterday. . . . That which is good becomes evil. All taste departs. That which old age does to people is evil in everything. The nostrils are stopped up, they breathe not. It is evil whether one stands or sits. Let thy servant be commanded to furnish the staff of old age.[1] Let my son stand in my place, and let me instruct him according to the word of those who have heard the manner of the ancestors, that (word) which the forefathers served, (variant: "which the gods have heard"). May they do likewise for thee; may revolt be suppressed among the people (of Egypt), may the Two Lands serve thee.'"

"Said his majesty: 'Instruct him after the word of old. May he do marvels among the children of the princes. . . .'"

The Wisdom of Ptahhotep then purports to have been uttered by a historical personage on a particular occasion. In the Fifth Dynasty, to which king Isesi belonged, there was indeed a line of viziers named Ptahhotep, who transmitted the office from father to son. The reign of Isesi fell about five hundred years earlier than the Feudal Age in which we find his wise vizier's wisdom in circulation. Ptahhotep petitions the king to appoint his son to the vizierial office in his place, because of advancing old age, the ills of which he graphically enumerates. In order

[1] Literally "old man's staff," which is a technical term for son and heir or successor. See BAR, I, 692, and GRIFFITH in the notes on *Bersheh*, I, pl. xxxiii. What is meant is, that the vizier, as the narrative shows, desires to be commanded to instruct his son as his successor.

that his son may be informed in the duties of so important an office, the vizier craves of the king permission to instruct him. While it is characteristic of the attitude of the inner official circle that the wisdom communicated should be designated as that which has descended from the fathers, its cautious mandates for right and wholesome living and for discreet official conduct may quite conceivably represent the sum total of the ripe experience of many generations of official life. While such men as the Misanthrope, Khekheperre-sonbu, and to a large extent also even Ipuwer had lost all confidence in the conventional virtue of the official world, the doctrines of the Eloquent Peasant and the Wisdom of Ptahhotep reveal to us that at least a nucleus of the best men of the official class and the court still felt confidence in the good old manner of living which had come down from their predecessors, if carefully conserved, and the principles of virtue persistently inculcated. Like all such fancied conservation, it contains clear evidences of the current and modern point of view, so much so indeed that there is ground for another interpretation of the historical setting, namely, that it was used merely to give prestige to a set of teachings which were for the most part modern. If so, the device is in sharp contrast with the open avowal of Khekheperre-sonbu that he sought new views and words which had not become hackneyed by generations of use.

Having received the king's permission, Ptahhotep enters upon the instruction of his son. "Beginning of the sayings of the good word which the hereditary prince, the count, the divine father, the priest, the eldest son of the king, of his body, the governor of the city, the vizier, Ptahhotep said, as instruction of the ignorant to knowledge, according to the correctness of the good word, as a profitable thing for him who is obedient to it, and as an evil thing for him who transgresses it."[1]

The introduction concludes with a short paragraph on the desirability of humility in wisdom in spite of its high value. Then begin the forty-three paragraphs into which the Wisdom of Ptahhotep is divided. There is not space here either for the entire text of this excessively difficult tractate or for the commentary necessary to make it intelligible to the modern reader. Nor even so, on the basis of our modern knowledge of the language, is it possible to render the document as a whole.[2]

The following table of the rubrics heading the paragraphs and suggesting in each case the subject discussed will serve, however, to indicate the ground which the wise man endeavored to cover. Where distinctly ethical problems are involved I have added to the rubric as much of the text as I found intelligible.

1. "If thou findest a wise man in his time, a leader of understanding more excellent than thou, bend thy arms and bow thy back"[3] (5, 10–12).

2. "If thou findest a wise man in his time, thy equal, ... be not silent when he speaks evil. Great is the approval by those who hear, and thy name will be good in the knowledge of the princes" (5, 13–14).

3. "If thou findest a wise man in his time, a poor man

---

[1] The Carnarvon Tablet ends here. It furnishes some valuable variants which have been incorporated above.

[2] We very much need an exhaustive treatment of the text, with careful word studies such as GARDINER has prepared for the *Admonitions of Ipuwer*. The summary offered above makes no pretension to rest upon any such study of the text, but perhaps presents enough for the purposes of this volume. See also GRIFFITH, in *Warner's Library of the World's Best Literature*.

[3] These references include the entire paragraph in each case. All refer to Pap. Prisse.

and not thy equal, be not overbearing against him when he is unfortunate" (6, 1-2).

4. "If thou art a leader (or 'administrator') issuing ordinances for the multitude, seek for thee every excellent matter, that thy ordinance may endure without evil therein. Great is righteousness (truth, right, justice), enduring . . .; it has not been disturbed since the time of Osiris" (6, 3-7).

5. "Put no fear (of thee?) among the people. . . . What the god commands is that which happens. Therefore live in the midst of quiet. What they (the gods?) give comes of itself" (6, 8-10).

6. "If thou art a man of those who sit by the seat of a man greater than thou, take what (food) he gives, . . . look at what is before thee, and bombard ¹ him not with many glances (don't stare at him). . . . Speak not to him until he calls. One knows not what is unpleasant to (his) heart. Speak thou when he greets thee, and what thou sayest will be agreeable to (his) heart" (6, 11-7, 3).

7. "If thou art a man of ⌈those who⌉ enter, whom (one) prince sends to (another) prince, . . . execute for him the commission according as he saith. Beware of ⌈altering⌉ a word which (one) prince ⌈speaks⌉ to (another) prince, by displacing the truth with the like of it" (7, 3-5).

8. "If thou ploughest and there is growth in the field, the god gives it (as) increase in thy hand. Satisfy not thine own mouth beside thy kin" (7, 5-6).

9. "If thou art insignificant, follow an able man and all thy proceedings shall be good before the god" (7, 7-8).

10. "Follow thy desire as long as thou livest. Do not more than is told (thee). Shorten not the time of following desire. It is an abomination to encroach upon the

¹ The word really means "to shoot."

time thereof. ⌜Take⌝ no ⌜care⌝ daily beyond the maintenance of thy house. When possessions come, follow desire, (for) possessions are not complete when he (the owner) is ⌜harassed⌝" (7, 9–10).

11. "If thou art an able man" (give attention to the conduct of thy son) (7, 10–8, 1).

12. "If thou art in the judgment-hall, standing or sitting" (8, 2–6).

13. "If thou art together with people" (8, 6–11).

14. "Report thy procedure without ⌜reservation⌝. Present thy plan in the council of thy lord" (8, 11–13).

15. "If thou art a leader" (or "administrator") (8, 14–9, 3).

16. "If thou art a leader (or 'administrator'), hear ⌜quietly⌝ the speech of the petitioner. He who is suffering wrong desires that his heart be cheered to do that on account of which he has come. . . . It is an ornament of the heart to hear kindly" (9, 3–6).

17. "If thou desirest to establish friendship in a house, into which thou enterest as lord, as brother, or as friend, wheresoever thou enterest in, beware of approaching the women. . . . A thousand men are undone for the enjoyment of a brief moment like a dream. Men gain (only) death for knowing them" (9, 7–13).

18. "If thou desirest that thy procedure be good, withhold thee from all evil, beware of occasion of avarice. . . . He who enters therein does not get on. It corrupts fathers, mothers, and mother's brothers. It ⌜divides⌝ wife and man; it is plunder (made up) of everything evil; it is a bundle of everything base. Established is the man whose standard is righteousness, who walks according to its way. He is used to make his fortune thereby, (but) the avaricious is houseless" (9, 13–10, 5).

19. "Be not avaricious in dividing. . . . Be not avaricious toward thy kin. Greater is the fame of the gentle than (that of) the harsh" (10, 5–8).

20. "If thou art successful, establish thy house. Love thy wife in husbandly embrace, fill her body, clothe her back. The recipe for her limbs is ointment. Gladden her heart as long as thou livest. She is a profitable field for her lord" (10, 8–12).[1]

21. "Satisfy those who enter to thee (come into thy office) with that which thou hast" (11, 1–4).

22. "Repeat not a word of ⌈hearsay⌉" (11, 5–7).

23. "If thou art an able man who sits in the council of his lord, summon thy understanding to excellent things. Be silent" (for speech is difficult) (11, 8–11).

24. "If thou art a strong man, establish the respect of thee by wisdom and by quietness of speech" (11, 12–12, 6).

25. "⌈Approach⌉ not a prince in his time"[2] (12, 6–9).

26. "Instruct a prince (or 'official') in that which is profitable for him" (12, 9–13).

27. "If thou art the son of a man of the council, commissioned to content the multitude, . . . be not partial. Beware lest he (the man of the multitude?) say, 'His plan is (⌈that of⌉) the princes. He utters the word in partiality" (13, 1–4).

28. "If thou art gentle ⌈in⌉ a matter that occurs" (13, 4–5).

29. "If thou becomest great after thou wert little, and gettest possessions after thou wert formerly poor in the city, . . . be not ⌈proud⌉-hearted because of thy wealth. It has come to thee as a gift of the god" (13, 6–9).

[1] Mohammed makes essentially the same remark in the Koran.
[2] "In his time" is seemingly an idiom for some particular mood. See also paragraphs 1–3 above.

30. "Bend thy back to thy superior, thy overseer of the king's house, and thy house shall endure because of his (or 'its') possessions and thy reward shall be in the place thereof. It is evil to show disobedience to a superior. One lives as long as he is gentle" (13, 9–14, 4).

31. "Do not practise corruption of children" (14, 4–6).

32. "If thou searchest the character of a friend, . . . transact the matter with him when he is alone" (14, 6–12).

33. "Let thy face be bright as long as thou livest. ⌜As for what goes out of the storehouse, it comes not in again; and as for loaves (already) distributed, he who is concerned therefor has still an empty stomach⌝" ("There is no use crying over spilt milk?") (14, 12–15, 2).

34. "Know thy merchants when thy fortunes are evil" (15, 2–5).

35. Quite uncertain (15, 5–6).

36. "If thou takest a wife" (15, 6–8).

37. "If thou hearkenest to these things which I have said to thee, all thy plans will progress. As for the matter of the righteousness thereof, it is their worth. The memory thereof shall ⌜circulate⌝ in the mouths of men, because of the beauty of their utterances. Every word will be carried on and not perish in this land forever. . . . He who understands ⌜discretion⌝ is profitable in establishing that through which he succeeds on earth. A wise man is ⌜satisfied⌝ by reason of that which he knows. As for a prince of good qualities, ⌜they are in⌝ his heart and his tongue. His lips are right when he speaks, his eyes see, and his ears together hear what is profitable for his son. Do right (righteousness, truth, justice), free from lying" (15, 8–16, 2).

38. "Profitable is hearkening for a son that hearkens. . . . How good it is when a son receives that which his

father says. He shall reach advanced age thereby. A hearkener is one whom the god loves. Who hearkens not is one whom the god hates. It is the heart (=understanding) which makes its possessor a hearkener or one not hearkening. The life prosperity and health of a man is his heart. The hearkener is one who hears and speaks. He who does what is said, is one who loves to hearken. How good it is when a son hearkens to his father! How happy is he to whom these things are said! ... His memory is in the mouth of the living who are on earth and those who shall be" (16, 3-12).

39. "If the son of a man receives what his father says, none of his plans will miscarry. Instruct as thy son one who hearkens, who shall be successful in the judgment of the princes, who directs his mouth according to that which is said to him. ... How many mishaps befall him who hearkens not! The wise man rises early to establish himself, while the fool is ⌈scourged⌉" (16, 13-17, 4).

40. "As for the fool who hearkens not, he accomplishes nothing. He regards wisdom as ignorance, and what is profitable as diseased. ... His life is like death thereby, ... he dies, living every day. Men pass by (avoid?) his qualities, because of the multitude of evils upon him every day" (17, 4-9).

41. "A son who hearkens is a follower of Horus. He prospers after he hearkens. He reaches old age, he attains reverence. He speaks likewise to his (own) children, renewing the instruction of his father. Every man who instructs is like his sire. He speaks with his children; then they speak to their children. Attain character, ... make righteousness to flourish and thy children shall live" (17, 10-18, 12).

42. Concerns "thy heart" (understanding) and "thy

mouth." "Let thy attention be steadfast as long as thou speakest, whither thou directest thy speech. May the princes who shall hear say, 'How good is that which comes out of his mouth!'" (18, 12-19, 3).

43. "So do that thy lord shall say to thee, 'How good is the instruction of his father from whose limbs he came forth! He has spoken to him; it is in (his) body throughout. Greater is that which he has done than that which was said to him.' Behold, a good son, whom the god gives, renders more than that which his lord says to him. He does right (righteousness, etc.), his heart acts according to his way. According as thou attainest me ('what I have attained'), thy limbs shall be healthy, the king shall be satisfied with all that occurs, and thou shalt attain years of life not less [⌈than⌉] I have passed on earth. I have attained one hundred and ten years of life, while the king gave to me praise above (that of) the ancestors (in the vizierial office) because I did righteousness for the king even unto the place of reverence (the grave)"[1] (19, 3-8).

In the Wisdom of Ptahhotep we have what purports to be the ripe worldly wisdom of a seasoned old statesman and courtier, with a long life of experience with men and affairs behind him. Nor do they in any way belie their assumed authorship. It is easy to picture a self-satisfied old prince looking back with vast complacency upon his long career, and drawing out of his wide experience, with no attempt at arrangement, the precepts of conduct, official and personal, which he has found valuable. As a matter of fact, however, it is evident that

[1] This is the end of the original, for the scribe's docket in red follows, reading as usual: "It is finished from its beginning to its end according to what was found in writing" (19, 9).

we have here a collection of precepts which had grown up among the officials of the Egyptian state when this compilation was made and put into the mouth of Ptahhotep. Some of them are doubtless much older than the collection itself; but in the main they reflect to us the conventional daily philosophy of the wisest among the official body in the Feudal Age.

Over half of these admonitions deal with personal character and conduct, while the remainder have to do with administration and official conduct.[1] In general they inculcate gentleness, moderation, and discretion without lack of self-assertion, displaying indeed the soundest good sense in the poise and balance to which they commend the young man. There is none of the sombre pessimism of the Misanthrope or Khekheperre-sonbu. Life is abundantly worth while. A wholesome amount of pleasure is to be taken, and official or other burdens are not to be allowed to curtail the hours of relaxation (see paragraph 10). Moreover, a man should always wear a cheerful face, for "there is no use in crying over spilt milk." Finally the dominant note is a commanding moral earnestness which pervades the whole homely philosophy of the old vizier's wisdom. The most prominent imperative throughout is "do right," and "deal justly with all."

So prominent are justice, character, and moral ideals in the surviving documents of this great age, that I am

---

[1] We may divide the paragraphs as numbered above roughly as follows:
Personal character and conduct, paragraphs 1-3, 6, 8, 10, 11, 13, 17, 18, 19, 22, 29, 31, 32, 33, 34, 36, 37, 38, 40, 41. Total, 23 paragraphs.
Administration and official conduct: 4, 5, 7, 9, 12, 14, 15, 16, 21, 23, 24, 25, 26, 27, 28, 30, 39, 42, 43. Total, 19 paragraphs.
Uncertain, paragraph 35.

confident we should place here the Installation of the Vizier, a traditional address orally delivered to the vizier by the king in person whenever a new incumbent was inducted into the vizierial office.[1] This remarkable address shows that the spirit of the Wisdom of Ptahhotep and the Eloquent Peasant was not exclusively a matter of homely proverbial philosophy, current precepts of conduct, or a picturesque story with a moral. This spirit of social justice pervaded even the very structure of the state and had reached the throne itself. The address is as follows:

[1] This document has survived in three different copies, each a hieroglyphic wall inscription, in three different tombs of the Eighteenth Dynasty at Thebes. The best preserved and most important of the three is in the tomb of Rekhmire, vizier under Thutmose III (1501-1447 B. C.). The other two copies are in the tomb of Woser, uncle and predecessor of Rekhmire, and the tomb of Hapu, vizier under Thutmose IV (1420-1411 B. C.). These two are little more than fragments. The inscription was published, on the basis of the Rekhmire text, by NEWBERRY, who first discovered it (*The Life of Rekhmara*, London, 1900, pls. ix-x). NEWBERRY placed the materials from the tombs of Woser and Hapu at GARDINER's disposal, who then re-edited the text with excellent commentary and translation (the *Installation of a Vizier*, *Recueil de travaux*, XXVI, 1-19). The document is exceedingly difficult in language and still shows serious lacunæ. Further study was given it by SETHE, who re-edited the text in his *Urkunden* (IX, 1086 *ff*.). He secured successive collations of all the originals from DAVIES, and published a final and much improved text with full commentary and translation (*Die Einsetzung des Veziers unter der 18. Dynastie*, Leipzig, 1909, in *Untersuchungen zur Geschichte und Altertumskunde Aegyptens*, V, 2). The above translation is an adaptation of SETHE, and should be used in place of my former translation in my *Ancient Records* (II, 665-670). While all the texts date from the fifteenth century B. C., the reasons for placing the document in the Middle Kingdom, at least several centuries earlier, seem to me conclusive. The document refers to a precedent from the Pyramid Age (Old Kingdom), and it is in spirit and thought closely related to the social documents of the Feudal Age above discussed. Employing the canons of historical criticism current elsewhere, if this document had not borne a date, it would

"Regulation laid upon the vizier X.[1] The council was conducted into the audience hall of Pharaoh, Life! Prosperity! Health! One (= the king) caused that there be brought in the vizier X, newly appointed."

"Said his majesty to him, 'Look to the office of the vizier; be watchful over all that is done therein. Behold it is the established support of the whole land.'

"'Behold, as for the vizierate, it is not sweet; behold, it is bitter, as ⌈he is named⌉. [Behold], he is copper enclosing the gold of his [lord's] house. Behold it (the vizierate) is not to show respect-of-persons to princes and councillors; it is not to make for himself slaves of any people.'

"'Behold, as for a man in the house of his lord, his ⌈conduct⌉ is good for him (the lord). (But) lo, he does not the same for another' (than the lord).[2]

have been placed in the Middle Kingdom by any unbiassed critic. It shows particularly close affinity to the Wisdom of Ptahhotep (Papyrus Prisse), duplicating not a few of its ideas, and even employing also the same form in some cases. For example regarding proper and kind treatment of a petitioner the two texts say:

"A petitioner desires that his utterance be regarded rather than the hearing of that on account of which he has come" (Installation, l. 17).

"He who is suffering wrong desires that his heart be cheered to do that on account of which he has come" (Wisdom of Ptahhotep, Prisse 9, 5; see paragraph 16, above).

There is not space here to array the parallel materials, but I hope to do this elsewhere in a special study. I may call attention to Prisse 11, 12–13, and 10, 6–7 as containing doctrines identical with those in the Installation. Perhaps the most conclusive evidence is the social policy of Ameni ("I did not exalt the great above the small"), almost an epitome of the Installation address, and of unquestionable Middle Kingdom date.

[1] Here of course was the name of the vizier, varying from incumbent to incumbent.

[2] The meaning of course is that the vizier is to be loyal to his lord, the king, to whose house he is attached.

"'Behold, when a petitioner comes from Upper or Lower Egypt (even) the whole land, equipped with . . . see thou to it that everything is done in accordance with law, that everything is done according to the custom thereof, [giving] to [⌈every man⌉] his right. Behold a prince is in a conspicuous place, water and wind report concerning all that he does. For behold, that which is done by him never remains unknown.'

"'When he takes up a matter [for a petition]er according to his case, he (the vizier) shall not proceed by the statement of a departmental officer.¹ But it (the matter under consideration) shall be known by the statement of one designated by him (the vizier), saying it himself in the presence of a departmental officer with the words: "It is not that I raise my voice; (but) I send the petitioner [according to] his [case to ⌈another court⌉] or prince." Then that which has been done by him has not been misunderstood.'

"'Behold the refuge of a prince is to act according to the regulation by doing what is said' (to him).² A petitioner who has been adjudged [⌈shall not say⌉]: 'My right has not been given to [me].'

"'Behold, it is a saying which was in the ⌈vizierial installation⌉ of Memphis in the utterance of the king in urging the vizier to moderation . . . "[Bewar]e of that which is said of the vizier Kheti. It is said that he discriminated against some of the people of his own kin [in favor of] strangers, for fear lest it should be said of him that he [favored] his [kin dishon]estly. When one of

---

¹ That is, an officer belonging to the staff of the vizier who has heard the matters reported at second hand, lest misunderstanding should result, when the vizier handles or acts on cases from another court.
² Compare PRISSE, 7, 9.

them appealed against the judgment which he thought ⌈to make⌉ him, he persisted in his discrimination." Now that is more than justice.'

"'Forget not to judge justice. It is an abomination of the god to show partiality. This is the teaching. Therefore do thou accordingly. Look upon him who is known to thee like him who is unknown to thee; and him who is near the king like him who is far from [his house]. Behold, a prince who does this, he shall endure here in this place.'

"'Pass not over a petitioner without regarding his speech. If there is a petitioner who shall appeal to thee, being one whose speech is not what is said,[1] dismiss him after having let him hear that on account of which thou dismissest him. Behold, it is said: "A petitioner desires that his saying be regarded rather than the hearing of that on account of which he has come."'

"'Be not wroth against a man wrongfully; (but) be thou wroth at that at which one should be wroth.'

"'Cause thyself to be feared. Let men be afraid of thee. A prince is a prince of whom one is afraid. Behold, the dread of a prince is that he does justice. Behold, if a man causes himself to be feared a multitude of times, there is something wrong in him in the opinion of the people. They do not say of him, "He is a man (indeed)." Behold, the ⌈fear⌉ of a prince [⌈deters⌉] the liar, when he (the prince) proceeds according to the dread of him. Behold, this shalt thou attain by administering this office, doing justice.'

"'Behold, men expect the doing of justice in the procedure [of] the vizier. Behold, that is its (justice's) cus-

---

[1] Meaning either what is said and thus proven by witnesses, or what *should* not be said, impropriety of speech.

tomary [⌈law⌉] since the god. Behold, it is said concerning the scribe of the vizier: "A just scribe," is said of him. Now, as for the hall in which thou "bearest" there is an audience-hall therein [⌈for⌉] ⌈the announcement⌉ of judgments. Now, as for "him who shall do justice before all the people," it is the vizier.'

"'Behold, when a man is in his office, he acts according to what is commanded him. [Behold] the success of a man is that he act according to what is said to him. Make no [⌈delay⌉] at all in justice, the law of which thou knowest. Behold, it becomes the arrogant that the king should love the timid more than the arrogant.'[1]

"'Now mayest thou do according to this command that is given thee—behold it is the manner of ⌈success⌉— besides giving thy attention to the ⌈crown⌉-lands, and making the establishment thereof. If thou happenest to inspect, then shalt thou send to inspect the overseer of ⌈land-measuring⌉ and the ⌈patrol of the overseer of land-measuring⌉. If there be one who shall inspect before thee, then thou shalt question him.'

"'[Behold the regulation] that is laid up[on] thee.'"

The chief emphasis throughout this remarkable state document is on social justice. The vizierate is not for the purpose of showing any preference "to princes and councillors" nor to enslave any of the people. All justice administered shall be according to law in every case, not forgetting that the vizier's position is a very conspicuous one, so that all his proceedings are widely known among the people. Even the waters and the winds report his doings to all. Nor does justice mean that any

[1] The same contrast between the "timid" and the "arrogant" or "violent-hearted" is found in Ipuwer (11, 13), and is another connection between the Installation and the Feudal Age documents.

injustice shall be shown those who may be of high station, as in the famous case of the ancient Memphite vizier Kheti, who made a decision against his own kin in spite of the inherent merits of the case. This is not justice. On the other hand, justice means strict impartiality, treating without distinction, known and unknown, him who is near the king's person and him who enjoys no connection with the royal house. Such administration as this will secure the vizier a long tenure of office. While the vizier must display the greatest discretion in his wrath, he must so demean himself as to ensure public respect and even fear, but this fear shall have its sole basis in the execution of impartial justice; for the true "dread of a prince is that he does justice." Hence he will not find it necessary repeatedly and ostentatiously to excite the fear of the people, which produces a false impression among them. The administration of justice will prove a sufficient deterrent. Men expect justice from the vizier's office, for justice has been its customary law since the reign of the Sun-god on earth, and he whom they proverbially call "him who shall do justice before all the people" is the vizier. A man's success in office depends upon his ability to follow instructions. Therefore let there be no delay in the dispensation of justice, remembering that the king loves the timid and defenceless more than the arrogant. Then with a reference to the lands which probably formed the royal fortune, and the inspection of the officials in charge of them, the king concludes this veritable magna charta of the poor with the words: "Behold the regulation that is laid upon thee."

It should be noted that this programme of social kindness and justice, in which the king loves the timid and defenceless more than the powerful and arrogant, is distinctly religious in motive. "It is an abomination of the god," says the king, "to show partiality." Moreover, justice has been the traditional law of the vizier's office since the time when the Sun-god ruled in Egypt. The rule of the Pharaoh which was supposed to continue the blood and the line of Re was likewise continuing the justice of the Sun-god's ancient régime on earth. The king lays his mandate unequivocally upon the vizier, but at the same time he does not hesitate to appeal to a higher court. The vizier must do justice because the great god of the state abhors injustice, and not solely because the king enjoins it. Twelve to thirteen hundred years later we find the Hebrew prophets boldly proclaiming the moral sovereignty of Jehovah as over that of the king, but how many generations of seemingly fruitless ministry were required before this contention of the prophets found expression in the spirit of the Hebrew government, much less in royal pronouncements such as this of the Feudal Age in Egypt. Was it the vision of the ideal king held up at the court by Ipuwer, the sombre picture of the corruption of men painted by the Misanthrope, the picturesque scene of official oppression disclosed in the story of the Eloquent Peasant, or the conventional tableau of father counselling son presented in the Wisdom of Ptahhotep, which finally so enveloped the throne in an atmosphere of social justice that the installation of the prime-minister and chief-justice of the realm, for such the vizier was, called forth from the king a speech from the throne, an official expression by the head of the state to its highest executive officer, embodying the fundamental principles of social justice? We have not been accustomed to associate such principles of government with the early East, nor, indeed, even with the modern Orient.

Indeed, when we examine the Laws of Hammurabi, which date from the same age, we find the administration of justice conditioned by clear recognition of social classes. For the same crime the penalty and the damages vary according to the social class of the individuals involved. In the Installation of the Egyptian vizier such distinctions are obliterated and all are to be treated alike. When Plato in his essay on Politics made the State the organized embodiment of justice, he probably little knew that fifteen hundred years earlier Egypt had adopted this ideal and endeavored to make it reality; or is this another evidence that Plato had been in Egypt, and an idea which he appropriated there?

The influence of such lofty ideals of social justice, which thus found the highest expression in government, was no doubt in large measure due to the form in which they circulated among all classes. Such doctrines, had they been enunciated as abstract principles, would have attracted little attention and exerted little or no influence. The Egyptian, however, always thought in concrete terms and in graphic forms. He thought not of theft but of a thief, not of love but of a lover, not of poverty but of a poor man: he sees not social corruption but a corrupt society. Hence the Misanthrope, a *man* in whom social injustice found expression in the picture of a despairing soul who tells of his despair and its causes; hence Ipuwer, a *man* in whom dwelt the vision to discern both the deadly corruption of society and the golden dream of an ideal king restoring all; hence the Eloquent Peasant, a *man* suffering official oppression and crying out against it; hence Ptahhotep, a *man* meeting the obligations of office with wholesome faith in righteous conduct and just administration to engender happiness, and passing on this experience to his son; hence even the Instruction of Amenemhet, a *king* suffering shameful treachery, losing faith in men and likewise communicating his experience to his son. The result is that the doctrines of these social thinkers were placed in a dramatic setting, and the doctrines themselves find expression in dialogue growing out of experiences and incidents represented as actual. In the East, and doubtless everywhere, such teachings, we repeat, make the most universal and the most powerful appeal in this form. It was the form into which the problem of suffering, as graphically exemplified in the story of Job, most naturally fell. The Story of Akhikar, recently recovered in its ancient Aramaic form, is unquestionably a discourse on the folly of ingratitude which belongs in the same class; while the most beautiful of all such tales, the parables of Jesus, adopt the method and the form for ages current in the East. When Plato wished to discourse on the immortality of the soul, he assumed as his dramatic setting the death of Socrates, and the doctrines which he wished to set forth took the form of conversation between Socrates and his friends.[1] It is hardly conceivable that this method of moralizing and philosophizing in dialogue after an introduction which throws the whole essentially into the form of a tale, a method which produced so many documents in Egypt, had no influence on the emergence of the dialogue form in Asia and Europe. It is not likely that the form originated independently among the Aramæans, Hebrews, and Greeks. The wide international circulation of the Akhikar tale, as we have said before, demonstrates how such literary products could travel, and it is perhaps significant that the

[1] The analogy of the Platonic dialogues was noticed by GARDINER, *Admonitions*, p. 17.

oldest form of the Akhikar tale was found in Egypt. In any case it is evident that the form of the teachings of these early social thinkers and reformers contributed much to give them a wide and powerful influence, an influence which finally reached the throne itself, as we have seen.

While we are, unhappily, unable to trace further the influence of these men in the practical legislation of this age, for the laws of Egypt have perished, the pervading power of their teaching is evident in the mortuary inscriptions of the period. We leave the court and journey to the provinces and baronies, where we find on the tomb door of such a baron as Ameni of Benihasan the following account of his administrative policy as lord of a barony:

"There was no citizen's daughter whom I misused, there was no widow whom I afflicted, there was no peasant whom I repulsed (evicted?), there was no herdman whom I repelled, there was no overseer of five whose people I took away for (unpaid) taxes. There was none wretched in my community, there was none hungry in my time. When years of famine came, I ploughed all the fields of the Oryx barony (his estate) as far as its southern and its northern boundary, preserving its people alive, furnishing its food so that there was none hungry therein. I gave to the widow as (to) her who had a husband. I did not exalt the great (man) above the small (man) in anything that I gave. Then came great Niles (inundations), possessors of grain and all things, (but) I did not collect the arrears of the field."[1]

In this record we seem to hear an echo of the Installation of the Vizier, especially in the statement, "I did not exalt the great man above the small man in anything

[1] BAR, I, 523.

that I gave." It is easy to believe that such a baron as this had been present at court and had heard the instructions of the Pharaoh at the vizier's inauguration. If the administration of Ameni was in any measure what he claims for it, we must conclude that the social teachings of the wise at the court were widely known among the great throughout the kingdom. Even though we may conclude that he has idealized his rule to a large extent, we have still to account for his desire to create such an impression as we gain from his biography. It is evident that the ideals of social justice, so insistently set forth in the literature of the age, had not only reached the king, but they had also exerted a profound influence among the ruling class everywhere.

Herein, then, we may discern a great transformation. The pessimism with which the men of the early Feudal Age,[1] as they beheld the desolated cemeteries of the Pyramid Age, or as they contemplated the hereafter, and the hopelessness with which some of them regarded the earthly life were met by a persistent counter-current in the dominant gospel of righteousness and social justice set forth in the hopeful philosophy of more optimistic social thinkers, men who saw hope in positive effort toward better conditions. We must regard the Admonitions of Ipuwer and the Tale of the Eloquent Peasant as striking examples of such efforts, and we must recognize in their writings the weapons of the earliest known group of moral and social crusaders. What more could such a man as Ipuwer have wished than the address delivered by the king at the installation of the vizier? A

---

[1] Such views are dated with considerable precision early in the Twelfth Dynasty by the Instruction of Amenemhet, the first king of the dynasty.

king capable of delivering such an address approaches the stature of that ideal king of whom Ipuwer dreamed.

There can be no doubt that that ideal king was Re, the moral glories of whose reign were to be renewed in his Pharaonic representative on earth. It is to the approval and to the traditional character of the reign of the Sun-god that the king appealed as the final basis for his instruction to the vizier. It is Re who is dominant in the thinking of these social philosophers of the Feudal Age. In the Song of the Harper even the mummy of the dead is set up before Re. It is to Re that the Misanthrope looks for justification in the hereafter, and Khekheperre-sonbu was a priest of the Sun-city of Heliopolis. Ipuwer's vision of the future ideal king emerges from reminiscence of the blessedness of Re's earthly reign among men; while the summary of the whole appeal of the Eloquent Peasant is contained in "that good word which came out of the mouth of Re himself: 'Speak truth, do truth (or "righteousness"), for it is great, it is mighty, it is enduring.'" The moral obligations emerging in the Solar theology thus wrought the earliest social regeneration and won the earliest battle for social justice of which we know anything in history. It is evident here also, as in the Pyramid Texts, that the connection of Osiris with ideals of righteousness and justice is secondary. He was tried and found innocent in the great hall at Heliopolis, that is before the *Solar* bar of justice, recognized, at the time when the Osiris myth was forming, as the tribunal before which he must secure acquittal, and his later exaltation as judge is but the Solarization of the Osirian functions on the basis of the Solar judgeship so common in the Pyramid Texts. In the Pyramid Texts, Osiris had already climbed upon the celestial throne of

Re; we shall see him now also appropriating Re's judgment-seat.[1]

We discern the Egyptians, then, developing at a surprisingly early date a sense of the moral unworthiness of man and a consciousness of deep-seated moral obligation to which he has been largely untrue. Their beginnings lie too far back to be discernible, but as they developed they found practical expression in the idealized kingship whence they were quickly reflected into the character and the activities of Re, the ideal king. The moral obligation which men felt within them became a fiat of the god, their own abomination of injustice soon became that of the god, and their own moral ideals, thus becoming likewise those of the god, gained a new mandatory power. The idealized kingship of Re, the possible recurrence of such a beneficent rule, brought with it golden visions of a Messianic kingdom. Furthermore, Re became the great moral arbiter before whom all might receive justice. Even Osiris had thus been subjected to the moral ordeal before the Sun-god in his great hall of justice at Heliopolis, as the Osirian myth narrates. It is not necessary to deny to early Osirian belief some ethical content, of which we found indications likewise in the local faiths of a number of Egyptian gods of the Pyramid Age; but here again it should not be forgotten that the Pyramid Texts have preserved traces of a view of Osiris which, far from making him the ideal king and the friend of man, discloses him as an enemy of the dead and hostile to men.[2] It is not until the Feudal Age that

---

[1] The Heliopolitan trial of Osiris is in itself enough to dispose of the extraordinary contention of BUDGE (in his two volumes on Osiris) that the Sun-god is a secondary phenomenon of foreign origin, imported into Egypt after the supremacy of the Osirian faith was established. [2] See above, pp. 75, 142-3.

Osiris unmistakably emerges as the champion of righteousness. Ptahhotep, with the complaisant optimism which characterizes his maxims, avers that righteousness has not been "disturbed since the time of Osiris," meaning the time when Osiris ruled on earth as a righteous king.[1] While the political triumph of Re largely created the religious atmosphere which environed these social philosophers of the court, we shall now observe Osiris and Re, side by side, in the moral thinking of the age.

It was now not only religious belief and social axiom, but also formally announced royal policy, that before the bar of justice the great and the powerful must expect the same treatment and the same verdict accorded to the poor and the friendless. It is not the province of these lectures to discover to what extent practical administration made these ideals effective. That is a matter of history for the investigation of which the materials are unhappily very scanty. Later conditions would indicate that the ideal remained largely unrealized. It can hardly be doubted, however, that such doctrines of social justice as we have found in this age contributed powerfully to develop the conviction that not the man of power and wealth, but the man of justice and righteousness, would be acceptable before the great god's judgment-seat. Here then ends the special and peculiar claim of the great and powerful to consideration and to felicity in the hereafter, and the democratization of blessedness beyond the grave begins. The friendless peasant pleading with the grand steward says to him, "Beware! Eternity approaches." Ameni, the great lord of Benihasan, sets forth upon his tomb door, as we have seen, the record of social justice in his treatment of all as the best passport he can devise

---

[1] See above, p. 232, paragraph 4 (Pap. Prisse 6, 5).

for the long journey. Over and over again the men of the Feudal Age reiterate in their tombs their claims to righteousness of character. "Sesenebnef has done righteousness, his abomination was evil, he saw it not,"[1] says an official of the time on his sarcophagus. The mortuary texts which fill the cedar coffins of this age[2] show clearly that the consciousness of moral responsibility in the hereafter has greatly deepened since the Pyramid Age. The balances of justice to which the peasant appealed so often and so dramatically are now really finding place in the drama of justification hereafter. "The doors of the sky are opened to thy beauty," says one to the deceased; "thou ascendest, thou seest Hathor. Thy evil is expelled, thy iniquity is wiped away, by those who weigh with the balances on the day of reckoning."[3] Just as the peasant so often called the grand steward the balances of justice, so the deceased may be possessed of character as true and unswerving as the scales themselves. Hence we find the Coffin Texts saying, "Lo, this —— (name of the deceased) is the balances of Re, wherewith he weighs truth" (or righteousness).[4] It is evident also whose are the balances of truth and who the judge who presides over them. It is as before the Sun-god, before whom even Osiris had been tried. A similar connection of the judgment with Re places it in the cabin of the Solar barque.[5]

The moral requirement of the great judge has become a matter of course. The dead says: "I have led the way before him and behind him. He loves righteousness and hates evil, upon his favorite ways of righteousness whereon

---

[1] GAUTIER et JÉQUIER, *Licht*, pl. xxv, horizontal line at top. Other references are BAR, I, 459, 509, 531, 532, 613, 745.
[2] These are forerunners of the Book of the Dead. An account of them will be found below, pp. 272-3
[3] *Rec.* 32, 78.   [4] *Rec.* 30, 189.   [5] *Rec.* 31, 23.

the gods lead."[1] When the dead man entered those righteous paths of the gods, it was with a sense of moral unworthiness left behind. "My sin is expelled," he said, "my iniquity is removed. I have cleansed myself in those two great pools which are in Heracleopolis."[2] Those ceremonial washings which were so common in the Pyramid Texts have now become distinctly moral in their significance. "I go upon the way where I wash my head in the Lake of Righteousness," says the dead man.[3] Again and very often the deceased claims that his life has been blameless: "I am one who loved righteousness, my abomination was evil."[4] "I sit down justified, I rise up justified."[5] "I have established righteousness, I have expelled evil."[6] "I am a lord of offering, my abomination is evil."[7]

A number of times the Osirian Horus appears as the moral champion of the dead, to whom he says: "I am thy son Horus, I have caused that thou be justified in the council."[8] This of course means the identification of the dead with Osiris, and the enjoyment of the same justification which had been granted Osiris. Hence Horus says to the dead: "O Osiris X! I have given to thee justification against thy enemies on this good day."[9] This justification was of course not that granted by Osiris, but by the Sun-god, as shown by such utterances of Horus as this: "I put righteousness before him (the deceased) like Atum" (the Sun-god).[10] Now, the justification before the Sun-god was accomplished by Thoth, as advocate of the

---

[1] *Rec.* 31, 22; see similar important references to "righteousness" on p. 21, but they are obscure.
[2] LEPSIUS, *Aelteste Texte*, pl. i, ll. 9–10 (Book of the Dead, 17th chap.). [3] *Ibid.*, pl. i, l. 12=pl. xvi, ll. 10–11 (Book of the Dead, 17th chap.). [4] *Annales du Service*, V, 237.
[5] *Rec.* 31, 28, l. 62.   [6] *Rec.* 31, 25.   [7] *Rec.* 30, 69.
[8] *Rec.* 33, 34.   [9] *Rec.* 33, 36.   [10] *Rec.* 33, 36.

accused, Thoth having been, according to the Solar myth, the vizier of the Sun-god. Hence we find in the Coffin Texts a "Chapter of Justification before Thoth, Hereditary Prince of the Gods," although the text of the chapter unfortunately consists of mortuary ceremonies on behalf of Osiris, and makes but one reference to justification in mentioning "the beautiful paths of justification."[1] In the justification of Osiris himself, Thoth had figured as his defender, and the justification in the foregoing chapter is probably Osirian, though it does not unequivocally make Osiris the judge. The ethical significance of Osiris is evident in a passage where the deceased, identified with Osiris, says: "I perish not, I enter as truth, I ⌈support⌉ truth, I am lord of truth, I go forth as truth, . . . I enter in as truth";[2] or again where Osiris says: "I am Osiris, the god who does righteousness, I live in it."[3]

But Osiris early discloses himself as the judge. We hear in the Coffin Texts of "the Great Council (or court of justice) of Osiris" as early as the Ninth or Tenth Dynasty (twenty-fourth to twenty-second centuries).[4] In the same text the dead (or possibly Horus) says: "I have commanded those who are in the Great Council in the cavern of Osiris; I have repeated it in the presence of Mat (Goddess of Truth), to cause that I prevail over that foe."[5] It is perhaps this council that is meant when the dead is assured, "Thou art justified on the day when judgment is rendered in the council of the Lord of Gemwet," although I am not certain that Osiris was the Lord of Gemwet.[6] According to another notion there were seven of these "councils" or courts of Osiris, and we find a

[1] LACAU'S, chap. XXIX, *Rec.* 30, 69 ff.   [2] *Rec.* 31, 16.
[3] *Annales*, V, 248.   [4] Assiut Coffin of Mesehet, *Rec.* 31, 173.
[5] *Ibid.*   [6] *Rec.* 29, 147.

prayer that the soul of the deceased may be justified "against his enemies in the sky, in the earth, and in these seven councils of Osiris."[1] Doubtless the popularity of Osiris had much to do with the spread of the conviction, now universal, that *every* soul must meet this ethical ordeal in the hereafter. It now became, or let us say that at the advent of the Middle Kingdom it had become, the custom to append to the name of every deceased person the epithet "justified."

In the Pyramid Texts this epithet had been received only by the Pharaoh, for *royal* Osirianism identified the king with the justified Osiris and prefixed "Osiris" to the king's name. A new element now entered the old *popular* Osirianism, and the process which was democratizing the splendid royal hereafter now began to identify every dead man with Osiris, so that he not only as of old entered the kingdom of Osiris to enjoy the god's protection and favor, but he now *became* Osiris and was conceived as king. Even in burials of simple folk, the mummy was fashioned and laid on the back like that of Osiris, and amulets representing the royal insignia of the Pharaoh were painted on the inside of the coffin or laid beside the body.[2] The popular power of the ancient god is evident in the new custom of prefixing the name of Osiris to that of the dead man. He might be and was frequently identified with the Sun-god too, but as a departed spirit it was by the name of Osiris that he was designated.

[1] Tomb of Harhotep, *Mém. de la Miss. arch. franç.*, I, 177-180. This appeal for justification is probably a magical formula. It is repeatedly addressed to the personified parts—rudder, mast, sail, etc.—of the sacred Osiris barque at Abydos, each being adjured to "justify" the soul of the deceased. (*Cf.* forty-eight names of a barque in LACAU, XXVII, *Rec.*, 30, 65 *ff.*, and Book of the Dead, xcix.) It is possible that "justify" implies little of ethical content here, and that it may be chiefly legal. On the use of "justified" as a juristic verdict, see SETHE, *Einsetzung des Vezirs*, p. 23, n. 96.

[2] See SCHAEFER, *Zeitschr. fuer aegypt. Sprache*, 43, 66 *ff.*

LECTURE VIII

POPULARIZATION OF THE OLD ROYAL HEREAFTER—TRIUMPH OF OSIRIS—CONSCIENCE AND THE BOOK OF THE DEAD—MAGIC AND MORALS

• THE scepticism toward preparations for the hereafter involving a massive tomb and elaborate mortuary furniture, the pessimistic recognition of the futility of material equipment for the dead, pronounced as we have seen these tendencies to be in the Feudal Age, were, nevertheless, but an eddy in the broad current of Egyptian life. These tendencies were undoubtedly the accompaniment of unrelieved pessimism and hopelessness, on the one hand, as well as of a growing belief in the necessity of moral worthiness in the hereafter, on the other; they were revolutionary views which did not carry with them any large body of the Egyptian people. As the felicity of the departed was democratized, the common people took up and continued the old mortuary usages, and the development and elaboration of such customs went on without heeding the eloquent silence and desolation that reigned on the pyramid plateau and in the cemeteries of the fathers. Even Ipuwer had said to the king: "It is, moreover, good when the hands of men build pyramids, lakes are dug, and groves of sycomores of the gods are planted."[1] In the opinion of the prosperous official class the loss of the tomb was the direst possible consequence of unfaithfulness to the king, and a wise man said to his children:

[2] Ipuwer, 13, 12-13.

"There is no tomb for one hostile to his majesty;
But his body shall be thrown to the waters."[1]

By the many, tomb-building was resumed and carried on as of old. To be sure, the kings no longer held such absolute control of the state that they could make it but a highly organized agency for the construction of the gigantic royal tomb; but the official class in charge of such work did not hesitate to compare it with Gizeh itself. Meri, an architect of Sesostris I, displays noticeable satisfaction in recording that he was commissioned by the king "to execute for him an eternal seat, greater in name than Rosta (Gizeh) and more excellent in appointments than any place, the excellent district of the gods. Its columns pierced heaven; the lake which was dug reached the river, the gates, towering heavenward, were of limestone of Troja. Osiris, First of the Westerners, rejoiced over all the monuments of my lord (the king). I myself rejoiced and my heart was glad at that which I had executed."[2] The "eternal seat" is the king's tomb, including, as the description shows, also the chapel or mortuary temple in front.

While the tombs of the feudal nobles not grouped about the royal pyramid, as had been those of the administrative nobles of the Pyramid Age, were now scattered in the baronies throughout the land, they continued to enjoy to some extent the mortuary *largesses* of the royal treasury. The familiar formula, "an offering which the king gives,"

[1] Stela of Sehetepibre at Abydos, BAR, I, 748. The Misanthrope refers to the similar fate of an abandoned body. See above, p. 190.
[2] Stela of Meri in the Louvre (C 3), BAR, I, 509. The excavations of the Metropolitan Museum of New York have indeed revealed the unusually sumptuous character of the surroundings of this pyramid of Sesostris I at Lisht.

so common in the tombs about the pyramids, is still frequent in the tombs of the nobles. It is, however, no longer confined to such tombs. With the wide popularization of the highly developed mortuary faith of the upper classes it had become conventional custom for every man to pray for a share in royal mortuary bounty, and all classes of society, down to the humblest craftsman buried in the Abydos cemetery, pray for "an offering which the king gives," although it was out of the question that the masses of the population should enjoy any such privilege.

It is not until this Feudal Age that we gain any full impression of the picturesque customs connected with the dead, the observance of which was now so deeply rooted in the life of the people. The tombs still surviving in the baronies of Upper Egypt have preserved some memorials of the daily and customary, as well as of the ceremonial and festival, usages with which the people thought to brighten and render more attractive the life of those who had passed on. We find the same precautions taken by the nobles which we observed in the Pyramid Age.

The rich noble Hepzefi of Siut, who flourished in the twentieth century before Christ, had before death erected a statue of himself in both the leading temples of his city, that is, *one* in the temple of Upwawet, an ancient Wolf-god of the place, from which it later received its name, Lycopolis, at the hands of the Greeks, and the *other* in the temple of Anubis, a well-known Dog- or Jackal-god, once one of the mortuary rivals of Osiris. The temple of Upwawet was in the midst of the town, while that of Anubis was farther out on the outskirts of the necropolis, at the foot of the cliff, some distance up the face of which Hepzefi had excavated his imposing cliff tomb. In this tomb likewise he had placed a third statue of himself, under charge of his mortuary priest. He had but one priest for the care of his tomb and the ceremonies which he wished to have celebrated on his behalf; but he had secured assistance for this man by calling in the occasional services of the priesthoods of both temples, and certain of the necropolis officials, with all of whom he had made contracts, as well as with his mortuary priest, stipulating exactly what they were to do, and what they were to receive from the noble's revenues in payment for their services or their oblations, regularly and periodically, after the noble's death.

These contracts, ten in number, were placed by the noble in bold inscriptions on the inner wall of his tomb-chapel, and they furnish to-day a very suggestive picture of the calendar of feasts celebrated in this provincial city of which Hepzefi was lord—feasts in all of which living and dead alike participated. The bald data from these contracts will be found in a table below (pp. 268-9), and on the basis of these the following imaginative reconstruction endeavors to correlate them with the life which they suggest. The most important celebrations were those which took place in connection with the new year, before its advent, as well as at and after its arrival. They began five days before the end of the old year, on the first of the five intercalary days with which the year ended. On this day we might have seen the priests of Upwawet in procession winding through the streets and bazaars of Siut, and issuing at last back of the town as they conducted their god to the temple of Anubis at the foot of the cemetery cliff. Here a bull was slaughtered for the visiting deity. Each of the priests carried in his hand a large conical white loaf of bread, and as they entered the court of the Anubis temple, each deposited his loaf at the base of Hepzefi's statue.[1]

Five days later, as the day declined, the overseer of the necropolis, followed by the nine men of his staff, climbed down from the cliffs, past many an open tomb-door which it was the duty of these men to guard, and entered the shades of the town below, now quite dark as it lay in the shadow of the lofty cliffs that overhung it. It is New Year's Eve, and in the twilight here and there the lights of the festival illumination begin to appear in doors and windows. As the men push on through the narrow streets in the outskirts of the town, they are suddenly confronted by the high enclosure wall of the temple of Anubis. Entering at the tall gate they inquire for the "great priest," who presently delivers to them a bale of torches. With these they return, slowly rising above the town as they climb the cliff again. As they look out over the dark roofs shrouded in deep shadows, they discover two isolated clusters of lights, one just below them, the other far out in the town, like two twinkling islands of radiance in a sea of blackness which stretches away at their feet. They are the courts of the two temples, where the illumination is now in full progress. Hepzefi, their ancient lord, sleeping high above them in his cliff tomb, is, nevertheless, present yonder in the midst of the joy and festivity which fill the temple courts. Through the eyes of his statue rising above the multitude which now throngs those courts, he rejoices in the beauty of the bright colonnades, he revels, like his friends below, in the sense of prodigal plenty spread out before him, as he beholds the offering loaves arrayed at his feet, where we saw the priests depositing them; and his ears are filled with the

[1] Contract 1.

roar of a thousand voices as the rejoicings of the assembled city, gathered in their temples to watch the old year die and to hail the new year, swell like the sound of the sea far over the dark roofs, till its dying tide reaches the ears of our group of cemetery guards high up in the darkness of the cliffs as they stand silently looking out over the town.

Just above is the great façade of the tomb where their departed lord, Hepzefi, lies. The older men of the party remember him well, and recall the generosity which they often enjoyed at his hands; but their juniors, to whom he is but an empty name, respond but slowly and reluctantly to the admonitions of the gray-beards to hasten with the illumination of the tomb, as they hear the voice of Hepzefi's priest calling upon them from above to delay no longer. The sparks flash from the "friction lighter" for an instant and then the first torch blazes up, from which the others are quickly kindled. The procession passes out around a vast promontory of the cliff and then turns in again to the tall tomb door, where Hepzefi's priest stands awaiting them, and without more delay they enter the great chapel. The flickering light of the torches falls fitfully upon the wall, where gigantic figures of the dead lord rise so high from the floor that his head is lost in the gloom far above the waning light of the torches. He seems to admonish them to punctilious fulfilment of their duties toward him, as prescribed in the ten contracts recorded on the same wall. He is clad in splendid raiment, and he leans at ease upon his staff. Many a time the older men of the group have seen him standing so, delivering judgment as the culprits were dragged through the door of his busy bureau between a double line of obsequious bailiffs; or again watching the progress of an important irrigation canal which was to open some new field to cultivation. Involuntarily they drop in obeisance before his imposing figure, like the scribes and artisans, craftsmen and peasants who fill the walls before him, in gayly colored reliefs vividly portraying all the industries and pastimes of Hepzefi's great estates and forming a miniature world, where the departed noble, entering his chapel, beholds himself again moving among the scenes and pleasures of the provincial life in which he was so great a figure. To him the walls seem suddenly to have expanded to include harvest-field and busy bazaar, workshop and ship-yard, the hunting-marshes and the banquet-hall, with all of which the sculptor and the painter have peopled these walls till they are indeed alive.

The torches are now planted around the offerings, thickly covering a large stone offering-table, behind which sits Hepzefi's statue in a niche in the wall; and then the little group slowly withdraws, casting many a furtive glance at a false door in the rear wall of the chapel, through which they know Hepzefi may at any moment issue from the shadow world behind it, to re-enter this world and to celebrate with his surviving friends the festivities of New Year's Eve.[1]

The next day, the first day of the new year, is the greatest feast-day in the calendar. There is joyful exchange of gifts, and the people of the estate appear with presents for the lord of the manor. Hepzefi's descendants are much absorbed in their own pleasure, but his cautious contracts, as still recorded in the town archives, ensure him from neglect. While the peasants and the leaseholders of the barony are crowding the gates of the manor-

[1] Contracts 9, 5 and 7.

house, bringing in their gifts to their living lord and thinking little, if at all, of his departed predecessor, we discover the little knot of ten necropolis guards, headed by their chief, again entering the outskirts of the town and proceeding to one of the treasuries of the estate where they are entitled to draw supplies. Presently they march away again, bearing five hundred and fifty fiat cakes, fifty-five white loaves, and eleven jars of beer. Pushing their way slowly through the holiday crowds they retrace their steps to the entrance of the cemetery at the foot of the cliffs, where they find a large crowd already gathered, every one among them similarly laden. Amid much shouting and merry-making, amid innumerable picturesque scenes of Oriental folk-life, such as are still common in the Mohammedan cemeteries of Egypt at the Feast of Bairam, the good towns-people of Siut carry their gifts of food and drink up the cliff to the numerous doors which honeycomb its face, that their dead may share the joyous feast with them. It is, indeed, the earliest Feast of All-Souls. The necropolis guards hasten up to Hepzefi's chapel with their supplies, which they quickly deliver to his priest, and are off again to preserve order among the merry crowds now everywhere pushing up the cliff.[1]

As the day wears on there are busy preparations for the evening celebration, for the illumination, and the "glorification of the blessed," who are the dead. The necropolis guards, weary with a long day of arduous duty in the crowded cemetery, descend for the second time into the town to the temple of Upwawet. Here they find the entire priesthood of the temple waiting to receive them. At the head of the line the "great priest"

[1] Contract 9.

delivers to the ten guards of the necropolis the torches for Hepzefi's "illumination." These are quickly kindled from those which the priests already carry, and the procession of guards and priests together moves slowly out of the temple court and across the sacred enclosure "to the northern corner of the temple," as the contract with Hepzefi prescribes, chanting the "glorification" of Hepzefi.[1] As they go the priests carry each a large conical loaf of white bread, such as they had laid before the statue of Hepzefi in the temple of Anubis five days before. Arrived at the "northern corner of the temple," the priests turn back to their duties in the crowded sanctuary, doubtless handing over their loaves to the necropolis guards, for, as stipulated, these loaves were destined for the statue of Hepzefi in his tomb. Threading the brightly lighted streets of the town, the little procession of ten guards pushes its way with considerable difficulty through the throngs, passing at length the gate of the Anubis temple, where the illumination is in full progress, and the statue of Hepzefi is not forgotten. As they emerge from the town again, still much hampered by the crowds likewise making their way in the same direction, the dark face of the cliff rising high above them is dotted here and there with tiny beacons moving slowly upward. These are the torches of the earlier towns-

---

[1] The nature of this ceremony, which was performed by the living, at the New Year's and other feasts, on behalf of their dead, while not clear in its details, must have been what its name technically defines it to have been. It means "the act of making glorious," and, as we have seen above, one of the epithets applied to the dead was "the glorious." It was therefore a ceremony for accomplishing the transformation of the deceased into a "glorious one," precisely as he was transformed also into a "soul" (ba) by an analogous ceremony performed by the living, a ceremony indeed which may have been much the same as that of glorification.

people, who have already reached the cemetery to plant them before the statues and burial-places of their dead. The guards climb to Hepzefi's tomb as they had done the night before and deliver torches and white bread to Hepzefi's waiting priest. Thus the dead noble shares in the festivities of the New Year's celebration as his children and former subjects were doing.¹

Seventeen days later, on the eve of the Wag-feast, the "great priest of Anubis" brought forth a bale of torches, and, heading his colleagues, they "illuminated" the statue of Hepzefi in the temple court, while each one of them at the same time laid a large white loaf at the feet of the statue. The procession then passed out of the temple enclosure and wound through the streets chanting the "glorification" of Hepzefi till they reached another statue of him which stood at the foot of the stairs leading up the cliff to his tomb. Here they found the chief of the desert patrol, or "overseer of the highland," where the necropolis was, just returning from the magazines in the town, having brought a jar of beer, a large loaf, five hundred flat cakes, and ten white loaves to be delivered to Hepzefi's priest at the tomb above.² The next day, the eighteenth of the first month, the day of the Wag-feast, the priests of Upwawet in the town each presented the usual large white loaf at Hepzefi's statue in their temple, followed by an "illumination" and "glorification" as they marched in procession around the temple court.³

Besides these great feasts which were thus enjoyed by the dead lord, he was not forgotten on any of the periodic minor feasts which fell on the first of every month and

¹ Contracts 9, 2, 5 and 7.   ² Contracts 7, 8 and 10.
³ Contract 4.

half-month, or on any "day of a procession." On these days he received a certain proportion of the meat and beer offered in the temple of Upwawet.[1] His *daily* needs were met by the laymen serving in successive shifts in the temple of Anubis. As this sanctuary was near the cemetery, these men, after completing their duties in the temple, went out every day with a portion of bread and a jar of beer, which they deposited before the statue of Hepzefi "which is on the lower stairs of his tomb."[2] There was, therefore, not a day in the year when Hepzefi failed to receive the food and drink necessary for his maintenance.[3]

Khnumhotep, the powerful baron of Benihasan, tells us more briefly of similar precautions which he took before his death. "I adorned the houses of the kas and the dwelling thereof; I followed my statues to the temple; I devoted for them their offerings: the bread, beer, water, wine, incense, and joints of beef credited to the mortuary priest. I endowed him with fields and peasants; I commanded the mortuary offering of bread, beer, oxen, and geese at every feast of the necropolis: at the Feast of the First of the Year, of New Year's Day, of the Great Year, of the Little Year, of the Last of the Year, the Great Feast, at the Great Rekeh, at the Little Rekeh, at the Feast of the Five (intercalary) Days on the Year, at ⌜. . .⌝ the Twelve Monthly Feasts, at the Twelve Mid-

---

[1] Contract 6. [2] Contract 8.
[3] The preceding account has attempted to indicate to some extent the place of the dead in the celebration of the calendar of feasts as they were in the life of the people. Perhaps imagination has been too liberally drawn upon. The bare data as furnished by the contracts of Hepzefi will be found in the table on pages 268 and 269; the contracts themselves may be found translated in my *Ancient Records*, I, 535–593.

CONTRACT	DATE	OCCASION	OFFERING OR SERVICE CONTRIBUTED	GIVER	RECIPIENT
First	1st of the 5 intercalary days	Procession of Upwawet to temple of Anubis	One white loaf per man	Each priest of the Upwawet temple	Statue of Hepzefi in temple of Anubis
Second	1st of 1st month	New Year's Day, when "the house" "gives gifts to its lord"; illumination	Same; also procession to "north corner of the temple"	Same	Statue of Hepzefi in charge of his priest (in his tomb)
Third	18th of 1st month	Feast of Wag	22 jars of beer, 2200 flat cakes, 55 white loaves	Official body of Upwawet temple (10 persons)	Hepzefi (in order to pay for bread, etc., received in Contract 4)
Fourth	18th of 1st month	Feast of Wag	a. One white loaf per man b. Procession, illumination, and glorification	Lay priesthood of Upwawet temple	Hepzefi
Fifth	a. 5th day of 5 intercalary days b. 1st day of 1st month c. 18th day of 1st month	a. New Year's Eve b. New Year's Day c. Feast of Wag	a. Bale of torches b. Bale of torches c. Bale of torches	a. Keeper of wardrobe of Upwawet temple b. Same c. Same	a. Hepzefi b. Hepzefi c. Hepzefi
Sixth	Probably 1st and 15th of each month and minor feasts	Procession, offerings, slaughter of bulls	1 roast of meat for each bull slaughtered in Upwawet temple, 1 measure of beer for every jar offered in Upwawet temple	Superior prophet of Upwawet	Hepzefi

TRIUMPH OF OSIRIS 269

Seventh	a. 5th of 5 intercalary days b. 1st of 1st month c. 17th of 1st month	a. New Year's Eve; illumination in Anubis temple b. New Year's Day; same c. Eve of Wag-feast; same	a. Bale of torches b. Bale of torches c. Bale of torches	a. Great priest of Anubis b. Same c. Same	Hepzefi
Eighth	a. 17th of 1st month b. Same c. Every day	a. Eve of Wag-feast b. Same c. Every day after daily offering in temple of Anubis	a. One white loaf per man b. Illumination and procession to lower stairs of tomb c. Loaf and jar of beer	a. Lay priests of Anubis b. Same c. Same	a. Statue of Hepzefi in temple of Anubis b. Same c. Statue of Hepzefi on lower stairs of his tomb
Ninth	a. 5th of 5 intercalary days b. 1st of 1st month c. Same	a. New Year's Eve; procession, illumination, glorification b. New Year's Day; same c. New Year's Day	a. Fetching bale of torches from great priest of Anubis to give to mortuary priest of Hepzefi (see Contract 7) b. Same c. 11 jars of beer, 550 flat cakes, 55 white loaves	a. Overseer of necropolis and his staff (10 men) b. Same c. Same	a. Hepzefi b. Same c. Statue of Hepzefi in charge of his mortuary priest (in his tomb)
Tenth	17th of 1st month	Eve of Wag-feast	1 jar beer, 1 large loaf, 500 flat cakes, 10 white loaves	Overseer of the highland (where necropolis was)	Same statue as in Contract 9

NOTE.—The "bale of torches" above enumerated is an interpretation of the word "gmḥt," which I rendered "wick" in my *Ancient Records*, following ERMAN (ÄZ, 1882, pp. 159–184).

CONTRACT	DATE	OCCASION	OFFERING OR SERVICE CONTRIBUTED	GIVER	RECIPIENT
First	1st of the 5 intercalary days	Procession of Upwawet to temple of Anubis	One white loaf per man	Each priest of the Upwawet temple	Statue of Hepzefi in temple of Anubis
Second	1st of 1st month	New Year's Day, when "the house" "gives gifts to its lord"; illumination	Same; also procession to "north corner of the temple"	Same	Statue of Hepzefi in charge of his priest (in his tomb)
Third	18th of 1st month	Feast of Wag	22 jars of beer. 2200 flat cakes, 55 white loaves	Official body of Upwawet temple (10 persons)	Hepzefi (in order to pay for bread, etc., received in Contract 4)
Fourth	18th of 1st month	Feast of Wag	a. One white loaf per man b. Procession, illumination, and glorification	Lay priesthood of Upwawet temple	Hepzefi
Fifth	a. 5th day of 5 intercalary days b. 1st day of 1st month c. 18th day of 1st month	a. New Year's Eve b. New Year's Day c. Feast of Wag	a. Bale of torches b. Bale of torches c. Bale of torches	a. Keeper of wardrobe of Upwawet temple b. Same c. Same	a. Hepzefi b. Hepzefi c. Hepzefi
Sixth	Probably 1st and 15th of each month and minor feasts	Procession, offerings, slaughter of bulls	1 roast of meat for each bull slaughtered in Upwawet temple, 1 measure of beer for every jar offered in Upwawet temple	Superior prophet of Upwawet	Hepzefi

TRIUMPH OF OSIRIS

Seventh	a. 5th of 5 intercalary days	a. New Year's Eve; illumination in Anubis temple	a. Bale of torches	a. Great priest of Anubis	
	b. 1st of 1st month	b. New Year's Day; same	b. Bale of torches	b. Same	Hepzefi
	c. 17th of 1st month	c. Eve of Wag-feast; same	c. Bale of torches	c. Same	
Eighth	a. 17th of 1st month	a. Eve of Wag-feast	a. One white loaf per man	a. Lay priests of Anubis	a. Statue of Hepzefi in temple of Anubis
	b. Same	b. Same	b. Illumination and procession to lower stairs of tomb	b. Same	b. Same
	c. Every day	c. Every day after daily offering in temple of Anubis	c. Loaf and jar of beer	c. Same	c. Statue of Hepzefi on lower stairs of his tomb
Ninth	a. 5th of 5 intercalary days	a. New Year's Eve; procession, illumination, glorification	a. Fetching bale of torches from great priest of Anubis to give to mortuary priest of Hepzefi (see Contract 7)	a. Overseer of necropolis and his staff (10 men)	a. Hepzefi
	b. 1st of 1st month	b. New Year's Day; same	b. Same	b. Same	b. Same
	c. Same	c. New Year's Day	c. 11 jars of beer, 550 flat cakes, 55 white loaves	c. Same	c. Statue of Hepzefi in charge of his mortuary priest (in his tomb)
Tenth	17th of 1st month	Eve of Wag-feast	1 jar beer, 1 large loaf, 500 flat cakes, 10 white loaves	Overseer of the highland (where necropolis was)	Same statue as in Contract 9

NOTE.—The "bale of torches" above enumerated is an interpretation of the word "gmḥt," which I rendered "wick" in my *Ancient Records*, following ERMAN (ÄZ, 1882, pp. 159–184).

monthly Feasts; every feast of the happy living and of the dead.[1] Now, as for the mortuary priest, or any person who shall disturb them, he shall not survive, his son shall not survive in his place."[2] The apprehension of the noble is evident, and such apprehensions are common in documents of this nature. We have seen Hepzefi equally apprehensive.

That these gifts to the dead noble should continue indefinitely was, of course, quite impossible. We of to-day have little piety for the grave of a departed grandfather; few of us even know where our great-grandfathers are interred. The priests of Anubis and Upwawet and the necropolis guards at Siut will have continued their duties only so long as Hepzefi's mortuary priest received his income and was true to his obligations in reminding them of theirs, and in seeing to it that these obligations were met. We find such an endowment surviving a change of dynasty (from the Fourth to the Fifth), and lasting at least some thirty or forty years, in the middle of the twenty-eighth century before Chirst.[3] In the Twelfth Dynasty, too, there was in Upper Egypt great respect for the ancestors of the Old Kingdom. The nomarchs of El-Bersheh, in the nineteenth and twentieth centuries before Christ, repaired the tombs of their ancestors of the Pyramid Age, tombs then over six hundred years old, and therefore in a state of ruin. The pious nomarch used to record his restoration in these words: "He (the nomarch) made (it) as his monument for his fathers, who are in the necropolis, the lords of this promontory; restoring what was found

---

[1] Lit. "every feast of the happy one in the (valley-) plain, and of the one on the mountain;" those who are on the plain still live, but those on the mountain are the dead in the cliff tombs.

[2] BAR, I, 630.   [3] BAR, I, 213.

in ruin and renewing what was found decayed, the ancestors who were before not having done it." We find the nobles of this province using this formula five times in the tombs of their ancestors.[1] In the same way, Intef, a baron of Hermonthis, says: "I found the chapel of the prince Nekhtyoker fallen to ruin, its walls were old, its statues were shattered, there was no one who cared for them. It was built up anew, its plan was extended, its statues were made anew, its doors were built of stone, that its place might excel beyond that of other august princes."[2] Such piety toward the departed fathers, however, was very rare, and even when shown could not do more than postpone the evil day. The marvel is that with their ancestors' ruined tombs before them they nevertheless still went on to build for themselves sepulchres which were inevitably to meet the same fate. The tomb of Khnumhotep, the greatest of those left us by the Benihasan lords of four thousand years ago, bears on its walls, among the beautiful paintings which adorn them, the scribblings of a hundred and twenty generations in Egyptian, Coptic, Greek, Arabic, French, Italian, and English. The earliest of these scrawls is that of an Egyptian scribe who entered the tomb-chapel over three thousand years ago and wrote with reed pen and ink upon the wall these words: "The scribe Amenmose came to see the temple of Khufu and found it like the heavens when the sun rises therein."[3] The chapel was some seven hundred years old when this scribe entered it, and its owner, although one of the greatest lords of his time, was so completely forgotten that the visitor, finding the name of Khufu in a casual geographical reference among the inscriptions on the wall, mistook the

[1] BAR, I, 688–9.   [2] Berlin, 13272; ERMAN, *Rel.*, pp. 143 *f.*
[3] NEWBERRY, *Benihasan*, I, pl. xxviii, 3.

place for a chapel of Khufu, the builder of the Great Pyramid. All knowledge of the noble and of the endowments which were to support him in the hereafter had disappeared in spite of the precautions which we have read above. How vain and futile now appear the imprecations on these time-stained walls!

But the Egyptian was not wholly without remedy even in the face of this dire contingency. He endeavored to meet the difficulty by engraving on the front of his tomb, prayers believed to be efficacious in supplying all the needs of the dead in the hereafter. All passers-by were solemnly adjured to utter these prayers on behalf of the dead.

The belief in the effectiveness of the uttered word on behalf of the dead had developed enormously since the Old Kingdom. This is a development which accompanies the popularization of the mortuary customs of the upper classes. In the Pyramid Age, as we have seen, such utterances were confined to the later pyramids. These concern exclusively the destiny of the Pharaoh in the hereafter. They were now largely appropriated by the middle and the official class. At the same time there emerge similar utterances, identical in function but evidently more suited to the needs of common mortals. These represent, then, a body of similar mortuary literature among the *people* of the Feudal Age, some fragments of which are much older than this age. Later the Book of the Dead was made up of selections from this humbler and more popular mortuary literature. Copious extracts from both the Pyramid Texts and these forerunners of the Book of the Dead, about half from each of the two sources, were now written on the inner surfaces of the heavy cedar coffins, in which the better burials of this age are found. The number of such mortuary texts is still constantly increasing as additional coffins from this age are found. Every local coffin-maker was furnished by the priests of his town with copies of these utterances. Before the coffins were put together, the scribes in the maker's employ filled the inner surfaces with pen-and-ink copies of such texts as he had available. It was all done with great carelessness and inaccuracy, the effort being to fill up the planks as fast as possible. They often wrote the same chapter over twice or three times in the same coffin, and in one instance a chapter is found no less than five times in the same coffin.[1]

---

[1] LACAU, XXII, *Rec.* 29, 143 *ff.* These texts as a class are sometimes designated as the Book of the Dead. As about half of them are taken from the Pyramid Texts, and the Pyramid Texts are sharply distinguished from the Book of the Dead (the former for the use of the king originally, the latter for universal use), it would seem not only incorrect, but also the obliteration of a useful distinction to term these Middle Kingdom texts the Book of the Dead. Hence I have for convenience termed them Coffin Texts, a designation drawn from the place in which they are found, and thus parallel with the Pyramid Texts. These Coffin Texts have never been collected and published as a whole. A very valuable collection taken from the coffins in the Cairo Museum has been made and published by LACAU, *Textes religieux, Recueil de travaux*, vols. 26–27, 28–33. LACAU's collection is not yet all in print, but it includes eight-six chapters. The character of the Coffin Texts as containing the earliest surviving fragments of the Book of the Dead was first recognised by LEPSIUS, who published the material in the Berlin collection (LEPSIUS, *Aelteste Texte des Todtenbuchs*, Berlin, 1867), and other texts were later published by BIRCH (*Egyptian Texts . . . from the Coffin of Amamu*, London, 1886). WILKINSON's tracing of an Eleventh Dynasty Coffin Text, now lost, was published by BUDGE, *Facsimiles of Egyptian Hieratic Papyri in the British Museum*, London, 1910, pl. xxxix–xlviii, pp. xxi–xxii. A similar body of texts from the sepulchre of the Middle Kingdom tomb of Harhotep was published by MASPERO, *Mémoires de la Mission arch. au Caire*, vol. I, 136–184. A useful statement of the available materials will be found by LACAU in his *Sarcophages antérieures au Nouvel Empire*, I (*Catalogue*

In so far as these Coffin Texts are identical with the Pyramid Texts we are already familiar with their general function and content.[1] The hereafter to which these citizens of the Feudal Age looked forward was, therefore, still largely celestial and Solar as in the Pyramid Age. But even these early chapters of the Book of the Dead disclose a surprising predominance of the celestial hereafter. There is the same identification with the Sun-god which we found in the Pyramid Texts. There is a chapter of "Becoming Re-Atum,"[2] and several of "Becoming a Falcon."[3] The deceased, now no longer the king, as in the Pyramid Texts, says: "I am the soul of the god, self-generator. . . . I have become he. I am he before whom the sky is silent, I am he before whom the earth is ⌜. . .⌝ . . . I have become the limbs of the god, self-generator. He has made me into his heart (understanding), he has fashioned me into his soul. I am one who has ⌜breathed⌝ the form of him who fashioned me, the august god, self-generator, whose name the gods know not. . . . He has made me into his heart, he has fashioned me into his soul, I was not born with a birth."[4] This identification of the deceased with the Sun-god alternates with old pictures of the Solar destiny, involving only association with the Sun-god. There is a chapter of "Ascending to the Sky to the Place where Re is,"[5] another of "Embarking in

général . . . du Musée du Caire, Cairo, 1904, pp. vi f. An exhaustive comparison and study of this entire body of mortuary texts is very much needed, and the work of LACAU is a valuable contribution to this end.

[1] See above, pp. 84–141. [2] LACAU, LII, *Rec.* 31, 10.
[3] A Solar symbol. LACAU, XVI, *Rec.* 27, 54 f.; LACAU, XXXVIII, *Rec.* 30, 189 f.; LACAU, XVII, *Rec.* 27, 55 f. The last is largely Osirian, but Re-Atum is prominent.
[4] *Annales du Service*, V, 235.
[5] LACAU, VI, *Rec.* 26, 225.

the Ship of Re when he has Gone to his Ka;[1] and a "Chapter of Entering Into the West among the Followers of Re Every Day."[2] When once there the dead man finds among his resources a chapter of "Being the Scribe of Re."[3] He also has a chapter of "Becoming One Revered by the King,"[4] presumably meaning the Sun-god, as the chapter is a magical formulary for accomplishing the ascent to the sky. In the same way he may become an associate of the Sun-god by using a chapter of "Becoming One of ⌈the Great⌉ of Heliopolis."[5]

The famous seventeenth chapter of the Book of the Dead was already a favorite chapter in this age, and begins the texts on a number of coffins. It is largely an identification of the deceased with the Sun-god, although other gods also appear. The dead man says:

> "I am Atum, I who was alone;
> I am Re at his first appearance.
> I am the Great God, self-generator,
> Who fashioned his names, lord of gods,
> Whom none approaches among the gods.
> I was yesterday, I know to-morrow.
> The battle-field of the gods was made when I spake.
> I know the name of that Great God who is therein.
> 'Praise-of-Re' is his name.
> I am that great Phœnix which is in Heliopolis."

Just as in the Pyramid Texts, however, so in these early Texts of the Book of the Dead, the Osirian theology has

[1] LACAU, XXXII, *Rec.* 30, 185 *f.*
[2] LACAU, XLI, *Rec.* 30, 191 *f.*
[3] LACAU, LIII, *Rec.* 31, 10 *f.* But the text is Osirian; see below, p. 277.
[4] LACAU, XV, *Rec.* 27, 53 *f.*
[5] LACAU, XL, *Rec.* 30, 191. *Cf. Book of the Dead*, chaps. LXXIX and LXXXII.

intruded and has indeed taken possession of them. Already in the Feudal Age this ancient Solar text had been supplied with an explanatory commentary, which adds to the line, "I was yesterday, I know to-morrow," the words, "that is Osiris." The result of this Osirianization was the intrusion of the Osirian *subterranean* hereafter, even in Solar and celestial texts. Thus this seventeenth chapter was supplied with a title reading, "Chapter of Ascending by Day from the Nether World."[1] This title is not original, and is part of the Osirian editing, which involuntarily places the sojourn of the dead in the Nether World though it cannot eliminate all the old Solar texts. The titles now commonly appended to these texts frequently conclude with the words, "in the Nether World." We find a chapter for "The Advancement of a Man in the Nether World,"[2] although it is devoted throughout to Solar and celestial conceptions. In the Pyramid Texts, as we have seen, the intrusion of Osiris did not result in altering the essentially *celestial* character of the hereafter to which they are devoted. In the Coffin Texts we have not only the commingling of Solar and Osirian beliefs which now more completely coalesce than before, but the

---

[1] The word which I have rendered "Ascending" is commonly rendered "going forth." A study of the use of the word (pr't) in mortuary texts shows clearly that it means to ascend. The following are some decisive examples of its use in the Pyramid Texts: of the rising of the sun (§§ 743 b, 800 a, 812 c, 919 a, 923 c, 971 e); of the rising of a star (§§ 871 b, 877 c) (compare the "Rising of Sothis"); of the ascent of a bird to the sky (§ 913 a); with the words "to the sky" added, not infrequently (e. g., § 922 a); on a ladder (§§ 974–5); in opposed parallelism with "descend" (§§ 821 b–c, 867 a, 922 a, 927 b). There is indeed in the Coffin Texts a "Chapter of Ascending (*pr't*) to the Sky to the Place where Re is" (*Rec.* 26, 225). These examples might be increased *ad infinitum*, and there can be no question regarding the rendering "Ascending."

[2] LACAU, XIII, *Rec.* 26, 232 *ff*.

result is that Re is intruded into the *subterranean* hereafter. The course of events may be stated in somewhat exaggerated form if we say that in the Pyramid Texts Osiris was lifted skyward, while in the Coffin Texts and the Book of the Dead, Re is dragged earthward.

The resulting confusion is even worse than in the Pyramid Texts. We shall shortly find Re appearing with subterranean functions on behalf of the dead, functions entirely unknown in the Pyramid Texts. The old Solar idea that the dead might become the scribe of Re, we have already found in the Coffin Texts; but while the title is given as "Being the Scribe of Re," the text begins, "I am Kerkeru, scribe of Osiris."[1] We can hardly conceive a mass of mortuary doctrine containing a "Chapter of Reaching Orion,"[2] a fragment of ancient celestial belief, side by side with such chapters as "Burial in the West,"[3] "That the Beautiful West Rejoice at the Approach of a Man,"[4] "Chapter of Becoming the Nile,"[5] which is, of course, a purely Osirian title although the text of the chapter is Solar; or a chapter of "Becoming the Harvest-god (Neper)," in which the deceased is identified with Osiris and with barley, as well as with Neper, god of harvest and grain.[6]

The Coffin Texts already display the tendency, carried so much further by the Book of the Dead, of enabling the deceased to transform himself at will into various beings. It was this notion which led Herodotus to conclude that the Egyptians believed in what we now call transmigration of souls, but this is a mistaken impression on his part. Besides identification with Re, Osiris, and other gods,

---

[1] LACAU, LIII, *Rec.* 31, 10 f.
[2] LACAU, LXII, *Rec.* 31, 19.
[5] LACAU, XIX, *Rec.* 27, 217 ff.
[3] LACAU, XI, *Rec.* 26, 229.
[4] LACAU, XLIII, *Rec.* 30, 192 f.
[6] LACAU, LVIII, *Rec.* 31, 15 f.

which, of course, involved belief in a transformation, the Coffin Texts also enable the deceased to "become the blazing Eye of Horus."[1] By the aid of another chapter he can accomplish the "transformation into an ekhet-bird"[2] or "into the servant at the table of Hathor."[3]

It is difficult to gain any coherent conception of the hereafter which the men of this age thus hoped to attain. There are the composite Solar-Osirian pictures which we have already found in the Pyramid Texts, and in which the priests to whom we owe these Coffin Text compilations allow their fancy to roam at will. The deceased citizen, now sharing the destiny of Osiris and called such by Horus, hears himself receiving words of homage and promises of felicity addressed to him by his divine son:

"I come, I am Horus who opens thy mouth, together with Ptah who glorifies thee, together with Thoth who gives to thee thy heart (understanding); . . . that thou mayest remember what thou hadst forgotten. I cause that thou eat bread at the desire of thy body. I cause that thou remember what thou hast forgotten. I cause that thou eat bread . . . more than thou didst on earth. I give to thee thy two feet that thou mayest make the going and coming of thy two soles (or sandals). I cause that thou shouldst carry out commissions with the south wind and shouldst run with the north wind. . . . I cause that thou shouldst ferry over ⌈Peterui⌉ and ferry over the lake of thy wandering and the sea of (thy) sandal as thou didst on earth. Thou rulest the streams and the Phœnix. . . . Thou leviest on the royal domains. Thou repulsest the violent who comes in the night, the

---

[1] LACAU, LXXX, Rec. 31, 166. [2] LACAU, XXX, Rec. 30, 71.
[3] LACAU, XXXI, Rec. 30, 72 f.

robber of early morning.¹ . . . Thou goest around the countries with Re; he lets thee see the pleasant places, thou findest the valleys filled with water for washing thee and for cooling thee, thou pluckest marsh-flowers and heni-blossoms, lilies and lotus-flowers. The birdpools come to thee by thousands, lying in thy path; when thou hast hurled thy boomerang against them, it is a thousand that fall at the sound of the wind thereof. They are ro-geese, green-fronts, quails, and kunuset.² I cause that there be brought to thee the young gazelles, ⌈bullocks⌉ of white bulls; I cause that there be brought to thee males of goats and grain-fed males of sheep. There is fastened for thee a ladder to the sky. Nut gives to thee her two arms. Thou sailest in the Lily-lake. Thou bearest the wind in an eight-ship. These two fathers (Re and Atum) of the Imperishable Stars and of the Unweariable Stars sail thee. They command thee, they tow thee through the district with their imperishable ropes." ³

In another Solar-Osirian chapter, after the deceased is crowned, purified, and glorified, he enters upon the Solar voyage as in the Pyramid Texts. It is then said of him: "Brought to thee are blocks of silver and ⌈masses⌉ of malachite. Hathor, mistress of Byblos, she makes the rudders of thy ship. . . . It is said to thee, 'Come into the broad-hall,' by the Great who are in the temple. Bared to thee are the Four Pillars of the Sky, thou seest the secrets that are therein, thou stretchest out thy two legs upon the Pillars of the Sky and the wind is sweet to thy nose." ⁴

---

¹ Thus far the picture is Osirian; it now becomes Solar.
² Varieties of wild fowl. ³ Lacau, XXII, *Rec.* 29, 143 *ff*.
⁴ Lacau, XX, *Rec.* 27, 221–6.

While the destiny, everywhere so evidently royal in the Pyramid Texts, has thus become the portion of any one, the simpler life of the humbler citizen which he longed to see continued in the hereafter is quite discernible, also in these Coffin Texts. As he lay in his coffin he could read a chapter which concerned "Building a house for a man in the Nether World, digging a pool and planting fruit-trees."[1] Once supplied with a house, surrounded by a garden with its pool and its shade-trees, the dead man must be assured that he shall be able to occupy it, and hence a "chapter of a man's being in his house."[2] The lonely sojourn there without the companionship of family and friends was an intolerable thought, and hence a further chapter entitled "Sealing of a Decree concerning the Household, to give the Household [to a man] in the Nether World." In the text the details of the decree are five times specified in different forms. "Geb, hereditary prince of the gods, has decreed that there be given to me my household, my children, my brothers, my father, my mother, my slaves, and all my establishment." Lest they should be withheld by any malign influence the second paragraph asserts that "Geb, hereditary prince of the gods, has said to release for me my household, ⌜my⌝ children, my brothers and sisters, my father, my mother, all my slaves, all my establishment at once, rescued from every god, from every goddess, from every death (or dead person)."[3] To assure the fulfilment of this decree there was another chapter entitled "Uniting of the Household of a Man with Him in the Nether World," which effected the "union of the household, father, mother, children, friends, ⌜connections⌝, wives, concubines, slaves, servants,

[1] LACAU, LXVII, Rec. 31, 24f.   [2] LACAU, XXXIV, Rec. 30, 186f.
[3] LACAU, LXXII, Rec. 31, 26-29.

everything belonging to a man, with him in the Nether World." [1]

The rehabilitation of a man's home and household in the hereafter was a thought involving, more inevitably even than formerly, the old-time belief in the necessity of food. It reminds us of the Pyramid Texts when we find a chapter of "Causing that X Raise Himself Upon his Right Side." [2] The mummy lies upon the left side, and he rises to the other side in order that he may partake of food. Hence, another "Chapter of Eating Bread in the Nether World," [3] or "Eating of Bread on the Table of Re, Giving of Plenty in Heliopolis." [4] The very next chapter shows us how "the sitter sits to eat bread when Re sits to eat bread. . . . Give to me bread when I am hungry. Give to me beer when I am thirsty." [5]

A tendency which later came fully to its own in the Book of the Dead is already the dominant tendency in these Coffin Texts. It regards the hereafter as a place of innumerable dangers and ordeals, most of them of a physical nature, although they sometimes concern also the intellectual equipment of the deceased. The weapon to be employed and the surest means of defence available to the deceased was some magical agency, usually a charm to be pronounced at the critical moment. This tendency then inclined to make the Coffin Texts, and ultimately the Book of the Dead which grew out of them, more and more a collection of charms, which were regarded as inevitably effective in protecting the dead or securing for him any of the blessings which were desired in the life beyond the grave. There was, therefore, a chapter of

[1] LACAU, II, *Rec.* 26, 67-73.   [2] LACAU, XXXIX, *Rec.* 30, 190 *f.*
[3] LACAU, XLV, *Rec.* 30, 193 *f.*
[4] LACAU, III, *Rec.* 26, 73 *ff.*   [5] LACAU, IV, *Rec.* 26, 76 *ff.*

"Becoming a Magician," addressed to the august ones who are in the presence of Atum the Sun-god. It is, of course, itself a charm and concludes with the words, "I am a magician."[1] Lest the dead man should lose his magic power, there was a ceremony involving the "attachment of a charm so that the magical power of man may not be taken away from him in the Nether World."[2] The simplest of the dangers against which these charms were supplied doubtless arose in the childish imagination of the common folk. They are frequently grotesque in the extreme. We find a chapter "preventing that the head of a man be taken from him."[3] There is the old charm found also in the Pyramid Texts to prevent a man from being obliged to eat his own foulness.[4] He is not safe from the decay of death; hence there are two chapters that "a man may not decay in the Nether World."[5] But the imagination of the priests, who could only gain by the issuance of ever new chapters, undoubtedly contributed much to heighten the popular dread of the dangers of the hereafter and spread the belief in the usefulness of such means for meeting them. We should doubtless recognize the work of the priests in the figure of a mysterious scribe named Gebga, who is hostile to the dead, so that a charm was specially devised to enable the dead man to break the pens, smash the writing outfit, and tear up the rolls of the malicious Gebga.[6] That men-

[1] LACAU, LXXVIII, *Rec.* 31, 164 ff.   [2] LACAU, VII, *Rec.* 26, 226.
[3] LACAU, VIII, *Rec.* 26, 226–7; also *Annales*, V, 241.
[4] LACAU, XXII, *Rec.* 29, 150; XXIV, *Rec.* 29, 156 f. Similar passages will be found in the *Book of the Dead*, LI, LIII, LXXXII, CII, CXVI, CXXIV, CLXXXIX. *Cf.* Pyr. §§ 127–8, and BD, CLXXVIII. References from LACAU.
[5] LACAU, XXV, XXVI, *Rec.* 29, 157–9.
[6] LACAU, IX, X, *Rec.* 26, 227 ff. He occurs also in the tomb of Harhotep, *Mém. de la Miss. franç. au Caire*, I, 166.

acing danger which was also feared in the Pyramid Texts, the assaults of venomous serpents, must likewise be met by the people of the Feudal Age. The dead man, therefore, finds in his roll charms for "Repulsing Apophis from the Barque of Re" and for "Repulsing the Serpent which ⌜Afflicts⌝ the Kas,"[1] not to mention also one for "Repulsing Serpents and Repulsing Crocodiles."[2] The way of the departed was furthermore beset with fire, and he would be lost without a charm for "Going Forth from the Fire,"[3] or of "Going Forth from the Fire Behind the Great God."[4] When he was actually obliged to enter the fire he might do so with safety by means of a "Chapter of Entering Into the Fire and of Coming Forth from the Fire Behind the Sky."[5] Indeed, the priests had devised a chart of the journey awaiting the dead, guiding him through the gate of fire at the entrance and showing the two ways by which he might proceed, one by land and the other by water, with a lake of fire between them. This Book of the Two Ways, with its map of the journey, was likewise recorded in the coffin.[6] In spite of such guidance it might unluckily happen that the dead wander into the place of execution of the gods; but from this he was saved by a chapter of "Not Entering Into the Place of Execution of the Gods;[7] and lest he should suddenly find himself condemned to walk head downward, he

---

[1] LACAU, XXXV, XXXVI, Rec. 30, 187–8.
[2] LACAU, LXXIII, Rec. 31, 29.
[3] LACAU, XXXVII, Rec. 30, 188 f.
[4] LACAU, XLIX, Rec. 30, 198.   [5] LACAU, XLVIII, Rec. 30, 197.
[6] Berlin Coffin, Das Buch von den zwei Wegen des seligen Toten, by H. SCHACK-SCHACKENBURG, Leipzig, 1903; also three coffins in Cairo, see LACAU, Sarcophages antérieures au Nouvel Empire, vol. I, Nos. 28083 and 28085, pls. lv., lvi, lvii; vol. II, No. 28089. Cf. also GRAPOW, Zeitschr. für aegypt. Sprache, 46, 77 ff.
[7] LACAU, LXIII, Rec. 31, 20.

was supplied with a "Chapter of Not Walking Head Downward."[1] These unhappy dead who were compelled to go head downward were the most malicious enemies in the hereafter. Protection against them was vitally necessary. It is said to the deceased: "Life comes to thee, but death comes not to thee. . . . They (Orion, Sothis, and the Morning Star) save thee from the wrath of the dead who go head downward. Thou art not among them. . . . Rise up for life, thou diest not; lift thee up for life, thou diest not."[2] The malice of the dead was a danger constantly threatening the newly arrived soul, who says: "He causes that I gain the power over my enemies. I have expelled them from their tombs. I have overthrown them in their (tomb-) chapels. I have expelled those who were in their places. I have opened their mummies, destroyed their kas. I have suppressed their souls. . . . An edict of the Self-Generator has been issued against my enemies among the dead, among the living, dwelling in sky and earth."[3] The belief in the efficacy of magic as an infallible agent in the hand of the dead man was thus steadily growing, and we shall see it ultimately dominating the whole body of mortuary belief as it emerges a few centuries later in the Book of the Dead. It cannot be doubted that the popularity of the Osirian faith had much to do with this increase in the use of mortuary magical agencies. The Osiris myth, now universally current, made all classes familiar with the same agencies employed by Isis in the raising of Osiris from the dead, while the same myth in its various versions told the people how similar magical power had been employed by Anubis, Thoth, and Horus on behalf of the dead and persecuted Osiris.

[1] Lacau, XLIV, Rec. 30, 193.   [2] Lacau, LXXXV, Rec. 32, 78.
[3] Lacau, LXXXIV, Rec. 31, 175.

Powerful as the Osiris faith had been in the Pyramid Age, its wide popularity now surpassed anything before known. We see in it the triumph of folk-religion as opposed to or contrasted with a state cult like that of Re. The supremacy of Re was a political triumph; that of Osiris, while unquestionably fostered by an able priesthood probably practising constant propaganda, was a triumph of popular faith among all classes of society, a triumph which not even the court and the nobles were able to resist. The blessings which the Osirian destiny in the hereafter offered to all proved an attraction of universal power. If they had once been an exclusively royal prerogative, as was the Solar destiny in the Pyramid Texts, we have seen that even the royal Solar hereafter had now been appropriated by all. One of the ancient tombs of the Thinite kings at Abydos, a tomb now thirteen or fourteen hundred years old, had by this time come to be regarded as the tomb of Osiris. It rapidly became the Holy Sepulchre of Egypt, to which all classes pilgrimaged. The greatest of all blessings was to be buried in the vicinity of this sacred tomb, and more than one functionary took advantage of some official journey or errand to erect a tomb there.[1] If a real tomb was impossible, it was nevertheless beneficial to build at least a false tomb there bearing one's name and the names of one's family and relatives. Failing this, great numbers of pilgrims and visiting officials each erected a memorial tablet or stela bearing prayers to the great god on behalf of the visitor and his family. Thus an official of Amenemhet II, who was sent by the king on a journey of inspection among the temples of the South, says on his stela found at Abydos: "I fixed my name at the place where

[1] BAR, I, 528 and 746.

is the god Osiris, First of the Westerners, Lord of Eternity, Ruler of the West, (the place) to which all that is flees, for the sake of the benefit therein, in the midst of the followers of the Lord of Life, that I might eat his loaf and 'ascend by day'; that my soul might enjoy the ceremonies of people kind in heart toward my tomb and in hand toward my stela."¹ Another under Sesostris I says: "I have made this tomb at the stairway of the Great God, in order that I may be among his followers, while the soldiers who follow his majesty give to my ka of his bread and his ⌈provision⌉, just as every royal messenger does who comes inspecting the boundaries of his majesty."² The enclosure and the approach to the temple of Osiris were filled with these memorials, which as they survive to-day form an important part of our documentary material for the history of this age. The body of a powerful baron might even be brought to Abydos to undergo certain ceremonies there, and to bring back certain things to his tomb at home, as the Arab brings back water from the well of Zemzem, or as Roman ladies brought back sacred water from the sanctuary of Isis at Philæ. Khnumhotep of Benihasan has depicted on the walls of his tomb-chapel this voyage on the Nile, showing his embalmed body resting on a funeral barge which is being towed northward, accompanied by priests and lectors. The inscription calls it the "voyage up-stream to know the things of Abydos." A pendent scene showing a voyage down-stream is accompanied by the words, "the return bringing the things of Abydos."³ Just what these sacred

¹ BAR, I, 613.   ² BAR, I, 528.
³ LEPSIUS, *Denkmaeler*, II, 126–7; NEWBERRY, *Benihasan*, I, pl. xxix, also p. 68, where both scenes are stated to depict the voyage *to* Abydos. It is clear, both from the inscriptions ("voyage up-stream" and "return") and from the scenes themselves, that the voyage *to*

"things of Abydos" may have been we have no means of knowing,[1] but it is evident that on this visit to the great god at Abydos, it was expected that the dead might personally present himself and thus ensure himself the favor of the god in the hereafter.

The visitors who thus came to Abydos, before or after death, brought so many votive offerings that the modern excavators of the Osiris tomb found it deeply buried under a vast accumulation of broken pots and other gifts left there by the pilgrims of thousands of years. There must eventually have been multitudes of such pilgrims at this Holy Sepulchre of Egypt at all times, but especially at that season when in the earliest known drama the incidents of the god's myth were dramatically re-enacted in what may properly be called a "passion play." Although this play is now completely lost, the memorial stone of Ikhernofret, an officer of Sesostris III, who was sent by the king to undertake some restorations in the Osiris temple at Abydos, a stone now preserved in Berlin, furnishes an outline from which we may draw at least the titles of the most important acts. These show us that the drama must have continued for a number of days, and that each of the more important acts probably lasted at least a day, the multitude participating in much that was done. In the brief narrative of Ikhernofret we discern eight acts.

Abydos and return are depicted. The vessel going up-stream shows canvas set as it should for sailing up-stream, while the other (the "return") shows the mast unstepped, as customary in coming downstream at the present day. *Moreover, both boats actually face to and from Abydos as they now stand on the tomb wall.* This device is not unknown elsewhere, *e. g.*, the ships of Hatshepsut, on the walls of the Der el-Bahri temple, face to and from Punt (BAR, II, 251 and p. 105).

[1] The word employed (ḫr't) is one of the widest latitude in meaning. Its original meaning is "that which belongs to" (a thing or person), then his "being, state, concerns, needs," and the like.

The first discloses the old mortuary god Upwawet issuing in procession that he may scatter the enemies of Osiris and open the way for him. In the second act Osiris himself appears in his sacred barque, into which ascend certain of the pilgrims. Among these is Ikhernofret, as he proudly tells in his inscription. There he aids in repelling the foes of Osiris who beset the course of the barque, and there is undoubtedly a general *melée* of the multitude, such as Herodotus saw at Papremis fifteen hundred years later, some in the barque defending the god, and others, proud to carry away a broken head on behalf of the celebration, acting as his enemies in the crowd below. Ikhernofret, like Herodotus, passes over the death of the god in silence. It was a thing too sacred to be described. He only tells that he arranged the "Great Procession" of the god, a triumphal celebration of some sort, when the god met his death. This was the third act. In the fourth Thoth goes forth and doubtless finds the body, though this is not stated. The fifth act is made up of the sacred ceremonies by which the body of the god is prepared for entombment, while in the sixth we behold the multitude moving out in a vast throng to the Holy Sepulchre in the desert behind Abydos to lay away the body of the dead god in his tomb. The seventh act must have been an imposing spectacle. On the shore or water of Nedyt, near Abydos, the enemies of Osiris, including of course Set and his companions, are overthrown in a great battle by Horus, the son of Osiris. The raising of the god from the dead is not mentioned by Ikhernofret, but in the eighth and final act we behold Osiris, restored to life, entering the Abydos temple in triumphal procession. It is thus evident that the drama presented the chief incidents in the myth.

As narrated by Ikhernofret, the acts in which he participated were these:

(1) "I celebrated the 'Procession of Upwawet' when he proceeded to champion his father (Osiris)."

(2) "I repulsed those who were hostile to the Neshmet barque, and I overthrew the enemies of Osiris."

(3) "I celebrated the 'Great Procession,' following the god in his footsteps."

(4) "I sailed the divine barque, while Thoth . . . the voyage."

(5) "I equipped the barque (called) 'Shining in Truth,' of the Lord of Abydos, with a chapel; I put on his beautiful regalia when he went forth to the district of Peker."

(6) "I led the way of the god to his tomb in Peker."

(7) "I championed Wennofer (Osiris) on 'That Day of the Great Battle'; I overthrew all the enemies upon the shore of Nedyt."

(8) "I caused him to proceed into the barque (called) 'The Great'; it bore his beauty; I gladdened the heart of the eastern highlands; I [put] jubilation in the western highlands, when they saw the beauty of the Neshmet barque. It landed at Abydos and they brought [Osiris, First of the Westerners, Lord] of Abydos to his palace."[1]

It is evident that such popular festivals as these gained a great place in the affections of the people, and over and over again, on their Abydos tablets, the pilgrims pray that after death they may be privileged to participate in these celebrations, just as Hepzefi arranged to do so in those at Siut. Thus presented in dramatic form the in-

[1] Stela of Ikhernofret, Berlin 1204, ll. 17-23. It was published by LEPSIUS, *Denkmaeler*, II, 135 b, and much more carefully by SCHAEFER, *Die Mysterien des Osiris in Abydos* (SETHE, *Untersuchungen*, IV, 2), Leipzig, 1904, with full discussion. Translation will also be found in BAR, I, 661-670 (some alterations above).

cidents of the Osiris myth made a powerful impression upon the people. The "passion play" in one form or another caught the imagination of more than one community, and just as Herodotus found it at Papremis, so now it spread from town to town, to take the chief place in the calendar of festivals. Osiris thus gained a place in the life and the hopes of the common people held by no other god. The royal destiny of Osiris and his triumph over death, thus vividly portrayed in dramatic form, rapidly disseminated among the people the belief that this destiny, once probably reserved for the king, might be shared by all. As we have said before, it needed but the same magical agencies employed by Isis to raise her dead consort, or by Horus, Anubis, and Thoth, as they wrought on behalf of the slain Osiris, to bring to every man the blessed destiny of the departed god. Such a development of popular mortuary belief, as we have already seen, inevitably involved also a constantly growing confidence in the efficiency of magic in the hereafter.

It is difficult for the modern mind to understand how completely the belief in magic penetrated the whole substance of life, dominating popular custom and constantly appearing in the simplest acts of the daily household routine, as much a matter of course as sleep or the preparation of food. It constituted the very atmosphere in which the men of the early Oriental world lived. Without the saving and salutary influence of such magical agencies constantly invoked, the life of an ancient household in the East was unthinkable. The destructive powers would otherwise have annihilated all. While it was especially against disease that such means must be employed, the ordinary processes of domestic and economic life were constantly placed under its protection. The mother never hushed her ailing babe and laid it to rest without invoking unseen powers to free the child from the dark forms of evil, malice, and disease that lurked in every shadowy corner, or, slinking in through the open door as the gloom of night settled over the house, entered the tiny form and racked it with fever. Such demons might even assume friendly guise and approach under pretext of soothing and healing the little sufferer. We can still hear the mother's voice as she leans over her babe and casts furtive glances through the open door into the darkness where the powers of evil dwell.

"Run out, thou who comest in darkness, who enterest in ⌜stealth⌝, his nose behind him, his face turned backward, who loses that for which he came."

"Run out, thou who comest in darkness, who enterest in ⌜stealth⌝, her nose behind her, her face turned backward, who loses that for which she came."

"Comest thou to kiss this child? I will not let thee kiss him."

"Comest thou to soothe (him)? I will not let thee soothe him.

"Comest thou to harm him? I will not let thee harm him.

"Comest thou to take him away? I will not let thee take him away from me.

"I have made his protection against thee out of Efetherb, it makes pain; out of onions, which harm thee; out of honey which is sweet to (living) men and bitter to those who are yonder (the dead); out of the evil (parts) of the Ebdu-fish; out of the jaw of the meret; out of the backbone of the perch."[1]

---

[1] Berlin Papyrus, P 3027 (I, 9 to II, 6). It belongs to the early Empire, or just before the Empire, about the sixteenth or

The apprehensive mother employs not only the uttered charm as an exorcism, but adds a delectable mixture of herbs, honey, and fish to be swallowed by the child, and designed to drive out the malignant demons, male and female, which afflict the baby with disease or threaten to carry it away. A hint as to the character of these demons is contained in the description of honey as "sweet to men (meaning the living) and bitter to those who are yonder (the dead)." It is evident that the demons dreaded were some of them the disembodied dead. At this point the life of the living throughout its course impinged upon that of the dead. The malicious dead must be bridled and held in check. Charms and magical devices which had proved efficacious against them during earthly life might prove equally valuable in the hereafter. This charm which prevented the carrying away of the child might also be employed to prevent a man's heart from being taken away in the Nether World. The dead man need only say: "Hast thou come to take away this my living heart? This my living heart is not given to thee;" whereupon the demon that would seize and flee with it must inevitably slink away.[1]

Thus the magic of daily life was more and more brought to bear on the hereafter and placed at the service of the dead. As the Empire rose in the sixteenth century B. C., we find this folk-charm among the mortuary texts inserted in the tomb. It is embodied in a charm now entitled "Chapter of Not Permitting a Man's Heart to be Taken Away from Him in the Nether World," [2] a chapter

seventeenth century B. C. Published by ERMAN, *Zaubersprueche für Mutter und Kind* (Abhandl. der Kgl. Preuss. Akad. der Wiss. zu Berlin, 1901).

[1] ERMAN, *ibid.*, 14–15.
[2] British Museum Papyrus of Ani, pl. xv, chap. XXIX.

TRIUMPH OF OSIRIS

which we found already in the Coffin Texts of the Middle Kingdom. These charms have now increased in number, and each has its title indicating just what it is intended to accomplish for the deceased. Combined with some of the old hymns of praise to Re and Osiris, some of which might be recited at the funeral,[1] and usually including also some account of the judgment, these mortuary texts were now written on a roll of papyrus and deposited with the dead in the tomb. It is these papyri which have now commonly come to be called the Book of the Dead. As a matter of fact, there was in the Empire no such book.[2] Each roll contained a random collection of such mortuary texts as the scribal copyist happened to have at hand, or those which he found enabled him best to sell his rolls; that is, such as enjoyed the greatest popularity. There were sumptuous and splendid rolls, sixty to eighty feet long and containing from seventy-five to as many as a hundred and twenty-five or thirty chapters. On the other hand, the scribes also copied small and modest rolls but a few feet in length, bearing but a meagre selection of the more important chapters. No two rolls exhibit the same collection of charms and chapters throughout, and it was not until the Ptolemaic period, some time after the fourth century B. C., that a more nearly canonical selection of chapters

[1] See Papyrus of Ani., pl. v, ll. 2–3, where the title of the section includes the words, "things said on the day of burial."
[2] The designation was first employed by LEPSIUS, who, however, realized that these rolls were not fixed and constant in content. See his *Todtenbuch* (p. 4), which was the earliest publication of so large a roll. The Theban Book of the Dead has been published by NAVILLE, *Das aegyptische Todtenbuch*, Berlin, 1886. Many individual rolls are now accessible in published form, notably that of Ani (see below, p. 304). No translation fully representing modern knowledge of the language exists. The best are those of BUDGE and of LE PAGE-RENOUF, continued by NAVILLE.

was gradually introduced. It will be seen, then, as we have said, that, properly speaking, there was in the Empire no *Book* of the Dead, but only various groups of mortuary chapters filling the mortuary papyri of the time. The entire body of chapters from which these rolls were made up, were some two hundred in number, although even the largest rolls did not contain them all. The independence or identity of each chapter is now evident in the custom of prefixing to every chapter a title—a custom which had begun in the case of many chapters in the Coffin Texts. Groups of chapters forming the most common nucleus of the Book of the Dead were frequently called "Chapters of Ascending by Day," a designation also in use in the Coffin Texts (see p. 276); but there was no current title for a roll of the Book of the Dead as a whole.

While a few scanty fragments of the Pyramid Texts have survived in the Book of the Dead, it may nevertheless be said that they have almost disappeared.[1] The Coffin Texts reappear, however, in increasing numbers and contribute largely to the various collections which make up the Book of the Dead. An innovation of which only indications are found in the Coffin Texts is the insertion in the Empire rolls of gorgeous vignettes illustrating the career of the deceased in the next world. Great confidence was placed in their efficacy, especially, as we shall see, in the scene of the judgment, which was now elaborately illustrated. It may be said that these illustrations in the Book of the Dead are another example of the elaboration of magical devices designed to ameliorate the life beyond the grave. Indeed, the Book of the Dead itself, as a whole, is but a far-reaching and complex illustration of the increasing dependence on magic in the hereafter.

[1] Later, especially in the Saitic Age, they were revived.

The benefits to be obtained in this way were unlimited, and it is evident that the ingenuity of a mercenary priesthood now played a large part in the development which followed. To the luxurious nobles of the Empire, the old peasant vision of the hereafter where the dead man might plough and sow and reap in the happy fields, and where the grain grew to be seven cubits (about twelve feet) high,[1] did not appear an attractive prospect. To be levied for labor and to be obliged to go forth and toil, even in the fields of the blessed, no longer appealed to the pampered grandees of an age of wealth and luxury. Already in the Middle Kingdom wooden figures of the servants of the dead were placed in the tomb, that they might labor for him in death as they had done in life. This idea was now carried somewhat further. Statuettes of the dead man bearing sack and hoe were fashioned, and a cunning charm was devised and written upon the breast of the figure: "O statuette,[2] counted for X (name of deceased), if I am called, if I am counted to do any work that is done in the Nether World, . . . thou shalt count thyself for me at all times, to cultivate the fields, to water the shores, to transport sand of the east to the west, and say, 'Here am I.'" This charm was placed among those in the roll, with the title, "Chapter of Causing that the Statuette Do the Work of a Man in the Nether World."[3] The device was further elaborated by finally placing one such little figure of the dead in the tomb for each day in the year, and they have been found in the Egyptian cemeteries in such numbers that museums

[1] Book of the Dead, chap. CIX.
[2] The word used is that commonly rendered "Ushebti," and translated "respondent." It is, however, of very obscure origin and of uncertain meaning.
[3] Book of the Dead, chap. VI.

and private collections all over the world, as has been well said, are "populated" with them.

With such means of gain so easily available, we cannot wonder that the priests and scribes of this age took advantage of the opportunity. The dangers of the hereafter were now greatly multiplied, and for every critical situation the priest was able to furnish the dead with an effective charm which would infallibly save him. Besides many charms which enabled the dead to reach the world of the hereafter, there were those which prevented him from losing his mouth, his head, his heart, others which enabled him to remember his name, to breathe, eat, drink, avoid eating his own foulness, to prevent his drinking-water from turning into flame, to turn darkness into light, to ward off all serpents and other hostile monsters, and many others. The desirable transformations, too, had now increased, and a short chapter might in each case enable the dead man to assume the form of a falcon of gold, a divine falcon, a lily, a Phœnix, a heron, a swallow, a serpent called "son of earth," a crocodile, a god, and, best of all, there was a chapter so potent that by its use a man might assume any form that he desired.

It is such productions as these which form by far the larger proportion of the mass of texts which we term the Book of the Dead. To call it the Bible of the Egyptians, then, is quite to mistake the function and content of these rolls.[1] The tendency which brought forth this mass of "chapters" is also characteristically evident in two other books each of which was in itself a coherent and

---

[1] The designation "Bible of the old Egyptians" is at least as old as the report of the Committee of the Oriental Congress, which sat in London in 1874 and arranged for publishing the Book of the Dead. See NAVILLE, *Todtenbuch*, Einleitung, p. 5.

connected composition. The Book of the Two Ways, as old, we remember, as the Middle Kingdom,[1] had already contributed much to the Book of the Dead regarding the fiery gates through which the dead gained entrance to the world beyond and to the two ways by which he was to make his journey.[2] On the basis of such fancies as these, the imagination of the priests now put forth a "Book of Him Who is in the Nether World," describing the subterranean journey of the sun during the night as he passed through twelve long cavernous galleries beneath the earth, each one representing a journey of an hour, the twelve caverns leading the sun at last to the point in the east where he rises.[3] The other book, commonly called the "Book of the Gates," represents each of the twelve caverns as entered by a gate and concerns itself with the passage of these gates. While these compositions never gained the popularity enjoyed by the Book of the Dead, they are magical guide-books devised for gain, just as was much of the material which made up the Book of the Dead.

That which saves the Book of the Dead itself from being exclusively a magical *vade mecum* for use in the hereafter is its elaboration of the ancient idea of the moral judgment, and its evident appreciation of the burden of conscience. The relation with God had become something more than merely the faithful observance of external rites. It had become to some extent a matter of the heart and of character. Already in the Middle Kingdom the wise man had discerned the responsibility of the inner man, of the heart or understanding. The

---
[1] See above, p. 283.
[2] See GRAPOW, *Zeitschr. für aegypt. Sprache*, 46, 77 ff.
[3] See JÉQUIER, *Le livre de ce qu'il y a dans l'Hades*. Paris, 1894.

man of ripe and morally sane understanding is his ideal, and his counsel is to be followed. "A hearkener (to good counsel) is one whom the god loves. Who hearkens not is one whom the god hates. It is the heart (understanding) which makes its possessor a hearkener or one not hearkening. The life, prosperity, and health of a man is in his heart."[1] A court herald of Thutmose III in recounting his services likewise says: "It was my heart which caused that I should do them (his services for the king), by its guidance of my affairs. It was . . . as an excellent witness. I did not disregard its speech, I feared to transgress its guidance. I prospered thereby greatly, I was successful by reason of that which it caused me to do, I was distinguished by its guidance. 'Lo, . . . ,' said the people, 'it is an oracle of God in every body.[2] Prosperous is he whom it has guided to the good way of achievement,' Lo, thus I was."[3] The relatives of Paheri, a prince of El Kab, addressing him after his death, pray, "Mayest thou spend eternity in gladness of heart, in the favor of the god that is in thee,"[4] and another dead man similarly declares, "The heart of a man is his own god, and my heart was satisfied with my deeds."[5] To this inner voice of the heart, which with surprising insight was even termed a man's god, the Egyptian was now more sensitive than ever before during the long course of the ethical evolution which we have been following. This

---

[1] See above, p. 236.
[2] Or "belly," meaning the seat of the mind.
[3] Louvre stela, C. 26, ll. 22–24. *Zeitschr. für aegypt. Sprache*, 39, 47.
[4] *Egypt Expl. Fund, Eleventh Mem.*, pl. ix, ll. 20–21. *Zeitschr. für aegypt. Sprache*, 39, 48.
[5] WRECZINSKI, *Wiener Inschriften*, 160, quoted by ERMAN, *Rel.*, p. 123.

sensitiveness finds very full expression in the most important if not the longest section of the Book of the Dead. Whereas the judgment hereafter is mentioned as far back as the Pyramid Age, we now find a full account and description of it in the Book of the Dead.[1] Notwithstanding the prominence of the intruding Osiris in the judgment we shall clearly discern its Solar origin and character even as recounted in the Book of the Dead. Three different versions of the judgment, doubtless originally independent, have been combined in the fullest and best rolls. The first is entitled, "Chapter of Entering Into the Hall of Truth (or Righteousness),"[2] and it contains "that which is said on reaching the Hall of Truth, when X (the deceased's name) is purged from all evil that he has done, and he beholds the face of the god. 'Hail to thee, great god, lord of Truth.[3] I have come to thee, my lord, and I am led (thither) in order to see thy beauty. I know thy name, I know the names of the forty-two gods who are with thee in the Hall of Truth, who live on evil-doers and devour their blood, on that day of reckoning character before Wennofer (Osiris).[4] Behold, I come to thee, I bring to thee righteousness and I expel for thee sin. I have committed no sin against people. . . . I have not done evil in the place of truth. I knew no wrong. I did no evil thing. . . . I did not do that which the god abom-

[1] It is commonly known as chap. CXXV.
[2] The word "truth" here is commonly written in the dual, which grammatically equals "the two truths." This strange usage is perhaps merely an idiom of intensification, as "morning" is written in the dual for "early morning."
[3] In the dual as above, and for the most part throughout this chapter.
[4] An important variant has, "Who live on righteousness (truth) and abominate sin." Some texts also insert here the name of Osiris, "Lo, the 'two beloved daughters, his two eyes of Truth' is thy name."

inates. I did not report evil of a servant to his master. I allowed no one to hunger. I caused no one to weep. I did not murder. I did not command to murder. I caused no man misery. I did not diminish food in the temples. I did not decrease the offerings of the gods. I did not take away the food-offerings of the dead (literally "glorious"). I did not commit adultery. I did not commit self-pollution in the pure precinct of my city-god. I did not diminish the grain measure. I did not diminish the span.[1] I did not diminish the land measure. I did not load the weight of the balances. I did not deflect the index of the scales. I did not take milk from the mouth of the child. I did not drive away the cattle from their pasturage. I did not snare the fowl of the gods. I did not catch the fish in their pools. I did not hold back the water in its time. I did not dam the running water.[2] I did not quench the fire in its time.[3] I did not withhold the herds of the temple endowments. I did not interfere with the god in his payments. I am purified four times, I am pure as that great Phœnix is pure which is in Heracleopolis. For I am that nose of the Lord of Breath who keeps alive all the people.'"[4] The address of the deceased now merges into obscure mythological allusions, and he concludes with the statement, "There arises no evil thing against me in this land, in the Hall of Truth, because I know the names of these gods who are therein, the followers of the Great God."

A second scene of judgment is now enacted. The

[1] A measure of length.
[2] This refers to diverting the waters of the irrigation canals at time of inundation at the expense of neighbors, still one of the commonest forms of corruption in Egypt.
[3] The text is clear, but the meaning is quite obscure.
[4] Book of the Dead, chap. CXXV; NAVILLE, *Todtenbuch*, I, CXXXIII, and II, 275–287.

judge Osiris is assisted by forty-two gods who sit with him in judgment on the dead. They are terrifying demons, each bearing a grotesque and horrible name, which the deceased claims that he knows. He therefore addresses them one after the other by name. They are such names as these: "Broad - Stride - that - Came - out - of-Heliopolis," "Flame-Hugger-that-Came-out-of-Troja," "Nosey-that-Came-out-of-Hermopolis," "Shadow-Eater-that-Came-out-of-the-Cave," "Turn-Face-that-Came-out of-Rosta," "Two-Eyes-of-Flame-that-Came-out-of-Letopolis," "Bone - Breaker - that-Came-out-of-Heracleopolis," "White - Teeth - that - Came - out - of - the-Secret-Land," "Blood - Eater-that-Came-out-of-the-Place-of-Execution," "Eater-of-Entrails-that-Came-out-of-Mebit." These and other equally edifying creations of priestly imagination the deceased calls upon, addressing to each in turn a declaration of innocence of some particular sin.

This section of the Book of the Dead is commonly called the "Confession." It would be difficult to devise a term more opposed to the real character of the dead man's statement, which as a declaration of innocence is, of course, the reverse of a confession. The ineptitude of the designation has become so evident that some editors have added the word negative, and thus call it the "negative confession," which means nothing at all. The Egyptian does *not* confess at this judgment, and this is a fact of the utmost importance in his religious development, as we shall see. To mistake this section of the Book of the Dead for "confession" is totally to misunderstand the development which was now slowly carrying him toward that complete acknowledgment and humble disclosure of his sin which is nowhere found in the Book of the Dead.

It is evident that the forty-two gods are an artificial

creation. As was long ago noticed, they represent the forty or more nomes, or administrative districts, of Egypt. The priests doubtless built up this court of forty-two judges in order to control the character of the dead from all quarters of the country. The deceased would find himself confronted by one judge at least who was acquainted with his local reputation, and who could not be deceived. The forty-two declarations addressed to this court cover much the same ground as those we have already rendered in the first address. The editors had some difficulty in finding enough sins to make up a list of forty-two, and there are several verbal repetitions, not to mention essential repetitions with slight changes in the wording. The crimes which may be called those of violence are these: "I did not slay men (5), I did not rob (2), I did not steal (4), I did not rob one crying for his possessions (18),[1] my fortune was not great but by my (own) property (41), I did not take away food (10), I did not stir up fear (21), I did not stir up strife (25)." Deceitfulness and other undesirable qualities of character are also disavowed: "I did not speak lies (9), I did not make falsehood in the place of truth (40), I was not deaf to truthful words (24), I did not diminish the grain-measure (6), I was not avaricious (3), my heart devoured not (coveted not?) (28), my heart was not hasty (31), I did not multiply words in speaking (33), my voice was not over loud (37), my mouth did not wag (lit. go) (17), I did not wax hot (in temper) (23), I did not revile (29), I was not an eavesdropper (16), I was not puffed up (39)." The dead man is free from sexual immorality: "I did not commit adultery with a

---

[1] The variants indicate "I did not ꞌtake possessionꞋ of my (own) property," or "I did not take ꞌpossessionꞋ except of just (or true) possessions."

woman (19), I did not commit self-pollution (20, 27);" and ceremonial transgressions are also denied: "I did not revile the king (35), I did not blaspheme the god (38), I did not slay the divine bull (13), I did not steal temple endowment (8), I did not diminish food in the temple (15), I did not do an abomination of the gods (42)." These, with several repetitions and some that are unintelligible, make up the declaration of innocence.[1]

Having thus vindicated himself before the entire great court, the deceased confidently addresses them: "Hail to you, ye gods! I know you, I know your names. I fall not before your blades. Report not evil of me to this god whom ye follow. My case does not come before you. Speak ye the truth concerning me before the All-Lord; because I did the truth (or righteousness) in the land of Egypt. I did not revile the god. My case did not come before the king then reigning. Hail to you, ye gods who are in the Hall of Truth, in whose bodies are neither sin nor falsehood, who live on truth in Heliopolis . . . before Horus dwelling in his sun-disk.[2] Save ye me from Babi,[3] who lives on the entrails of the great, on that day of the great reckoning. Behold, I come to you without sin, without evil, without wrong. . . . I live on righteousness, I feed on the righteousness of my heart. I have done that which men say, and that wherewith the gods are content. I have satisfied the god with that which he desires. I gave bread to the hungry, water to the thirsty, clothing to the naked, and a ferry to him who was without a boat. I made divine offerings for the gods and food-offerings for

---

[1] Book of the Dead, chap. CXXV; Naville, *Todtenbuch*, I, CXXXIV-V; II, pp. 289-309.

[2] It should be noted that this is another evidence of the Solar origin of this court.

[3] A hostile demon of the Nether World.

the dead. Save ye me; protect ye me. Enter no complaint against me before the Great God. For I am one of pure mouth and pure hands, to whom was said 'Welcome, welcome' by those who saw him."[1] With these words the claims of the deceased to moral worthiness merge into affirmations that he has observed all ceremonial requirements of the Osirian faith, and these form more than half of this concluding address to the gods of the court.

The third record of the judgment was doubtless the version which made the deepest impression upon the Egyptian. Like the drama of Osiris at Abydos, it is graphic and depicts the judgment as effected by the balances. In the sumptuously illustrated papyrus of Ani[2] we see Osiris sitting enthroned at one end of the judgment hall, with Isis and Nephthys standing behind him. Along one side of the hall are ranged the nine gods of the Heliopolitan Ennead, headed by the Sun-god.[3] *They* afterward announce the verdict, showing the originally Solar origin of this third scene of judgment, in which Osiris has now assumed the chief place. In the midst stand "the balances of Re wherewith he weighs truth," as we have seen them called in the Feudal Age;[4] but the judgment in which they figure has now become Osirianized. The balances are manipulated by the ancient mortuary god Anubis, behind whom stands the divine scribe Thoth, who presides over the weighing, pen and writing palette

---

[1] Book of the Dead, chap. CXXV; NAVILLE, *Todtenbuch*, I, CXXXVII, ll. 2–13; II, pp. 310–317.

[2] British Museum Papyrus 10470. See *Fac-simile of the Papyrus of Ani, in the British Museum. Printed by order of the Trustees.* London, 1894, pls. iii–iv.

[3] The number has been adjusted to the exclusion of Osiris, who sits as chief judge. Isis and Nephthys are placed together and counted as one.

[4] See above, p. 253.

in hand, that he may record the result. Behind him crouches a grotesque monster called the "Devouress," with the head of a crocodile, fore quarters of a lion and hind quarters of a hippopotamus, waiting to devour the unjust soul. Beside the balances in subtle suggestiveness stands the figure of "Destiny" accompanied by Renenet and Meskhenet, the two goddesses of birth, about to contemplate the fate of the soul at whose coming into this world they had once presided. Behind the enthroned divinities sit the gods "Taste" and "Intelligence." In other rolls we not infrequently find standing at the entrance the goddess "Truth, daughter of Re," who ushers into the hall of judgment the newly arrived soul. Ani and his wife, with bowed heads and deprecatory gestures, enter the fateful hall, and Anubis at once calls for the heart of Ani. In the form of a tiny vase, which is in Egyptian writing the hieroglyph for heart, one side of the balances bears the heart of Ani, while in the other side appears a feather, the symbol and hieroglyph for Truth or Righteousness. At the critical moment Ani addresses his own heart: "O my heart that came from my mother! O my heart belonging to my being! Rise not up against me as a witness. Oppose me not in the council (court of justice). Be not hostile to me before the master of the balances. Thou art my ka that is in my body. . . . Let not my name be of evil odor with the court, speak no lie against me in the presence of the god."

Evidently this appeal has proven effective, for Thoth, "envoy of the Great Ennead, that is in the presence of Osiris," at once says: "Hear ye this word in truth. I have judged the heart of Osiris [Ani][1] His soul stands as a witness concerning him, his character is just by the great

[1] Omitted by the scribe.

balances. No sin of his has been found." The Nine Gods of the Ennead at once respond: "⌈How good⌉ it is, this which comes forth from thy just mouth. Osiris Ani, the justified, witnesses. There is no sin of his, there is no evil of his with us. The Devouress shall not be given power over him. Let there be given to him the bread that cometh forth before Osiris, the domain that abideth in the field of offerings, like the Followers of Horus."

Having thus received a favorable verdict, the fortunate Ani is led forward by "Horus, son of Isis," who presents him to Osiris, at the same time saying: "I come to thee, Wennofer; I bring to thee Osiris Ani. His righteous heart comes forth from the balances and he has no sin in the sight of any god or goddess. Thoth has judged him in writing; the Nine Gods have spoken concerning him a very just testimony. Let there be given to him the bread and beer that come forth before Osiris-Wennofer like the Followers of Horus." With his hand in that of Horus, Ani then addresses Osiris: "Lo, I am before thee, Lord of the West. There is no sin in my body. I have not spoken a lie knowingly nor (if so) was there a second time. Let me be like the favorites who are in thy following."[1] Thereupon he kneels before the great god, and as he presents a table of offerings is received into his kingdom.

These three accounts of the judgment, in spite of the grotesque appurtenances with which the priests of the time have embellished them, are not without impressiveness even to the modern beholder as he contemplates these rolls of three thousand five hundred years ago, and realizes that these scenes are the graphic expression of the same moral consciousness, of the same admonishing voice within, to which we still feel ourselves amenable. Ani

[1] Papyrus of Ani, pl. iv.

importunes his heart not to betray him, and his cry finds an echo down all the ages in such words as those of Richard:

> "My conscience hath a thousand several tongues,
> And every tongue brings in a several tale,
> And every tale condemns me for a villain."

The Egyptian heard the same voice, feared it, and endeavored to silence it. He strove to still the voice of the heart; he did not yet confess, but insistently maintained his innocence. The next step in his higher development was humbly to disclose the consciousness of guilt to his god. That step he later took. But another force intervened and greatly hampered the complete emancipation of his conscience. There can be no doubt that this Osirian judgment thus graphically portrayed and the universal reverence for Osiris in the Empire had much to do with spreading the belief in moral responsibility beyond the grave, and in giving general currency to those ideas of the supreme value of moral worthiness which we have seen among the moralists and social philosophers of the Pharaoh's court several centuries earlier, in the Feudal Age. The Osiris faith had thus become a great power for righteousness *among the people*. While the Osirian destiny was open to all, nevertheless all must prove themselves morally acceptable to him.

Had the priests left the matter thus, all would have been well. Unhappily, however, the development of belief in the efficacy of magic in the next world continued. All material blessings, as we have seen, might infallibly be attained by the use of the proper charm. Even the less tangible mental equipment, the "heart," meaning the understanding, might also be restored by magical agencies.

It was inevitable that the priests should now take the momentous step of permitting such agencies to enter also the world of moral values. Magic might become an agent for moral ends. The Book of the Dead is chiefly a book of magical charms, and the section pertaining to the judgment did not continue to remain an exception. The poignant words addressed by Ani to his heart as it was weighed in the balances, "O my heart, rise not up against me as a witness," were now written upon a stone image of the sacred beetle, the scarabeus, and placed over the heart as a mandate of magical potency preventing the heart from betraying the character of the deceased. The words of this charm became a chapter of the Book of the Dead, where they bore the title, "Chapter of Preventing that the Heart of a Man Oppose Him in the Nether World."[1] The scenes of the judgment and the text of the Declaration of Innocence were multiplied on rolls by the scribes and sold to all the people. In these copies the places for the name of the deceased were left vacant, and the purchaser filled in the blanks after he had secured the document. The words of the verdict, declaring the deceased had successfully met the judgment and acquitting him of evil, were not lacking in any of these rolls. Any citizen whatever the character of his life might thus secure from the scribes a certificate declaring that Blank was a righteous man before it was known who Blank would be. He might even obtain a formulary so mighty that the Sun-god, as the real power behind the judgment, would be cast down from heaven into the Nile, if he did not bring forth the deceased fully justified before his court.[2] Thus the earliest moral development which

[1] Book of the Dead, chap. XXX.
[2] Book of the Dead, ed. NAVILLE, chap. LXV, ll. 10-16.

we can trace in the ancient East was suddenly arrested, or at least seriously checked, by the detestable devices of a corrupt priesthood eager for gain.

It is needless to point out the confusion of distinctions involved in this last application of magic. It is the old failure to perceive the difference between that which goeth in and that which cometh out of the man. A justification mechanically applied from without, and freeing the man from punishments coming from without, cannot, of course, heal the ravages that have taken place within. The voice within, to which the Egyptian was more sensitive than any people of the earlier East, and to which the whole idea of the moral ordeal in the hereafter was due, could not be quieted by any such means. The general reliance upon such devices for escaping ultimate responsibility for an unworthy life must have seriously poisoned the life of the people. While the Book of the Dead discloses to us more fully than ever before in the history of Egypt the character of the moral judgment in the hereafter, and the reality with which the Egyptian clothed his conception of moral responsibility, it is likewise a revelation of ethical decadence. In so far as the Book of the Dead had become a magical agency for securing moral vindication in the hereafter, irrespective of character, it had become a positive force for evil.

So strong was the moral sense of the Egyptian, however, that he did not limit the value of a worthy life to its availability in rendering him acceptable to Osiris in the next life. Herein lies the limitation of the Osirian ethics which bade a man think only of moral consequences beyond the grave. After all, Osiris was a god of the dead. The old social philosophers of the Feudal Age had preached the righteousness of Re, the Sun-god, and demanded social justice *here* because Re demanded it. They were not without their descendants in the Empire— men who found in the Solar faith an obligation to righteous living here and now, and who discerned earthly rewards in so living. The Sun-god was not chiefly a god of the dead. He reigned in the earthly affairs of men, and during the earthly life men felt the moral obligation which he placed upon them hourly. One of the architects of Amenhotep III, addressing a hymn of praise to the Sun-god, says: "I was a valiant leader among thy monuments, doing righteousness for thy heart. I know that thou art satisfied with righteousness. Thou makest great him who doeth it on earth. I did it and thou didst make me great."[1] Similarly, when the Pharaoh made oath he swore, "As Re loves me, as my father Amon (long since identified with Re) favors me;"[2] and the conqueror Thutmose III in making this oath to the truth of what he says, and affirming his respect for the truth in the sight of his god, refers to the Sun-god's presence thus: "For he knoweth heaven and he knoweth earth, he seeth the whole earth hourly."[3] While it is true that the subterranean hereafter of the Osiris faith depicts the Sun-god as journeying from cavern to cavern beneath the earth, passing through the realm of Osiris and bringing light and joy to the dead who dwell there, this is a conception unknown to the early Solar theology as found in the Pyramid Texts.[4] In the Empire the Sun-god is preeminently a god of the world of living men, in whose af-

[1] British Museum Stela, No. 826, published by BIRCH, *Transactions of the Soc. of Bib. Arch.*, VIII, 143; and in PIERRET'S *Recueil*, I. I had also my own copy of the original.
[2] BAR, II, 318, 570.   [3] BAR, II, 570.
[4] It is not likely that the "caves" referred to in Pyr. § 852 have any connection with the subterranean caverns of the Osirian faith.

fairs he is constantly present and active. Men feel their responsibility to him here and now, and that dominion deepening constantly in the hearts of men is now also to expand with the expanding horizon of the imperial age until, for the first time in history, there dawns upon the eyes of these early Nile-dwellers the vision of the world-god.

LECTURE IX

THE IMPERIAL AGE—THE WORLD-STATE MAKES ITS IMPRESSION ON RELIGION—TRIUMPH OF RE—EARLIEST MONOTHEISM—IKHNATON (AMENHOTEP IV)

In the Feudal Age the *social* realm had made its impression upon religion as in the Pyramid Age the Egyptian state, the *political* realm had done. Both these were limited to the territory of Egypt. The Pyramid Age had gained a dim vision of the vast extent of the Sun-god's domain, and had once addressed him by the sounding title "Limitless."[1] But this remained, as it were, a momentary glimpse without effect upon the Solar theology as a whole. The Sun-god ruled only Egypt, and in the great Sun-hymn of the Pyramid Texts[2] he stands guardian on the Egyptian frontiers, where he builds the gates which restrain all outsiders from entering his inviolable domain. In the Pyramid Age, too, the Sun-god had already begun the process of absorbing the other gods of Egypt, a process resulting even at so remote a date in a form of national pantheism, in which all the gods ultimately coalesced into forms and functions of one. But even this process, though it did not cease, had left the supreme god's dominion still restricted to Egypt. He was very far from being a world-god. The Egyptians indeed had not as yet gained the world-idea, the world-empire over which they might install the world-ruler. The influences of an environment restricted to the limits

[1] Pyr. § 1434. [2] See above, pp. 13–14.

of the Nile valley had now, however, gone as far as they
could, when a career of imposing foreign expansion of
national power enlarged the theatre of thought and action.
The Solar theology had been sensitively responsive to
conditions in the Nile-valley world. It proved to be not
less sensitive to the larger world, to include which the
Egyptian horizon had now expanded.

Egypt's imperial expansion northward and southward
until the Pharaoh's power had united the contiguous
regions of Asia and Africa into the first stable Empire in
history is the commanding fact in the history of the East
in the sixteenth century B. C. The consolidation of that
power by Thutmose III's twenty years' campaigning in
Asia is a stirring chapter of military imperialism in which
for the first time in the East we can discern the skilfully
organized and mobile forces of a great state as they are
brought to bear with incessant impact upon the nations
of western Asia, until the Egyptian supremacy is undisputed from the Greek Islands, the coasts of Asia Minor,
and the highlands of the Upper Euphrates on the north
to the Fourth Cataract of the Nile on the south. This
great military leader himself made the remark which we
have quoted above regarding his god: "He seeth the whole
earth hourly." If this was true it was because the sword
of the Pharaoh had carried the power of Egypt's god to
the limit of Egypt's Empire.[1] Fifty years earlier, indeed,
Thutmose I proclaimed his kingdom as far as "the circuit
of the sun."[2] In the Old Kingdom the Sun-god was conceived as a Pharaoh, whose kingdom was Egypt. With
the expansion of the Egyptian kingdom into a world-empire it was inevitable that the domain of the god

[1] See Thutmose III's Hymn of Victory, BAR, II, 655-662.
[2] BAR, II, 98.

should likewise expand. As the kingdom had long since found expression in religion, so now the Empire was a powerful influence upon religious thought.

While this was a more or less mechanical and unconscious process, it was accompanied by an intellectual awakening which shook the old Egyptian traditions to the foundations and set the men of the age to thinking in a larger world. Thutmose III was the first character of universal aspects, the first world-hero. As such he made a profound impression upon his age. The idea of universal power, of a world-empire, was visibly and tangibly bodied forth in his career. There is a touch of universalism now discernible in the theology of the Empire which is directly due to such impressions as he and his successors made. Egypt is forced out of the immemorial isolation of her narrow valley into world-relations, with which the theology of the time must reckon—relations with which the Sun-god, as we have seen, was inextricably involved. Commercial connections, maintained from an immemorially remote past, had not sufficed to bring the great world without into the purview of Egyptian thinking. The limits of the dominion of the Egyptian gods had been fixed as the outer fringes of the Nile valley long before the outside world was familiar to the Nile-dwellers; and merely commercial intercourse with a larger world had not been able to shake the tradition. Many a merchant had seen a stone fall in distant Babylon and in Thebes alike, but it had not occurred to him, or to any man in that far-off age, that the same natural force reigned in these widely separated countries. The world was far indeed from the lad lying beneath the apple-tree and discovering a universal force in the fall of an apple. Many a merchant of that day, too, had seen the sun rise behind the Babylonian ziggurats as it did among the clustered obelisks of Thebes, but the thought of the age had not yet come to terms with such far-reaching facts as these. It was universalism expressed in terms of imperial-power which first caught the imagination of the thinking men of the Empire, and disclosed to them the universal sweep of the Sun-god's dominion as a physical fact. Monotheism is but imperialism in religion.

It is no accident, therefore, that about 1400 B. C., in the reign of Amenhotep III, the most splendid of the Egyptian emperors, we find the first of such impressions. Two architects, Suti and Hor, twin brothers, whom Amenhotep III was employing at Thebes, have left us a Sun-hymn on a stela now in the British Museum,[1] which discloses the tendency of the age and the widening vision with which these men of the Empire were looking out upon the world and discerning the unlimited scope of the Sun-god's realm.

> "Hail to thee, beautiful god of every day!
> Rising in the morning without ceasing,
> [⌈Not⌉] wearied in labor.
> When thy rays are visible,
> Gold is not considered,
> It is not like thy brilliance.
> Thou art a craftsman shaping thine own limbs;
> Fashioner without being fashioned;[2]

[1] British Museum Stela, No. 826. This important monument much needs an adequate publication. It is accessible only in two very incorrect copies, published by BIRCH, *Trans. Soc. Bib. Arch.*, VIII, 143, and PIERRET, in his *Recueil*, I. I had also my own copy made in student days, and not much more reliable than the publications. I have not yet seen SCOTT-MONCRIEFF's recent volume of British Museum stelæ, and do not know whether it was included by him. The above translation could undoubtedly be corrected in parts on the basis of a better text.

[2] Or "Begetter without being born," as already in the Middle Kingdom; see above, p. 274.

Unique in his qualities, traversing eternity;
Over ways ⌈with⌉ millions under his guidance.
Thy brilliance is like the brilliance of the sky,
Thy colors gleam more than the hues of it.[1]
When thou sailest across the sky all men behold thee,
(Though) thy going is hidden from their sight.
When thou showest thyself at morning every day,
. . . under thy majesty, though the day be brief,
Thou traversest a journey of leagues,
Even millions and hundred-thousands of time.
Every day is under thee.
When thy setting ⌈comes⌉,
The hours of the night hearken to thee likewise.
When thou hast traversed it
There comes no ending to thy labors.
All men, they see by means of thee.
Nor do they finish when thy majesty sets,
(For) thou wakest to rise in the morning,
And thy radiance, it opens the eyes (again).
When thou settest in Manu,
Then they sleep like the dead.
Hail to thee! O disk of day,
Creator of all and giver of their sustenance,
Great Falcon, brilliantly plumaged,
Brought forth to raise himself on high of himself,
Self-generator, without being born.
First-born Falcon in the midst of the sky,
To whom jubilation is made at his rising and his setting likewise.
Fashioner of the produce of the soil,

. . . .

Taking possession of the Two Lands (Egypt), from great to small,
A mother, profitable to gods and men,
A craftsman of experience, . . .
Valiant herdman who drives his cattle,
Their refuge and giver of their sustenance,
Who passes by, running the course of Khepri (the Sun-god),

[1] The word "hues" is the word commonly meaning "skin." That it has the meaning "hue" or similar is shown by similar passages in NAVILLE, *Mythe d'Horus*, pl. xii, l. 2; *Amarna Hymn of Tutu*, l. 2, and *Amarna Hymn of Api*, ll. 2–3.

> Who determines his own birth,
> Exalting his beauty in the body of Nut,
> Illuminating the Two Lands (Egypt) with his disk,
> The primordial being, who himself made himself;
> Who beholds that which he has made,
> Sole lord taking captive all lands every day,
> As one beholding them that walk therein;
> Shining in the sky ⌜a being as the sun⌝.
> He makes the seasons by the months,
> Heat when he desires,
> Cold when he desires.
> He makes the limbs to languish
> When he enfolds them,
> Every land is in rejoicing
> At his rising every day, in order to praise him."

It is evident in such a hymn as this that the vast sweep of the Sun-god's course over all the lands and peoples of the earth has at last found consideration, and the logical conclusion has also followed. The old stock phrases of the earlier hymns, the traditional references to the falcon, and the mythological allusions involved have not wholly disappeared, but the momentous step has been taken of extending the sway of the Sun-god over all lands and peoples. No earlier document left us by the thought of Egypt contains such unequivocal expression of this thought as we find here:

> "Sole lord, taking captive all lands every day,
> As one beholding them that walk therein."

It is important to observe also that this tendency is connected directly with the social movement of the Feudal Age. Such epithets applied to the Sun-god as

> "Valiant herdman who drives his cattle,
> Their refuge and the giver of their sustenance,"

of course carry us back to the address of Ipuwer and his "shepherd of all men."[1]   The other remarkable epithet,

"A mother, profitable to gods and men,"

carries with it the idea of similar solicitude for mankind. The humane aspects of the Sun-god's sway, to which the social thinkers of the Feudal Age chiefly contributed, have not disappeared among the powerful political motives of this new universalism.

This hymn of the two architects is, however, likewise a revelation of one of the chief difficulties in the internal situation of the Pharaoh at this time. The hymn bears the title: "Adoration of Amon when he rises as Harakhte (Horus of the Horizon)"; that is to say, the hymn is addressed to Amon as Sun-god. Amon, the old obscure local god of Thebes, whose name is not to be found in the great religious documents of the earlier age like the Pyramid Texts,[2] had by this time gained the chief place in the state theology, owing to the supreme position held by the ruling family of his native town in the Empire. Theologically, he had long succumbed to the ancient tendency which identified the old local gods with the Sun-god, and he had long been called "Amon-Re." His old local characteristics, whatever they may have been, had been supplanted by those of the Sun-god, and the ancient local Amon had been completely Solarized. In this way it had been possible to raise him to the supreme place in the pantheon. At the same time this supremacy was

---

[1] See above, p. 211.
[2] His name occurs four times in the Turin *Book of the Dead*, published by LEPSIUS. It does not occur at all in the Pyramid Texts, unless the reference in Pyr. § 1095 is to him, which seems to me not entirely certain.

not confined to theological theory. Economically and administratively, Amon actually received the first place among the gods. For the first time in the history of the country the great organizer, Thutmose III, seems to have merged the priesthoods of all the temples of the land into one great sacerdotal organization, at the head of which he placed the High Priest of Amon.[1] This is the earliest national priesthood as yet known in the early East, and the first *pontifex maximus*. This Amonite papacy constituted a powerful political obstacle in the way of realizing the supremacy of the ancient Sun-god.

When Amenhotep III's son, Amenhotep IV, succeeded his father, about 1375 B. C., a keen struggle arose between the royal house, on the one hand, and the sacerdotal organization dominated by Amon, on the other. It is evident that the young king favored the claims of the old Sun-god as opposed to those of Amon, but early in his reign we find him ardently supporting a new form of the old Solar faith, which may have been the result of a compromise between the two. At a time when the Asiatic situation was exceedingly critical, and the Pharaoh's supremacy there was threatened, he devoted himself with absorbing zeal to the new Solar universalism which we have discerned under his father. The Sun-god was given a designation which freed the new faith from the compromising polytheistic tradition of the old Solar theology. He was now called "Aton," an ancient name for the physical sun, and probably designating his disk. It oc-

---

[1] Hapuseneb, the first High Priest of Amon, who occupied the position at the head of the new sacerdotal organization, was grand vizier under queen Hatshepsut, but it is more likely that her husband, Thutmose III, effected this organization than that she should have done it. However this may be, the evidence will be found in BAR, II, 388 *ff*.

curs twice in the hymn of the two architects of Amenhotep III, translated above, and it had already gained some favor under this king, who named one of his royal barges "Aton-Gleams."[1] There was an effort made to make the name "Aton" equivalent in some of the old forms to the word "god"; thus the traditional term "divine offering" (lit. "god's offering") was now called "Aton offering."[2] Not only did the Sun-god receive a new name, but the young king now gave him a new symbol also. The most ancient symbol of the Sun-God, as we have seen, was a pyramid, and as a falcon the figure of that bird was also used to designate him. These, however, were intelligible only in Egypt, and Amenhotep IV had a wider arena in view. The new symbol depicted the sun as a disk from which diverging beams radiated downward, each ray terminating in a human hand. It was a masterly symbol, suggesting a power issuing from its celestial source, and putting its hand upon the world and the affairs of men. As far back as the Pyramid Texts the rays of the Sun-god had been likened to his arms and had been conceived as an agency on earth: "The *arm* of the sunbeams is lifted with king Unis,"[3] raising him to the skies. Such a symbol was suited to be understood throughout the world which the Pharaoh controlled. There was also some effort to define the Solar power thus symbolized. The full name of the Sun-god was "Harakhte (Horizon-Horus), rejoicing in the horizon in his name 'Heat which is in Aton.'" It was enclosed in two royal cartouches, like the double name of the Pharaoh, a device suggested by the analogy of the Pharaoh's power, and another clear evidence of the impression which the Empire as a state had now made on

---

[1] BAR, II, 869; see also the author's *History of Egypt*, p. 360.
[2] BAR, II, 987.   [3] Pyr. § 334.

the Solar theology. But the name enclosed in the cartouches roughly defined the actual physical force of the sun in the visible world, and was no political figure. The word rendered "heat" sometimes also means "light." It is evident that what the king was deifying was the force by which the Sun made himself felt on earth. In harmony with this conclusion are the numerous statements in the Aton hymns, which, as we shall see, represent Aton as everywhere active on earth by means of his "rays." While it is evident that the new faith drew its inspiration from Heliopolis, so that the king assuming the office of High Priest of Aton called himself "Great Seer," the title of the High Priest of Heliopolis, nevertheless most of the old lumber which made up the externals of the traditional theology was rejected. We look in vain for the sun-barques, and in the same way also later accretions, like the voyage through the subterranean caverns of the dead, are completely shorn away.[1]

To introduce the Aton faith into Thebes, Amenhotep IV erected there a sumptuous temple of the new god, which, of course, received liberal endowments from the royal treasury. If the Aton movement was intended as a compromise with the priests of Amon, it failed. The bitterest enmities soon broke out, culminating finally in the determination on the king's part to make Aton sole god of the Empire and to annihilate Amon. The effort to obliterate all trace of the existence of the upstart Amon resulted in the most extreme measures. The king changed his own name from "Amenhotep" ("Amen rests" ro "is satisfied")

---

[1] The decree for the burial of the sacred bull of Heliopolis, Mnevis, at Amarna (DAVIES, *Amarna*, V, p. 30) is clearly a compromise with the Heliopolitan priests, but of course does not mean "animal worship."

to "Ikhnaton," which means "Aton is satisfied," and is a translation of the king's old name into a corresponding idea in the Aton faith.[1] The name of Amon, wherever it occurred on the great monuments of Thebes, was expunged, and in doing so not even the name of the king's father, Amenhotep III, was respected. These erasures were not confined to the name of Amon. Even the word "gods" as a compromising plural was expunged wherever found, and the names of the other gods, too, were treated like that of Amon.[2]

Finding Thebes embarrassed with too many theological traditions, in spite of its prestige and its splendor, Ikhnaton forsook it and built a new capital about midway between Thebes and the sea, at a place now commonly known as Tell el-Amarna. He called it Akhetaton, "Horizon of Aton." The name of the Sun-god is the only divine name found in the place, and it was evidently intended as a centre for the dissemination of Solar monotheism. Here several sanctuaries[3] of Aton were erected, and in the boundary landmarks, imposing stelæ which the king set up in the eastern and western cliffs, the place was formally devoted to his exclusive service. A similar Aton city was founded in Nubia, and in all likelihood there was another in Asia. The three great portions of the Empire, Egypt, Nubia, and Syria, were thus each given a centre

[1] See SETHE, *Zeitschr. für aegypt. Sprache*, 44, 116–118, where this new rendering of the name is demonstrated. The rendering in the author's history, p. 364, is to be changed accordingly.

[2] It has been widely stated that the hostility of Ikhnaton did not extend beyond his erasure of Amon; but this is an error. I found other gods expunged in Nubia. See also my remarks in *Zeitschr. für aegypt. Sprache*, 40, 109–110.

[3] There were at least four. The earlier Boundary Stelæ give five (DAVIES, *Amarna*, V, p. 30), but one is evidently a dittography of the preceding in the ancient scribes copy.

of the Aton faith. Besides these sanctuaries of Aton were also built at various other places in Egypt.[1]

This was, of course, not accomplished without building up a powerful court party, which the king could oppose, to the evicted priesthoods, especially that of Amon. The resulting convulsion undoubtedly affected seriously the power of the royal house. The life of this court party, which now unfolded at Akhetaton, centred about the propagation of the new faith, and as preserved to us in the wall reliefs which fill the chapels of the cliff tombs, excavated by the king for his nobles in the face of the low cliffs of the eastern plateau behind the new city, it forms, perhaps, the most interesting and picturesque chapter in the story of the early East.[2] It is to the tombs of these partisans of the king that we owe our knowledge of the content of the remarkable teaching which he was now propagating. They contain a series of hymns in praise of the Sun-god, or of the Sun-god and the king alternately, which afford us at least a glimpse into the new world of thought, in which we behold this young king and his

[1] A list of the Aton temples will be found in my essay in the *Zeitschr. für aegypt. Sprache*, 40, 106–113. The Nubian city of Ikhnaton was found in 1907 by the University of Chicago Expedition. See my *Monuments of Sudanese Nubia*, pp. 51–82.

[2] These tombs were frequently visited and studied in the early days of Egyptology, and fragmentarily published. No complete publication, however, was issued until 1903–8, when N. DE G. DAVIES published his valuable *Rock Tombs of El Amarna*, vols. I–VI, London, 1903–8, which includes everything at Amarna except the town site and the tomb of the king. I copied the most important hymns there in 1895, and these two sources are the bases of the renderings given above. For a presentation of the Amarna situation, historically considered, especially the life of the court in the new environment, the reader may refer to the author's *History of Egypt*, pp. 358–378. A popular discussion and description of the remarkable reliefs in the tombs will be found in the author's *Two Thousand Miles Up the Nile*, soon to be published.

associates lifting up their eyes and endeavoring to discern God in the illimitable sweep of his power—God no longer of the Nile valley only, but of all men and of all the world. We can do no better at this juncture than to let these hymns speak for themselves. The longest and most important is as follows:[1]

UNIVERSAL SPLENDOR AND POWER OF ATON

"Thy dawning is beautiful in the horizon of the sky,
  O living Aton, Beginning of life!
When thou risest in the eastern horizon,
Thou fillest every land with thy beauty.
Thou art beautiful, great, glittering, high above every land,
Thy rays, they encompass the lands, even all that thou hast made.
Thou art Re, and thou carriest them all away captive;[2]
Thou bindest them by thy love.
Though thou art far away, thy rays are upon earth;
Though thou art on high, thy ⌜footprints are the day⌝.

NIGHT

"When thou settest in the western horizon of the sky,
The earth is in darkness like the dead;
They sleep in their chambers,
Their heads are wrapped up,
Their nostrils are stopped,
And none seeth the other,
While all their things are stolen

---

[1] The best text is that of DAVIES, *Amarna*, VI, pl. xxix. Full commentary will be found in my *De hymnis in solem sub rege Amenophide IV. conceptis*, Berlin, 1894, though unfortunately based on the older text of Bouriant. Some changes in the above translation, as compared with that in the author's *History*, are due to a few new readings in DAVIES's text, as well as to further study of the document also. The division into strophes is not in the original, but is indicated here for the sake of clearness. The titles of the strophes I have inserted to aid the modern reader.

[2] There is a pun here on the word Re, which is the same as the word used for "all."

Which are under their heads,
And they know it not.
Every lion cometh forth from his den,
All serpents, they sting.
Darkness . . .
The world is in silence,
He that made them resteth in his horizon.

DAY AND MAN

"Bright is the earth when thou risest in the horizon.
When thou shinest as Aton by day
Thou drivest away the darkness.
When thou sendest forth thy rays,
The Two Lands (Egypt) are in daily festivity,
Awake and standing upon their feet
When thou hast raised them up.
Their limbs bathed, they take their clothing,
Their arms uplifted in adoration to thy dawning.
(Then) in all the world they do their work.

DAY AND THE ANIMALS AND PLANTS

"All cattle rest upon their pasturage,
The trees and the plants flourish,
The birds flutter in their marshes,
Their wings uplifted in adoration to thee.
All the sheep dance upon their feet,
All winged things fly,
They live when thou hast shone upon them.

DAY AND THE WATERS

"The barques sail up-stream and down-stream alike.
Every highway is open because thou dawnest.
The fish in the river leap up before thee.
Thy rays are in the midst of the great green sea.

CREATION OF MAN

"Creator of the germ in woman,
Maker of seed in man,
Giving life to the son in the body of his mother,

Soothing him that he may not weep,
Nurse (even) in the womb,
Giver of breath to animate every one that he maketh!
When he cometh forth from the body . . . on the day of his birth,
Thou openest his mouth in speech,
Thou suppliest his necessities.

CREATION OF ANIMALS

"When the fledgling in the egg chirps in the shell,
Thou givest him breath therein to preserve him alive.
When thou hast ⌜brought him together⌝,
To (the point of) bursting it in the egg,
He cometh forth from the egg
To chirp ⌜with all his might⌝.
He goeth about upon his two feet
When he hath come forth therefrom.

THE WHOLE CREATION

"How manifold are thy works!
They are hidden from before (us),
O sole God, whose powers no other possesseth.[1]
Thou didst create the earth according to thy heart [2]
While thou wast alone:
Men, all cattle large and small,
All that are upon the earth,
That go about upon their feet;
[All] that are on high,
That fly with their wings.
The foreign countries, Syria and Kush,
The land of Egypt;

[1] The shorter hymns follow the phrase "sole God," with the addition, "beside whom there is no other" (see DAVIES, *Amarna*, I, XXXVI, l. 1, and III, XXIX, l. 1).
This use of the word sp for "quality" or "power" will be found also in the hymn of Suti and Hor translated above (Brit. Mus. Stela 826, l. 3); Great Hymn to Amon (1, 5), and similarly on the late statue of Hor (Louvre 88, BRUGSCH, *Thes.*, VI, 1251, l. 1).

[2] The word "heart" may mean either "pleasure" or "understanding" here.

Thou settest every man into his place,
Thou suppliest their necessities.
Every one has his possessions,
And his days are reckoned.
The tongues are divers in speech,
Their forms likewise and their skins are distinguished.
(For) thou makest different the strangers.

WATERING THE EARTH IN EGYPT AND ABROAD

"Thou makest the Nile in the Nether World,
Thou bringest it as thou desirest,
To preserve alive the people.[1]
For thou hast made them for thyself,
The lord of them all, resting among them;
Thou lord of every land, who risest for them,
Thou Sun of day, great in majesty.
All the distant countries,
Thou makest (also) their life,
Thou hast set a Nile in the sky;
When it falleth for them,
It maketh waves upon the mountains,
Like the great green sea,
Watering their fields in their towns.

"How excellent are thy designs, O lord of eternity!
There is a Nile in the sky for the strangers
And for the cattle of every country that go upon their feet.
(But) the Nile, it cometh from the Nether World for Egypt.

THE SEASONS

"Thy rays nourish[2] every garden;
When thou risest they live,
They grow by thee.
Thou makest the seasons
In order to create all thy work:
Winter to bring them coolness,
And heat that ⌈they may taste⌉ thee.

---

[1] The word is one used only of the people of Egypt.
[2] The word used implies the nourishment of a mother at the breast.

Thou didst make the distant sky to rise therein,
In order to behold all that thou hast made,
Thou alone, shining in thy form as living Aton,
Dawning, glittering, going afar and returning.
Thou makest millions of forms
Through thyself alone;
Cities, towns, and tribes, highways and rivers.
All eyes see thee before them,
For thou art Aton of the day over the earth.

. . . .

REVELATION TO THE KING

"Thou art in my heart,
There is no other that knoweth thee
Save thy son Ikhnaton.
Thou hast made him wise
In thy designs and in thy might.
The world is in thy hand,
Even as thou hast made them.
When thou hast risen they live,
When thou settest they die;
For thou art length of life of thyself,
Men live through thee,
While (their) eyes are upon thy beauty
Until thou settest.
All labor is put away
When thou settest in the west.

. . . .

Thou didst establish the world,
And raise them up for thy son,
Who came forth from thy limbs,
The king of Upper and Lower Egypt,
Living in Truth, Lord of the Two Lands,
Nefer-khepru-Re, Wan-Re (Ikhnaton),
Son of Re, living in Truth, lord of diadems,
Ikhnaton, whose life is long;
(And for) the chief royal wife, his beloved,
Mistress of the Two Lands, Nefer-nefru-Aton, Nofretete,
Living and flourishing for ever and ever."

This great royal hymn doubtless represents an excerpt, or a series of fragments excerpted, from the ritual of Aton, as it was celebrated from day to day in the Aton temple at Amarna. Unhappily, it was copied in the cemetery in but one tomb, where about a third of it has perished by the vandalism of the modern natives, leaving us for the lost portion only a very inaccurate and hasty modern copy of thirty years ago (1883). The other tombs were supplied, with their devotional inscriptions, from the current paragraphs and stock phrases which made up the knowledge of the Aton faith as understood by the scribes and painters who decorated these tombs. It should not be forgotten, therefore, that the fragments of the Aton faith which have survived to us in the Amarna cemetery, our chief source, have thus filtered mechanically through the indifferent hands, and the starved and listless minds of a few petty bureaucrats on the outskirts of a great religious and intellectual movement. Apart from the Royal Hymn, they were elsewhere content with bits and snatches copied in some cases from the Royal Hymn itself, or other fragments patched together in the form of a shorter hymn, which they then slavishly copied in whole or in part from tomb to tomb. Where the materials are so meagre, and the movement revealed so momentous, even the few new contributions furnished by the short hymn are of great value.[1] In four cases the hymn is attributed to the king himself; that is, he is represented as reciting it to Aton. The lines are as follows:

[1] The short hymn was put together in a composite text of all versions in the second (unpublished) portion of my *De hymnis in solem*, and this was later supplemented by my own copies. DAVIES has also put together a composite text from five tombs in his *Amarna*, IV, pls. xxxii–xxxiii. The above translation is based on both sources.

"Thy rising is beautiful, O living Aton, lord of Eternity;
  Thou art shining, beautiful, strong;
  Thy love is great and mighty,
  Thy rays ⌜are cast⌝ into every face.
  Thy glowing hue brings life to hearts,
  When thou hast filled the Two Lands with thy love.
  O God who himself fashioned himself,
  Maker of every land,
  Creator of that which is upon it:
  Men, all cattle large and small,
  All trees that grow in the soil.
  They live when thou dawnest for them,
  Thou art the mother and the father of all that thou hast made.
  As for their eyes, when thou dawnest,
  They see by means of thee.
  Thy rays illuminate the whole earth,
  And every heart rejoices because of seeing thee,
  When thou dawnest as their lord.

"When thou settest in the western horizon of the sky,
  They sleep after the manner of the dead,
  Their heads are wrapped up,
  Their nostrils are stopped,
  Until thy rising comes in the morning,
  In the eastern horizon of the sky.
  Their arms are uplifted in adoration of thee,
  Thou makest hearts to live by thy beauty,
  And men live when thou sendest forth thy rays,
  Every land is in festivity:
  Singing, music, and shoutings of joy
  Are in the hall of the Benben[1]-house,
  Thy temple in Akhet-Aton, the seat of Truth,
  Wherewith thou art satisfied.
  Food and provision are offered therein;
  Thy pure son performs thy pleasing ceremonies,
  O living Aton, at his festal processions.
  All that thou hast made dances before thee,
  Thy august son rejoices, his heart is joyous,

---

[1] See above, p. 71.

O living Aton, born in the sky every day.
He begets his august son Wanre (Ikhnaton)
Like himself without ceasing,
Son of Re, wearing his beauty, Nefer-khepru-Re, Wanre (Ikhnaton),
Even me, thy son, in whom thou art satisfied,
Who bears thy name.
Thy strength and thy might abide in my heart,
Thou art Aton, living forever. . . .
Thou hast made the distant sky to rise therein,
In order to behold all that thou hast made,
While thou wast alone.
Millions of life are in thee to make them live,
It is the breath of life in the nostrils to behold thy rays.[1]
All flowers live and what grows in the soil
Is made to grow because thou dawnest.
They are drunken before thee.
All cattle skip upon their feet;
The birds in the marsh fly with joy,
Their wings that were folded are spread,
Uplifted in adoration to the living Aton,
The maker . . ."[2]

In these hymns there is an inspiring universalism not found before in the religion of Egypt. It is world wide in its sweep. The king claims that the recognition of the Sun-god's universal supremacy is also universal, and that all men acknowledge his dominion. On the great boundary stela likewise he says of them, that Aton made them "for his own self; all lands, the Ægæans bear their dues, their tribute is upon their backs, for him who made their life, him by whose rays men live and breathe the air."[3]

---

[1] Variant: "Breath, it enters the nostrils when thou showest thyself to them."
[2] The remainder of the line is lost. Only one of the five texts which exist from the beginning goes as far as this point. It also stopped at this place, so that only part of a line has been lost.
[3] Stela K, DAVIES, *Amarna*, V, pl. xxix, l. 7.

It is clear that he was projecting a world religion, and endeavoring to displace by it the nationalism which had preceded it for twenty centuries.

Along with this universal power, Ikhnaton is also deeply impressed with the eternal duration of his god; and although he himself calmly accepts his own mortality and early in his career at Amarna makes public and permanently records on the boundary stelæ instructions for his own burial, nevertheless he relies upon his intimate relation with Aton to insure him something of the Sun-god's duration. His official titulary always contains the epithet after his name, "whose lifetime (or duration) is long."

But in the beginning of all, Aton called himself forth out of the eternal solitude, the author of his own being. The king calls him "My rampart of a million cubits, my reminder of eternity, my witness of the things of eternity, who himself fashioned himself with his own hands, whom no artificer knew."[1] In harmony with this idea, the hymns love to reiterate the fact that the creation of the world which followed was done while the god was yet alone. The words "while thou wert alone" are almost a refrain in these hymns. He is the universal creator who brought forth all the races of man and distinguished them in speech and in color of the skin. His creative power still goes on calling forth life, even from the inanimate egg. Nowhere do we find more marked the naïve wonder of the king at the Sun-god's life-giving power than in this marvel, that within the egg-shell, which the king calls the "stone" of the egg—within this lifeless stone, the sounds of life respond to the command of Aton, and, nourished by the breath which he gives, a living creature issues forth.

[1] Boundary Stela K, *ibid.*, V, pl. xxix, l. 9.

This life-giving power is the constant source of life and sustenance, and its immediate agency is the rays of the Sun. It is in these rays that Aton is present on earth as a beneficent power. Thus manifested, the hymns love to dwell upon his ever-present universal power. "Thou art in the sky, but thy rays are on earth;" "Though thou art far away, thy rays are on earth;" "Thy rays are in the midst of the great green sea;" "Thy rays are on thy beloved son;" "He who makes whole the eyes by his rays;" "It is the breath of life in the nostrils to behold thy rays;" "Thy child (the king), who came forth from thy rays;" "Thou didst fashion him (the king) out of thine own rays;" "Thy rays carry a million royal jubilees;" "When thou sendest forth thy rays, the Two Lands are in festivity;" "Thy rays embrace the lands, even all that thou hast made;"[1] "Whether he is in the sky or on earth, all eyes behold him without [ceasing]; he fills [every land] with his rays, and makes all men to live; with beholding whom may my eyes be satisfied daily, when he dawns in this house of Aton and fills it with his own self by his beams, beauteous in love, and lays them upon me in satisfying life for ever and ever."[2] In these last words the king himself expresses his own consciousness of the god's presence, especially in the temple, by his rays. The obvious dependence of Egypt upon the Nile made it impossible to ignore this agency of life, and there is nothing which discloses more clearly the surprising rationalism of Ikhnaton than the fact that he strips off without hesitation the venerable body of myth and tradition which deified the Nile as Osiris, and attributes the inundation to natural forces controlled by his god, who

[1] See my *De hymnis in solem*, pp. 21-22.
[2] Boundary Stela K, Davies, *Amarna*, V, pl. xxix, ll. 10-11.

in like solicitude for other lands has made a Nile for them in the sky.

It is this recognition of the fatherly solicitude of Aton for all creatures which lifts the movement of Ikhnaton far above all that had before been attained in the religion of Egypt or of the whole East before this time. "Thou art the father and the mother of all that thou hast made" is a thought which anticipates much of the later development in religion even down to our own time. The picture of the lily-grown marshes, where the flowers are "drunken" in the intoxicating radiance of Aton, where the birds unfold their wings and lift them "in adoration of the living Aton," where the cattle dance with delight in the sunshine, and the fish in the river beyond leap up to greet the light, the universal light whose beams are even "in the midst of the great green sea"—all this discloses a discernment of the presence of God in nature, and an appreciation of the revelation of God in the visible world such as we find a thousand years later in the Hebrew psalms, and in our own poets of nature since Wordsworth.

It is evident that, in spite of the political origin of this movement, the deepest sources of power in this remarkable revolution lay in this appeal to nature, in this admonition to "consider the lilies of the field." Ikhnaton was a "God-intoxicated man," whose mind responded with marvellous sensitiveness and discernment to the visible evidences of God about him. He was fairly ecstatic in his sense of the beauty of the eternal and universal light. Its beams enfold him on every monument of his which has survived. He prays, "May my eyes be satisfied daily with beholding him, when he dawns in this house of Aton and fills it with his own self by his beams, beauteous in love, and lays them upon me in satisfying life for ever and ever." In this light—which more than once, as here, he identifies with love, or again with beauty, as the visible evidence of the presence of God—he revels with an intoxication rarely to be found, and which may be properly compared to the ecstatic joy felt by such a soul as Ruskin in the contemplation of light. Ruskin, as he sees it playing over some lovely landscape, calls it "the breathing, animated, exulting light, which feels and receives and rejoices and acts—which chooses one thing and rejects another—which seeks and finds and loses again—leaping from rock to rock, from leaf to leaf, from wave to wave, glowing or flashing or scintillating according to what it strikes, or in its holier moods absorbing and enfolding all things in the deep fulness of its repose, and then again losing itself in bewilderment and doubt and dimness, or perishing and passing away, entangled in drifting mist, or melted into melancholy air, but still—kindling or declining, sparkling or still—it is the living light, which breathes in its deepest, most entranced rest, which sleeps but never dies."[1] That is the loftiest modern interpretation of light, a veritable gospel of the beauty of light, of which the earliest disciple was this lonely idealist of the fourteenth century before Christ. To Ikhnaton, too, the eternal light might sleep, when he that made the world has "gone to rest in his horizon," but to him also as with Ruskin it "sleeps but never dies."

In this aspect of Ikhnaton's movement, then, it is a gospel of the beauty and beneficence of the natural order, a recognition of the message of nature to the soul of man, which makes it the earliest of those revivals which we call in the case of such artists as Millet and the Barbizon school, or of Wordsworth and his successors, "a return to

[1] RUSKIN, *Modern Painters*, vol. I, p. 250.

nature." As the earliest of such movements known to us, however, we cannot call it a "return." We should not forget also that this intellectual attitude of the king was not confined to religion. The breath of nature had also touched life and art at the same time, and quickened them with a new vision as broad and untrammelled as that which is unfolded in the hymns. The king's charmingly natural and unrestrained relations with his family, depicted on public monuments without reserve, is another example of his powerful individuality and his readiness to throw off the shackles of tradition without hesitation in the endeavor to establish a world of things as they are, in wholesome naturalness. The artists of the time, one of them indeed, as he says, under the king's own instructions, put forth works dominated by the same spirit. Especially do they reflect to us that joy in nature which breathes in the religion of Ikhnaton. We have come to speak habitually of an Amarna age, in religion, in life, in art, and this fact of itself is conclusive evidence of the distinctive intellectual attitude of Ikhnaton.

It is remarkable that the hymns as an expression of religious aspiration contain so little reference to character and to ethical matters. We have seen that the Solar theology was closely identified from the beginning with the development of the moral consciousness in Egypt. Recognizing as it does more clearly than ever was done before the beneficent goodness of the Sun-god's sway, it is inconceivable that the Amarna movement should have rejected the highly developed ethics of Heliopolis. Its close connection with the Heliopolitan theology is evident throughout. The identification of the royal line with that of the Sun-god by the Heliopolitan priests in the Pyramid Age had resulted, as we have seen, in transferring to Re the humane qualities of beneficent dominion with which the Pharaohs of the Feudal Age were imbued. The Pharaoh was the "good shepherd" or "good herdman," and this figure of the paternal and protecting sovereign had been transferred to Re. Re had thus gained wondrously in qualities of humane and paternal sympathy, as a result of this development in the conception of the kingship in the Feudal Age. The social forces which had contributed this high ideal of kingship were thus the ultimate influences, which, through the kingship, enriched and humanized the otherwise rather mechanical and perfunctory political conception of Re's dominion. The human appeal which he now made was thus akin to that of Osiris himself. This tendency of the Solar faith was entirely in sympathy with the teaching of Ikhnaton. Under his father we have found a Sun-hymn calling the Sun-god "the valiant herdman driving his herds," a hint clearly connecting the Aton faith with the social and moral movement of the Feudal Age, which we have just recalled. Nevertheless it is evident that it was the beneficence and beauty rather than the righteousness of the Sun-god, on which Ikhnaton loved to dwell, in the hymns to his god. Outside of the hymns, however, there is a marked prominence of the ancient word "truth," or, as we have observed so often, "justice" or "righteousness." To the official name of the king, there is regularly appended the epithet, "living in truth,"[1] and although it is difficult

---

[1] It is difficult to define the exact meaning of this phrase. The Sun-god was the father of the goddess who personified Truth, and his close connection with truth is evident throughout. In the sixty-fifth chapter of the Book of the Dead, he lives "in truth" or "on truth," using the same words applied to Ikhnaton. But the passage exhibits a very materialistic conception of truth, for the Sun-god lives "on truth" as the Nile lives "on fish." (See GRAPOW, *Zeitschr.*

to interpret the phrase exactly, it is evident that the conception of Truth and Right, personified as a goddess, the daughter of the Sun-god at a remote age, occupied a prominent place in the Aton movement, and not least in the personal faith of the king. The new capital was called the "seat of truth" in the short hymn, and we frequently find the men of Ikhnaton's court glorifying truth. One of his leading partisans, Eye, says: "He (the king) put truth in my body and my abomination is lying. I know that Wanre (Ikhnaton) rejoices in it (truth)."[1] The same man affirms that the Sun-god is one "(whose) heart is satisfied with truth, whose abomination is falsehood."[2] Another official states in his Amarna tomb: "I will speak truth to his majesty, (for) I know that he lives therein. . . . I do not that which his majesty hates, (for) my abomination is lying in my body. . . . I have reported truth to his majesty, (for) I know that he lives therein. Thou art Re, begetter of truth. . . . I took not the reward of lying, nor expelled the truth for the violent."[3] Re was still the author of truth or righteousness at Amarna as before, and if we hear of no judgment hereafter in the Amarna tombs, it was clearly only the rejection of the cloud of gods and demi-gods, with Osiris at their head, who had been involved in the judgment as we find it in the Book of the Dead. These were now banished, and the dramatic scene of the judgment seems to have disappeared with them, although it is clear that the ethical requirements of the Solar faith, the faith in which they emerged and developed, were not relaxed in Ikhnaton's

für aegypt. Sprache, 49, 51.) The chapter is a magical charm to force the Sun-god to justify the deceased. It was doubtless such materialistic notions of ethical concepts which led the priests to employ magic in the realm of ethics and ethical values.

[1] BAR, II, 993, 1002.   [2] BAR, II, 994.   [3] BAR, II, 1013.

teaching. The sacerdotal invasion of the moral realm with mechanical magical agencies for insuring justification was also evidently repelled by Ikhnaton. The familiar heart scarab now no longer bears a charm to still the accusing voice of conscience, but a simple prayer, in the name of Aton, for long life, favor, and food.[1]

Such fundamental changes as these, on a moment's reflection, suggest what an overwhelming tide of inherited thought, custom, and tradition had been diverted from its channel by the young king who was guiding this revolution. It is only as this aspect of his movement is clearly discerned that we begin to appreciate the power of his remarkable personality. Before his time religious documents were usually attributed to ancient kings and wise men, and the power of a belief lay chiefly in its claim to remote antiquity and the sanctity of immemorial custom. Even the social prophets of the Feudal Age attribute the maxims of Ptahhotep to a vizier of the Old Kingdom, five or six centuries earlier. Until Ikhnaton the history of the world had been but the irresistible drift of tradition. All men had been but drops of water in the great current. Ikhnaton was the first individual in history. Consciously and deliberately, by intellectual process he gained his position, and then placed himself squarely in the face of tradition and swept it aside. He appeals to no myths, to no ancient and widely accepted versions of the dominion of the gods, to no customs sanctified by centuries—he appeals only to the present and visible evidences of his god's dominion, evidences open to all, and as for tradition, wherever it had left material manifestations of any sort in records which could be reached, he endeavored to an-

[1] See SCHAEFER, *Zeitschr. für aegypt. Sprache*, 48, 45 f., and *Proceedings of the Soc. of Biblical Arch.*, XVII, 155, No. 3.

nihilate it. The new faith has but one name at Amarna. It is frequently called the "teaching," and this "teaching" is attributed solely to the king. There is no reason to question this attribution. But we should realize what this "teaching" meant in the life of the Egyptian people as a whole.

Here had been a great people, the onward flow of whose life, in spite of its almost irresistible momentum, had been suddenly arrested and then diverted into a strange channel. Their holy places had been desecrated, the shrines sacred with the memories of thousands of years had been closed up, the priests driven away, the offerings and temple incomes confiscated, and the old order blotted out. Everywhere whole communities, moved by instincts flowing from untold centuries of habit and custom, returned to their holy places to find them no more, and stood dumfounded before the closed doors of the ancient sanctuaries. On feast days, sanctified by memories of earliest childhood, venerable halls that had resounded with the rejoicings of the multitudes, as we have recalled them at Siut, now stood silent and empty; and every day as the funeral processions wound across the desert margin and up the plateau to the cemetery, the great comforter and friend, Osiris, the champion of the dead in every danger, was banished, and no man dared so much as utter his name.[1] Even in their oaths, absorbed from childhood with their mothers' milk, the involuntary names must not

---

[1] In mortuary doctrines this Amarna movement was unable wholly to eradicate the old customs. The heart scarab is mentioned above; "ushebti" statuettes were also known. There is one in Zurich, see WIEDEMANN, *Proceed. of the Soc. of Bib. Arch.*, VII, 200–3; also one in Cairo, see MASPERO, *Musée égyptien*, III, pl. xxiii, pp. 27–28. They contain prayers for sustenance at the tomb, in the name of Aton. Osiris is not named.

THE IMPERIAL AGE AND MONOTHEISM 341

be suffered to escape the lips; and in the presence of the magistrate at court the ancient oath must now contain only the name of Aton. All this to them was as if the modern man were asked to worship X and swear by Y. Groups of muttering priests, nursing implacable hatred, must have mingled their curses with the execration of whole communities of discontented tradesmen—bakers who no longer drew a livelihood from the sale of ceremonial cakes at the temple feasts; craftsmen who no longer sold amulets of the old gods at the temple gateway; hack sculptors whose statues of Osiris lay under piles of dust in many a tumble-down studio; cemetery stone-cutters who found their tawdry tombstones with scenes from the Book of the Dead banished from the cemetery; scribes whose rolls of the same book, filled with the names of the old gods, or even if they bore the word god in the plural, were anathema; actors and priestly mimes who were driven away from the sacred groves by gendarmes on the days when they should have presented to the people the "passion play," and murmuring groups of pilgrims at Abydos who would have taken part in this drama of the life and death and resurrection of Osiris; physicians deprived of their whole stock in trade of exorcising ceremonies, employed with success since the days of the earliest kings, two thousand years before; shepherds who no longer dared to place a loaf and a jar of water under yonder tree and thus to escape the anger of the goddess who dwelt in it, and who might afflict the household with sickness in her wrath; peasants who feared to erect a rude image of Osiris in the field to drive away the typhonic demons of drought and famine; mothers soothing their babes at twilight and fearing to utter the old sacred names and prayers learned in childhood, to drive away from their little ones the lurking demons of the dark. In the midst of a whole land thus darkened by clouds of smouldering discontent, this marvellous young king, and the group of sympathizers who surrounded him, set up their tabernacle to the daily light, in serene unconsciousness of the fatal darkness that enveloped all around and grew daily darker and more threatening.

In placing the movement of Ikhnaton against a background of popular discontent like this, and adding to the picture also the far more immediately dangerous secret opposition of the ancient priesthoods, the still unconquered party of Amon, and the powerful military group, who were disaffected by the king's peace policy in Asia and his lack of interest in imperial administration and maintenance, we begin to discern something of the powerful individuality of this first intellectual leader in history. His reign was the earliest age of the rule of ideas, irrespective of the condition and willingness of the people upon whom they were to be forced. As Matthew Arnold has so well said, in commenting on the French Revolution: "But the mania for giving an immediate political application to all these fine ideas of the reason was fatal. . . . Ideas cannot be too much prized in and for themselves, cannot be too much lived with; but to transfer them abruptly into the world of politics and practice, violently to revolutionize the world at their bidding—that is quite another thing." But Ikhnaton had no French Revolution to look back upon. He was himself the world's first revolutionist, and he was fully convinced that he might entirely recast the world of religion, thought, art, and life by the invincible purpose he held, to make his ideas at once practically effective. And so the fair city of the Amarna plain arose, a fatuous island of the blest in a sea of discontent, a vision of fond hopes, born in a mind fatally forgetful that the past cannot be annihilated. The marvel is that such a man should have first arisen in the East, and especially in Egypt, where no man except Ikhnaton possessed the ability to forget. Nor was the great Mediterranean world which Egypt now dominated any better prepared for an international religion than its Egyptian lords. The imperial imagination of Ikhnaton reminds one of that of Alexander the Great, a thousand years later, but it was many centuries in advance of his age.

We cannot wonder that when the storm broke it swept away almost all traces of this earliest idealist. All that we have to tell us of him is the wreck of his city, a lonely outpost of idealism, not to be overtaken and passed till six centuries later those Bedouin hordes who were now drifting into Ikhnaton's Palestinian provinces had coalesced into a nation of social, moral, and religious aspirations, and had thus brought forth the Hebrew prophets.

LECTURE X

THE AGE OF PERSONAL PIETY—SACERDOTALISM AND FINAL DECADENCE

THE fall of Ikhnaton is shrouded in complete obscurity. The ultimate result was the restoration of Amon by Tutenkhamon, one of Ikhnaton's feeble successors. The old régime returned. Tutenkhamon's account of his restoration of the gods is an interesting revelation of the religious and intellectual attitude of the leading men of affairs when Ikhnaton had passed away. The new king refers to himself as "the good ruler, who did excellent things for the father of all gods (Amon), who restored for him that which was in ruin as everlasting monuments; cast out for him sin in the Two Lands (Egypt), so that righteousness endured . . .; and made lying to be the abomination of the land, as in the beginning. For when his majesty was crowned as king, the temples of the gods and goddesses were [desolat]ed from Elephantine as far as the marshes of the Delta [1] . . . (hammered out). Their holy places were ⌈forsaken⌉ and had become overgrown tracts, . . . their sanctuaries were like that which has never been, and their houses were trodden roads. The land was in an evil pass, and as for the gods, they had forsaken this land. If people were sent to Syria to extend

---

[1] "Marshes of the Delta" (ḫ'wt ydḫw) is not in the published edition of the text, but close study of a large-scale photograph shows that it is still discernible, though with great difficulty, on the stone.

the borders of Egypt, they prospered not at all; if men prayed to a god for succor, he came not; . . . if men besought a goddess likewise, she came not at all. Their hearts were ⌈deaf⌉ in their bodies, and they diminished what was done. Now, after days had passed by these things, [his majesty] appeared upon the throne of his father, he ruled the regions of Horus. . . . His majesty was making the plans of this land and the needs of the two regions were before his majesty, as he took counsel with his own heart, seeking every excellent matter and searching for profitable things for his father Amon, fashioning his august emanation of pure gold, and giving to him more than was done before."[1]

Thus was the memory of the great idealist execrated. When in a state document it was necessary to refer to him, he was called "the criminal of Akhetaton." The reestablished priesthood of Amon rejoiced in the restoration of their power, especially when the ephemeral successors of Ikhnaton were followed by the able rule of Harmhab, a military leader who had contrived gradually to secure control of the situation. A hymn to Amon from this period reveals the exultant triumph of his devotees as they sing to him:

"Thou findest him who transgresses against thee;
Woe to him who assails thee!
Thy city endures;

[1] These new and interesting facts are drawn from a large stela of Tutenkhamon found by LEGRAIN in the Karnak temple in 1905, and published by him in *Recueil de trav.*, XXIX, 162–173. I am indebted to M. LEGRAIN for kind permission to make a series of large-scale photographs of the monument, on which it is possible to read the important northern limits of the persecution of the gods by Ikhnaton, not before noted. The stela was usurped by Harmhab, who inserted his name over that of Ikhnaton.

> But he who assails thee falls.
> Fie upon him who transgresses against thee in every land.
> . . . .
> The sun of him who knows thee not goes down, O Amon!
> But as for him who knows thee, he shines.
> The forecourt of him who assailed thee is in darkness,
> But the whole earth is in light.
> Whosoever puts thee in his heart, O Amon,
> Lo, his sun dawns." [1]

This very hymn, however, betrays its connection with the old Solar faith and the paternal interpretation of Re, as it goes on to the praise of Amon as the "good shepherd" and the "pilot," ideas which, we recall, arose in the social movement of the Feudal Age. Indeed, notwithstanding the restoration of Amon, the ideas and the tendencies which had given birth to the revolution of Ikhnaton were far from disappearing. It was not possible to carry them on, under a monotheistic form, involving the annihilation of the old gods; but the human and beneficent aspects of Aton, in his care for all men, had taken hold upon the imagination of the thinking classes, and we find the same qualities now attributed to Amon. Men sang of him:

> "Lord of truth, father of gods,
>   Maker of men and creator of animals,
> Lord of that which is,
>   Creator of the tree of life,
>   Maker of herbs, sustaining the cattle alive." [2]

The hymn from which these lines are quoted does not hesitate to call the god thus praised Re or Atum, showing

---

[1] Ostrakon 5656 a in the British Museum, published in BIRCH, *Inscriptions in the Hieratic Character*, pl. xxvi. The historical connection of the passages cited was first noted in a brilliant interpretation by ERMAN, *Zeitschr. für aegypt. Sprache*, 42, 106 ff.

[2] Great Hymn to Amon, Cairo Papyrus, No. 17 (MARIETTE, II, pls. 11–13).

that the Aton movement had left the traditional prestige of the Heliopolitan Re unblemished. Another passage contains evident echoes of the Aton faith:

> "Hail to thee! Re, lord of Truth,
>   Whose sanctuary is hidden, lord of gods,
>   Khepri in the midst of his barque,
>   Who commanded and the gods became;
>   Atum, who made the people,
>   Who determined the fashion of them,
>   Maker of their sustenance,
>   Who distinguished one color (race) from another;
>   Who hears the prayer of him who is in captivity,
>   Who is kindly of heart when one calls upon him,
>   Who saves the timid from the haughty,
>   Who separates the weak from the ⌈strong⌉,
>   Lord of Knowledge, ⌈in⌉ whose mouth is Taste;
>   For love of whom the Nile comes,
>   Lord of sweetness, great in love,
>   At whose coming the people live."

Even the old monotheistic phrases have here and there survived, and this hymn employs them without compunction, though constantly referring to the gods. It says:

> "Sole ⌈likeness⌉, maker of what is,
>   Sole and only one, maker of what exists.
>   From whose eyes men issued,
>   From whose mouth the gods came forth,
>   Maker of herbs for the cattle,
>   And the tree of life for mankind,
>   Who maketh the sustenance of the fish [in] the stream,
>   And the birds that ⌈traverse⌉ the sky,
>   Who giveth breath to that which is in the egg,
>   And maketh to live the son of the worm,
>   Who maketh that on which the gnats live,
>   The worms and the insects likewise,
>   Who supplieth the needs of the mice in their holes,
>   Who sustaineth alive the ⌈birds⌉ in every tree.

> Hail to thee, who hast made all these,
> Thou sole and only one, with many arms,
> Thou sleeper waking while all men sleep,
> Seeking good things for his cattle.
> Amon, enduring in all things,
> Atum-Harakhte,
> Praise to thee in all that they say,
> Jubilation to thee, for ⌈thy tarrying with us⌉,
> Obeisance to thee, who didst create us,
> 'Hail to thee,' say all cattle;
> 'Jubilation to thee,' says every country,
> To the height of heaven, to the breadth of earth,
> To the depths of the sea."

A hymn to Osiris of the same age says to him: "Thou art the father and the mother of men, they live from thy breath."[1] There is a spirit of humane solicitude in all this, which, as we have seen, appeared as early as the social teaching of the Feudal Age. Especially the preference for the "timid" as over against the "haughty" and overbearing, and the discerning "taste" and "knowledge," which are the royal and divine prerogatives, we have already discovered in social tractates like Ipuwer, and even in a state document like the Installation of the Vizier in the Twelfth Dynasty. That God is the father and mother of his creatures was, of course, a doctrine of the Aton faith. Such hymns also still preserve the universalism, the disregard for national lines, which was so prominent in the teaching of Ikhnaton. As we look further into the simpler and less ecclesiastical professions of the thirteenth and twelfth centuries before Christ, the two centuries after Ikhnaton, the confidence of the worshipper in the solicitude of the Sun-god for all, even the least of his creatures, has developed into a devotional

[1] *Zeitschr. für aegypt. Sprache*, 38, 31.

spirit, and a consciousness of personal relation with the god, which was already discernible in Ikhnaton's declaration to his god: "Thou art in my heart." The surviving influence of the Aton faith and the doctrines of social justice of the Feudal Age now culminated, therefore, in the profoundest expression or revelation of the devotional religious spirit ever attained by the men of Egypt. Furthermore, although rooted in the teaching of an exclusive few heretofore, these beliefs in an intimate and personal relation between the worshipper and his god had now, with the lapse of centuries and by slow and gradual process, become widespread among the people. An age of personal piety and inner aspiration to God now dawned among the masses. It is a notable development and, like so many of the movements which we have followed in these lectures, the earliest of its kind as yet discernible in the history of the East, or for that matter in the history of man. We are able to follow it only at Thebes, and it is not a little interesting to be able to look into the souls of the common folk who thronged the streets and markets, who tilled the fields and maintained the industries, who kept the accounts and carried on the official records, the hewers of wood and the drawers of water, the men and women upon whose shoulders rested the great burden of material life in the vast capital of the Egyptian Empire during the twelfth and thirteenth centuries before Christ.

A scribe in one of the treasury magazines of the Theban necropolis prays to Amon, as to him

> "Who cometh to the silent,
> Who saveth the poor,
> Who giveth breath to every one he loveth,
> . . . .
> Give to me [thy] hand,

> Save me,
> Shine upon me,
> For thou makest my sustenance.
> Thou art the sole god, there is no other,
> Even Re, who dawneth in the sky,
> Atum maker of men,
> Who heareth the prayers of him who calls to him,
> Who saveth a man from the haughty,
> Who bringeth the Nile for him who is among them,
> Who leadeth — for all men,
> When he riseth, the people live,
> Their hearts live when they see him
> Who giveth breath to him who is the egg,
> Who maketh the people and the birds to live,
> Who supplieth the needs of the mice in their holes,
> The worms and the insects likewise." [1]

To a god, the least of whose creatures are the object of his care, these men of Thebes might bring their misfortunes and their daily cares, confident in his kindness and beneficence. A painter of tomb scenes in the necropolis erected a stela in one of the necropolis sanctuaries, telling how Amon, in gracious mercy, had saved his son from sickness.[2] Amon is to him the "august god, who heareth petitions, who cometh at the cry of the afflicted poor, and giveth breath to him who is bowed down," and the story of Amon's goodness he tells thus:

> "Praise to Amon!
> I make hymns in his name,
> I give to him praise,
> To the height of heaven,

---

[1] Berlin Statuette, No. 6910.
[2] Berlin, No. 23077, published by ERMAN, *Sitzungsber. der Kgl. Preuss. Akad.*, 1911, XLIX, pp. 1087 ff. ERMAN first called attention to the character of this group of necropolis votive stelæ in an essay, *Denksteine aus dem thebanischen Gräberstadt*, ibid., pp. 1086 ff.

And the breadth of earth;
I tell of his prowess
To him who sails down-stream,
And to him who sails up-stream.

"Beware of him!
Repeat it to son and daughter,
To great and small,
Tell it to generation after generation,
Who are not yet born.
Tell it to the fishes in the stream,
To the birds in the sky,
Repeat it to him who knoweth it not
And to him who knoweth it.
Beware of him.

"Thou, O Amon, art the lord of the silent,
Who cometh at the cry of the poor.
When I cry to thee in my affliction,
Then thou comest and savest me.
That thou mayest give breath to him who is bowed down,
And mayest save me lying in bondage.[1]
Thou, Amon-Re, Lord of Thebes, art he,
Who saveth him that is in the Nether World,
. . . .
When men cry unto thee,
Thou art he that cometh from afar."

"Nebre, painter of Amon in the necropolis, son of Pai, painter of Amon in the necropolis, made this in the name of his lord, Amon, Lord of Thebes, who cometh at the cry of the poor; making for him praises in his name, because of the greatness of his might, and making for him prayers before him and before the whole land, on behalf of the painter Nakht-Amon,[2] when he lay sick unto death, being ⌈in⌉ the power of Amon, because of his sin."

[1] So ERMAN.   [2] The son of Neb-Re, whose life Amon saves.

"I found that the lord of gods came as the north wind, while fragrant air was before him, that he might save the painter Nakht-Amon, son of the painter of Amon in the necropolis, Nebre, born of the housewife, Peshed."

"He saith, 'Though the servant be wont to commit sin, yet is the lord wont to be gracious. The lord of Thebes spends not the whole day wroth. If he be wroth for the space of a moment, it remaineth not . . . turns to us in graciousness, Amon turns ⌜with⌝ his breath.'" [1]

"By thy ka, thou wilt be gracious, and that which is turned away will not be repeated."

"He saith, 'I will make this stela in thy name, and I will record this hymn in writing upon it, if thou wilt save for me the painter Nakht-Amon.' Thus I spake to thee, and thou hearkenedst to me. Now behold I do that which I said. Thou art the lord of the one who calls upon him, who is satisfied with righteousness, the lord of Thebes."

"Made by the painter, Nebre and [his] son Khai."

Similarly in a year of unseasonable weather and resulting distress a man prays: "Come to me, O Amon, save me in this year of distress. As for the sun, when it happens that he shines not, then winter comes in summertime, the months are ⌜retarded⌝ and the days are belated. The great cry out to thee, O Amon, and the small seek after thee. Those who are in the arms of their nurses say, 'Give us breath, O Amon.' Then is Amon found coming in peace with the sweet air before him. He transforms me into a vulture-wing, like a barque manned, ⌜saying⌝, 'Strength to the shepherds in the field, the washers on the dike, the ⌜guards⌝ who come forth from the district, the gazelles in the desert.'"

[1] So ERMAN.

THE AGE OF PERSONAL PIETY 353

"Thou findest that Amon doeth according to thy desire, in his hour of peace, and thou art praised in the midst of the officials and established in the place of truth. Amon-Re, thy great Nile ascendeth the mountains, thou lord of fish, rich in birds; and all the poor are satiated."[1]

The Sun-god, or his supplanter, Amon, has thus become the champion of the distressed, "Who heareth the petition, who heareth the prayers of him who crieth out to him, who cometh at the voice of him who mentions his name,"[2] "the loving god who heareth prayers, [who giveth the hand] to the poor, who saveth the weary."[3] So the injured mother, neglected by her son, "raises her arms to the god, and he hears her cry."[4] The social justice which arose in the Middle Kingdom is now a claim which every poor man pleads before the god, who has himself become a "just judge, not accepting a bribe, uplifting the insignificant, [protecting] the poor, not extending thy hand to the rich."[5] And so the poor man prays: "O Amon, lend thine ear to him who stands alone in the court (of justice), who is poor while his [opponent] is rich. The court oppresses him (saying), 'Silver and gold for the scribes! Clothing for the servants!' But Amon transforms himself into the vizier, that he may cause the poor man to triumph; the poor man is just and the poor man ⌜overcomes⌝ the rich. Pilot [in] front who knoweth the water, Amon, thou Rudder, . . . who giveth bread to him who has none, and preserveth alive the servant of his house."[6] For the god is now that "Amon-Re who first became king, O god of the beginning, thou vizier of the poor man, not taking the corrupt reward, not saying,

[1] Papyrus Anastasi, IV, 10, 1-7.
[2] Ibid., 1108.
[3] Erman, ibid., 1107.
[4] Maximes d'Ani, 7, 3.
[5] Zeitschr. für aegypt. Sprache, 38, 24.
[6] Papyrus Anastasi, II, 8, 5-9, 3.

'Bring witnesses;' Amon-Re who judgeth the earth with his finger, whose words are before the heart. He assigneth him that sinneth against him to the fire, and the just [to] the West."[1] Rich and poor alike may suffer the displeasure of the god aroused by sin. An oath taken lightly or falsely calls down the wrath of the god, and he smites the transgressor with sickness or blindness, from which relief may be obtained as we have seen, if repentance follows and the offender humbly seeks the favor of his god.[2] Now for the first time conscience is fully emancipated. The sinner pleads his ignorance and proneness to err. "Thou sole and only one, thou Harakhte who hath none other like him, protector of millions, savior of hundred-thousands, who shieldeth him that calleth upon him, thou lord of Heliopolis; punish me not for my many sins. I am one ignorant of his own body, I am a man without understanding. All day I follow after my own dictates as the ox after his fodder."[3] This is in striking contrast with the Book of the Dead, in which the soul admits no sin and claims entire innocence. But now in this posture of unworthiness and humility there is inner communion with God night and day. "Come to me, O Re-Harakhte, that thou mayest guide me; for thou art he that doeth, and none doeth without thee, but thou art he who doeth it. Come to me, Atum, thou art the august god. My heart goes out to Heliopolis. . . . My heart rejoiceth and my bosom is glad. My petitions are heard, even my daily prayers, and my hymns by night. My supplications shall flourish in my mouth, for they are heard this day."[4]

[1] Papyrus Anastasi, II, 6, 5–7.
[2] ERMAN, *ibid.*, 1102–3, 1104, 1098–1110, 1101–2, 1107.
[3] Papyrus Anastasi, II, 10, 5–11, 2.
[4] *Ibid.*, II, 10, 1–10, 5.

THE AGE OF PERSONAL PIETY 355

In the old hymns, made up of objective descriptions, quotations from the myths, and allusions to mythical incidents, all matters entirely external to the life of the worshipper, every man might pray the same prayer; but now prayer becomes a revelation of inner personal experience, an expression of individual communion with God. It is a communion in which the worshipper discerns in his god one nourishing the soul as a shepherd feeds his flock. "O Amon, thou herdman bringing forth the herds in the morning, leading the suffering to pasture; as the herdman leads the herds [to] pasture, so dost thou, O Amon, lead the suffering to food, for Amon is a herdman, herding him that leans upon him. . . . O Amon-Re, I love thee and I have filled my heart with thee. . . . Thou wilt rescue me out of the mouth of men in the day when they speak lies; for the Lord of Truth, he liveth in truth. I will not follow the anxiety in my heart, (for) that which Amon hath said flourisheth."[1] There are, to be sure, external and material means which will further this spiritual relation with the god. The wise man sagely admonishes to "celebrate the feast of thy god, repeat his seasons; the god is wroth [with] him who transgresses [against] him."[2] Nevertheless, even in the opinion of the sages, who are wont to compromise with traditional customs, the most effective means of gaining the favor of God is contemplative silence and inner communion. "Be not of many words, for in silence shalt thou gain good. . . . As for the precinct of God, his abomination is crying out; pray thou with a desiring heart whose every word is hidden,

---

[1] *Inscriptions in the Hieratic Character*, XXVI, British Museum Ostrakon, No. 5656 a, ll. 6–7, 14–15, verso ll. 1–3 (after a collation by ERMAN. *Cf. Zeitschr. für aegypt. Sprache*, 42, 106).
[2] *Maximes d'Ani*, 2, 3–5.

and he will supply thy need, and hear thy speech and receive thy offering."[1] It is in such an attitude as this that the worshipper may turn to his God as to a fountain of spiritual refreshment, saying, "Thou sweet Well for him that thirsteth in the desert; it is closed to him who speaks, but it is open to him who is silent. When he who is silent comes, lo, he finds the well."[2] This attitude of silent communion, waiting upon the gracious goodness of God, was not confined to the select few, nor to the educated priestly communities. On the humblest monuments of the common people Amon is called the god "who cometh to the silent," or the "lord of the silent," as we have already observed.[3] It is in this final development of devotional feeling, crowning the religious and intellectual revolution of Ikhnaton, and also forming the culmination of the doctrines of social justice emerging in the Feudal Age, that the religion of Egypt reached its noblest and most exalted period. The materials for the age of the decadence which followed are too scanty to reveal clearly the causes of the stagnation which now ensued, a decline from which the religious life of Egypt never recovered.

In morals and in the attitude toward life the sages continued to maintain a spirit of wholesome regard for the highest practical ideals, an attitude in which we discern a distinct advance upon the teachings of the fathers. Reputation was strictly to be guarded. "Let every place which thou lovest be known," says the sage;[4] and drunkenness and dissolute living are exhibited in all their disastrous consequences for the young. To the young man the dangers of immorality are bared with naked frank-

[1] *Ibid.*, 3, 1–4.
[2] Papyrus Sallier, I, 8, 2–3.
[3] See above, pp. 349, 351.
[4] *Maximes d'Ani*, 3, 12.

ness. "Guard thee from the woman from abroad, who is not known in her city; look not on her, ... know her not in the flesh; (for she is) a flood great and deep, whose whirling no man knows. The woman whose husband is far away, 'I am beautiful,' says she to thee every day. When she has no witnesses, she stands and ensnares thee. O great crime worthy of death when one hearkens, even when it be not known abroad. (For) a man takes up every sin [after] this *one*."[1] As for the good things of life, they are to be regarded with philosophical reserve. It is foolish to count upon inherited wealth as a source of happiness. "Say not, 'My maternal grandfather has a house on the estate of So and So.' Then when thou comest to the division (by will) with thy brother, thy portion is (only) a storage-shed."[2] In such things indeed there is no stability. "So it is forever, men are naught. One is rich, another is poor. ... He who was rich last year, he is a vagrant this year. ... The watercourse of last year, it is another place this year. Great seas become dry places, and shores become deeps."[3] We have here that Oriental resignation to the contrasts in life which seems to have developed among all the peoples of the early East.[4]

The speculations of the thinking class, especially those which we have found in intimations of pantheism as far back as the Pyramid Age, had also now gained currency among the common people, although of course in the concrete form in which such reflections always find expression in the East. A picturesque tale of the twelfth century

---
[1] *Ibid.*, 2, 13-17.   [2] *Ibid.*, 5, 7-8.   [3] *Ibid.*, 7, 8-9.
[4] See, for example, the song of Sindebad the porter in the court of the rich man's house. Algiers edition of *Sindebad the Sailor*, Arabic text, p. 4.

B. C. expresses in graphic form the thought of the people concerning these complicated and elusive matters. It is now commonly known as the Tale of the Two Brothers.[1] The two gods who appear as the chief characters in the tale are pictured in the naïve imagination of the folk as two peasants, whose names, Anubis and Bata, have disclosed them as gods of the town of Kasa,[2] who had a place in the religion of Egypt at an enormously remote date.[3] Anubis, the elder brother, is married; Bata, the younger, lives with them almost as their son, when the idyllic round of picturesque rustic life is forever ended by an attempt on the part of the wife, enamoured of the younger brother, to establish improper relations with him. The youth indignantly refuses, exemplifying the current wisdom of the wise man as we have already met it. The incident later found place in the Hebrew tradition of Joseph in Egypt. Deceived by his wife into believing a perverted version of the affair foisted upon him by the false woman, Anubis lies in wait to slay his brother. Warned by his cattle, however, the youth flees, and his brother's pursuit

---

[1] Preserved in a papyrus of the British Museum called *Papyrus D'Orbiney;* published in *Select Papyri . . . in the British Museum*, London, 1860, part II, pls. ix–xix. It has been often translated. A good rendering by GRIFFITH will be found in PETRIE's *Egyptian Tales*, London, 1895, Second Series, pp. 36–65.

[2] See GARDINER, *Proceedings of the Soc. of Bibl. Arch.*, XXVII, 1905, p. 185, and SPIEGELBERG, *Zeitschr. für aegypt. Sprache*, 44, pp. 98–99.

[3] NAVILLE has called attention to the probable occurrence of Bata in the Pyramid Texts (*Zeitschr. für aegypt. Sprache*, 43, 77–83). NAVILLE seems to have overlooked the fact that Bata occurs as early as Menes's time. Indeed he is to be found on a tablet of Menes published by NAVILLE in the very article in question (p. 79, fig.'3); for the bird represented there perched on the building or sanctuary has before him a "t." The bird is to be read "B'," which with the "t" gives us the reading Bata.

is cut off by the Sun-god, who places between them a torrent filled with crocodiles. Then Bata, calling upon the Sun-god "who distinguisheth between good and evil" to judge between them, reproaches his brother with his easy credulity as they converse across the stream and tells him that all is now over. As for the youth himself, he must depart to the "Valley of the Cedar," a place which must have been on the Phœnician coast, as there were no cedars in Egypt. There he will await the coming of Anubis to succor him, whenever Anubis observes commotion in the jar of beer which he drinks. Anubis returns and slays his unfaithful wife, while the youth wanders on to the Valley of the Cedar. Maintaining himself there as a hunter, the Sun-god sends him a beautiful wife to solace his loneliness. Although she escapes the sea that would have carried her away, a stray lock of her perfumed hair wandering to Egypt betrays her to the Pharaoh, who searches for her far and wide, and, like Cinderella, she is at last brought to the palace. She at once prays the king to send emissaries to cut down the cedar with which the life of Bata, her husband, is mysteriously involved. When this is done, Bata falls dead, and his treacherous wife feels free to live in splendor at the court. Then Bata's brother, Anubis, observes a commotion in the beer he is drinking, and he sets out at once to search for Bata, whose body he soon finds in the "Valley of the Cedar." For three years he sought the cedar blossom in which was the soul of Bata, and wearying, he was about to return to Egypt, when in the fourth year, as he was walking by the cedar, he chanced upon it. Then he hastened to place it in a jar of water, and having given the water to Bata to drink, his dead brother revived, and they embraced each other and talked together. Bata now informs his brother that he must assume the form of a sacred bull, and going in this guise to the court, he will reckon with the faithless beauty whom the gods gave him. But the court beauty compasses the death of the bull, and from his blood which spatters the door-posts of the palace two beautiful persea-trees spring up, one on either side of the doorway. When the Pharaoh's favorite induces him to cut these down, a chip from one of them flies into her mouth, and as a result she bears a son, who proves to be Bata himself. The Pharaoh makes him heir to the throne, to which Bata finally succeeds, and after a long and happy reign is followed as king by his brother, the faithful Anubis.

It is easy to discern in the imperishable life of Bata, as it emerges in one form after another, especially in the cedar and the persea-tree, a folk version of some of the Osiris incidents interwoven with the myth of the Sun-god. But it will be noticed that Bata is alternately the persea of Osiris and the bull of the Sun, who still remains, as he has been throughout its history, the great god of Egypt. "The god of this land is the Sun in the horizon, (while) his statues are on earth," says the sage;[1] but the other gods have now in the thought of the time completely coalesced with him. This Solar pantheism now took definite form in the thought of the theologian, and we ultimately find an "Amon-Re-Wennofer (Osiris)" as king of Egypt, with his name inclosed in a cartouche like an earthly ruler.[2] Amon as Sun-god becomes the all-pervasive, life-giving air. "He emits air, refreshing the throat, in his name of 'Amon,' who abides (mn) in all things, the soul of Shu (god of the air) for all gods, the substance of life, who created the tree of life, . . . flood-

---

[1] *Maximes d'Ani*, 6, 16.
[2] BRUGSCH, *Reise nach der grossen Oase*, pl. xvii.

ing the Two Lands (Egypt), without whom none liveth in Egypt."[1] As god of the universal air, "his voice is heard though he is not seen, refreshing every throat, strengthening the heart of the pregnant woman in travail, and the man-child born of her."[2] In the words of an old Sun-hymn of Aton times, the worshipper says, "Thou art he who fashions his body with his own hands in any form he desires;"[3] and Amon, "lord of Thebes shines in his forms, which are in every province,"[4] indicating that the local gods of the provinces or nomes are but forms and names of Amon. The priests narrated too how this had come to pass. "Thou didst establish thy throne in every place thou lovest, in order that thy names might be many. Cities and nomes bear thy beauty, and there is no ⌈region⌉ without thy image." Then they told how in the beginning Amon had gone from one great sanctuary to the other, and how in each one he had established himself as the god of the place. At Heliopolis he had become Atum, at Memphis he had become Ptah, at Heracleopolis he had become Harsaphes. Not only are the gods but forms of Amon, Amon is in all, and he *is* all. "Thy form is the Nile, the first-born, older than the gods; thou art the great waters, and when they penetrate into the soil, thou makest it to live by thy flood. Thou art the sky, thou art the earth, thou art the Nether World, thou art the water, thou art the air that is between them. Men rejoice because of thee, (for) thou ceasest not[5] to care for all that is."[6]

---

[1] *Ibid.*, pl. xv, ll. 5-6.
[2] *Ibid.*, pl. xvi, ll. 38-39.
[3] *Ibid.*, pl. xv, ll. 14-16.
[4] *Ibid.*, pl. xv, ll. 2-3.
[5] Text has "he ceaseth not."
[6] *Ibid.*, pls. xxv-xxvi, ll. 22-41. All the above texts from BRUGSCH's *Grosse Oase* are from the temple of Hibeh in the oasis of el Khargeh, and date from the reign of Darius II, the last quarter of the fifth century B. C.

Thus those pantheistic speculations which we found as far back as the Pyramid Age, after two thousand years of slow development have finally resulted in identifying the world with God.

In form all the old faiths went on as before, maintaining all the old externals. This was especially true of mortuary practices, which developed under the Empire as never before. All men of whatever class, no matter how poor and needy, desired and received some mortuary equipment, when laid away in the grave, which might enable the departed to share in the blessed destiny of Osiris. The material equipment of the dead for eternity, in spite of the impressive demonstration of its futility furnished by the desolate pyramid cemeteries, had now become a vast industry which all classes of society called into requisition. The sages cautioned even the young to make ready their tombs. "Say not 'I am (too) young to be taken.' Thou knowest not thy death. Death comes and takes the child who is in his mother's arms, like the man who has reached old age."[1] "Adorn thy seat which is in the valley, the tomb which shall hide thy body. Put it before thee in thy affairs, which are made account of in thy eyes, like the very old whom thou layest to rest in the midst of their ⌜dwelling⌝. There is no blame to him who doeth it, it is good that thou be likewise equipped. When thy messenger comes ⌜to take thee he shall find thee equipped⌝."[2] Neither should a man forget those who already lie there: "Put water for thy father and thy mother who rest in the valley. . . . Thy son shall do likewise for thee."[3]

Under such influences as these grew up the vast cemetery of Thebes, in which myriads of the common people

---

[1] *Maximes d'Ani*, 4, 2–4.   [2] *Ibid.*, 3, 14–4, 2.   [3] *Ibid.*, 3, 4–6.

of a class who had never before enjoyed Osirian burial were now laid away. The great mass of material remains from such cemeteries, however, reveals only the popularization of tendencies and beliefs long before observable among the higher and the educated classes. It is rarely that such tendencies were more than mechanically and thoughtlessly followed by the common folk, and seldom do we find such important developments among them as those manifestations of personal piety among the poor, to which we have already given attention.

With the decline of the Empire from the thirteenth century onward, the forces of life both within and without were exhausted and had lost their power to stimulate the religion of Egypt to any further vital development. Stagnation and a deadly and indifferent inertia fell like a stupor upon the once vigorous life of the nation. The development which now ensued was purely institutional and involved no progress in thought. The power of the priesthood as a political influence is observable as far back as the rise of the Fifth Dynasty, in the middle of the twenty-fifth century B. C. In the Empire, however, vast temples, richly endowed, became an economic menace. Moreover, the great Pharaohs of this age began to recognize oracles of Amon as mandatory. Thutmose III was seated on his throne by a conspiracy of the priests of Amon, supported by an oracle of the great god recognizing him as king.[1] When Thutmose III, therefore, made the High Priest of Amon primate of all the priesthoods of Egypt, the chief sacerdotal official of the state, he was but paying his political debts. This Amonite papacy suffered severely at the hands of Ikhnaton, as we have seen. After his overthrow, however, it recovered all it had lost

[1] BAR, II, 131-149.

and much more. Ramses II even allowed an oracle of Amon to guide him in the appointment of the god's high priest,[1] and under such circumstances it was easy for the high priests of Amon to make the office hereditary. Unable to resist the political power of this state within the state, a constant victim of its economic encroachments, Egypt rapidly degenerated into a sacerdotal state, and by 1100 B. C. the Pharaoh had yielded the sceptre to the head of the state church. It was in the course of this long development which placed the sacerdotal party in control of the throne, that the outward and official manifestations of religion took on those forms of dignity and splendor such as no Oriental religion had before displayed. The sanctuaries of this age will always form one of the most imposing survivals from the ancient world. Not only in their grandeur as architecture, but also in their sumptuous equipment, these vast palaces of the gods lifted the external observances of religion to a plane of splendor and influence which they had never enjoyed before. Enthroned in magnificence which not even the sumptuous East had ever seen, Amon of Thebes became in the hands of his crafty priesthood a mere oracular source for political and administrative decisions. Even routine legal verdicts were rendered by the nod of the god, and such matters as wills and testaments were subject to his oracles.[2] The old prayer of the oppressed, that Amon might become the vizier of the poor man, was receiving a very literal fulfilment, and with results little foreseen by the men who had framed this prayer. As Thebes degenerated into a sacerdotal principality after 1000 B. C.,

---

[1] SETHE, *Zeitschr. für aegypt. Sprache*, 44, 30 ff.
[2] For the most important of such oracles as yet known, see BAR, IV, 650-8, 725-8, 795, etc.

and the great cities of the north, especially of the Delta, eclipsed the splendor of the old imperial capital, Amon slowly lost his pre-eminence, although he was not wholly neglected. Even the venerable supremacy of the Sungod was encroached upon by the other gods of the north. On the other hand, it is evident that Osiris, who was more independent of state patronage and support, rather gained than lost in popularity.

When the decadence, which had continued for five hundred years, was slowly transformed into a restoration, after 700 B. C., the creative age of inner development was forever past. Instead of an exuberant energy expressing itself in the spontaneous development of new forms and new manifestations, as at the beginning of the Empire, the nation fell back upon the past, and consciously endeavored to restore and rehabilitate the vanished state of the old days before the changes and innovations introduced by the Empire.[1] Seen through the mist of two thousand years, what was to *them* ancient Egypt was endowed with the ideal perfection of the divine régime which had preceded it. In the endeavor to reconstitute modern religion, society, and government upon ancient lines, the archaizers must consciously or unconsciously have been constantly thwarted by the inevitable mutability of the social, political, and economic conditions of a race. The two thousand years which had elapsed since the Pyramid Age could not be annihilated. Through the deceptive mantle of antiquity with which they cloaked contemporary conditions, the inexorable realities of the present were discernible. The solution of the difficulty, when perceived, was the same as that attempted by the Hebrews

[1] These and the following remarks largely after the author's *History of Egypt*, pp. 570 ff.

in a similar dilemma: it was but to attribute to the modern elements also a hoary antiquity, as the whole body of Hebrew legislation was attributed to Moses. The theoretical revival was thus rescued.

The ancient mortuary texts of the pyramids were revived, and although frequently not understood, were engraved upon the massive stone sarcophagi. The Book of the Dead, which now received its last redaction, shows plain traces of this influence. In the tomb-chapels we find again the fresh and pleasing pictures from the life of the people in marsh and meadow, in workshop and ship-yard. They are perfect reproductions of the relief scenes in the mastaba tombs of the Pyramid Age, so perfect indeed that at the first glance one is not infrequently in doubt as to the age of the monument. Indeed a man named Aba, at Thebes, sent his artists to an Old Kingdom tomb near Siut to copy thence the reliefs for use in his own Theban tomb, because the owner of the ancient tomb was also named Aba.

There is a large black granite stela in the British Museum,[1] a copy, dating from the dawn of the Restoration, of an ancient papyrus book of the Old Kingdom, a "work of the ancestors, which was eaten of worms." Thus the writings and sacred rolls of bygone days were now eagerly sought out, and, with the dust of ages upon them, they were collected, sorted, and arranged. The past was supreme. The priest who cherished it lived in a realm of shadows, and for the contemporary world he had no vital meaning. Likewise in Babylon the same retrospective spirit was now dominant in the reviving empire of Nebuchadnezzar. It was soon to take possession

---

[1] No. 797. See my essay in *Zeitschr. für aegypt. Sprache*, 39, Tafel I, II, and *infra*, pp. 41–47, especially p. 46, note.

of the returning Hebrew exiles. The world was growing old, and men were dwelling fondly and wistfully on her far-away youth. In this process of conserving the old, the religion of Egypt sank deeper and deeper in decay, to become, what Herodotus found it, a religion of innumerable external observances and mechanical usages, carried out with such elaborate and insistent punctiliousness that the Egyptians gained the reputation of being the most religious of all peoples. But such observances were no longer the expression of a growing and developing inner life, as in the days before the creative vitality of the race was extinct. To be sure, many of the finest of the old teachings continued as purely literary survivals, and new ones unconsciously crept in, chiefly due to foreign influence.[1]

In the days of the Greek kings, the Osirian faith finally submerged the venerable Sun-god, with whose name the greatest movements in the history of Egyptian religion were associated, and when the Roman emperor became an Oriental Sun-god, *sol invictus*, the process was in large measure due to the influence of Asiatic Solar religion rather than to the Solar Pharaoh, who, as we have seen in the Pyramid Texts, had been sovereign and Sun-god at the same time many centuries before such doctrines are discernible in Asia. Whether they are in Asia the result of Egyptian influence is a question still to be investigated. In any case, as Osiris-Apis or Serapis, Osiris gained the supreme place in the popular as well as the state religion, and through him the subterranean hereafter, rather than

[1] Especially Babylonian astrology, see Cumont's brilliant book, *Astrology and Religion Among the Greeks and Romans*, New York, 1912, pp. 73–77, although the Egyptian origin of Ikhnaton's movement is too evident to make possible M. Cumont's suggestion of influences from Asia in it.

the Sun-god's glorious celestial kingdom of the dead, passed over into the Roman world. The imposing *mêlée* of thought and religion from the most remote and racially divergent sources, with which the historian is confronted as he surveys the Mediterranean world at the beginning of the Christian era, was not a little modified by the current which constantly mingled with it from the Nile. It has not been the purpose of these lectures to include this period of far-reaching syncretism of the Græco-Roman world; but as we stand at the close of the long religious development which we have been endeavoring to trace, we may ask ourselves the question whether the ancient religion of Egypt, as we have found it in old native sources long antedating Greek civilization, now passed out unalloyed into the great Mediterranean world. It has of course long since been evident that the religions of the Mediterranean, from the fourth century B. C. onward, or beginning perhaps even earlier, were gradually Orientalized, and in this process of Orientalization the progress of Christianity was but a single phenomenon among others like it. We all know that it was not the Christianity of Judea in the first decades after the crucifixion which conquered the Roman world. It seems equally evident that it was the religion of Egypt as viewed, interpreted, and apprehended by generations of Greeks, it was this Hellenized composite of old Egyptian religion and Greek preconceptions [1] which passed out into the Mediterranean world to make Isis a household word in Athens, to give her a sanctuary even in such a provincial city as Pompeii, and to leave such monuments in Rome

[1] Perhaps we should also add here the astrological elements which had invaded Egypt from Syria, and after being Egyptianized passed on to Rome. See CUMONT, *ibid.*, pp. 76-77.

as Hadrian's obelisk on the Monte Pincio, which in Egyptian hieroglyphs still proclaims to the modern world not only the deification of the beautiful Greek youth, Hadrian's favorite, as "Osiris-Antinous," but at the same time the enthronement of the ancient mortuary god of Egypt in the palace of the Cæsars.

I believe it was Louis Agassiz who, after studying the resistless action of the Swiss glaciers and watching the massive boulders and fragments of rock brought down in the grip of the ice, to be dropped at the bidding of the summer sun in a wandering rampart of tumbled rocks skirting the mouth of the valley, at length realized that this glacial action had been going on for ages, and the imposing truth burst upon him that the geological processes of past æons which have made the earth are still going on at the present day, that they have never ceased, that they will never cease.

We have been tracing in broad lines the development of the religion of a great people, unfolding in the course of over three thousand years as the forces within and the forces around this ancient man wrought and fashioned his conception of the divine powers. God as discerned everywhere in the ancient Oriental world was a human experience. The ancient ideas of God are but the expression of the best that man has felt and thought embodied in a supreme character of which he dreamed. What was intended by Ingersoll, I suppose, as a biting gibe, "An honest god is the noblest work of man," is nevertheless profoundly true. We have seen the Egyptian slowly gaining his honest god. We gained ours by the same process, beginning among the Hebrews. It would be well if we of the modern world as we look back over these ages lying behind us might realize with Agassiz in the geological world,[1] that religion is still in the making, that the processes which brought forth inherited religion have never ceased, that they are going on around us every day, and that they will continue as long as the great and complex fabric of man's life endures.

[1] It is, however, a remarkable fact in this connection, that Agassiz never accepted evolution in the *organic* world.

INDEX

ABA: proper name, 366
Absorption of divine qualities, 129
Abusir, 11, 70, 74, 78, 82
Abydos, 26, 38, 39, 64, 86, 96, 100, 159, 179, 256, 259, 285, 286, 287, 288, 289, 341
Administration, 238
Admonitions of an Egyptian sage, 199
Admonitions of Ipuwer, 204 ff., 213, 230, 243 n,. 245, 249, 257, 318, 348
Akhetaton: Tell el-Amarna, 322 f., 330
Akhikar, story of, 215, 247
Alexander the Great, 16
Amamu, coffin, 273 n.
Amenemhet I: king, 202, 203
Amenemhet II: king, 285
Amenemhet III: king, 73
"Amenhotep": meaning, 321
Amenhotep III: king, 52, 310, 315, 319, 320, 322
Amenhotep IV: king, 319 ff.
Ameni of Benihasan, 240 n., 248, 252
Amenmose: scribe, 271
Amon: god, 310, 318, 321, 322, 342, 344, 345, 346, 349, 350, 351, 352, 353, 360, 363, 364
Amon-Re: god, 318
Amon-Re-Wennofer: Osiris, 360
Ancestors, respect for, 270
Ani and wife: scribe, 306 f.
Anubis: god of the dead, 27, 33, 37, 62, 100, 113, 131, 149, 225, 259, 260, 261, 266, 270, 284, 290, 304, 358 f.
Api, Amarna hymn of, 316 n.
Apophis: deity, 283
Art as affected by Aton faith, 336
"Ascendest": use of word, 161
"Ascending": meaning, 276 n.
Ascending by Day: Chapters of, 276, 294
Ascent of the sky, 109, 154
Atlas: Greek deity, 11
Aton as universal creator, 332
Aton faith, 322 ff., 347

Aton, fatherly solicitude, 334
Aton, source of life, 333
Atum: Sun-god, 8, 9, 11, 13, 18, 19, 36, 42, 44, 45, 76, 96, 107, 108, 111, 112, 113, 123, 125, 127, 154, 157, 161, 185, 254, 275, 279, 282, 319 ff., 346 f., 350, 354, 361

BA: soul, 56, 57, 59, 61, 62, 265 n.
Ba, soul, began to exist at death, 56
Babi: demon, 303
Barque of Osiris, 288
Bastet: goddess, 173
Bata: god in folk-tale, 358 f.
Beetle, sacred, 308
Beliefs, archaic, 50
Ben (ben-ben) at Heliopolis, 11, 76, 330
Blessedness hereafter. See Felicity
Bodily members enumerated, 110
Body, part of personality, 55
Body, permanent survival, 70
Body, resuscitation of, 57, 61
"Book of him who is in the Nether World," 297
Book of the Dead, 22, 34, 134, 253 n., 272, 273, 274, 277, 281, 284, 293, 294, 295, 296, 297, 299, 301, 308, 309, 318 n., 337 n., 338, 341, 354
Book of the Dead: genesis of, 293 f.
"Book of the Gates," 297
"Book of the Two Ways," 283, 297
Busiris: Dedu, 39
Buto: capital of Delta, 86, 118, 145
Byblos: place name, 26

CALENDAR of festivals, 68, 77, 260, 267 n., 290
Cartouches: use of, 320
Celebrations, religious, 68
Celestial hereafter, 101, 159, 274, 276
Celestial hereafter not Osirian, 142, 148
Celestial Nile, 122
Celestial ocean, 10
Celestial revenues of Pharaoh, 131
Ceremonial transgressions, 303

INDEX

Ceremonial washings, 254
Chapel, tomb-, 62
Character, personal, 179, 238, 302, 336
Charm: quoted, 133
Charm to open gates of sky, 114
Charms, 93, 94, 135, 292, 307
Charms against dangers of hereafter, 296
Charms, collections of, 281
Charms in mortuary texts, 292
Charms in Pyramid Texts, 80 n.
Charms, Pyramid Texts used as, 94
Charms: Ushebtis, 295
Coffin Texts, 23 n., 253, 255, 273, 274, 276, 277, 278, 280, 281, 293, 294
Coffins, inscribed, 272
Commercial relations, 314
Communion with god, 354, 355
Concrete forms of thought, 246
"Confession," negative, 301
Conscience, 198, 297, 354
Crimes denied, 302
Cult, 7

DAHSHUR, pyramid, 73, 81
Daily life, pictured in Pyramid Texts, 88
Dangers of hereafter, 282
Dead, designations of, 56 n.
Dead, dreaded as demons, 292
Dead lived near the tomb, 51
Dead, malice of, 284
Dead, place of the, 99
Dead, realms of the, 70 ff., 118 ff.
Dead, required restoration of senses, 58 f.
Dead, sojourn in Nether World, 276
Dead, transformations of, 277, 296
Dead, two beliefs as to abode, 51
Death, protest against, 91
Death, views of, 190
Debhen: official, 65
Declaration of innocence, 301 ff., 308
Dedication of pyramid and temple, 75
Der el-Bahri: Thebes, 16, 287 n.
"Devouress": demon, 306
Dewamutef, son of Horus, 112, 133
Dewat, 122, 136, 139, 144
Dialogue form of discourse, 247
Dialogue of a Misanthrope, 188 ff., 199, 203, 215, 230, 238, 245, 246, 250, 358 n.

EAST: place of ascent of sky, 116
"East": place of the dead, 101, 102
"East of the sky" more sacred than West, 104
East of the Sky, place of living again, 102
Edfu: place name, 9
Editors of Pyramid Texts, 93
Egyptian thinking, graphic, 7, 219 f., 246
Eloquent Peasant, tale of the. See Tale
Endowments, testamentary, 67, 81, 270
"Ennead": meaning, 42
Equipment of the dead, material, 75, 84
"Equipped": meaning, 169
"Equipped" mouths, 94
"Equipped" one, 60
Ethical decadence, 309
Ethical ordeal, future. See Judgment
Ethical requirements, 338
Ethical significance of Osiris, 255
Ethical teaching in Osirian faith, 176
Ethics, 336
Exorcism, 292
"Expeller of Deceit," 175
Eye of Horus. See Horus-Eye
Eye of Khnum, 107

FACULTIES, reconstitution of, 61
Falcon, 133, 274, 320
Falcon, sacred bird of Sun-god, 109
Falcon, symbol of Horus, 9
Feast, oldest religious, 39
Feasts, calendar of. See Calendar
Feasts, list of, 267
Felicity in hereafter, 135, 177, 257
Felicity, not dependent on material means, 84
Ferry-boat over Lily-lake, 105 f.
Ferrying over, 155, 157
Ferryman, 119, 130, 157
Ferryman of Re, 172
Festivals, Osirian, 289
Fetekta, servant of Re, 119
Field of Life, 136
Field of Offering, 133, 137
Field of Rushes, 161, 172
Filial piety, 167
"First of the Westerners," 38, 100, 104 n., 143, 159, 162, 258, 286, 289
Floats of reeds, two, 108, 158

INDEX

Folk-religion: Osirian, 285
Folk-tales, 10, 46
"Followers of Horus," 171, 306
"Followers of Osiris," 158
Food supply in hereafter, 129, 281
Forty-two gods of judgment, 299 ff.
Funeral barge, 286
Funerary furniture, prehistoric, 50
Funerary ritual, 93
Future, ultimate, 196

Gasuti, bull of the sky (Saturn), 112
Gates of celestial country opened, 114
Geb: Earth-god, 9, 11, 18, 21, 22, 24, 30, 34, 36, 41, 42, 58, 63, 111, 113, 117, 118 n., 139, 143, 172, 173, 280
Gebga: mysterious scribe, 282
Genii of the dead, four, 156, 157
Gizeh: place name, 258
Gizeh, cemetery, 83, 84
Gizeh, pyramids of, 15
"Glorious," 56 n.
"Glorious," dead called, 94
"Glorious one," 60, 148, 162, 265 n.
"Gods," 322
Gods, possible hostility of, 115
Graphic forms of thought, 7, 219 f., 246
"Grasper of Forelocks," 127
"Great God, Lord of the Sky," 171

Hammurabi, laws of, 246
Hapi, son of Horus, 112, 133
Hapu: vizier, 239 n.
Hapuseneb: High-priest of Amon, 319 n.
Harakhte: Horus of Horizon, 9, 109, 121, 155, 156, 318, 320
Hardedef: son of Khufu, 182, 184
Harhotep, tomb of, 256 n.
Harhotep: tomb inscriptions, 273 n., 282 n.
Harkhuf of Elephantine, 169
Harmhab: king, 345
Harsaphes: god, 361
Hathor, the eye of Re: goddess, 124, 253, 278, 279
Hatshepsut: queen, 287 n., 319 n.
"Heart": seat of intelligence, 44, 55, 59
Heart scarab, 308, 339, 340 n.
Heliopolis, 10, 11, 15, 28, 33, 34, 40, 43, 44, 71, 72, 76, 110, 116, 118 n., 147, 148, 152, 175, 176, 199, 250, 251, 275, 281, 303, 321, 354, 361

Heliopolitan theology, 149, 336
Hepzefi of Siut, 67, 259, 270, 289
Hereafter as a place of dangers, 281
Hereafter, conception of, 278
Hereafter, continuation of life in, 49 f., 81, 280
Hereafter, dangers of, 296
Hereafter, democratization of, 252, 257
Hereafter, glorious, 103
Hereafter, material welfare in, 165
Hereafter, Osirian, 285
Hereafter, Osirian doctrine, 159
Hereafter, royal felicity in, 88
Hereafter, royal survival in, 75
Hereafter, sojourn in, 53
Hereafter, Solar and Osirian conceptions, 140
Hereafter, views of, 295
Heralds announcing the king, 118
Herodotus, 277, 288, 290, 367
High Priest of Amon, 319
Hor: architect, 315, 326 n.
Horus: god, 8, 9, 10, 18, 26, 28, 29, 30, 32, 33, 34, 35, 36, 37, 39, 40, 41, 42, 53, 57, 59, 62, 63, 78, 81, 86, 100, 105, 108, 112, 118, 119, 120, 122, 133, 140, 143, 145, 147, 148, 152, 154, 160, 162, 164, 166, 172, 173, 175, 236, 254, 255, 278, 284, 288, 290, 303, 306, 345
Horus, battle with Set, 31
Horus, filial piety of, 29
Horus, good offices to the king, 146
Horus of Dewat, 133
Horus of the East, 155 f.
Horus of the Gods, 155 f.
Horus of the Horizon, 155 f., 318
Horus of the Shesmet, 155 f.
Horus, Solar, 41
Horus, sons of, 111, 112 n., 183, 156, 175
Horus-Eye, 12, 13, 31, 59, 78, 104, 107 n., 162, 278
Horuses, four, 9, 114, 124, 133, 154, 155, 156, 157, 172
Hostile creatures to dead, 51
Hymn, magical, to Sun-god, 121
Hymn to Amon, 345 f., 349, 350
Hymn to Aton, royal, 329
Hymn to Osiris, 348
Hymn to Osiris as Nile, 96
Hymn to Sun, earliest, 13
Hymn to Sun-god, 124, 310, 312, 315
Hymn to the Sky-goddess, 96, 148

Hymn to the Sun, 95, 96, 98, 211 n.
Hymns, ancient religious, 93
Hymns not necessarily charms, 95
Hymns, old, 355
Hymns, religious, 97
Hymns to Aton, 321, 323, 336, 361
Hymns to the gods, 17

IDEALS, practical, 356
Ikhernofret: officer, 287 ff.
"Ikhnaton": meaning, 322
Ikhnaton: king, 344, 345 n., 363
Imhotep: architect of Zoser, 182, 184
Immorality, 356
Immortality, 179, 184
"Immortality" not an Egyptian belief, 61
Imperialism, effect on religion, 313
Imperial power, reaction on thought, 5
"Imperishable Ones": the dead, 101
Imperishable Stars, 92, 107, 130, 134, 136, 137, 138, 139, 149, 158, 159, 163, 279
Imset, son of Horus, 112, 133
Incense, significance of, 126
Inmutef: priestly title, 14
Innocence, declaration of, 301ff., 308
Innocence of evil-doing, 168
Installation of the Vizier, 239, 246, 248, 249, 348
Instruction of Amenemhet, 247, 249 n.
Intef: baron, 271
Intelligence, part of personality, 55
Inti of Deshasheh, 171
Ipuwer, Admonitions of, 204 ff., 213, 230, 243 n., 245, 249, 257, 318, 348
Irreconcilable beliefs, 163 f.
Isesi: king, 228
Isis: goddess, 9, 11, 24, 26, 27, 29, 30, 32, 34, 37, 38, 39, 57, 104 n., 113, 119, 125, 135, 137, 145, 147, 154, 156, 162, 286, 290, 304, 306, 368

JACKAL, a god of the west, 120
Judge in the hereafter, 176
Judgment, future, 169, 173, 179, 253, 256, 294, 297, 299 ff., 309, 338
Judgment: Osirian, 307
"Justice," 174 n.
Justice, 238, 242, 244, 252, 253
Justice to the poor, 226
Justification of the dead, 54, 178, 197, 254, 255, 339

Justification, Solar, 174
Justification through magic, 309
"Justified," 33, 147, 175, 256 n.

KA (kas), 45, 52 f., 55, 57 n., 69 n., 76, 77, 111, 112, 122, 130, 134, 137, 174, 267, 275, 283, 284, 286, 305, 352
Ka a superior genius, 52
Ka, exclusive possession of king, 55
Ka, not an element of personality, 55
Kebehet, daughter of Anubis, 112, 113, 116, 136
Kebehsenuf, son of Horus, 112, 133
Kegemne: vizier, 228
Kerkeru: scribe of Osiris, 277
Khafre: king, 15, 68
Khai: proper name, 352
Khekheperre-sonbu: priest, 199, 200, 230, 238, 247, 250
Khenti-Amentiu: "First of the Westerners," 38, 143
Khepri: Sun-god, 9, 10, 13, 112, 161, 316
Kheti: vizier, 241, 244
Khnumhotep of Benihasan, 267, 271, 286
Khufu: king, 15, 182, 184, 271
King. *See also* Pharaoh
King as counsellor of Re, 120
King became Osiris, 145 f.
King identified with god, 160
King not exempt from judgment, 172, 177
Kingship, conception of, 17
Kingship, relation of Osiris to, 39
Kingship, the idealized, 251

LADDER to sky, 111, 112, 116, 153, 156, 158
"Landing": euphemism for "death," 92
Laws of Egypt, 248
Lexicography of Pyramid Texts, 90
Life after death, 49 f. *See also* Hereafter
Life-giving power of Aton, Sun-god, 333
Life hereafter, indefinite, 81
"Lily-lake," 105 f., 116, 125 n., 139, 279
Literary quality of Pyramid Texts, 97
"Look-behind," the ferryman, 105 f.
Luxor, 16, 52

MAFDET: deity, 133
Magic, 284, 309. *See also* Charms
Magic and magic power, 94, 95
Magic in hereafter, 290, 292, 307
Magic jar, 106
Magical agencies, 281, 339
Magical charm, 338 n.
Magical charms, 93
Magical devices, 132
Magical equipment, mortuary, 60
Magical formulæ, 291
Magical hymn to Sun-god, 121
Magical power, 116
Mastaba reliefs, 113
Mat: goddess of truth, 173, 255, 338
Material equipment of the dead, 32, 362
Medum, pyramids, 83
Memphis, 43, 241, 361
Memphite theology, 46, 166
Menkure: king, 15
Meri: architect, 258
Merire: Pepi I, 172
Mernere: king, 19, 77, 84, 85, 108, 160, 172
Messianic kingdom, 251
Messianism, 212 *ff*.
Methen, keeper of gate of sky, 119
"Mighty": used of the dead, 61
Migration of literary materials, 215
Mnevis: sacred bull, 321 n.
Mohammed, 234 n.
Monotheism, 6, 315
Monotheistic phrases, 347
"Mooring": euphemism for "death," 92, 186
Moral aspirations limited, 176
Moral consciousness, 37, 306, 336
Moral decadence, 209
Moral distinctions, 309
Moral earnestness, 238
Moral ideals, 238
Moral ideas, 8
Moral life obligation to, 187
Moral obligations, 250, 251
Moral ordeal in future. *See* Judgment
Moral requirements, 253
Moral responsibility, 170, 253, 307, 309
Moral sense, 33, 309
Moral sense, emergence of, 165
Moral thinking, 252
Moral unworthiness, 251
Moral unworthiness of society, 202
Moral values, 5

Moral worthiness, 173, 304
Moral worthiness, claims of, 167
Morning Star, 133, 134, 138, 173, 284
Mortuary belief dominated by magic, 284
Mortuary contracts, 260
Mortuary gifts, 258, 270
Mortuary inscriptions, 248, 285
Mortuary literature, 272
Mortuary magical equipment, 60
Mortuary maintenance, 78
Mortuary paintings, 56
Mortuary practices, 259, 362
Mortuary practices, Osirian, 62
Mortuary priest, servant of the ka, 54
Mortuary priests, 98, 270
Mortuary processions, 260, 266
Mortuary statuettes: Ushebtis, 295
Mortuary texts, 253, 273, 366
Mortuary texts for king only, 99
Mortuary texts on rolls, 293
Mummy, devices to make it a living body, 59
Mythology of Egypt, 46
Myths, 12, 85, 355
Myths, fragments of old, 93
Myths, lost, 91
Myths, old, 96

NAKHT-AMON: painter, 351
Name, 107, 116, 134, 301
Name, good, on earth, 188
National organization, first, 5
Nebre: painter, 351
Neferhotep: priest, 182, 185
Neferhotepes, queen, 82
Neferirkere, king, 16, 78, 82
Neferkere: Pepi II, 139, 146, 174
"Negative confession," 301
Neit: goddess, 125
Nekheb, 130
Nekhtyoker: prince, 271
Nekure, prince, 68
Nemaathap: royal mother, 81
Neper: harvest god, 277
Nephthys: goddess, 9, 11, 26, 27, 30, 32, 34, 38, 59 n., 97, 104 n., 113, 119, 125, 137, 145, 147, 154, 156, 162, 304
Neshmet barque, 289
Nether World, 99, 144, 160, 276, 281
Nether World the domain of Osiris, 36
New Year celebrations, 261

Nile, 21
Nile as Osiris, 333
Nile, influence on Egyptian religion, 8
Nile-god, 52
Nun: god, 34, 125, 133
Nuserre: king, 82
Nut: Sky-goddess, 11, 24, 95, 123, 133, 135, 136, 137, 139, 143, 148, 161, 162, 279, 317

OBELISK, 15
Obelisk: symbol of Sun-god, 70
Offering ritual, 79, 90 n., 150, 151, 159
Offerings for king, 78
Offerings for the dead, 62
Offerings to the dead: Horus-eye, 59
Official conduct, 238
Onkhu: priest, 200
Ophir of the Old Testament, 66
Orion: the sky, 128, 139, 144, 277, 284
Osirian editing of texts, 172 n., 276
Osirian ethics, 309
Osirian faith, 37 *f.*, 78, 102, 139, 157, 176, 274, 285, 304, 307, 310, 367
Osirian faith: popular religion, 140, 142
Osirian litigation at Heliopolis, 175
Osirian "passion play," 26, 287, 290, 341
Osirian point of view, 42
Osirian theology, 43, 148
Osirianization of Egyptian religion, 142 *ff.*, 176
Osirianization of hereafter, 276
Osirianization of Pyramid Texts, 150 *ff.*
Osiris: god, 8, 9, 11, 18 *ff.*, 25, 26, 27, 28, 29, 30, 32, 34, 35, 36, 37, 39, 40, 42, 53, 57 n., 59, 62, 73 n., 74, 75, 76, 96, 97, 100, 104 n., 119, 139, 140, 143, 144, 145, 147, 148, 149, 150, 153, 154, 155, 156, 157, 158, 159, 160, 161, 162, 163, 164, 170, 171, 174, 176, 188, 250, 251, 252, 253, 254, 255, 256, 258, 259, 276, 277, 278, 284, 285, 286, 288, 289, 290, 299, 301, 304, 305, 306, 309, 310, 337, 338, 340, 341, 348, 360, 362, 365, 367
Osiris, a mortuary god, 54
Osiris and Set, correlation of, 40
Osiris as judge, 255

Osiris as Nile, 18, 146
Osiris as sea or ocean, 20
Osiris, associated with vegetable life, 22
Osiris barque, 256 n.
Osiris celestialized, 149
Osiris, charges against, 32
Osiris, identifications of, 23
Osiris, identified with soil or earth, 21
Osiris, lord of Dewat, 150
Osiris myth, 24, 37, 63, 145, 152, 251, 284, 287, 288, 290
Osiris receives the kingdom, 36
Osiris Solarized, 160
Osiris, source of fertility, 20
Osiris, the principle of life, 23
Osiris, triumph of, 33
Osiris-Apis: Serapis, 367
Osiris-Wennofer: god, 306

PAHERI: prince, 298
Pai: painter, 351
Pantheism, 312, 357
Pantheistic speculations, 362
Papremis: place name, 288, 290
"Passion play": Osirian, 287, 290, 341
Pepi: king, 53, 57, 58, 76, 78, 81, 88, 89, 91, 92, 94, 102, 106, 107, 108, 109, 110, 111, 113, 114, 115, 116, 117, 118, 126, 130, 131, 132, 133, 134, 136, 137, 150, 153, 158, 162, 163, 171, 172, 173, 174, 175, 177, 178
Pepi I: king, 19, 84, 85, 154, 158
Pepi I, addressed as Osiris, 19
Pepi II, king, 19, 66, 76, 79, 81, 85, 111, 112
Pepi II, as Osiris, 19
Persen: noble, 82
Personal aspiration to god, 349
Personal relation to god, 349
Personality, Egyptian conception, 51, 55, 61, 70, 179, 181
Personality never dissociated from body, 56
Pessimism, 203, 216, 249, 257
Pharaoh, 15, 16, 17, 64, 70, 75, 81, 100, 103, 105, 114, 117, 130 n., 135, 154, 173, 240, 272, 310, 318, 319, 320, 364
Pharaoh a cosmic figure, 125
Pharaoh as priest before Re, 121
Pharaoh as son of Sun-god, 122
Pharaoh becomes a great god, 123

INDEX 377

Pharaoh, deceased, as scribe of Re, 120
Pharaoh, entrance to sky, 149
Pharaoh, identified with Re, 122
Pharaoh on Sun-god's throne, 124
Pharaoh preying on the gods, 127
Pharaoh receives homage as Sun-god, 125
Pharaoh. *See also* King
Phœnix, 11, 71, 72, 77, 274, 278, 296, 300
Physical restoration of dead, 57
Pilgrimages to Abydos, 285
Pleasure, life of, 194
Plutarch, 25, 28
Poetic form of the Pyramid Texts, 97
Poor, complaints of the, 219
Popularization of mortuary customs, 272
Portrait statues, 65, 168, 179, 259, 267
Prayer, 355
Prayer for the dead: effectiveness, 272
Prayers for dead king, 93
Prayers in Pyramid Texts, 80 n.
Prayers used as charms, 95
"Prepared" one, 60
Priesthood, 179, 309, 342
Priesthood of Amon, 319, 321
Priesthood, political, 363
Priesthood, state, 142
Priests, maintenance of, 81
"Primæval," title of Osiris, 22
Privileges accruing from endowments, 68
Procession, Osirian, 289
Psychology of the dead, 61
Ptah: god, 11, 43, 44, 45 n., 47, 278, 361
Ptah-tatenen: god, 45, 46
Punt: Ophir, 66
Purification of the dead, 103, 155, 171
Pyramid, 15, 140
Pyramid causeway, 74
Pyramid complex, 74
Pyramid residence city, 75
Pyramid, sacred symbol, 70
Pyramid, symbol of Sun-god, 320
Pyramid temple, 74
Pyramid Texts, 10, 12, 18, 19, 20, 25, 26, 31, 33 n., 34, 35, 38, 40, 52, 56, 57, 60, 61, 63, 69 n., 72, 73 n., 77, 79, 84, 85, 87, 97, 101, 102, 103, 104, 114, 115, 122, 124, 126, 131, 135, 142, 144, 145, 146, 148, 149, 150, 155, 158, 159, 163, 171, 172, 175, 176 n., 177, 178, 209, 250, 251, 254, 272, 273, 274, 275, 276, 277, 278, 279, 280, 281, 282, 285, 294, 310, 312, 318, 320, 358
Pyramid Texts: a compilation, 92
Pyramid Texts: a terra incognita, 90
Pyramid Texts: function to insure king felicity in hereafter, 88, 92
Pyramid Texts not a coherent whole, 135 *f.*
Pyramid Texts not used by nobles, 99
Pyramid Texts Osirianized, 150 *ff.*
Pyramid Texts recited, 98
Pyramid-tomb, 72, 74
Pyramidion (ben-ben), 71
Pyramids, 178, 179
Pyramids, inscribed, 84
Pyramids: material equipment, 84

Ramses II: king, 364
Ramses IV: king, 18
Rationalism of Ikhnaton, 333
Re: Sun-god, 8, 9, 10, 17, 18, 24, 33, 36, 43, 53, 66, 78, 79, 87, 102, 103, 106, 107, 108, 109, 110, 111, 115, 117, 118, 119, 120, 121, 122, 123, 124, 125, 126, 131, 132, 133, 134, 135, 136, 137, 138, 139, 140, 148, 149, 152, 154, 159, 160, 161, 162, 163, 164, 170, 171, 172, 174, 175, 185, 187, 196, 211, 221, 225, 245, 250, 251, 252, 253, 274, 275, 277, 279, 281, 285, 304, 305, 310, 324, 328, 337, 346, 350
Re-Atum: Solar god, 10, 119, 120, 139, 160, 161, 274
Re-Harakhte: god, 354
Re-Khepri: god, 21
Reed floats, two, 108, 158
Rekhmire: vizier, 239 n.
Religious development institutional, 363.
Religious faculty, the, 4
Religious literature, ancient, 96
Renaissance, 365
Responsibility, personal, 297
Resurrection of Osiris, 31 *f.*, 39, 160, 288, 341
Resurrection the act of a god, 57
"Righteousness," 174–5, 253, 254 n., 310
Ritual at Abydos, 96

Ritual for benefit of king, 77
Ritual, funerary and offering, 93
Ritual of Aton, 329
Ritual of offerings, 79 n.
Ritual of worship, 93
Royal cemetery, Abydos, 64

Sahure, king, 82, 168
Sakkara: pyramids at, 84
Satis, goddess of cataract, 103
Scarab, 31
Scepticism, 179, 185, 257
Sebek-o: coffin of, 73 n.
Sebni of Elephantine, 62, 65
Sed-Feast, 39
Sehetepibre: stela, 258 n.
Sehpu: herald of king, 118
Sekhem: son of Osiris, 152
Sekhmet: goddess, 82
Self-consciousness, 198
Serapis: Osiris, 367
Serket: goddess, 125
Serpent-charms, 95, 135
Sesenebnef: official, 253
Sesostris I: king, 71, 202, 258, 286
Sesostris II: king, 199
Sesostris III: king, 287
Set: god, 14, 25, 27, 28, 29, 30, 33, 34, 35, 36, 40, 41, 53, 59, 78, 79, 104, 105, 112, 118 n., 119, 125, 143, 152, 153, 154, 157, 161, 166, 288
Set, enemy of Osiris, 41
Set, symbol of darkness, 40
Set-Horus feud, Osirian absorption of, 41
Seti I: king, 20
Shesha, 112
Shesmu, 128
Shu: god, 11, 19, 34, 77, 113, 114, 133, 360
Sky, east of, place of living again, 102
Sky, place of future blessedness, 99
Snefru: king, 81, 82, 228
Social classes, 246
Social conditions, 208
Social ethics, 228
Social forces, 199 ff.
Social ideals, 212, 214 f.
Social justice, 5, 216, 226, 243, 244, 246, 249, 252, 349, 353, 356
Society, redemption of, 215
Sokar: god, 21, 175
Solar barque, 122, 130, 253, 283
Solar faith, 74, 102, 176, 310, 319, 338, 346

Solar faith: state theology, 140, 142
Solar henotheism, 43
Solar hereafter, 139, 145
Solar monotheism, 322
Solar pantheism, 360
Solar theology, 43, 148, 149, 160, 250, 312, 313, 321, 336, 337
Solar universalism, 319
Solarization of Osiris, 250
"Son of Re": title of kings, 15
Song of mourning, 179 f.
Song of the Harper, 180 f., 185, 191, 194, 250
Song, palace, 17
Soped: Solar god, 74 n.
Sothis, star of Isis, 22, 284
Sovereignty of Re, 174
Speculation among common people, 357
State religion: Solar, 285
Statues, portrait funerary, 69
Status of dead king, 120
Stelæ erected at Abydos, 285
Subterranean hereafter, 159–160, 276, 277, 310, 367
Subterranean journey of the dead, 297
Subterranean kingdom of the dead, 37
Sun as Re, 10
Sun, influence on Egyptian religion, 8
Sun's disk: symbol of Aton, 320
Sun-god, 8, 10, 11, 12, 13, 14, 16, 25, 39, 40, 45 n., 62, 70, 71, 72, 76, 78, 100, 101, 103, 105, 106, 109, 111, 112, 115, 116, 120, 121, 122, 129, 131, 142, 155, 157, 158, 159, 171, 176, 188, 196, 211, 245, 251, 253, 274, 275, 304, 308, 309, 310, 312, 313, 317, 319, 320, 322, 323, 331, 337, 353, 359, 360, 365
Sun-god and Osiris, correlation of, 39
Sun-god, identification with, 274
Sun-god supreme, 12
Sun-god's realm, 315
Sun-gods, old local, 43
Sun-hymn, earliest, 13
Sun-hymn used as charm, 98
Suti: architect, 315, 326 n.
Symbol of god Aton, 320

Tale of the Eloquent Peasant, 228 n., 230, 239, 245, 249, 250
Tale of the Two Brothers, 21, 26, 136 n., 215, 216, 358 f.

INDEX

"Teaching" of Ikhnaton, 340
Tefnut: goddess, 11, 19, 77, 114, 133
Tell el-Amarna, 322 *f.*
Teti: king, 57, 59, 85, 106, 114, 123, 133, 137, 138, 142, 147, 154, 155, 158, 178
Thoth: god, 12, 34, 35, 45, 81, 107, 119, 129, 137, 147, 224, 254, 255, 278, 284, 288, 289, 290, 304, 305, 306
Thutenakht: official, 217 *ff.*
Thutmose I: king, 313
Thutmose III: king, 239 n., 298, 310, 313, 314, 318, 363
Thutmose IV: king, 239 n.
Tomb, 257
Tomb at Abydos, 285
Tomb-building, 258
Tomb decoration, 262, 366
Tomb: duty of son to provide, 63
Tomb, monumental, 62
Tomb, royal, 75, 103
Tomb, royal, of sacred significance, 72
Tombs, 178, 259, 362
Tombs of First Dynasty, 64
Tombs, restoration of, 270
Tombs: Tell el-Amarna, 323
Translation of king to sky, 137 *f.*
Transmigration of souls, 277
Tree of life, 133
"Triumphant," 33
Troja: quarries, 65, 258
"Truth," 166, 225 n., 299 n., 304, 337
Tutenkhamon: king, 344 *f.*
Tutu, Amarna hymn of, 316 n.
"Two Truths," 34

Uneg: son and body-servant of Re, 121

Unis: king, 18, 58, 85, 87, 91, 93, 98, 100, 107, 109, 110, 111, 113, 116, 119, 120, 123, 126, 128, 129, 130, 132, 137, 146, 150, 151, 153, 154, 158, 174, 178, 320
Unis, king, identified with Nile, 18
Universalism, 314, 315, 348
Universalism, Solar, 331
Unwearlable stars, 279
Upwawet: god, 32, 145, 259, 260, 264, 266, 270, 288, 289
Uræus, 110
Usages of religion, 7
Userkaf: king, 68, 167
Ushebtis: Respondents, 295, 340 n.
"Utterances": Pyramid Texts, 93, 98

"Victorious," 33
Vignettes in Book of Dead, 294
Vital principle identified with breath, 55
Vizier: vizierate, 240, 243
Vocabulary of Pyramid Texts, 90
Votive offerings, 287
Voyage with Re across the sky, 121

Wag-feast, 266
Wealth, 357
Wennofer: Osiris, 289, 299, 306
Weshptah: vizier, 66
"West" the place of dead, 100, 101
Wisdom literature, 227 n.
Wisdom of Ptahhotep, 216, 226 *ff.*, 240, 245, 246, 252, 339
World-religion, 332
Woser: vizier, 239 n.

Yemen-kau, 139

Zau: name, 64, 66, 167
Zoser: king, 182, 184

www.ingramcontent.com/pod-product-compliance
Lightning Source LLC
Chambersburg PA
CBHW040320300426
44112CB00020B/2819